# Reaping Richer Returns

# Reaping Richer Returns

## Public Spending Priorities for African Agriculture Productivity Growth

Aparajita Goyal and John Nash

A copublication of the Agence Française de Développement and the World Bank

# Africa Development Forum Series

The **Africa Development Forum Series** was created in 2009 to focus on issues of significant relevance to Sub-Saharan Africa's social and economic development. Its aim is both to record the state of the art on a specific topic and to contribute to ongoing local, regional, and global policy debates. It is designed specifically to provide practitioners, scholars, and students with the most up-to-date research results while highlighting the promise, challenges, and opportunities that exist on the continent.

The series is sponsored by Agence Française de Développement and the World Bank. The manuscripts chosen for publication represent the highest quality in each institution and have been selected for their relevance to the development agenda. Working together with a shared sense of mission and interdisciplinary purpose, the two institutions are committed to a common search for new insights and new ways of analyzing the development realities of the Sub-Saharan Africa region.

## Advisory Committee Members

*Agence Française de Développement*
**Gaël Giraud,** Executive Director, Research and Knowledge
**Mihoub Mezouaghi,** Deputy Director, Research and Knowledge
**Guillaume de Saint Phalle,** Head, Knowledge Management Division
**Françoise Rivière,** Head, Research Division

*World Bank*
**Albert G. Zeufack,** Chief Economist, Africa Region
**Markus P. Goldstein,** Lead Economist, Africa Region

## Sub-Saharan Africa

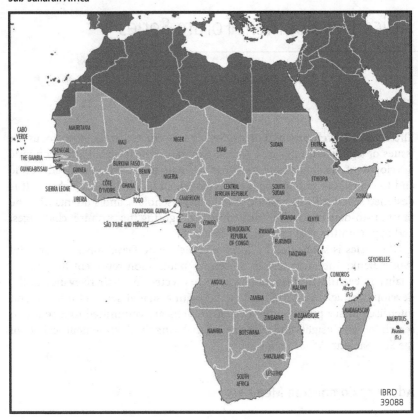

*Source:* World Bank (IBRD 39088R, September 2015).

# Titles in the Africa Development Forum Series

*Tourism in Africa: Harnessing Tourism for Growth and Improved Livelihoods* (2014) by Iain Christie, Eneida Fernandes, Hannah Messerli, and Louise Twining-Ward

* *Safety Nets in Africa: Effective Mechanisms to Reach the Poor and Most Vulnerable*, «Les fi lets sociaux en Afrique : Méthodes effi caces pour cibler les populations pauvres et vulnérables en Afrique» (2015) edited by Carlo del Ninno and Bradford Mills

* *Land Delivery Systems in West African Cities: The Example of Bamako, Mali*, «Le système d'approvisionnement en terres dans les villes d'Afrique de l'Ouest: L'exemple de Bamako» (2015) by Alain Durand-Lasserve, Maÿlis Durand-Lasserve, and Harris Selod

*Enhancing the Climate Resilience of Africa's Infrastructure: The Power and Water Sectors* (2015) edited by Raffaello Cervigni, Rikard Liden, James E. Neumann, and Kenneth M. Strzepek

* *Africa's Demographic Transition: Dividend or Disaster?* «La transition demographique de l'Afrique» (2015) edited by David Canning, Sangeeta Raja, and Abdo S. Yazbeck

*The Challenge of Fragility and Security in West Africa* (2015) by Alexandre Marc, Neelam Verjee, and Stephen Mogaka

*Highways to Success or Byways to Waste: Estimating the Economic Benefits of Roads in Africa* (2015) by Ali A. Rubaba, Federico Barra, Claudia Berg, Richard Damania, John Nash, and Jason Russ

*Confronting Drought in Africa's Drylands: Opportunities for Enhancing Resilience* (2016) edited by Raffaello Cervigni and Michael Morris

*Mining in Africa: Are Local Communities Better Off?* (2017) by Punam Chuhan-Pole, Andrew L. Dabalen, and Bryan Christopher Land

*Reaping Richer Returns: Public Spending Priorities for African Agriculture Productivity Growth* (2017) by Aparajita Goyal and John Nash

* Available in French

All books in the Africa Development Forum series are available for free at
https://openknowledge.worldbank.org/handle/10986/2150

# Contents

## Figures

## Tables

# Foreword

A vibrant, sustainable, and resilient agriculture sector is vital for Sub-Saharan Africa's economic future. While the productivity of African agriculture has grown, it still lags behind comparable rates in Asia and Latin America, and it has not delivered the development dividends needed to significantly reduce poverty in rural areas across Sub-Saharan Africa. Consider this: nearly two-thirds of Africa's population still rely on agriculture to make a living, and for Africa's poorest households, food makes up almost three-quarters of consumption expenditures. As a result of limited agricultural productivity, Africa's growing urban populations are also confronted with higher food prices. To make a significant dent in poverty, enhancing the productivity and competitiveness of African agriculture must become a priority.

Clearly, the status quo must change. One key element that can accelerate change and unleash growth is to catalyze a shift toward more effective, efficient, and climate-resilient public spending in agriculture. This book comes at an opportune time, and the research effort was motivated by the confluence of several factors related to public spending on agriculture in Africa.

First is the elevated prominence of this topic in policy-making circles, underscored by the Maputo Declaration of 2003, and more recently, the Malabo Declaration of 2014, which calls for enhancing investment finance in agriculture as a means to ending hunger and halving poverty by 2025 through inclusive agricultural growth and transformation. Furthermore, assisting countries to develop national agricultural investment programs and to improve the efficiency and quality of expenditures has become a cornerstone of the New Partnership for Africa's Development (NEPAD) and its Comprehensive Africa Agriculture Development Programme (CAADP).

Second, Africa's development partners have been actively supporting this effort and in doing so have accumulated a large and growing body of experience and knowledge that can provide useful lessons. The World Bank, in particular, through a program with the Bill and Melinda Gates Foundation, has been assisting countries to carry out agriculture public expenditure reviews

(AgPERs), and more recently has been developing tools to help mainstream them as standard instruments for budgeting and policy making.

Third, as this book well demonstrates, agricultural spending in Sub-Saharan Africa is not only below that of other developing regions but its impact is also vitiated by subsidy programs and transfers that tend to benefit elites to the detriment of poor people and the agricultural sector itself. Shortcomings of the budgeting processes also reduce spending effectiveness. In light of this scenario, addressing the quality of public spending and the efficiency of resource use becomes an even more important issue than simply addressing the level of spending. The rigorous analysis presented in this book provides options for reform with a view to enhancing investment in the sector and eventually development impact.

The evidence shows that the efficient use of public funds has been instrumental in laying the foundations for agricultural productivity growth around the world, providing important lessons for African policy makers and development partners. Investments in rural public goods, combined with better policies and institutions, drive agricultural productivity growth. The dividends from investments to strengthen markets and to develop and disseminate improved technologies can be enormous. Similarly, improvement of the policy environment through trade and regulatory policy complements spending by enhancing incentives for producers and innovators to take advantage of public goods, thereby crowding in private investment. Reforming the design and implementation of these subsidy programs while prioritizing government spending in favor of high-return core public goods and policies could produce significant gains. For this reason, this book argues for a rebalancing of the composition of public agricultural spending to reap richer development dividends.

We hope that the findings presented here will resonate with policy makers concerned with agricultural policies, and more specifically with public spending programs that aim to improve the productivity of African agriculture. The target audiences include ministries of agriculture, as well as ministries of finance, planning, and rural development, which are concerned with maximizing the development impact of public expenditures across different sectors. In addition, the study seeks to reinforce the work of regional initiatives, such as CAADP, that are working with individual country governments to enhance the efficiency of agricultural budgets and increase investments in agriculture. Ultimately, we hope that the findings will help catalyze growth in Sub-Saharan Africa's agricultural sector for the benefit of all Africans.

*Makhtar Diop*
Vice President, Africa Region
The World Bank

# Preface

An important aspect of evidence-based policy making for improving productivity—and thereby reducing poverty and boosting shared prosperity—is the use of rigorous research to inform policy choices. Making such choices on public spending for increasing agricultural productivity is critical in this regard. One objective of this study is, therefore, to analyze the effectiveness of different types of agricultural public expenditures for drawing conclusions about what works and what does not for sustainable productivity growth. Another is to provide evidence-based guidance and pragmatic policy advice to governments, development partners, civil society, and the private sector on the cost-effectiveness of major programs in meeting their objectives and their collateral consequences. A third is to identify common problems that impede spending effectiveness—whether in the political economy or in the more technical realm—and to examine how these constraints can be overcome.

As with any such effort, it comes with caveats and limitations. First, this work is mainly about how to craft spending to address the productivity challenge in Africa, and how spending choices affect poverty. It also touches on how spending can be used to address other objectives, such as improving resilience and enhancing nutrition, though these are not the main areas of focus. And to the extent that enhancing productivity is an essential ingredient in a strategy to transform agriculture, the messages of this book are relevant for this broader objective as well, but they are not intended as a checklist for a comprehensive transformation strategy.

Second, this is not an operational manual for carrying out an agriculture public expenditure review (AgPER)—it is intended mainly to provide rigorous analysis for crafting and evaluating agricultural budgets. Readers interested in such a "how to" manual should refer to the World Bank's "Practitioners' Toolkit for Agriculture Public Expenditure Analysis."

Third, this volume is not concerned with project-level implementation in specific spending categories. A good overview of this topic, covering many kinds of projects, has been covered in the World Bank's *Agriculture Investment Sourcebook.*

Finally, many topics identified in preparing the book are highly relevant to public agricultural spending policy, but fall outside its scope. Excellent candidates for future research include

- Identifying areas for transforming African agriculture; using policy and spending to address employment, resilience, and nutrition
- Assessing investment support instruments with regard to their effectiveness in incentivizing structural change and deeper sector transformation
- Using ground-truthing and case studies to explore the differences in administrative complexity and the costs of various public-spending instruments
- Integrating cost considerations in impact evaluations of various types of spending to enable benefit-cost analyses, which are fairly rare outside the categories of research and subsidies
- Studying how to achieve an optimal balance between support for smallholder farming versus large-scale farming

Pursuing these topics could do much to transform African agriculture, reduce extreme poverty, and boost shared prosperity in the region.

# Acknowledgments

This volume is part of the African Regional Studies Program, an initiative of the Africa Region Vice Presidency at the World Bank. This series of studies aims to combine high levels of analytical rigor and policy relevance, and to apply them to various topics important for the social and economic development of Sub-Saharan Africa. Quality control and oversight are provided by the Office of the Chief Economist in the Africa Region (AFRCE). This study, in particular, is an outcome of collaborative effort of the AFRCE, Poverty Global Practice, Agriculture Global Practice, Development Economics Research Group (DECRG), International Fertilizer Development Center (IFDC), International Food Policy Research Institute (IFPRI), Bill and Melinda Gates Foundation, and academic experts from Michigan State University and Stanford University.

The team was led by Aparajita Goyal and John Nash and included Joshua Ariga, Samuel Benin, Bill Burke, Alvina Erman, Erick Fernandes, Habtamu Fuje, Madhur Gautam, Ruth Hill, Hanan Jacoby, Thom Jayne, Nicole Mason, Stephen Mink, Tewodaj Mogues, and Yurie Tanimichi. Background papers for chapters were authored by Samuel Benin (chapter 2); Thom Jayne, Nicole Mason, Joshua Ariga, and Bill Burke (chapter 3); Stephen Mink (chapter 4); and Tewodaj Mogues and Alvina Erman (chapter 5). These are available as working papers, as indicated in individual chapters. Additional inputs were also received from Kathleen Beegle, Luc Christiaensen, Chris Delgado, and David Nielson. Excellent research assistance was provided by Sinafikeh Gemessa, Abdul Nabourema, and Sehoon Park.

The team would like to acknowledge the generous support of the AFRCE, Bill and Melinda Gates Foundation, and Consultative Group for International Agricultural Research Program on Policies, Institutions, and Markets. Invaluable advice was provided by Karen Brooks, Mark Cackler, Shanta Devarajan, Dina Umali-Deininger, Pablo Fajnzylber, Francisco Ferreira, Mark Lundell, Bill Maloney, Mamta Murthi, Martien van Nieuwkoop, Punam Chuhan Pole, Ana Revenga, Ethel Sennhauser, Juergen Voegele, Jan Walliser, and Albert Zeufack.

Thanks to Nabil Chaherli, Andrew Dabalen, Keith Fuglie, Holger Kray, Don Larson, Robert Townsend, and anonymous reviewers selected by the AFRCE for insightful peer review comments. Useful suggestions were also provided by Simeon Ehui, Massimo Mastruzzi, Elliot Mghenyi, and Alan Rennison. Several World Bank staff, as well as policy makers, academics, and other stakeholders, provided comments at various stages of the development of this study. Thanks also to Srilatha Shankar, Salam Hailou, Cindy Fisher, Volana Andriamasinoro, Mapi Buitano, Marina Galvani, Alexandre Hery, Sarwat Hussain, Beatrice Berman, Stephen McGroarty, Abdia Mohamed, and Kofi Tsikata for administrative, communication, design, and outreach efforts. Bruce Ross-Larson was the principal editor. All errors and omissions are the responsibility of the team.

# About the Authors

**Aparajita Goyal** is senior economist in the Poverty and Equity Global Practice, Africa Region of the World Bank. Her work focuses on microeconomic issues of development, with a particular emphasis on technological innovation in agriculture, access to markets, and intellectual property rights. She has worked on operations, policy advice, and analytical activities in Africa, Latin America, and South Asia. Her research has been published in leading academic journals such as *American Economic Review, Journal of Human Resources*, and *Journal of Development Economics*, and has also been featured in popular press such as *Frontline, The Economist*, and *The Wall Street Journal*, among others. Since joining the World Bank through the Young Professionals Program, she has worked in the Development Economics Research Group, Office of the Chief Economist for the Latin America and the Caribbean Region, and the Agriculture Global Practice. She holds a PhD in economics from the University of Maryland, an MSc from the London School of Economics, and a BA in economics from St. Stephen's College, University of Delhi, India.

**John Nash** is lead economist in the Agriculture Global Practice of the Sub-Saharan Africa Region of the World Bank. Prior to joining the World Bank in 1986, he was an assistant professor at Texas A&M University and an economic advisor to the chairman of the Federal Trade Commission of the United States. At the Bank, John has worked in regional vice presidencies serving Africa, Europe and Central Asia, and Latin America and the Caribbean, as well as units carrying out global research and strategic leadership in sustainable development. Among his recent major publications are (co-authored) *Reaping Richer Returns: Public Spending Priorities for Agriculture Productivity Growth; Highways to Success or Byways to Waste: Estimating the Economic Benefits of Roads in Africa; Low Carbon, High Growth: Latin American Responses to Climate Change; Natural Resources in Latin America and the Caribbean: Beyond*

*Booms and Busts?*; *Agricultural Exports from Latin America and the Caribbean: Harnessing Trade to Feed the World and Promote Development*; and *Unlocking Africa's Agricultural Potential: An Action Agenda for Transformation*. He holds an MSc and PhD in economics from the University of Chicago and a BS in economics from Texas A&M University.

# Abbreviations

| | |
|---|---|
| AfDB | African Development Bank |
| AgPER | agriculture public expenditure review |
| AOI | agriculture orientation index |
| ASARECA | Association for Strengthening Agricultural Research in East and Central Africa |
| ASTI | Agricultural Science and Technology Indicators |
| AU | African Union |
| BCR | benefit-cost ratio |
| CAADP | Comprehensive Africa Agriculture Development Programme |
| CDD | community-driven development |
| CGE | computable general equilibrium |
| CGIAR | Consultative Group on International Agricultural Research |
| COFOG | Classification of Functions of Government (United Nations) |
| CORAF | Council for Agricultural Research and Development |
| CSA | climate-smart agriculture |
| DALY | disability-adjusted life year |
| DID | difference-in-differences |
| ECA | United Nations Economic Commission for Africa |
| ECOWAS | Economic Community of West African States |
| ERS | Economic Research Service |
| EU | European Union |
| FAO | Food and Agriculture Organization |
| FDI | foreign direct investment |

| | |
|---|---|
| FE | fixed effects |
| ICT | information and communications technology |
| IFDC | International Fertilizer Development Center |
| IFPRI | International Food Policy Research Institute |
| IPCC | Intergovernmental Panel on Climate Change |
| IPR | intellectual property rights |
| IRR | internal rate of return |
| ISP | input subsidy program |
| LCU | local currency unit |
| M&E | monitoring and evaluation |
| MTEF | medium-term expenditure framework |
| MVCR | marginal value-cost ratio |
| NAIP | national agricultural investment plan |
| NEPAD | New Partnership for Africa's Development |
| ODA | official development assistance |
| R&D | research and development |
| ReSAKSS | Regional Strategic Analysis and Knowledge Support System |
| ROR | rate of return |
| SOE | state-owned enterprise |
| SPEED | Statistics on Public Expenditures for Economic Development |
| TFP | total factor productivity |
| UN | United Nations |
| USAID | United States Agency for International Development |
| USDA | United States Department of Agriculture |
| VCR | value-cost ratio |
| WAEMU | West African Economic and Monetary Union |
| WDI | World Development Indicators |

# Overview

The lack of sustainable agricultural productivity growth underlies pervasive rural poverty in Sub-Saharan Africa. While many developing countries in other regions have successfully raised their agricultural productivity, Sub-Saharan Africa tends to lag behind. Yet boosting agricultural productivity in Sub-Saharan Africa would not only raise the incomes of farm households, which make up more than half the region's population, but also lower food costs for the nonfarm population and promote the development of agro-industry. This in turn would promote broader economic growth by stimulating demand for nonfarm goods and services. Higher productivity would also free up resources such as labor for the growth of other economic sectors. For these reasons, improving agricultural productivity in Sub-Saharan Africa remains an important strategy for reducing poverty, enhancing inclusive growth, and promoting structural transformation in the region.

Investments in rural public goods combined with better policies and institutions have driven agricultural productivity growth around the world. The dividends from investments to strengthen markets, expand water access, and develop and adopt improved technologies can be enormous. And improving the policy environment through trade and regulatory policy reforms complements such spending by enhancing the incentives for producers and innovators to take advantage of public goods, thus crowding in private investment. Despite high returns to such investments, Sub-Saharan countries tend to underinvest in them. Rebalancing the composition of public agricultural spending toward high return investments could reap massive payoffs.

Agriculture public spending in Sub-Saharan Africa is not only lower than other developing regions on several metrics of volume but also is vitiated by subsidy programs and transfers that favor the better-off with insignificant gains for agriculture productivity growth or for the poor. Shortcomings of the budgeting process also reduce spending effectiveness. Therefore, addressing the quality of public spending and the efficiency of resource use is perhaps even more important than addressing the level of spending.

Improving the efficiency of public spending requires managing the political pressures that determine budget allocations. Groups of producers that control a large proportion of national wealth often have the means to influence public policies to their benefit. And political pressures sometimes influence spending toward short gestation projects and programs rather than those that are longer in term but also higher in impact. How then to marshal political support for reform and more effective spending? By increasing transparency about the distributional effects of policies, by improving targeting and gradually phasing out subsidies, by using mechanisms to enhance credibility of government commitment to investments with long time horizons, and by packaging and sequencing reforms in ways that reduce opposition.

The dearth of rigorous evaluations and limited access to data and public information on expenditures as well as its beneficiaries reduce the effectiveness of formal accountability mechanisms that might be provided by political checks and balances, a free press, and well-intentioned civil society organizations. Rigorous evidence and wide dissemination could reduce this information gap and increase transparency.

Efficient public spending is only one ingredient of a strategy for agricultural transformation, and must be complemented by a host of additional policies. Indeed, in a poor policy environment, even spending in areas that would otherwise deliver high returns will be unproductive or counterproductive. Although these complementary policies and investments are essential, this book is not about them—it is about public spending in and for agriculture. But as we will demonstrate, the efficient use of public funds has laid the foundation for transformation in other parts of the world, and a key objective here is to explore how public agricultural spending can play that role in Sub-Saharan Africa as well.

## Enhance Agricultural Productivity to Reduce Poverty

### Extreme Poverty Is Broad and Deep

Extreme poverty is becoming concentrated in Sub-Saharan Africa, which accounted for 43 percent of global poverty in 2012,[1] and its breadth and depth remain a dominant challenge (World Bank, WDI database). While the region's gross domestic product (GDP) growth has picked up in recent years, it has been driven mostly by higher production of mineral and hydrocarbon resources. This has not rapidly reduced poverty or boosted shared prosperity—the World Bank's twin goals (Ferreira, Leite, and Ravallion 2010). Even after experiencing nearly two decades of economic growth, most Africans continue to earn their livelihoods in the traditional economy. Much more than in any other region, agriculture dominates African economies, accounting for a third of the GDP regionwide and employing two-thirds of the labor force, with the poorest countries most heavily reliant on it.

*Growth Must Be Revitalized Where the Poor Work*

Clearly one element to progress toward the twin goals is to revitalize growth where a large majority of the continent's poor live and work. Evidence indicates that agricultural growth reduces poverty in developing countries by around three times more than growth in other sectors (Ivanic and Martin 2014; Christiaensen and Kaminski 2015). Improving agricultural productivity is also critical for fostering structural transformation and managing the urban transition by increasing incomes and enabling people to move out of agriculture (Gollin, Lagakos, and Waugh 2013). Investments and policies to foster growth in the rural economy thus emerge as critical for accelerating poverty reduction and fostering inclusive growth in the region.

## African Agriculture Has Been Growing, But Not Sustainably

Growth in agricultural production in Africa has undeniably picked up in recent years, and was close to that of other developing regions in 1985–2012 (figure O.1). In those other regions, production increases were mainly associated with yield growth due to intensive use of inputs and improved production technologies. In Africa, however, production increases were largely the result of expanding the area under cultivation (Deininger et al. 2011). Such expansion cannot be sustained indefinitely, even with Africa's relative land abundance.

**Figure O.1** Production Increases in Africa Came Largely from Expanding the Area under Cultivation Rather Than Input Intensification or Total Factor Productivity Growth

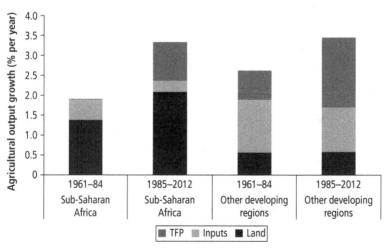

*Source:* USDA Economic Research Service data.
*Note:* TFP = total factor productivity.

The Green Revolution that boosted yields in other countries largely bypassed Africa. A comparison with Asia and South America over two decades shows Africa in the 1990s with lower total factor productivity growth than its comparators (TFP is a comprehensive measure of overall efficiency in the use of all inputs) (Fuglie 2015). And while other regions enjoyed faster growth in the 2000s than in the 1990s, Africa's rate fell even lower, further magnifying the TFP gap (figure O.2).

### Conditions Are in Place to Transform African Agriculture

Although TFP needs to be the primary driver of sustainable agricultural growth, Africa's potential for agricultural prosperity is enhanced by an abundance of vital inputs. Of the world's surface area suitable for the sustainable expansion of production—that is, unprotected, unforested land with low population density—Africa has the largest share by far, accounting for almost 45 percent of the global total. Although some large areas of the continent are arid or semi-arid, the water resources in Africa are also, on average, substantially underused. Only 2.5 percent of renewable water resources in Africa are being used, half the 5 percent rate worldwide.

On the supply side, the prospects are promising to increase both capital and the labor devoted to agricultural production. If the investment climate can be improved, the potential for attracting a higher share of global

**Figure O.2** Total Factor Productivity Growth in Africa Lags behind Other Regions—and the Gap Is Widening

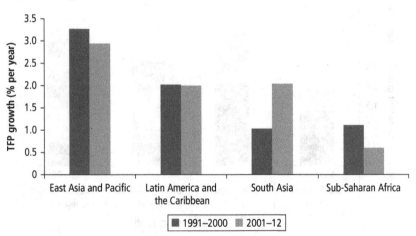

*Source:* USDA Economic Research Service data.
*Note:* TFP = total factor productivity.

resources can be realized. Africa's inward foreign direct investment (FDI) stock in agriculture accounts for a mere 7 percent of the total stock in developing countries, compared with 78 percent for those of Asia and 15 percent for those of Latin America and the Caribbean. There is also the prospect of a growing labor force for agriculture. With the creation of jobs in upstream or downstream agribusinesses, this "youth dividend" could drive growth in the sector. But failing to create these jobs would mean rising unemployment or accelerated migration to already-crowded cities (Brooks et al. 2013).

## African Markets Are Growing Rapidly

On the demand side, African regional markets are growing rapidly—driven by population, urban, and income growth—and are forecast to reach a trillion dollars by 2030 (figure O.3) (World Bank 2013a). The rising demand for food to nourish rapidly growing urban populations has so far been filled mostly with imports. From the 1990s to the 2000s, the balance of trade in food staples was moving from deficit to surplus in Europe and Central Asia, South Asia, and East Asia and Pacific. But in Sub-Saharan Africa, the deficits widened (World Bank 2012). Food trade deficits are understandable in a region such as the Middle East and North Africa, which has limited advantage in food production. But in Sub-Saharan Africa, where all the natural ingredients for

**Figure O.3** The Retail Value of Food and Beverages in Sub-Saharan Africa Is Set to Hit US$1 Trillion

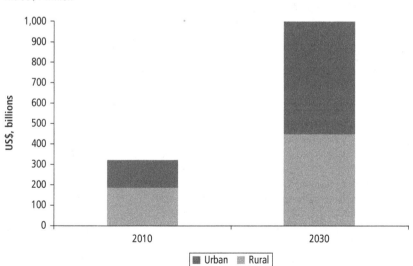

*Source:* World Bank 2013a.

efficient production are in place, the deficits signal that something fundamental is amiss. If not reversed, the consequences of missed opportunities to capture regional markets will only increase over time. But if African agriculture becomes more competitive and regional producers capture these markets, the benefits could be enormous. Taking full advantage of these opportunities will need smart policy choices to reduce trade barriers, which currently greatly impede regional trade, as well as smart spending in the public and private sectors to make Africa's production more competitive with imports.

**Improving Public Spending on Agriculture Can Boost Productivity**

A crucial element in enhancing agricultural productivity growth is improving the provision of productive investments through more and better public spending in agriculture (box O.1). This opportunity has been recognized by African

## BOX O.1

### How Productive Is Public Spending in Agriculture?

Past estimates put the elasticity of agriculture output with respect to public spending in African agriculture in the range of 0.1 to 0.3. But most of these studies were conducted with data prior to 2003. Recent trends in agricultural spending on the continent are quite different from the earlier trends, especially following the commitment by African leaders in 2003 to increase their annual spending on agriculture to 10 percent of total national expenditure. For example, the share of agricultural spending in total spending and the agricultural growth rate from 2001–10 both declined as compared to shares in the 1980s and 1990s. New evidence is needed on the returns to public agricultural spending that accounts for the recent declines in spending and productivity.

To address this lacuna, research for this book (Benin 2015) used data from 34 African countries, including the post-2003 period, to undertake a careful estimation of the effects of overall public agricultural spending and public spending on agricultural research—and then to present estimated rates of return for each country. An aggregate agricultural productivity function (value added per hectare) was estimated with capital, labor, fertilizer, animal feed, rainfall, irrigation, and an index of technology level, which yielded elasticities of productivity for each of these variables. These elasticities were then used to estimate rates of return to spending in individual countries and groups of countries by the number of years participating in the Comprehensive Africa Agriculture Development Programme (CAADP) and by agroecological zones. The aggregate elasticity of agriculture productivity to public agricultural spending in the sample countries was 0.04, with a rate of return of 11 percent. That is significantly lower than past estimates. But the elasticity to research spending was estimated to be substantially higher than for overall expenditure, at 0.09, with rates of return ranging from 24 percent to 126 percent.

policy makers, and over the past few years, ministries of agriculture and finance have intensified efforts to improve both the quantity (volume) and quality (effectiveness) of public spending. In 2003, African nations launched the Comprehensive Africa Agriculture Development Programme (CAADP), including a commitment to invest 10 percent of national public spending in agriculture, a commitment popularly known as the Maputo Declaration. This target was recently reiterated in the 2014 Malabo Declaration, and CAADP has led the charge to support national teams working on agriculture sector expenditure to conduct basic agriculture public expenditure reviews and related specialized analyses. A cornerstone of CAADP's work and that of its development partners, including the World Bank, has been to assist countries in developing national agricultural investment plans, make progress toward the quantitative goal, and improve the quality of spending.

## Spending Choices Make a Difference

Increasing the volume of public spending in agriculture will be important but not sufficient to kindle agriculture growth and poverty reduction. Actions will also be needed to improve the efficiency and effectiveness of public spending. The expectation that high-quality public spending should bolster growth has strong empirical validation. This book shows significant differences in the rates of return to different categories of agricultural spending. Indeed, many studies find quite low returns to aggregate spending on agriculture. But almost all find high returns to specific types of spending, such as investments in core public goods related to technology generation and diffusion, market links, and rural infrastructure. The implication is that a large part of the spending in some countries goes to low-return activities, dragging down the overall returns relative to what they could have been if more spending were allocated to the higher-return activities. The inevitable conclusion is that choices about how to allocate public agricultural spending matter a lot.

The importance of getting the greatest impact from public spending is further magnified in the recent period, when fiscal resources became more constrained with the end of the commodities boom. Previously high prices have afflicted commodity-dependent countries with a Dutch disease effect. Appreciating exchange rates from the large inflows of foreign exchange from commodities depressed internal prices for other tradable sectors, including agriculture, and made domestic products less competitive with imports. This has long been a problem in countries like Gabon, Nigeria, and the Democratic Republic of Congo, with their hydrocarbon and mineral sectors. The end of the boom is in one sense good news for the agricultural sector. But it also reduces public sector budgets, reinforcing the message that agricultural budgets need to be well spent—or risk getting disproportionately cut.

## Other Complementary Policies and Investments Are Necessary as Well

Enhanced public spending in agriculture is only one ingredient of a strategy for agricultural transformation. Investments in broader rural infrastructure, health, and education matter too, and wise investments must be complemented by a host of other policies. Indeed, in a poor policy environment, even spending in areas generally considered high return will be unproductive or counterproductive. But smart use of public funds—not only by agriculture ministries but also by other ministries dealing with hard and soft infrastructure in rural areas—has laid the foundation for transformation in other parts of the world. A key for policy makers and development practitioners is knowing what kinds of spending decisions can yield higher returns in achieving public policy objectives. What are the options to rebalance agricultural public spending and improve the budgeting process to increase the efficiency of limited resources for inclusive growth? Answering this question is the main objective of this book, so that public spending can do for Africa what it has done elsewhere.

## Why Governments Should Invest in Agriculture

Before discussing "what" African governments should be spending public funds on, it may be useful to briefly understand the "why." Why should governments be spending on agriculture at all? The rationale for public investments derives from two fundamental sources: economic inefficiencies caused by market failures and inequalities in the distribution of goods and services (box O.2).

---

### BOX O.2

### Correcting Market Failures and Inequalities

Agricultural production is quintessentially a private enterprise. But production requires public goods and services that the private sector, on both theoretical and practical grounds, cannot provide efficiently. One characteristic of such goods and services is that they are nonexcludable—if provided to one consumer, other potential beneficiaries cannot be kept from enjoying them. A second is that they are nonrivalrous—consumption by one does not reduce the consumption of another. Nonexcludability implies that potential beneficiaries cannot be charged for the good, so the producer cannot capture its full social value. Nonrivalry implies that it is inefficient to charge anything for the good, since the cost of supplying an additional unit (letting another consumer enjoy the benefits) is zero. These characteristics cause social and private returns to diverge, leading to private investments below the social optimum. That is why the public sector needs to play a role in their provision.

---

## Considering Pathways to Benefits

To guide decisions on areas appropriate for government spending, it helps to consider what kinds of goods and services are necessary to catalyze agricultural growth, and to what extent each is a "public good." To do this, we conceptualize the beneficial effects of public spending in agriculture along four pathways: generating technology, disseminating technology, reducing transaction costs, and attracting private capital. Each can be identified with particular classes of spending to provide goods or services that have public good characteristics and that are crucial for fostering robust agriculture productivity growth and poverty reduction in rural contexts.

- *To generate knowledge.* Technology-advancing effects are associated with public spending on agricultural research and development (R&D) to create basic knowledge, which is both nonexcludable and nonrivalrous. Sometimes the knowledge can be embodied in a commercial product (as with hybrid seeds and chemicals), with benefits that are excludable and rivalrous, but the basic knowledge itself is not. Investments in R&D are among the most important public goods and a critical component of public agricultural spending.

- *To disseminate knowledge and build human capital.* Effects that enhance human capital can be associated with public spending on extension, training, and information services that transfer knowledge and skills to those engaged in agricultural production. These investments create significant positive externalities through demonstration effects and peer-to-peer learning of benefits from adopting new productivity-enhancing technology. As agricultural production processes become increasingly knowledge intensive, with higher demand for precise and timely information, such investments become more important.

- *To reduce transaction costs.* Similarly, effects that reduce transaction costs can derive from public spending on soft and hard infrastructure that might improve access to input and output markets. Transaction costs are an important determinant of market integration, and investments that lower the costs of searching for and exchanging information—and of bargaining, decision making, and enforcing contracts—tend to enhance market participation. Investments in rural roads, market information dissemination, and land market development, for example, are important in reducing transaction costs.

- *To attract private capital.* The crowding-in effects of public agricultural spending on private capital occurs when public and private investments are complements in production. An example is public investment in large irrigation infrastructure such as dams and canals, which then make it profitable for farmers to make small on-farm investments in water management and a wider range of production technologies.

### Reducing Inequality and Poverty

Public spending in agriculture is also justified on equity grounds, especially salient given the concentration of the poor in rural areas, most of whom rely primarily on agriculture (directly or indirectly) for their livelihoods. One argument for fertilizer subsidies is that they could potentially help poor farmers break out of a low-productivity poverty trap. The equity justification for spending, of course, is stronger for programs that can actually be targeted at the poor and for programs that demonstrate a high income multiplier. For instance, impacts of spending on extension are just as progressive as those from several kinds of social spending, and are far superior to spending on subsidies. Also to be recognized is that many programs aimed at rural poverty reduction—either directly (as with rural safety nets) or indirectly (as with programs to support structural transformation by helping the rural poor find jobs in urban areas)—fall outside the scope of this study.

### Ensuring Productive Spending

Not all public spending is productive. This is a clear implication of the low estimated net benefits from total agricultural spending compared with the high benefits of some categories of agricultural spending (Benin et al. 2012; Fan, Gulati, and Thorat 2008). Apparently, where aggregate spending has no measurable impact, the negative effects of ineffective spending overwhelm the positive effects of more effective spending (Devarajan, Swaroop, and Zou 1996). Public spending may be unproductive or even reduce the productivity of other spending for two basic reasons. First, governments sometimes spend on things that are not public goods. They tend to be inefficient suppliers of private goods, and when they enter these markets, there is a serious risk of displacing the private sector. Second, even when there are clear failures in particular markets, government spending will not necessarily improve the situation. Inherent characteristics of government interventions can sometimes lead to "government failures," which may exacerbate the original problems caused by the market failures and produce unintended adverse ancillary effects. Empirically though, public spending on public goods has typically been much more productive than public spending on private goods (López and Galinato 2007).

## How Much Public Spending—And for What?

### Ten Percent on Agriculture?

In the 2003 Maputo Declaration, African heads of state and government agreed that spending was far too low in agriculture and set a goal of investing 10 percent of their total national spending in agriculture. This goal was reaffirmed in the Malabo Declaration in 2014, and assisting countries to increase the quantity and quality of public agricultural spending has been a major objective of the CAADP. There is also an aspirational goal of increasing agricultural annual growth to 6 percent for Sub-Saharan countries, though growth is not a policy variable under the direct control of governments the way public spending is.

Of course, for the objective of getting the biggest increase in national welfare from the overall budget, nothing is special about the 10 percent target for agriculture. The optimal distribution among sectors will depend on many country-specific factors (box O.3). In particular, to the extent that ministries of agriculture (and related ministries) can demonstrate that their programs are an efficient and high-impact use of public funds, they can make a stronger case to ministries of finance and planning for increasing their budgets. In this sense, enhancing the quality of spending is the first order of business, and this book sees this objective as the priority. Nonetheless, the quantity of spending is a meaningful indicator of government commitment to agriculture, so it is worth considering how Africa stacks up to other regions, and to the Maputo and Malabo targets.

## BOX O.3

### How Much of the Government Budget Should Be Devoted to Agriculture?

How much of the government budget should be devoted to agriculture, and how much to other sectors? What is "too little" and what is "enough"? The answers are conceptually straightforward but difficult to put into practice. In principle, to maximize welfare on a given budget, spending should be distributed such that the marginal dollar in each activity yields the same increase in national welfare (however *welfare* is defined). If this were not true—if, for example, an additional dollar devoted to agriculture increased welfare more than the incremental dollar to health spending—overall welfare could be increased by taking a dollar from health and spending it on agriculture.

In a two-sector world (agriculture and nonagriculture), this condition for distributing spending so as to maximize welfare can be expressed as equation (O.1):

$$\frac{dW}{dS_A} = \frac{dW}{dS_{NA}},$$
(O.1)

where $W$ is welfare and $S_A$ and $S_{NA}$ are spending on agriculture and nonagriculture.

*(continued next page)*

## Box 0.3 (continued)

Of course, how much welfare is increased by an incremental public dollar spent in agriculture depends on how much that dollar will increase agricultural production, as well as how much the additional production will increase welfare. This optimal allocation condition can be expressed in a ratio of spending in each sector, such that:

$$\frac{S_A}{S_{NA}} = \left(\frac{E_{WA}}{E_{W,NA}}\right) \times \left(\frac{E_{A,}S_A}{E_{NA,}S_{NA}}\right), \tag{O.2}$$

where $E_{WA}$ is the elasticity of welfare to agricultural production (and likewise for non-agricultural production), and $E_{A,}S_A$ is the elasticity of agricultural production to public spending in agriculture (and likewise for nonagricultural production).

The optimality condition in equation (O.2) provides a useful framework for thinking about spending allocations whereby the optimal ratio of public spending in agriculture versus nonagriculture is equal to the ratio of the welfare elasticity of each sector's production times the ratio of each sector's elasticity of production with respect to public spending in the sector. The problem in operationalizing this to provide practical guidance to policy makers is that it would require empirical estimation of all these elasticities (in every sector) for a given country. There have been attempts in cross-country samples to estimate the elasticity of welfare (measured by either national GDP or poverty reduction) with respect to agricultural production, and the elasticity of production with respect to public spending.[a] But there is no strong reason to assume that for any given country, the elasticities would be equal to the global or regional average.

In the absence of a practical way to rigorously answer the question of how much public spending should be allocated to agriculture, there have been some efforts to provide rules of thumb, which may seem intuitive and reasonable. For example, De Ferranti et al. (2005) show that with some special (and quite restrictive) simplifying assumptions, the optimal allocation is such that each sector's share of spending is its share of national GDP.[b] This index—the share of spending on agriculture relative to agriculture's share in the economy—is calculated for a number of Latin American countries over time to analyze whether there has been a systematic underallocation or "anti-agricultural bias" in public spending, with the general conclusion of no such bias in that region.

An alternative approach is to examine the experiences of countries that have undergone successful agricultural transformations. Analysis of 12 East and South Asian countries during their periods of high agricultural growth—the Green Revolution—shows that, on average, these countries devoted around 10 percent of total public spending to agriculture.[c] Many other factors certainly contributed to success, but public support was an important ingredient. Thus, the Maputo target is similar to what the Asian countries were spending on agriculture in this period. Likewise, the New Partnership for Africa's Development (NEPAD) target of spending 1 percent of agricultural GDP on research is quite similar to the level that Brazil devoted to its successful research agency, Embrapa, as well as the level of spending on research in some high-income countries.

*(continued next page)*

## Box O.3 (continued)

In applying such rules of thumb, it is also sensible to make adjustments based on economic reasoning using equation (O.2). For example, countries differ greatly in the contribution of agriculture to national GDP, and a 1 percent increase in agricultural production will generally result in a smaller percentage increase in overall GDP in a country in which agriculture is 10 percent of the economy than in a country in which it is 30 percent. That is, the value of $E_{WA}$ will be smaller in the latter than in the former, and so—all other things equal—the share of spending going to agriculture should be smaller as well. And the elasticity of production with respect to spending $(E_A, S_A)$ will be higher in countries with high agricultural potential (both because of favorable natural endowments and because the overall policy environment is conducive to a positive supply response)—and where the spending is "smarter." In such countries with a higher value of $E_A, S_A$ agriculture's share of spending should be higher.

*Sources:* De Ferranti et al. 2005; Correa and Schmidt 2014.
a. For example, see De Ferranti et al. (2005) with a focus on Latin America.
b. For agriculture, this would mean that the agriculture orientation index (AOI) is equal to 1.
c. The figures were 15.4 percent (1972), 10.5 percent (1975), 12.4 percent (1980), 10.9 percent (1985), and 9.6 percent (1990).

## Lagging behind Other Regions

Public agricultural spending in Africa has lagged behind that in other developing regions on several metrics. Agricultural spending as a share of overall public spending—the metric used in the Maputo Declaration—is substantially lower than that in other regions, particularly East Asia and the Pacific and South Asia (figure O.4). In 2014, only Burkina Faso, Malawi, Mozambique, and Zimbabwe had barely met or surpassed the 10 percent target (Malawi and Mozambique consistently surpassed it). Three countries—Niger, Rwanda, and Zambia—were close behind at 9 percent. On another metric—public spending on agriculture as a share of agricultural GDP—spending is also substantially lower in Africa than in other regions. This is also the case on the metric of spending per capita; in Africa, spending per capita was on average US$19, almost a third lower than that in the next lowest region, South Asia.

## Conditions and Contexts Differ Widely—But Trends Indicate a Widespread Problem

While almost all African countries are spending below the 10 percent target, country conditions and thus spending contexts differ widely across Sub-Saharan Africa (figure O.5). For instance, the spending target is arguably less meaningful for such countries as South Africa and Botswana, with relatively small agricultural GDP shares in the overall economy (box O.3). An alternative

**Figure O.4** Public Agricultural Spending Lags behind Other Regions, 2000–14

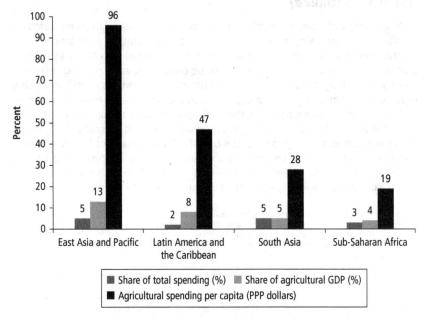

Source: IFPRI Statistics on Public Expenditures for Economic Development database.
Note: The figure represents public agricultural spending across regions. GDP = gross domestic product;
PPP = purchasing power parity.

indicator of the public budgetary commitment to agriculture accounts for
sector size—the Agriculture Orientation Index (AOI)—is agriculture's share of
public spending relative to its share in the economy.[2] An AOI value of 1 would
indicate that the government spends a share of its budget on agriculture exactly
proportional to agriculture's contribution to GDP. As with other indicators, this
is a blunt tool to measure policy, and only under special assumptions would
spending be allocated exactly in proportion to each sector's contribution to the
economy. Still, intuitively, large deviations would at least suggest a deeper
inquiry by policy makers.

As it turns out, no country in Africa has an AOI of 1, although some come
close (figure O.6). There is a strong tendency for the countries with small agricultural sectors to devote proportionately more of the budget to supporting it
(higher AOIs). Overall, however, most African countries spend much smaller
proportions of the public budget on agriculture than the sector's share in the
economy. Of the 47 countries for which the AOI can be computed, it is less than
0.3 in 31 countries.

While the numerical goal of 10 percent is somewhat arbitrary and the failure
to meet this target is arguably not so worrisome, the AOI also appears to

**Figure O.5** Almost All African Countries Fall Short of the 10 Percent Target of Government Spending, 2014

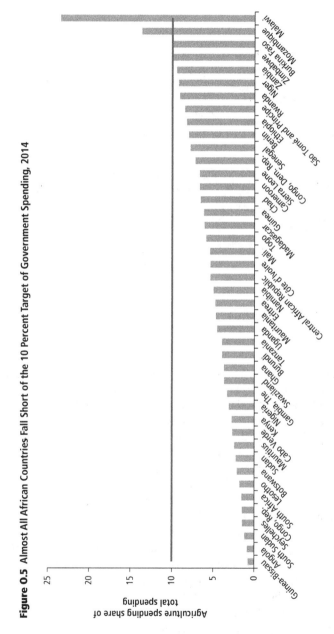

*Source:* IFPRI Regional Strategic Analysis and Knowledge Support System data.
*Note:* The figure represents public agricultural spending in Sub-Saharan countries.

**Figure O.6** No Country in Africa Spends as Much on Agriculture as Agriculture Contributes to the Economy

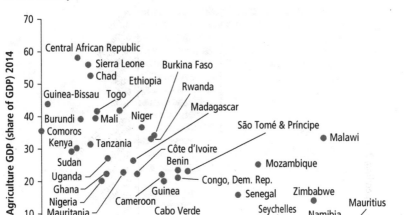

*Source:* World Bank calculations using SPEED database.
*Note:* AOI = agriculture orientation index; GDP = gross domestic product.

demonstrate underspending in most countries. Even more problematic is the persistent negative trend across three decades in agricultural spending as a share of both agricultural GDP and total public spending in Sub-Saharan Africa.

Perhaps even more important than the level of spending is the inefficiency of resource use within the existing budget envelope. Within any given overall budget envelope for agricultural public spending, the allocation across different activities needs to be balanced to achieve the highest returns for the overall portfolio. There is no one-size-fits-all formula for deciding what that optimal allocation across programs, investments, and activities should be. This allocation will differ greatly across countries, depending on country circumstances and political preferences. Even so, it is useful to consider what kinds of expenditures have generally been most productive, and to examine how current composition of spending appears to reflect these lessons—or not. The evidence on returns to different spending categories is a bit lopsided, in the sense that much more research integrating benefits and costs has been done on certain categories of spending such as R&D than on other types of spending. Why? Efforts at data collection in this area have been more systematic, and the specific kind of spending under this rubric is perhaps more homogeneous than other categories as well.

**Figure O.7** Public Agricultural Research Spending Lags in Sub-Saharan Africa, 2000–11

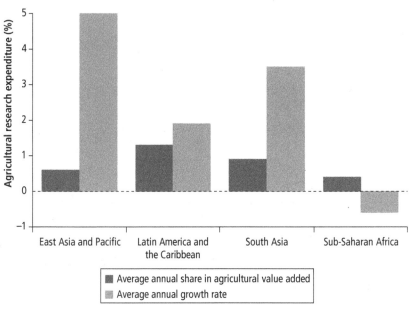

*Source:* IFPRI Agricultural Science and Technology Indicators data.

## Research Has High Returns but Is Severely Underfunded

Spending on agricultural R&D is worth an especially close look, given the strong evidence that returns to investments in this area are consistently high around the world. A large sample of studies estimated rates of return averaging 43 percent in developing countries and 34 percent in Sub-Saharan Africa. Yet agricultural R&D capacity in Sub-Saharan Africa has remained low by international norms. Over the last decade, spending on agricultural research constituted about 0.4 percent of agricultural GDP in Sub-Saharan Africa, compared with 1.3 percent in Latin America and the Caribbean, 0.6 percent in East Asia and the Pacific, and 0.9 percent in South Asia (figure O.7). In addition, Africa was the only region where agricultural research spending fell on average over this period. These are troubling signs that agricultural research is severely underfunded in Africa.

### Most Countries Fall Short of NEPAD's 1 Percent Target

It is not surprising that in 2006, in its commitment to implementing an agriculture-led development agenda, the African Union's NEPAD set an additional target to increase public spending on agricultural R&D to at least

**Figure O.8** Only Six Public Budgets in Sub-Saharan Africa Spend More Than One Percent of Agricultural GDP on Research, 2011

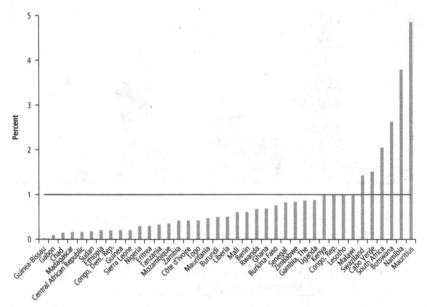

*Source:* IFPRI Agricultural Science and Technology Indicators data.
*Note:* The figure represents agricultural research spending as a share of agricultural GDP. GDP = gross domestic product.

1 percent of agricultural GDP, a target that few countries have met (figure O.8). As noted earlier, most high-income countries spend around 1 percent of their agricultural GDP on research, as does Brazil, a country widely regarded to have an effective research agency, Embrapa. A closer look at the relative shift in the patterns of spending in agricultural R&D in Sub-Saharan countries over time reveals important cross-country differences and challenges. Over 2000–11, half the Sub-Saharan countries experienced near-zero or negative growth in agricultural R&D spending (figure O.9). Despite the well-documented considerable payoffs to agricultural research and the demonstrated political commitment to agricultural R&D in Africa, many Sub-Saharan countries have continued to underinvest in this activity.

*Agricultural R&D Spending Is Low Despite the Enormous Rewards*
Spending on R&D has driven agriculture's transformation around the world. During periods of rapid growth, Brazil, China, and India invested heavily in agricultural research, with their collective share in developing country public spending on agricultural R&D rising from a third in 1981 to almost half in 2000

**Figure O.9** Half the Countries Have Zero or Negative Spending Growth, 2000–11

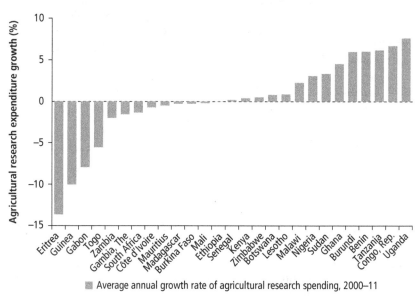

Average annual growth rate of agricultural research spending, 2000–11

*Source:* IFPRI Agricultural Science and Technology Indicators data.
*Note:* The figure represents annual growth in agricultural R&D spending. The figure excludes Cabo Verde, the Central African Republic, Chad, the Democratic Republic of Congo, Guinea-Bissau, Liberia, Mauritania, Mozambique, Namibia, Rwanda, Sierra Leone, and Swaziland because time series data did not date back to 2000. R&D = research and development.

(Alston et al. 2000; Pardey et al. 2007). And investments in national and international agricultural research have been demonstrated to be among the most important determinants of long-term productivity growth in Sub-Saharan Africa as well. For example, the Consultative Group on International Agricultural Research (CGIAR) has played an important role in raising agricultural productivity growth in Sub-Saharan Africa. Spending by CGIAR in the region has generated US$6 in benefits for every dollar spent on research in Africa. Returns to national agricultural R&D spending have been lower, but still significant, averaging about US$3 in benefits for every US$1 spent on R&D.

Given the economies of scale in research, one would expect that resources devoted to research would bear more fruit in larger countries. And indeed, this seems to be the case. Large countries have earned higher returns to R&D than small countries, but even in small countries, returns were still high enough to justify the investment, particularly around adaptive research (table O.1). Moreover, national and international agricultural research efforts in Sub-Saharan Africa are complementary: countries that have made a greater

**Table 0.1** Returns to Agricultural Research in Sub-Saharan Africa

| Countries | Returns to agricultural research | | |
|---|---|---|---|
| | Benefit-cost ratio | IRR (%) | IRR (%) without CGIAR |
| **Large countries** | | | |
| Côte d'Ivoire, Ethiopia, Ghana, Kenya, Nigeria, Sudan | 4.4 | 43 | 36 |
| **Midsize countries** | | | |
| Madagascar, Mali, Mozambique, Senegal, Uganda | 2.6 | 29 | 23 |
| **Small countries** | | | |
| Botswana, Burundi, Gabon, The Gambia, Swaziland | 1.6 | 17 | 13 |

*Source:* Fuglie and Rada 2013.
*Note:* The benefit-cost ratio discounts future benefits at a yearly rate of 10 percent. CGIAR = Consultative Group on International Agricultural Research; IRR = internal rate of return.

national investment in agricultural research are better able to adapt and deliver new technologies to farmers emanating from international centers (Fuglie and Rada 2013).

African research institutions can learn from Brazil's Embrapa, whose success is attributable to institutional characteristics and policy choices in addition to adequate funding, such as high investment in human capital, effective collaboration with private sector and international research centers, as well as an open innovation system and intellectual property rights to facilitate technology development and diffusion. Other lessons emerging from Africa's own experience in investing in technology generation and dissemination will be useful in shaping future spending decisions in this area.

## Rebalance Spending to Reap Richer Returns

### Reduce the Barriers to Disseminating Foreign Technology and Developing Domestic Technology

An important principle for expenditure policy is that governments cannot afford to be the only, or even the main, developers of new technology. In Africa, governments currently fund more than 90 percent of the ongoing R&D. But with scarce budget resources, countries need to adopt policies to reduce barriers to spill-ins of technology from abroad and to encourage private investment in technology generation. Current requirements for lengthy and expensive tests to register new seed varieties (imported or domestic) in many African countries practically guarantee that African farmers will not benefit from advances in other parts of the world or from private domestic R&D.

These barriers could be reduced by following the practices in such countries as India and South Africa, which allow the introduction of new varieties with no performance testing but which require truth in labeling to protect farmers from false claims (Gisselquist, Nash, and Pray 2002). This has been particularly effective in South Africa, where farmers benefit from a much higher rate of introducing new varieties than in other African countries, even accounting for the size of the market. Barriers can at least be lowered by mutual recognition of new varieties already registered in neighboring countries, the approach of the European Union (EU), and is being pursued in several regional regulatory frameworks in Africa, but progress has been slow. The two approaches are not mutually exclusive and countries could potentially consider unilateral action to reduce barriers while waiting for regional agreements to take shape (Keyser 2013).

### Invest in Land Governance

One key public good that is greatly undersupplied across Africa is the legal and institutional framework for land governance. Only about 10 percent of rural land in Africa is registered. The rest is undocumented or under informal arrangements that make it vulnerable to "land grabbing" or expropriation, a particular problem for women. It takes twice as long (65 days) and costs twice as much (9.4 percent of the property value) to transfer land in Sub-Saharan Africa than in Organisation for Economic Co-operation and Development (OECD) countries (31 days; 4.4 percent). The poor institutional framework is reflected in the low demand for land administration professionals: Ghana, Kenya, and Uganda, for example, all have fewer than 10 land surveyors per million population, compared with 197 in Malaysia and 150 in Sri Lanka (Byamugisha 2013). These conditions undermine land market development and secure tenure, weakening incentives to make on-farm investments and impeding rural credit market development.

Significant investments will be needed to reverse soil degradation and depletion, so improving land security will be hugely important to create conditions for sustainably boosting productivity. Many Sub-Saharan countries have either legislation in place or initiatives under way to address communal land rights and gender equality, the basis for sound land administration. In addition, they have made a commitment to implement more land policy reforms, primarily second-generation reforms, through a declaration adopted by the African heads of state and government in their July 2009 Summit in Libya, to develop and implement comprehensive land policies, guided by the African Union's *Framework and Guidelines on Land Policy in Africa* (AUC-ECA-AfDB Consortium 2010). Implementing the main elements of a strategy to raise standards of land governance across Africa is estimated to require increased spending of some US$4.3 billion.

## Bolster Extension

Another crucial element in crafting spending decisions to encourage greater adoption of modern technologies is to improve the effectiveness of extension services. Particularly where information constraints are a major bottleneck in the uptake of modern inputs and production techniques, public funding (although not necessarily provision) of extension can be a cost-effective use of public funds. Moreover, higher returns to investments in agricultural extension are expected if the rate of developing new technologies for Sub-Saharan Africa is increasing, enabling farmers to adjust more quickly to changing circumstances.

Extension services are coming back on the agenda, and in a few countries now make up substantial shares of the budget. But there is the risk that extension will once again be viewed as ineffective. Attention to extension services peaked in the 1980s and early 1990s, when money was poured into systems that mainly promoted agricultural technology adoption in a centralized, linear, one-size-fits-all method (Davis 2008). In the late 1990s, when many of these traditional systems were shown to be deficient in their quality and relevance, public spending on extension declined. However, the rapid adoption of digital technologies in rural areas shows promise in reviving some aspects of extension services and consequently improving productivity. Innovative models are being implemented in Kenya and Nigeria. New tools and approaches have helped overcome information problems that hinder market access for many small-scale farmers, promote knowledge and skill development, and stimulate opportunities for agricultural supply chain management (Deichmann, Goyal, and Mishra 2016).

The balance between R&D and extension has long been an issue, with critics suggesting that many of these extension agents had nothing to extend owing to weak R&D—and that extension systems tended to be the poor relation at the bottom of the funding chain. As a result entire budgets were spent on recurrent items such as salaries, while there was no fuel for vehicles and thus no farm visits (Thirtle and van Zyl 1994). In funding the new generation of extension programs, the lessons from the past need to be taken into account to better balance spending across subcategories and make extension more effective, particularly in reaping the benefits from irrigation (box O.4).

## Improve Post-Harvest Practices and Market Access

Investments in post-harvest processing facilities, access to markets, and accompanying infrastructure and policy reforms that foster commercial agriculture are critical for transforming African agriculture. A large literature on the impacts of investments to improve market access for farmers has found that benefits are significant, come in different forms, and can be realized

**BOX O.4**

## Africa's Potential for Increasing Irrigation

The irrigated area as a share of total cultivated area is estimated at 6 percent for Africa, compared with 37 percent for Asia and 14 percent for Latin America. Food production in Africa remains almost entirely rainfed, despite highly variable and in many cases insufficient rainfall together with a high incidence of droughts. The potential for profitable irrigation development for Sub-Saharan Africa remains large, given the existing water resources, the high value of irrigated agriculture on the continent, and the large number of rural poor who could benefit from productivity improvements as a result of irrigation.

The returns to many irrigation projects in the past were relatively low in Africa, and the negative externalities high. But recent advances in planning and design techniques have provided the ability to minimize adverse environment and social consequences of large irrigation infrastructure. Recent studies show that irrigated land can be expanded from 13 million hectares to 24 million hectares in economically viable ways, with returns ranging from 17 percent for large-scale irrigation to 43 percent for small-scale irrigation (You et al. 2011). Sub-Saharan Africa has significant unexploited potential to develop both large- and small-scale irrigation, but economic viability depends on keeping costs down. Although there is significant potential for rehabilitating existing irrigated areas in the region, the expertise, knowledge, and capacity to manage irrigation investments are low (Rosegrant, Ringler, and Zhu 2009).

through several channels. Reduction in transport costs reduces both trade costs and interregional price gaps (Casaburi, Glennerster, and Suri 2013). The spillover effects are that farmers pay less for their inputs and get more for their outputs, increasing incomes (Chamberlin et al. 2007; Stifel and Minten 2008).

Proximity to rural roads has significant effects on poverty and agricultural productivity overall. This is particularly critical in Africa, where less than half of the rural population lives close to an all-season road. Trader surveys in Benin, Madagascar, and Malawi find that transport costs account for 50–60 percent of total marketing costs (Dercon et al. 2008; World Bank 2008). In Tanzania, the maize price pass-through from broader markets to farmers was significantly lower even 25 miles away from a paved road (Delgado, Minot, and Tiongco 2005). Higher profitability from road access also increases the value of farmers' land (Donaldson, forthcoming; Jacoby 2000). Not surprisingly, access to markets facilitates economic diversification in rural areas and creates incentives to adopt modern production technologies by farmers.

### Shift Government Spending from Private to Public Goods

Research from Latin America and the Caribbean finds that it is crucial to shift public spending from providing goods and services to specific groups of producers toward the increased provision of public goods. On average, 51 percent of total government spending in rural areas was on subsidies to private goods during 1985–2001. A reallocation of 10 percentage points of public expenditures from subsidies to public goods would increase per capita agricultural income by about 2.3 percent without increasing total spending (López and Galinato 2007; Valdes 2008). These findings from cross-country analysis for Latin America are consistent with the analysis for Asia, where spending on rural infrastructure, agricultural research, and dissemination had large poverty alleviation effects (box O.5). Governments in Africa and other developing regions have invested heavily in state-owned enterprises (SOEs), or parastatals, to perform commercial functions that generally are carried out more efficiently by the private sector, crowding out private investment and dragging down overall sectoral performance. While this situation has improved over time, SOEs are still more involved than they should be in the agriculture sector, particularly in marketing inputs and outputs.

**BOX O.5**

## Reform Policies and Invest Well: Lessons from Asia's Agricultural Transformation

Many parts of Asia have achieved impressive gains in agricultural productivity and poverty reduction over the past half-century. By contrast, sustained productivity growth remains elusive in most of Africa. What can African policy makers learn from Asia's experience? Conditions naturally differ in many respects between Africa and Asia, but it is instructive to understand the mix of public investments and policies of many Asian countries, and their relative importance in driving growth and reducing poverty. Spending on productive investments related to the development and diffusion of technological improvements, greater connectivity in rural areas, and irrigation development did the most to reduce poverty.

In India, the relative performance of subsidies evolved over time, with somewhat higher returns in the early years of the Green Revolution but declining rapidly thereafter. Fertilizer, power, and irrigation subsidies were among the least significant contributors over the four decades.

The findings of these studies provide potentially important implications for enhancing agricultural growth and poverty reduction in Africa. There are strong reasons to believe that the policy reforms and investments that generated high payoffs in Asia can drive growth and reduce poverty in most of Africa as well.

## Target Spending to Reduce Poverty

The scope is considerable for crafting investments to magnify their pro-poor impacts. Rural roads and irrigation infrastructure can be geographically targeted at areas where there are concentrations of poverty. Research can be aimed at crops, livestock, and technologies that are likely to be most useful to the poor rather than, say, for example, plantation export crops. Efforts to connect farmers to markets can be focused on smallholders. Analysis indicates that such investments can have a large payoff in both economic growth and poverty reduction (box O.6).

These must be conscious decisions in the design and targeting of spending programs, and there are likely to be trade-offs between distributional objectives and the goal of boosting the growth of agricultural GDP. Of course, this kind of pro-poor targeting has limits, since the investments will benefit the landless poor only indirectly, for instance. As far as we know, there are no comprehensive cross-country studies on the extent to which current spending policies are taking advantage of opportunities to target in this way. Anecdotal evidence

## BOX 0.6

## Impacts of Policy Options to Raise Agricultural Productivity in Sub-Saharan Africa

Recent research has quantified the potential improvement in productivity from policy reforms and several kinds of spending on agriculture or in rural areas. While comprehensive development of Africa's agricultural sector requires investments across multiple areas, a TFP decomposition shows that productivity improvements in Africa have been led by investments in development of new technologies, wider adoption of new technologies (proxied by farmer education), and policy reforms to strengthen economic incentives to farmers (table BO.6.1).

**Table BO.6.1** Drivers of Agriculture Productivity in Sub-Saharan Africa

|  | Contribution to cumulative TFP growth (%) |
| --- | --- |
| Agriculture research and development | 51 |
| Improvement in agriculture's terms of trade with market and trade policy reform | 20 |
| Reduction in conflict | 18 |
| Increase in farmer education | 8 |
| HIV/AIDS therapy to adult population infected | 2 |

*Sources:* Fuglie and Rada 2013.
*Note:* HIV/AIDS = human immunodeficiency virus/acquired immune deficiency syndrome; TFP = total factor productivity.

suggests that decisions are being made this way (for example, almost all World Bank projects to improve market linkages are aimed at smallholders), but there undoubtedly is room for improvement.

## Address Emerging Priorities Arising from Climate Change

Public spending policy will need to remain flexible to cope with future challenges, and for agriculture, probably none is more urgent than climate change. It is a threat for agriculture across the world, but the lack of resilience of poor farmers makes it particularly serious in Sub-Saharan Africa. Projections show yield decreases in the near term of 5 percent, potentially growing to 15–20 percent across all crops and Sub-Saharan regions by the end of the century (World Bank 2013b). Agriculture is also an important contributor to greenhouse emissions, particularly from deforestation, and Africa is the only region where the majority of production increases have come from expanding cultivated areas, generally at the expense of forests. In Africa, as around the world, a more climate-resilient agriculture is needed to achieve the triple win of enhancing agricultural productivity, mitigating emissions of greenhouse gases, and helping farmers adapt to climate change.

Most investments to mitigate climate change (low-carbon growth) and adapt to it (resilience building) will need to be made by farmers and other private agents. But proactive government policies, planning, and investments will be required to provide information, incentives, and an enabling environment to encourage communities, households, and the private sector to change their behaviors and investment choices. Many climate-resilient investments will not be very different from productive investment choices, even not taking climate change into account. Building resilience has overall benefits in any case, but their value is amplified by the changes that will occur with global warming.

For public spending priorities, climate-smart agriculture entails using landscape-scale approaches to invest in managing climate risks through developing drought or flood-resistant technologies, understanding and planning for transitions to new adapted cropping and livestock systems and livelihood options, and reducing greenhouse gas emissions from livestock practices and land use changes that cause deforestation and losses of biomass and soil carbon. Increasing resilience, restoring degraded lands, and managing ecosystem services better will play key roles in all of these. Efforts to craft budgetary and policy choices to create a more climate-smart agriculture will have to cope with special challenges rooted in many uncertainties, distributional issues, and the long-term nature of the problem. To help meet these challenges, public expenditure reviews (PERs) will need to do a better job than in the past of incorporating considerations of climate change.

## Redress the Current Excessive Focus on Unproductive Fertilizer Subsidies

### Subsidies Are Resurging

The resurgence of input subsidy programs in Africa has arguably been the region's most important policy development for public agricultural spending in recent years. Ten African governments spend roughly US$1.2 billion annually on input subsidies alone (figure O.10), primarily on fertilizers. These programs were almost phased out in the 1990s, during a period of structural adjustment in Africa, but they have made a strong comeback due partly to residual support for subsidies among African leaders, even while pressured to phase them out, and partly to the uncertainties about food supply during the 2007–08 global food and fertilizer price instability. Input subsidies continue to be vastly popular among African politicians as a highly demonstrable way to support their constituents.

### Fertilizer Use Is Supposedly Suboptimal

The economic rationale for fertilizer subsidies comes mainly from the motivation that, because of credit and information constraints, fertilizer use is suboptimal in most of Africa. The subsidies could overcome these problems by

**Figure O.10** The 10 Largest African Governments Spend US$1.2 Billion a Year on Input Subsidies Alone

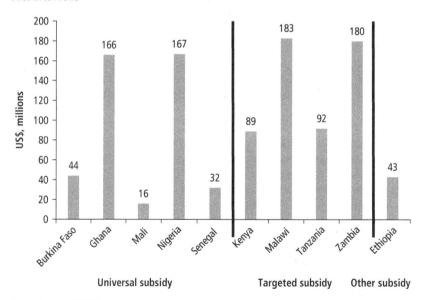

*Source:* Jayne et al. 2016.

reducing the costs that farmers incur and the barriers of affordability, access, and learning. This justification is often based on the fact that fertilizer is used much less intensively in Africa than in other regions, particularly Asia, and that fertilizer use in demonstration plots provides high returns.

Even so, there are reasons to question the assumption of suboptimal use. Experimental evidence from farmer-managed fields indicates response rates that are considerably lower than on researcher-managed fields. On the demonstration plots, crops are grown under conditions much closer to optimal than in most farmers' fields, with better soil and more plentiful water. But in much of Africa, water management is scarce, and soil has been degraded, greatly reducing the responsiveness of crops to higher chemical fertilizer use (Christiaensen and Kaminski 2015). Facile comparisons of average fertilizer application rates between Africa and Asia suggesting that higher application rates in Africa would produce results comparable to those in Asia can be highly misleading. Indeed, policy discussions of low productivity in Africa tend to overemphasize fertilizer use and underemphasize the poor farming practices and rainfed conditions that limit African farmers' ability to use fertilizer as profitably as in other regions (Jayne et al. 2016).

In any case, the evidence from the high agricultural growth periods in South Asia shows that fertilizer subsidies played little or no role in substantially boosting productivity (Fan, Gulati, and Thorat 2008; Gautam 2015). Studies in four Asian countries—Bangladesh, India, Indonesia, and Pakistan—conclude that fertilizer subsidies were not significant in farmers' adoption of technology. They instead identify technology research, irrigation expansion, and other investments such as roads as the main drivers (Rashid et al. 2013; Smith and Urey 2002). At the height of the Green Revolution, farmers in three of the four countries (not in Bangladesh) were net-taxed for fertilizer (that is, domestic prices for fertilizers were higher than the world market price), indicating that it was profitability and not subsidies that drove technology adoption during this era (Rashid et al. 2013).

## The Returns to Subsidies Are Low and Variable

Evidence has recently been accumulating on some of the largest input subsidy programs in Sub-Saharan Africa—Ethiopia, Ghana, Kenya, Malawi, Nigeria, Tanzania, and Zambia—based on farm-level surveys.[3] The analysis points to several conclusions with important policy implications:

- Crop response rates of smallholder farmers are highly variable and usually low because of the inability to use fertilizer efficiently and profitably due to low water availability and poor soil, to chronically late deliveries of fertilizer, to poor management practices, and to insufficient complementary inputs to enable farmers to obtain higher rates of fertilizer efficiency.

**Table O.2** Benefits Are Low in Relation to Costs—and Go to Richer Farmers

| Country | Characteristics of recipient households acquiring subsidized fertilizer | Financial benefit-cost ratio | Economic benefit-cost ratio |
|---|---|---|---|
| Malawi | Households with larger landholding and asset wealth get more | 0.62 | 0.80 |
| Zambia | Households with more land get slightly more | 0.56 | 0.92 |
| Kenya | Households with higher landholding receive more subsidized fertilizer | 0.79 | 1.09 |

*Source:* Jayne et. al. 2016.
*Note:* This table represents summary evidence of impacts from farm and household studies. Ratios are estimated based on five-year estimated response rates. The ratios reported here use baseline calculations, making adjustments to the average partial effect of 1 kilogram of subsidized fertilizer on total smallholder fertilizer use, as suggested by Chirwa and Dorward (2013) and Jayne et al. (2016). Costs are those of the fertilizer only, while reported yields were those observed using both the fertilizer and seeds. For this reason, the benefits overestimate the benefits of fertilizer use alone, and the benefit-cost ratios could be considered upper bounds of the ratio for subsidized fertilizer.

- The increment in total fertilizer use is smaller than is distributed through the program because even with "smart" subsidies, the crowding out of commercial fertilizer sales—as well as outright diversion and theft—remain major problems.
- Subsidies are unlikely to address their multiple objectives effectively. It is often argued that subsidizing fertilizer is desirable both to boost agricultural production and to help poor farmers. Yet there is strong evidence that most of the benefits do not go to poor farmers (targeting is regressive with respect to asset wealth and landholding size), and the gains in overall food production have been transitory and much smaller than the costs (table O.2).

## Add Alternative and Complementary Investments to the Policy Mix

In areas where fertilizer or other modern production technologies are actually underused, many policy levers are available to encourage greater uptake. The optimal choice of instruments depends to a large extent on the constraint. If the main bottleneck is that farmers have few choices of appropriate input technologies for the main agroecological systems in a country, the best solution may be to focus on regulatory reform to encourage spillovers from abroad and investment in domestic research. If the problem is a lack of information on the part of farmers, extension services may be the best policy lever. If one of the underlying causes for low fertilizer use is insufficient cash flow for farmers to buy inputs, efficiently promoting the emergence and growth of rural credit markets (including support for land market development) would address this.

Much can be done using innovative ways of doing banking and taking advantage of new applications of information technologies.

A number of countries have recently implemented changes to improve the efficiency and effectiveness of their input subsidy programs. Countries have replaced public with private procurement and delivery mechanisms, and even put in place electronic delivery systems for subsidies (as in Nigeria). These appear to be steps in the right direction. But there is not yet rigorous empirical evidence to assess whether these changes have significantly improved the performance of the programs, much less whether they have changed the benefit-cost ·calculus from negative to positive. And some claims echo those for the earlier generation of smart subsidies, which proved to be exaggerated. The new reforms are worth monitoring, but until they are proven effective, they cannot be assumed to be good models for spending decisions.

Notwithstanding the large body of evidence that even "smart" input subsidies have seldom produced benefits commensurate with their fiscal costs, they remain politically attractive. Where subsidies continue to be used, they should at least be reduced to a modest amount in national agriculture budgets, with a clear exit strategy, and combined with complementary expenditures. In the longer term, no program will sustainably raise fertilizer use until it becomes profitable for farmers to buy fertilizer on commercial markets after they graduate from the subsidy program. This brings back the issue of complementary investments. Creating demand will require lowering the farm gate prices of fertilizers in Africa, where they are high relative to other regions. This has clear implications for government spending priorities: spending needs to be aimed at streamlining logistics and reducing costs and risks in fertilizer supply chains (Jayne et al. 2013). Much of this investment is most appropriate for the private sector, but governments can support the effort by improving the infrastructure for fertilizer distribution, reducing regulatory barriers, and improving profitability through reduced transport costs.

Other steps required to stimulate demand for fertilizer are enhancing research and extension, and investing in soil analysis and mapping, to improve soil fertility management to raise fertilizer response rates. Input promotion during the high agricultural productivity periods in Asia and South America, for example, addressed systemic constraints to productivity through integrated investments in new technologies, extension support, irrigation, and market linkages. Countries in Sub-Saharan Africa could get a bigger impact within the existing expenditure envelope by moving away from a heavy focus on fertilizer subsidies toward a package of complementary investments. Reforming the design and implementation of these subsidy programs while rebalancing government spending in favor of high-return core public goods and policies could produce massive dividends.

## Budget for Greater Impact

A third dimension of a strategy to maximize impacts of public spending in agriculture is ensuring that the budgetary process supports efficient implementation. There is considerable variance in budget preparation and execution capacity among countries, but there is undoubtedly scope for improvement, as reflected from the analysis of 20 existing country-level agriculture PER studies sponsored by a joint World Bank–Gates Foundation program, examined as background for this book.

### Start from a Solid Foundation

Budgeting needs to start from a stronger foundation of sector strategies and national agricultural investment plans, few of which currently provide much guidance on budget preparation. The investment plans need to give more detailed and quantitative guidance on translating recommendations to spending priorities, and adjustments from the most recent implementation period need to be accompanied by a monitorable results framework.

### Improve Budget Execution

In many countries, the rate of budget execution is dismal (figure O.11). Improving budget execution rates is essential for demonstrating that the sector can make good use of additional public resources, and for persuading ministries of finance that their budgets must be increased. So resources are used effectively, the focus ought to be on improving the implementation of development expenditures, the predictability of releases from ministries of finance, the procurement planning and implementation system, and the budget information management systems to inform within-year budget implementation.

### Strengthen Monitoring and Evaluation

Countries need to strengthen monitoring and evaluation (M&E) capacity as part of accountability systems that shift resources toward effective spending. Ministries of agriculture need more resources and staff doing M&E and in exchange to be held accountable for demonstrating that budgets are effectively spent. The ministries of finance need to increase recurrent spending for this purpose. And budget analysis capacity has to be established in the sector ministries for expenditure monitoring and adjustment within the budget year. Budget information systems appear to be improving with the expanded rollout of computerized systems by ministries of finance and accountant-general offices.

**Figure O.11** Execution Rates of Total Agricultural Budgets Can Be Dismal

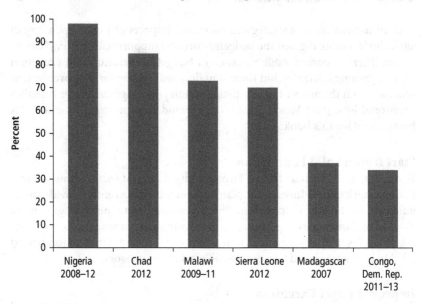

*Source:* Mink 2016.

## Capture Off-Budget Financing—and Make Flows to SOEs More Transparent

Ministries of finance need to put in place budget information systems that, in some form, capture off-budget external partner financing of projects that deliver public goods and services, which in some countries is a significant share of the budget (figure O.12). Two fiscal management reforms that can significantly improve the technical efficiency of expenditure management are implementing a treasury single account system and a centralized civil service information system.

In addition to crowding out the private sector, SOEs have sometimes required large and highly variable funding, reducing transparency and predictability. SOEs can run up off-budget debt on their own account, and when this reaches an unsustainable level, they require a large infusion of funds from the regular budget for re-capitalization. For example, the Togolese Cotton Company in 2007 required a transfer equivalent to 52 percent of the ministry of agriculture's budget to pay off its debt. It was liquidated and replaced by a public-private enterprise, which required another "extraordinary" transfer to cover the government's share of the capitalization. Most countries in West Africa now use Organization for the

**Figure O.12** Off-Budget Shares of Public Agricultural Spending Can Be Substantial

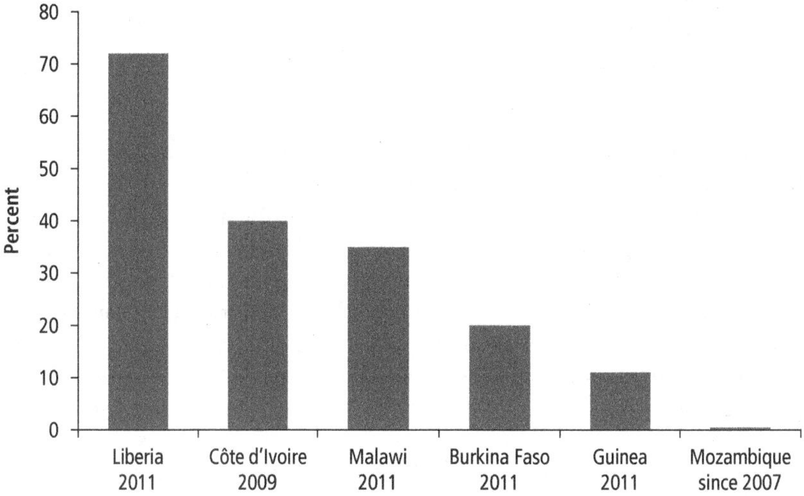

*Source:* Mink 2016.

Harmonization of Business Law in Africa (OHADA) accounting rules, which limit the use of practices that make expenditures nontransparent and unpredictable.[4]

### Shift to Program Budgeting and Build Local Capacity

Two other aspects of budget processes are likely to grow in priority, but require attention over several years to build the capacity for improving the quality of budget outcomes.

- The first is a shift to program budgeting, as some countries have committed to do. Backward-looking reconfiguration of sector public spending by program categories to provide the recent history of composition and trends helps benchmark the programs and the specifics of their expenditure foundation.

- The second is decentralization and deconcentration in countries that are moving from political commitment to implementation in both the administration and the fiscal management of government functions. This flags the importance of building expenditure implementation capacity at the local level, and in the case of decentralization, of expenditure planning capacity as well. Where implementation momentum is accelerating, budget information systems and information sharing need to be developed across the different levels of government, including often geographically remote sector agencies and institutes, to enable budget planning that leverages potential synergies and avoids duplication in sector spending.

### Boost Key Categories of Recurrent Spending and Administration

Some countries seem to be underfunding certain categories of recurrent expenditures, resulting in a ratio of recurrent spending to investments that is low and declining. It is perhaps understandable that politically attuned ministers are reluctant to divert budget resources from front-line activities of direct constituency benefit to unglamorous back-office functions. But in some countries, despite a significant scale-up of public spending on the sector, there has been no or little increase in these core administrative functions, which can provide the sorts of information essential to steering the endeavor based on evidence.

Examples of public functions that involve mainly recurrent expenditures and appear to be underfunded are maintenance, core budget planning and implementation, M&E, and sector regulatory functions. Maintenance is a category of recurrent spending that seems to be systematically short-changed. Some countries seem not to be adequately funding recurrent goods and services that are necessary to maintain capital investments, and their continued neglect risks negative outcomes for sector performance. Underfunding budget planning, monitoring, and evaluation capacity in ministries reduces the quality and impact of public spending on agriculture. Inadequate support to undertake project M&E reduces the ability to track results and make adjustments to improve impacts or reorient approaches. Most countries that have had rapid investment growth have also allowed a decline in the ratio of M&E budgets (nonwage goods and service spending) to investment budgets. Recurrent budget planning is typically conducted as an incremental adjustment to prior year levels. Yet significant policy shifts, such as expanding reliance on private markets for input provision, do not appear to be accompanied by funding regulatory capacity for input quality in markets, a recurrent function.

## Manage the Political Economy

### High-Return Categories of Spending Are Often Underfunded

Some categories of spending that have been shown to have significant positive effects on productivity and welfare are often underfunded, and others that generally show unfavorable results often capture large shares of the budget. Explaining such discrepancies between impact and prominence in the public budget requires understanding how the public resource allocation process is shaped by agents' incentive structures, the characteristics of the investments, and the broader governance environment in which agents operate (Mogues and Erman 2016). Budget decisions will always be politically influenced, but understanding that the sources of bias are likely to drive inefficient or ineffective policies can help avoid those outcomes.

## Move Beyond the Status Quo

Many African countries have long pursued policies of implicit or explicit agricultural taxation, creating a pro-urban, anti-agricultural bias (Anderson 2009; Krueger, Schiff, and Valdes 1988). One explanation is that rural populations exhibit greater difficulty of organizing collective action among dispersed populations that lack easy means of communication (Olson 1985). But if the difficulty of organizing collective action can be overcome, there is also strength in numbers (Acemoğlu and Robinson 2001). One way to at least partially offset this natural disadvantage of rural populations is to improve the information base of key actors so that they better understand the effects of alternative policy choices. Policy processes exhibit a status quo bias, such that policies that have outlived their usefulness still continue. Governments tend to favor the status quo because those who benefit from the current state are usually the ones with the power to have ensured enactment of those policies in the first place (Fernandez and Rodrik 1991). And their political support for current policies is increased by those who have altered their behavior to become beneficiaries after policies were put in place (Coate and Morris 1999).

## Visibility Guides Spending

Different classes of spending influence how politically attractive they are. Types of spending with highly visible results that are easily attributable are more attractive. Visible infrastructure investments and direct cash or in-kind transfers are more easily connected to the efforts and spending decisions of public officials. These can even be conveniently advertised—for example, through labels on the fertilizer voucher ticket indicating who is responsible for subsidizing the fertilizer—thus serving as an effective tool for patronage (Chinsinga 2011). In contrast, if a farmer observes that the quality of information provided by a new agricultural extension officer has improved, it may be difficult for her to ascertain whether that is because the new extension officer is more motivated, or whether the agricultural ministry has done a better job in selecting, training, and incentivizing extension officers. The greater visibility (and therefore attributability) of large-scale irrigation schemes in Mozambique, for instance, has made them more attractive than small schemes, despite the weaker agricultural performance of the large ones (Mogues and do Rosario 2015).

## Time Lags in Investment

Goods and services with a long lag between the time when resources are allocated and the time when the benefits become available are less politically attractive for several reasons. A longer lag tends to break the perceptible link between politicians' decisions and public officials' resource allocations, and politicians may have a short time horizon for their tenure in office. The inability to extract short-term political credit sometimes acts as a disincentive for policy makers to commit to long-term agricultural R&D investments, thus jeopardizing future research planning and outputs. Given low investments by governments, agricultural research in many Sub-Saharan countries is highly dependent on donor funding, which by nature is mostly short term and ad hoc, often causing major fluctuations in a country's yearly agricultural investments. In contrast to the long gestation to realize benefits of investing in research, public spending to subsidize agricultural inputs usually requires a span of only a few months from the time of the investment until the subsidized fertilizer reaches farmers.

## Monitor Corruption

Areas of public spending involving large infrastructure or other capital investments (such as irrigation) create opportunities for public officials to improve the chances of a private agent winning contracts, or to loosen regulatory burdens on the agent, in return for private payments to the official. Underperformance of irrigation infrastructures in countries beset with corruption is notorious for another reason as well. Incentives for technical staff to properly maintain structures are severely weakened without side payments, given the rents that can be extracted in a context of insecurity about access to functioning irrigation systems (Wade 1982; Walter and Wolff 2002).

## From Top-Down to More Participatory Budgeting Institutions

Institutional mechanisms to make spending more pro-poor have a mixed record and vary in their strengths and vulnerabilities. In some African countries, the potential benefits of participatory budgeting have been vitiated by a top-down process closely managed by the party in power, as in Mozambique (Nylen 2014). The benefit has also been constrained by earmarking transfers from the federal government, as in Kenya and Uganda (Ranis 2012), or by high administrative and maintenance costs, as in Uganda (Francis and James 2003). Where spending decisions are decentralized, concrete mechanisms to strengthen electoral accountability need to be put in place to ensure local administrators are responsive to the needs of individuals and not only to local elite groups. This must be matched by building local officials' public management capacity, and improving citizens' information base on the actions as well as the performance of local governments. The inefficiencies and poor targeting of subsidies can be at least reduced through operational features that improve the clarity and reduce the ambiguity of eligibility criteria, paired with an increase of transparency and information about which localities, and within localities which households, are eligible to receive the transfers.

## Overcome Inertia in Policy Making

Too often, countries fail to adopt and implement policies that are known to be necessary for sustained economic development. In addition, for reasons described above, there is significant inertia in policy making. How, then, can change occur?

### Be Ready to Take Advantage of Opportunities for Reform

Major past reform programs have been necessitated by the realization that more of the same is not fiscally sustainable. External (oil and other commodity) price shocks have often exposed inefficient and unsustainable policies (World Bank 2008). Much of the restructuring and privatizing of marketing boards in Africa came about when they became fiscally unsustainable, partially because of movements in the international prices of the commodities (Akiyama et al. 2001). Severe budgetary constraints have often disturbed the political equilibria that supported those policies and opened space for reforms, often with the strategic and financial support of external actors such as international financial institutions. These reforms involved profound changes in agricultural policies, including major shifts in public spending programs. Among them was a reduction in input subsidies, common in the 1980s and 1990s. But as economic recovery progressed, some of the same programs and policies (including input subsidies) re-emerged, albeit in improved versions, because they remained politically attractive (Jayne et al. 2016). The lesson here is not that reforms must always await the advent of shocks, but that reformers ought to be ready with plans and evidence to influence reforms and be alert to opportunities that may arise.

### Consider Compensating Losers

Improvements in the quality of spending have sometimes been greatly facilitated by partially compensating losers. Comprehensive reforms in Mexico, Romania, and Turkey that reduced agriculture subsidies and privatized SOEs greatly improved the efficiency of spending and ushered in rapid sectoral growth. They were accompanied by area-based cash payments (much more efficient and less costly to the government than the policies they replaced), without which these reforms likely would not have been politically feasible to enact or sustain.

### Find Ways to Commit to Long-Gestation Policies with High Returns

Other forces can be harnessed to facilitate policy reform. As noted earlier, two major barriers to reform are the lack of understanding by the citizenry of the distributional effects of policies (which also reduces attributability of positive impacts) and the difficulty that politicians have in making a credible commitment to policies with long gestations. Farmer cooperatives and other producer organizations can help identify beneficial policies, disseminate this information to their members, and then lobby for their enactment. The formation of member-driven groups can be effective in promoting policy change as opposed to the top-down organizations. Other agents of civil society in a country (press, local nongovernmental organizations [NGOs], and even competing parties) can also increase the transparency of policy and the availability of information. Rigorous impact evaluations of projects and programs hold promise for revealing the distributional and welfare effects of spending policies, and their wide dissemination would go a long way toward increasing public understanding.

### Enhance Credibility by Committing to an External Agent

This is an important principle underlying international trade treaties. The agricultural reform program in Mexico, for example, was motivated by the determination to join the North American Free Trade Agreement and the consequent need to firmly "lock in" the policies that would make this possible. In a similar vein, regional agreements and institutions in Africa, such as the CAADP, can play this role if commitments are taken seriously. CAADP's peer reviews of national agricultural investment plans and the joint sector review process with an emphasis on "mutual accountability" mechanisms could potentially enhance credibility. As noted earlier, the fungibility of resources makes it difficult for donors and development partners to have a significant influence over the size and composition of agricultural budgets through the mechanism of funding individual projects. But with agricultural PERs becoming more common, they provide a tool to get a comprehensive view of the entire budget, identify shifts in overall spending patterns, increase transparency, and facilitate more effective input into budget planning and implementation.

### Improve the Efficiency of Spending

Irrespective of spending targets, the evidence in this book shows that countries in Sub-Saharan Africa have consistently lagged behind countries in other developing regions in the quantity of public agricultural spending. Even so, raising the volume of spending requires political consensus—among development partners, government decision makers (particularly ministries of finance), and above all electorates—that money invested in agriculture will be well spent. Measures to raise the efficiency of existing spending in agriculture—and demonstrating that it has a high impact on growth and poverty reduction—will make the case for higher levels of spending much more persuasive. The conclusions and recommendations in this book try to give policy makers options for doing just this.

## Notes

1. Hereafter *Africa* for simplicity.
2. AOI = [(Ag PE/Total PE)]/(Ag GDP/GDP)]; PE = public expenditure.
3. Most empirical work refers to the fertilizer components of these programs. While many programs distributed packets of fertilizer and seeds together, the cost of fertilizer was 10–14 times the cost of seeds.
4. "Organisation pour l'Harmonisation en Afrique du Droit des Affaires," which translates into English as "Organization for the Harmonization of Business Law in Africa."

## References

Acemoğlu, D., and J. Robinson. 2001. "Inefficient Redistribution." *American Political Science Review* 95 (3): 649–61.

Akiyama, T., J. Baffes, D. Larson, and P. Varangis. 2001. "Commodity Market Reforms: Lessons of Two Decades." *Regional and Sectoral Studies*. Washington, DC: World Bank.

Alston, J., M. Marra, P. Pardey, and T. Wyatt. 2000. "Research Returns Redux: A Meta-analysis of the Returns to Agricultural R&D." *Australian Journal of Agricultural and Resource Economics* 44 (2): 185–215.

Anderson, K. 2009. *Distortions to Agricultural Incentives: A Global Perspective, 1955–2007*. Washington, DC: World Bank.

AUC-ECA-AfDB Consortium. (African Union Commission; UN Economic Commission for Africa; African Development Bank). 2010. *Framework and Guidelines on Land Policy in Africa: Land Policy in Africa: A Framework to Strengthen Land Rights, Enhance Productivity and Secure Livelihoods*. Addis Ababa, Ethiopia: AUC-ECA-AfDB Consortium. http://www.uneca.org/sites/default/files/PublicationFiles/fg_on_land_policy_eng.pdf.

Banful, A. 2011. "Old Problems in the New Solutions? Politically Motivated Allocation of Program Benefits and the "New" Fertilizer Subsidies." *World Development* 39 (7): 1166–76.

Benin, S. 2015. "Returns to Agricultural Public Spending in Africa South of the Sahara." IFPRI Discussion Paper 01491 (December). IFPRI, Washington, DC.

Benin, S., L. McBride, and T. Mogues. 2016. "Why Do Countries Underinvest in Agricultural R&D?" In *Agricultural Research in Africa: Investing in Future Harvests*, edited by J. Laynam, N. Beintema, J. Roseboom, and O. Badiane. Washington, DC: IFPRI.

Benin, S., T. Mogues, G. Cudjoe, and J. Randriamamonjy. 2012. "Public Expenditures and Agricultural Productivity Growth in Ghana." In *Public Expenditures for Agricultural and Rural Development in Africa*, edited by T. Mogues and S. Benin. London and New York: Routledge, Taylor, and Francis Group.

Bosker, M., and H. Garretsen. 2012. "Economic Geography and Economic Development in Sub-Saharan Africa. *World Bank Economic Review* 26 (3): 443–85.

Brooks, K., S. Zorya, A. Gautam, and A. Goyal. 2013. "Agriculture as a Sector of Opportunity for Young People in Africa." Policy Research Working Paper 6473, World Bank, Washington, DC.

Byamugisha, F. 2013. *Securing Africa's Land for Shared Prosperity: A Program to Scale Up Reforms and Investments*. Africa Development Forum Series. Washington, DC: World Bank and Agence Française de Développement.

Casaburi, L., R. Glennerster, and T. Suri. 2013. "Rural Roads and Intermediated Trade: Regression Discontinuity Evidence from Sierra Leone." Massachusetts Institute of Technology, Cambridge, MA. http://www.mit.edu/~tavneet/Casaburi_Glennerster_Suri.pdf.

Chamberlin, J., L. You, S. Wood, and U. Wood-Sichra. 2007. "Generating Plausible Crop Distribution Maps for Sub-Saharan Africa Using a Spatial Allocation Model." *Information Development* 23 (2–3): 151–59.

Chinsinga, B. 2011. "Seeds and Subsidies: The Political Economy of Input Programmes in Malawi." *IDS Bulletin* 42 (4): 59–68.

Chirwa, E., and A. Dorward. 2013. *Agricultural Input Subsidies: The Recent Malawi Experience*. Oxford, U.K.: Oxford University Press.

Christiaensen, L., and J. Kaminski. 2015. "Structural Change, Economic Growth, and Poverty Reduction: Micro Evidence From Uganda." Mimeo. World Bank, Washington, DC.

Coate, S., and S. Morris. 1999. "Policy Persistence." *American Economic Review* 89 (5): 1327–36.

Correa, P., and C. Schmidt. 2014. "Public Research Organizations and Agricultural Development in Brazil: How Did Embrapa Get It Right?" *Economic Premise* 145 (June). http://siteresources.worldbank.org/EXTPREMNET/Resources/EP145.pdf.

Davis, K. 2008. "Extension in Sub-Saharan Africa: Overview and Assessment of Past and Current Models and Future Prospects." *Journal of International Agricultural and Extension Education* 15 (3): 15–28.

De Ferranti, D., G. Perry, W. Foster, D. Lederman, and A. Valdes. 2005. *Beyond the City: The Rural Contribution to Development*. Washington, DC: World Bank.

Deichmann, U., A. Goyal, and D. Mishra. 2016. "Will Digital Technologies Transform Agriculture in Developing Countries?" Policy Research Working Paper 7669. World Bank, Washington, DC.

Deininger, K., D. Byerlee, J. Lindsay, A. Norton, H. Selod, and M. Stickler. 2011. *Rising Global Interest in Farmland: Can It Yield Sustainable and Equitable Benefits?* Washington, DC: World Bank.

Delgado, C., N. Minot, and M. Tiongco. 2005. "Evidence and Implications of Non-Tradability of Food Staples in Tanzania 1983–1998," *Journal of Development Studies* 41 (3): 376–93.

Dercon, S., D. Gilligan, J. Hoddinott, and T. Woldehanna. 2008. "The Impact of Agricultural Extension and Roads on Poverty and Consumption Growth in Fifteen Ethiopian Villages." *American Journal of Agricultural Economics* 91 (4): 1007–21.

Devarajan, S., V. Swaroop, and H. F. Zou. 1996. "The Composition of Public Expenditure and Economic Growth." *Journal of Monetary Economics* 37 (2–3): 313–44.

Donaldson, D. Forthcoming. "Railroads of the Raj: Estimating the Impact of Transportation Infrastructure." *American Economic Review.*

Dorward, A., E. Chirwa, V. Kelly, T. S. Jayne, and R. Slater. 2008. *Evaluation of the 2006/07 Agricultural Input Subsidy Programme, Malawi.* Final Report. Lilongwe, Malawi: Ministry of Agriculture and Food Security.

Drechsel, P., L. Gyiele, D. Kunze, and O. Cofie. 2001. "Population Density, Soil Nutrient Depletion, and Economic Growth in Sub-Saharan Africa." *Ecological Economics* 38 (2): 251–58.

Fan, S., A. Gulati, and S. Thorat. 2008. "Investment, Subsidies, and Pro-Poor Growth in Rural India." *Agricultural Economics* 39 (2): 163–70.

Fernandez, R. and D. Rodrik. 1991. "Resistance to Reform: Status Quo Bias in the Presence of Individual-Specific Uncertainty." *American Economic Review* 81 (5): 1146–55.

Ferreira, F. H., P. G. Leite, and M. Ravallion. 2010. "Poverty Reduction without Economic Growth? Explaining Brazil's Poverty Dynamics, 1985–2004." *Journal of Development Economics* 93 (1): 20–36.

Francis, P., and R. James. 2003. "Balancing Rural Poverty Reduction and Citizen Participation: The Contradictions of Uganda's Decentralization Program." *World Development* 31 (2): 325–37.

Fuglie, K. O. 2015. "Accounting for Growth in Global Agriculture." *Bio-based and Applied Economics* 4 (3): 221–54.

Fuglie, K. O., and N. E. Rada. 2013. "Resources, Policies, and Agricultural Productivity in Sub-Saharan Africa." *Economic Research Report 145*. Washington, DC: United States Department of Agriculture Economic Research Service.

Gachassin, M., B. Najman, and G. Raballand. 2010. "The Impact of Roads on Poverty Reduction: A Case Study of Cameroon." Policy Research Working Paper Series. World Bank, Washington, DC.

Gautam, M. 2015. "Agricultural Subsidies: Resurging Interest in a Perennial Debate." Keynote address at the 74th Annual Conference of Indian Society of Agricultural Economics, Dr. Babasaheb Ambedkar Marathwada University, Aurangabad, India, December 18.

Gisselquist, D., J. Nash, and C. Pray. 2002. "Deregulating Technology Transfer in Agriculture: Impact on Technical Change, Productivity, and Incomes." *World Bank Research Observer* 17: 237–65.

Gollin, D., D. Lagakos, and M. E. Waugh. 2013. "The Agricultural Productivity Gap." Policy Note w19628, National Bureau of Economic Research, Cambridge, MA.

IFPRI (International Food Policy Research Institute). Agricultural Science and Technology Indicators (ASTI) database, Washington, DC (accessed September 15, 2015), www.asti .cgiar.org/data/.

———. Regional Strategic Analysis and Knowledge Support System (ReSAKSS) database, Washington, DC (accessed September 15, 2015), http://www.resakss.org/about.

———. Statistics on Public Expenditures for Economic Development (SPEED) database, Washington, DC (accessed September 15, 2015), http://www.ifpri.org/book-39 /ourwork/programs/priorities-public-investment/speed-database.

Ivanic, M., and W. Martin. 2014. "Short- and Long-Run Impacts of Food Price Changes on Poverty." World Bank Policy Research Working Paper 7011. World Bank, Washington, DC.

Jacoby, H. 2000. "Access to Markets and the Benefits of Rural Roads." *Economic Journal* 110 (465): 713–37.

Jayne, T. S., N. M. Mason, W. J. Burke, and J. Ariga. 2016. "Agricultural Input Subsidy Programs in Africa: An Assessment of Recent Evidence." International Development Working Paper 145, Michigan State University, East Lansing. http://fsg.afre.msu.edu /papers/idwp145.pdf.

Jayne, T. S., D. Mather, N. M. Mason, and J. Ricker-Gilbert. 2013. "How Do Fertilizer Subsidy Programs Affect Total Fertilizer Use in Sub-Saharan Africa? Crowding Out, Diversion, and Benefit/Cost Assessments." *Agricultural Economics* 44 (6): 687–703.

Keefer, P., and S. Khemani. 2005. "Democracy, Public Expenditures, and the Poor: Understanding Political Incentives for Providing Public Services." *World Bank Research Observer* 20 (1): 1–27.

Keyser, J. C. 2013. "Regional Trade of Food Staples and Crop Inputs in West Africa." Africa Trade Policy Note 36, World Bank, Washington, DC.

Khandker, S., Z. Bakht, and G. Koolwal. 2006. "The Poverty Impact of Rural Roads: Evidence from Bangladesh." World Bank Policy Research Working Paper 3875, World Bank, Washington, DC.

Krueger, A., M. Schiff, and A. Valdes. 1988. "Agricultural Incentives in Developing Countries: Measuring the Effects of Sectoral and Economy-wide Policies." *World Bank Economic Review* 2 (3): 255–72.

López, R., and G. I. Galinato. 2007. "Should Governments Stop Subsidies to Private Goods? Evidence from Rural Latin America." *Journal of Public Economics* 91: 1071–94.

Mink, S. 2016. "Findings Across Agricultural Public Expenditure Reviews in African Countries." Discussion Paper 01522, April. IFPRI, Washington, DC.

Minten, B., and S. Kyle. 1999. "The Effect of Distance and Road Quality on Food Collection, Marketing Margins, and Traders' Wages: Evidence from the Former Zaire." *Journal of Development Economics* 60 (2): 467–95.

Mogues, T. 2011. "The Bang for the Birr: Public Expenditures and Rural Welfare in Ethiopia." *Journal of Development Studies* 47 (5): 735–752.

Mogues, T., and D. do Rosario. 2015. "The Political Economy of Public Expenditures in Agriculture: Applications of Concepts to Mozambique." *South African Journal of Economics* 27 (3): 452–73.

Mogues, T., and A. Erman. 2016. "Institutional Arrangements to Make Public Spending Responsive to the Poor—(Where) Have They Worked? Review of the Evidence on Four Major Intervention Types." Discussion Paper 01519, IFPRI, Washington, DC.

Mogues, T., B. Yu, S. Fan, and L. Mcbride. 2012. "The Impacts of Public Investment in and for Agriculture: Synthesis of the Existing Evidence." Discussion paper 01217, IFPRI, Washington, DC.

Mu, R., and D. van de Walle. 2007. "Rural Roads and Poor Area Development in Vietnam." Working Paper 4340, World Bank, Washington, DC.

Nylen, W. 2014. "Participatory Budgeting in a Competitive-Authoritarian Regime: A Case Study (Maputo, Mozambique)." IESE Cadernos 13E, Instituto de Estudos Sociais e Económicos, Scientific Council, Maputo, Mozambique.

Olson, M. 1965. *The Logic of Collective Action: Public Goods and the Theory of Groups.* Cambridge, MA: Harvard Economic Studies.

———. 1985. "Space, Agriculture, and Organization." *American Journal of Agricultural Economics* 67 (5): 928–37.

Pardey, P., J. James, J. Alston, S. Wood, B. Koo, E, Binenbaum, T. Hurley, and P. Glewwe. 2007. "Science, Technology, and Skills." Background paper for *World Development Report 2008*, World Bank, Washington, DC.

Ranis, G. 2012. *Vertical and Horizontal Decentralization and Ethnic Diversity in Sub-Saharan Africa.* Discussion Paper 1017, Economic Growth Center, Yale University, New Haven, CT.

Rashid, S., P. Dorosh, M. Malek, and S. Lemma. 2013. "Modern Input Promotion in Sub-Saharan Africa: Insights from Asian Green Revolution." *Agricultural Economics* 44: 705–21.

Rosegrant, M. W., C. Ringler, and T. Zhu. 2009. "Water for Agriculture: Maintaining Food Security under Growing Scarcity." *Annual Review of Environment and Resources* 34 (1): 205.

Sadoulet, E., and A. de Janvry. 1995. *Quantitative Development Policy Analysis.* Baltimore, MD: Johns Hopkins University Press.

Smith, L. E. D., and I. Urey. 2002. "Agricultural Growth and Poverty Reduction: A Review of Lessons from the Post-Independence and Green Revolution Experience of India." Report for the research project on Institutions and Economic Policies for Pro-Poor Growth, Department of Agricultural Economics, Imperial College, London.

Stifel, D., and B. Minten. 2008. "Isolation and Agricultural Productivity." *Agricultural Economics* 39 (1): 1–15.

Thirtle, C., and J. van Zyl. 1994. "Explaining Total Factor Productivity Growth and Returns to Research and Extension in South African Commercial Agriculture, 1947–91." *South African Journal of Agricultural Extension* 23 (1): 21–27.

Tittonell, P., and K. Giller. 2013. "When Yield Gaps Are Poverty Traps: The Paradigm of Ecological Intensification in African Smallholder Agriculture." *Field Crops Research* 143: 76–90.

UN (United Nations). Commodity Trade Statistics (Comtrade) database, New York, http://comtrade.un.org/.

USDA (United States Department of Agriculture). Economic Research Service (ERS) database, Washington, DC, http://www.ers.usda.gov/.

Valdes, A. 2008. "Agricultural Public Spending: Description and Assessment Relevant to Latin America." Background paper for the *Mexico Agricultural and Rural Development Public Expenditure Review*, World Bank, Washington, DC.

Wade, R. 1982. "The System of Administrative and Political Corruption: Canal Irrigation in South India." *Journal of Development Studies* 18 (3): 287–328.

Walter, H., and B. Wolff. 2002. "Principal-Agent Problems in Irrigation: Inviting Rent-seeking and Corruption." *Quarterly Journal of International Agriculture* 41(1–2): 99–118.

World Bank. 2008. *World Development Report 2008: Agriculture for Development.* Washington, DC.

———. 2012. *Africa Can Help Feed Africa: Removing Barriers to Regional Trade in Food Staples.* World Bank Africa Region Poverty Reduction and Economic Management, Washington, DC.

———. 2013a. *Growing Africa: Unlocking the Potential of Agribusiness.* Washington, DC.

———. 2013b. *Turn Down the Heat: Confronting the New Climate Normal.* Washington, DC.

———. World Development Indicators database, Washington, DC, http://data.worldbank.org/data-catalog/world-development-indicators.

You, L., C. Ringler, U. Wood-Sichra, R. Robertson, S. Wood, T. Zhu, and Y. Sun. 2011. "What Is the Irrigation Potential for Africa? A Combined Biophysical and Socioeconomic Approach." *Food Policy* 36: 770–82.

# Chapter 1

# Why Look at Public Spending for Agriculture in Africa?

Extreme poverty in the world is becoming increasingly concentrated in Sub-Saharan Africa, which accounted for 43 percent of global poverty in 2012, and its breadth and depth remain a dominant challenge (World Bank, WDI database). While gross domestic product (GDP) growth has picked up in recent years, it is driven mostly by higher production of mineral and hydro-carbon resources. This growth model has not rapidly reduced poverty or boosted shared prosperity, the World Bank's twin goals. Even after experiencing nearly two decades of economic growth, most Africans continue to earn their livelihoods in the traditional economy. Much more than in any other region, agriculture dominates African economies, accounting for a third of the GDP regionwide and employing two-thirds of the labor force, with the poorest countries most heavily reliant on it.

Further underscoring the need to encourage growth in rural areas, evidence shows that growth in agriculture is one of the most effective ways to reduce poverty, with growth in the sector reducing poverty by around three times as much as growth in other productive sectors. A 1 percent improvement in agricultural productivity translates into about a 0.9 percentage point reduction in poverty in developing countries, compared with a reduction of 0.3–0.4 percentage point from a 1 percent increase in productivity in other sectors (Ivanic and Martin 2014). Agriculture is also critical for managing Africa's urban transition. To date, this process has been driven largely by populations being pushed out of rural areas, rather than by cities attracting a larger workforce. The urban transition would be a more positive process if it were driven by improving economic opportunities in the cities that gradually pull rural residents in, rather than by declining conditions and periodic disasters in rural areas that push residents out. A key element of a transition strategy, therefore, is to enhance living standards and increase resilience in rural areas.

## Conditions Are in Place for Transforming African Agriculture

The Green Revolution that boosted yields in other countries largely bypassed Africa. A comparison of Africa's performance in total factor productivity growth (TFP, a comprehensive measure of overall efficiency in using all inputs) with that in other developing regions over two decades shows that Sub-Saharan Africa was lagging in the 1990s and fell even farther behind in the 2000s (figure 1.1) (Fuglie 2015). In other regions, production increases were mainly associated with yield growth due to the better use of inputs and adoption of improved production technologies. But in Sub-Saharan Africa, the increases in production were largely the result of expanding the area under cultivation. In fact, it is the only developing region in the world where the contribution of area expansion exceeded the contribution of growth in yields (figure 1.2) (Deininger et al. 2011). And growth in cereal yields in Sub-Saharan Africa has consistently lagged that in all other regions (figure 1.3). Over four decades, yields in

**Figure 1.1** Total Factor Productivity Growth in Africa Lags behind Other Regions—and the Gap Is Widening

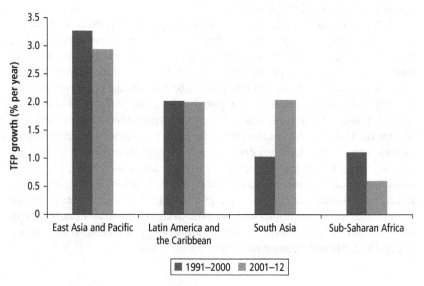

Source: USDA Economic Research Service data.
Note: TFP = total factor productivity.

**Figure 1.2**  Production Increases in Africa Came Largely from Expanding the Area under Cultivation Rather Than Input Intensification or Total Factor Productivity Growth

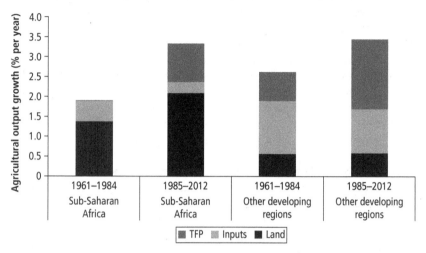

*Source:* USDA Economic Research Service data.
*Note:* TFP = total factor productivity growth.

**Figure 1.3**  Cereal Yields in Africa Have Barely Increased in Four Decades

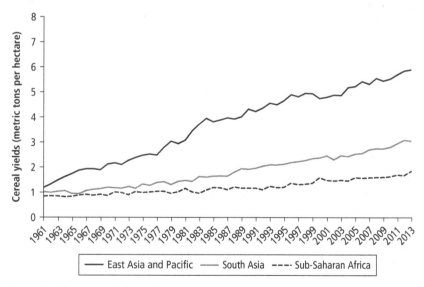

*Source:* World Development Indicators database.

Sub-Saharan Africa have barely doubled, while tripling in South Asia and increasing around sixfold in East Asia and the Pacific.

Even so, the potential for increasing production and productivity in African agriculture is enormous. With an abundance of land and water, Africa has the resources for agricultural prosperity. Of the world's surface area suitable for sustainable expansion of production—that is, unprotected, unforested land, with low population density—Africa has the largest share by far, accounting for roughly 45 percent of the global total. Although some large areas of the continent are arid or semiarid, the available water resources in Africa are, on average, greatly underused. Only 2–3 percent of renewable water resources in Africa are being used, compared with 5 percent worldwide.

On the supply side, the prospects are encouraging for increasing capital and labor devoted to agriculture. If the investment climate can be improved, there is much potential to attract a higher share of global resources. The inward foreign direct investment (FDI) stock in agriculture in Africa is only 7 percent of the total stock in developing countries compared with 78 percent in Asia and 15 percent in Latin America.

There is also the prospect of a growing labor force for agriculture, if Africa can create the jobs to absorb this "youth dividend." With the creation of jobs in upstream or downstream agribusinesses, this youth dividend could drive growth in the sector. However, failing to create these job openings in agriculture would mean rising unemployment, with the adverse effects that entails.

On the demand side, African regional markets are growing rapidly, driven by population and income growth and urbanization, and forecast to reach US$1 trillion by 2030 (figure 1.4) (World Bank 2013). The rising demand for food to nourish rapidly growing urban populations in the region has mostly been filled with imports. From the 1990s to the 2000s, the balance of trade in food staples was moving from deficit (imports exceeding exports) to surplus in Europe and Central Asia, South Asia, and East Asia and the Pacific; in Sub-Saharan Africa, however, this gap greatly expanded.

Food trade deficits are understandable in a region such as the Middle East and North Africa, which has limited comparative advantage in food production. But in Sub-Saharan Africa, with all the natural ingredients for efficient production, deficits of this nature signal that something fundamental is amiss. If not reversed, the consequences of the missed opportunity to capture regional markets will grow over time as that market expands. But as African agriculture becomes more competitive and regional producers can capture more of these markets, the benefits would be enormous.

**Figure 1.4** Retail Value of Food and Beverages, Sub-Saharan Africa

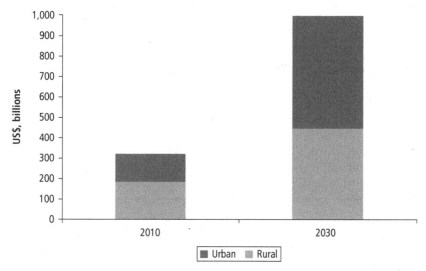

*Source:* World Bank 2013.

## Enhancing Agricultural Growth Requires Improving Public Spending in Agriculture

African policy makers are refocusing their attention on improving agricultural performance, and one essential ingredient in the strategy is to improve public spending in agriculture. Over the past few years, ministries of agriculture and finance have intensified efforts to improve the volume and effectiveness of public spending. The African Union's Maputo Declaration (2003) recognized that agriculture in most African countries was neglected in the public budget and set a notional target for countries to increase public agricultural spending to 10 percent of total public expenditure—a target recently reiterated in its 2014 Malabo Declaration.

Increasing the volume of public spending in agriculture will be important, but will not by itself be enough to kindle growth. Actions will also be needed to improve the efficiency and effectiveness of public spending. To address this, the Comprehensive Africa Agriculture Development Programme (CAADP) has led the charge in supporting national teams working on agricultural sector expenditure programming to conduct basic agriculture sector public expenditure reviews and to carry out related specialized analyses. Assisting countries to develop national agricultural investment plans (NAIPs) that make progress toward the quantitative goal and improve the quality of expenditures has become a cornerstone of CAADP's work with that of its development partners, including the World Bank.

## Why Governments Spend on Agriculture

Much of this book is concerned with "how" governments should spend public funds, but before getting to that point, it is useful to briefly consider the "why." Why should governments be involved in spending on agriculture at all? The rationale for public investments derives from two fundamental sources: economic inefficiencies resulting from market failures and inequality in the distribution of goods and services.

Agricultural production is quintessentially a private enterprise. Yet production requires a number of goods and services that, on both theoretical and empirical grounds, the private sector is unable to provide efficiently. The nonexcludable (if the good is provided to one consumer, other potential beneficiaries cannot be kept from enjoying it) and nonrivalrous (consumption by one does not reduce the availability of consumption by another) characteristics of these goods create a divergence between social and private returns leading to investments that are below the social optimum. Nonexcludability implies that potential beneficiaries cannot be charged for the good, so the producer cannot capture its full social value. Nonrivalry implies that it is inefficient to charge anything for the good, since the cost of supplying an additional unit (that is, letting another consumer enjoy the benefits) is zero. These are classic characteristics of a "public good" and a good that has one or both would be underprovided to some extent by the private sector.

Of course, enhanced public spending in agriculture is only one ingredient in a strategy for agricultural transformation. Investments in health, education, and rural infrastructure matter as well, and wise investments must be complemented by a host of other policies. Indeed, in a poor policy environment, even spending in areas generally considered high return will be unproductive or counterproductive. But smart use of public funds—not only by agriculture ministries but also by other ministries dealing with hard and soft infrastructure in rural areas—has laid the foundation for transformation in other parts of the world. A key question for policy makers and development practitioners is what kinds of spending decisions can yield the highest returns in achieving public policy objectives. What are the options to rebalance public agricultural spending and improve the budgeting process to increase the efficiency of limited resources for inclusive growth? Answering this question is the main objective of this book, so that public expenditure can do for Africa what it has done elsewhere.

## Considering Pathways to Benefits

To guide decisions on areas appropriate for government spending, it is useful to consider what kinds of goods and services are necessary to catalyze agricultural growth, and to what extent each is a "public good." To do this, we conceptualize the beneficial effects of public spending in agriculture along four pathways: generating technology, disseminating technology, reducing transaction costs, and attracting private capital. Each can be identified with particular classes of spending to provide goods or services that have public good characteristics and that are crucial for fostering robust agriculture productivity growth and poverty reduction in rural contexts.

- *To generate knowledge.* Effects that advance technology are associated with public spending on agricultural research and development (R&D) to create basic knowledge, which is both nonexcludable and nonrivalrous. Sometimes the knowledge can be embodied in a commercial product (as with hybrid seeds and chemicals), with benefits that are excludable and rivalrous, but the basic knowledge itself is not. Investments in R&D are among the most important public goods and a critical component of public agricultural spending. Numerous studies show that investments in R&D have tremendously enhanced agricultural productivity around the world over the past five decades, reducing poverty and increasing food security (Alston, Pardey, and Piggott 2006; Evenson and Gollin 2003; Pardey et al. 2007). In Sub-Saharan Africa, economic analysis finds strong and consistent evidence that investment in agricultural research yields high returns per dollar spent. These returns include benefits not only to the farm sector but also to the food industry and consumers in more abundant food at lower prices. Studies using different methods and coverage give a range of estimates of returns to agricultural research, but there is a consensus that the payoff from government investment in agricultural research has been high in Africa (Alene and Coulibaly 2009; Fuglie and Rada 2013; Thirtle, Piesse, and Lin 2003). One area where investment in knowledge may give high returns in raising productivity is improving information on soils (such as soil mapping), which would lay the foundation for programs to enhance soil quality.

- *To disseminate knowledge and build human capital.* Effects that enhance human capital can be associated with public spending on extension, training, and information services that transfer knowledge and skills to those engaged in agricultural production. These investments create significant positive externalities through demonstration effects and peer-to-peer learning of benefits from the adoption of new productivity-enhancing technology. As agricultural production processes become increasingly knowledge intensive, with higher demand for precise and timely information, such investments are becoming increasingly important. Studies find positive effects of public extension systems on agricultural productivity and the adoption of improved agriculture technologies (Evenson 2001; Fan and Zhang 2008). Evidence also points to significant research-extension linkages and shows that the returns to extension services tend to be higher when technological change is rapid (Anderson and Feder 2007). The transmission of technologies depends on how fast new technologies become available, and the overall productivity gain tends to be limited by the weakest link in this chain. The new technological improvements available on the shelf, for instance, require effective extension and adaptive research to prosper in local contexts.

- *To reduce transaction costs.* Similarly, effects that reduce transaction costs can derive from public spending on soft and hard infrastructure that might improve access to input and output markets. Transaction costs are an important determinant of market integration, and investments that lower the cost of searching and exchanging information and of bargaining, decision making, and enforcing contracts tend to enhance market participation (Sadoulet and de Janvry 1995). Investments in rural roads, market information dissemination, and development of land markets, for example, are important in reducing transaction costs. Rural roads are a critical element of public infrastructure for agricultural growth—reducing travel times, transport costs, and in-transit spoilage; raising the prices farmers receive for their products; and lowering the prices they pay for inputs (Calderón and Servén 2004; Dorosh, Dradri, and Haggblade 2009). However, the high costs of identifying and charging a multitude of small-scale beneficiaries may make it infeasible for a private investor. Similarly, institutional investments to overcome barriers to collective action and reduce transaction costs to improve collection, storage, processing, quality control, and price information can optimize supply chain management in remote areas (Aker and Mbiti 2010; Deichmann, Goyal, and Mishra 2016; Torero 2015). Improving land governance is also a public good with special importance for agriculture. Securing land tenure and reducing costs of transferring land, important in their own right, can also give farmers an important source of collateral and pave the way for the development of rural credit markets.

- *To attract private capital.* The crowding-in effects of agricultural public spending on private capital comes about to the extent that public and private investments are complements in production. An example is public investment in large irrigation infrastructure such as dams and canals, which then make it profitable for farmers to make small on-farm investments in water management and a wider range of production technologies. The large number of atomistic beneficiaries makes it difficult to collect payments by private investors of large infrastructure projects. It is also sometimes argued that spending on programs to subsidize greater use of inputs (fertilizers and improved seeds) have the objective of demonstrating to poor farmers the benefits of using improved inputs and break out of a low-productivity poverty trap, thereby encouraging them to continue to spend their own money after input subsidies end (Jayne et al. 2015). Well-designed subsidy programs can in principle address these constraints, although whether they do so in practice is another question to which we return in the book.

## Reducing Inequality and Poverty

Public spending in agriculture is also often justified on equity grounds, especially salient for spending in agriculture, given the concentration of the poor in rural areas, most of whom rely primarily on agriculture (directly or indirectly) for their livelihoods. One argument for fertilizer subsidies, for example, is that they could potentially help poor farmers break out of a low-productivity poverty trap. The equity justification for spending, of course, is stronger for programs that can actually be targeted at the poor, rather than diffusing their benefits, and for programs that demonstrate a high income multiplier effect. For instance, impacts of spending on extension have been found to compare favorably to several kinds of social sector spending with respect to progressivity, and were far superior to spending on subsidies. Also to be recognized is that many programs aimed at rural poverty reduction—either directly (as with rural safety nets) or indirectly (as with programs to support structural transformation by helping the rural poor find jobs in urban areas)—fall outside the scope of this study.

## Ensuring Productive Spending

Not all public spending is productive. This is a clear implication of the relatively low estimated net benefits from total agricultural spending compared with the high benefits of certain categories of agricultural spending (Benin et al. 2012; Fan and Zhang 2008; Mogues 2011). Apparently, where aggregate spending has no measurable impact, the negative effects of ineffective spending overwhelm the positive effects of more effective spending (Devarajan, Swaroop, and Zou 1996). Public spending may be unproductive or even reduce the productivity of other spending for two basic reasons. First, governments sometimes spend on things that are not public goods. Governments tend to be inefficient suppliers of private goods, and when they enter these markets, there is a serious risk of displacing the private sector. Second, even when there are clear failures in particular markets, government spending will not necessarily improve the situation. Inherent characteristics of government interventions can sometimes lead to "government failures," which may exacerbate the original problems caused by the market failures and produce unintended adverse ancillary effects. Empirically though, public spending on public goods has typically been much more productive than public spending on private goods (López and Galinato 2007).

### How Much to Agriculture?

How much should governments spend on agriculture? There is no easy answer. But a conceptual and analytical framework provides guidance on some factors governments need to include in the decision calculus (box 1.1). In the next chapter, we turn to the empirical questions of how much African governments have historically allocated to agriculture, how this has trended over time, and how it compares to other regions.

---

### BOX 1.1

## How Much of the Government Budget Should Be Devoted to Agriculture?

How much of the government budget should be devoted to agriculture, and how much to other sectors? What is "too little" and what is "enough"? The answers are conceptually straightforward but difficult to put into practice. In principle, to maximize welfare on a given budget, spending should be distributed such that the marginal dollar in each activity yields the same increase in national welfare (however *welfare* is defined). If this were not true—if, for example, an additional dollar devoted to agriculture increased welfare more than the incremental dollar to health spending—overall welfare could be increased by taking a dollar from health and spending it on agriculture (Correa and Schmidt 2014).

In a two-sector world (agriculture and nonagriculture), this condition for distributing spending so as to maximize welfare can be expressed as equation (1.1):

$$\frac{dW}{dS_A} = \frac{dW}{dS_{NA}}, \tag{1.1}$$

where $W$ is welfare and $S_A$ and $S_{NA}$ are spending on agriculture and nonagriculture.

Of course, how much welfare is increased by an incremental public dollar spent in agriculture depends on how much that dollar will increase agricultural production,

---

*(continued next page)*

## Box 1.1 (continued)

as well as how much the additional production will increase welfare. This optimal allocation condition can be expressed in a ratio of spending in each sector, such that:

$$\frac{S_A}{S_{NA}} = \left(\frac{E_{WA}}{E_{W,NA}}\right) \times \left(\frac{E_{A,SA}}{E_{NA,S_{NA}}}\right), \tag{1.2}$$

where $E_{WA}$ is the elasticity of welfare to agricultural production (and likewise for non-agricultural production), and $E_{A,SA}$ is the elasticity of agricultural production to public spending in agriculture (and likewise for nonagricultural production).

The optimality condition in equation (1.2) provides a useful framework for thinking about spending allocations whereby the optimal ratio of public spending in agriculture versus nonagriculture is equal to the ratio of the welfare elasticity of each sector's production times the ratio of each sector's elasticity of production with respect to public spending in the sector. The problem in operationalizing this to provide practical guidance to policy makers is that it would require empirical estimation of all these elasticities (in every sector) for a given country. There have been some attempts in cross-country samples to estimate the elasticity of welfare (measured by either national GDP or poverty reduction) with respect to agricultural production, and the elasticity of production with respect to public spending.[a] But there is no strong reason to assume that for any given country, the elasticities would be equal to the global or regional average.

In the absence of a practical way to rigorously answer the question of how much public spending should be allocated to agriculture, there have been some efforts to provide rules of thumb, which may seem intuitive and reasonable. For example, De Ferranti et al. (2005) show that with some special (and quite restrictive) simplifying assumptions, the optimal allocation is such that each sector's share of spending is its share of national GDP. (For agriculture, this would mean that the Agriculture Orientation Index [AOI], discussed below, is equal to 1.) This index—the share of spending on agriculture relative to agriculture's share in the economy—is calculated for a number of Latin American countries over time to analyze whether there has been a systematic underallocation or "anti-agricultural bias" in public spending, with the general conclusion of no such bias in that region.

An alternative approach is to examine the experiences of countries that have undergone successful agricultural transformations. Analysis of 12 East Asian and Pacific and South Asian countries during their periods of high agricultural growth—the Green Revolution—shows that, on average, these countries devoted around 10 percent of total public spending to agriculture.[b] Many other factors certainly contributed to success, but public support was an important ingredient. Thus, the Maputo target is similar to what the Asian countries were spending on agriculture in this period. Likewise, the New Partnership for Africa's Development (NEPAD) target of spending 1 percent of agricultural GDP on research is quite similar to the level that Brazil devoted to its successful research agency, Embrapa, as well as the level of spending on research in some high-income countries.

(continued next page)

## Box 1.1 (continued)

In applying such rules of thumb, it is also sensible to make adjustments based on economic reasoning using equation (1.2). For example, countries differ greatly in the contribution of agriculture to national GDP, and a 1 percent increase in agricultural production will generally result in a smaller percentage increase in overall GDP in a country in which agriculture is 10 percent of the economy than in a country in which it is 30 percent. That is, the value of $E_{WA}$ will be smaller in the latter than in the former, and so—all other things equal—the share of spending going to agriculture should be smaller as well. And the elasticity of production with respect to spending ($E_{A,SA}$) will be higher in countries with high agricultural potential (both because of favorable natural endowments and because the overall policy environment is conducive to a positive supply response)—and where the spending is "smarter." In such countries with a higher value of $E_{A,SA}$, agriculture's share of spending should be higher.

a. For example, see De Ferranti et al. (2005) with a focus on Latin America.
b. The figures were 15.4 percent (1972), 10.5 percent (1975), 12.4 percent (1980), 10.9 percent (1985), and 9.6 percent (1990).

# References

Aker, J. C., and I. M. Mbiti. 2010. "Mobile Phones and Economic Development in Africa." Working Paper 211, Center for Global Development, Washington, DC.

Alene, A. D., and O. Coulibaly. 2009. "The Impact of Agricultural Research on Productivity and Poverty in Sub-Saharan Africa." *Food Policy* 34: 198–209.

Alston, J., P. Pardey, and R. Piggott, eds. 2006. *Agricultural R&D in the Developing World.* Washington, DC: International Food Policy Research Institute.

Anderson, J., and G. Feder. 2007. "Agricultural Extension." In *Handbook of Agricultural Economics*, edited by R. Evenson and P. Pingali. Amsterdam: Elsevier.

Benin, S., L. McBride, and T. Mogues. 2016. "Why Do Countries Underinvest in Agricultural R&D?" In *Agricultural Research in Africa: Investing in Future Harvests*, edited by J. Laynam, N. Beintema, J. Roseboom, and O. Badiane. Washington, DC: International Food Policy Research Institute.

Benin, S., T. Mogues, G. Cudjoe, and J. Randriamamonjy. 2012. "Public Expenditures and Agricultural Productivity Growth in Ghana." In *Public Expenditures for Agricultural and Rural Development in Africa*, edited by T. Mogues and S. Benin. London and New York: Routledge, Taylor and Francis Group.

Brooks, K., S. Zorya, and A. Gautam. 2013. "Employment in Agriculture: Jobs for Africa's Youth." In *Global Food Policy Report*, 48–57. Washington, DC: International Food Policy Research Institute.

Calderón, C., and L. Servén. 2004. "The Effects of Infrastructure Development on Growth and Income Distribution." Policy Research Working Paper 270, World Bank, Washington, DC.

Correa, P., and C. Schmidt. 2014. *Public Research Organizations and Agricultural Development in Brazil: How Did Embrapa Get It Right?* World Bank Economic Premise Series 145 (June). Washington, DC: World Bank. http://siteresources.worldbank.org /EXTPREMNET/Resources/EP145.pdf.

De Ferranti, D., G. Perry, W. Foster, D. Lederman, and A. Valdes. 2005. *Beyond the City: The Rural Contribution to Development.* Washington, DC: World Bank.

Deichmann, U., A. Goyal, and D. Mishra. 2016. "Will Digital Technologies Transform Agriculture in Developing Countries?" Policy Research Working Paper 7669, World Bank, Washington, DC.

Deininger, K., D. Byerlee, J. Lindsay, A. Norton, H. Selod, and M. Stickler. 2011. *Rising Global Interest in Farmland: Can It Yield Sustainable and Equitable Benefits?* Washington, DC: World Bank.

Devarajan, S., V. Swaroop, and H. F. Zou. 1996. "The Composition of Public Expenditure and Economic Growth." *Journal of Monetary Economics* 37 (2–3): 313–44.

Dorosh, P. A., S. Dradri, and S. Haggblade. 2009. "Regional Trade, Government Policy and Food Security: Recent Evidence from Zambia." *Food Policy* 34 (4): 350–66.

Evenson, R. 2001. "Economic Impacts of Agricultural Research and Extension." In Vol. 1 of *Handbook of Agricultural Economics,* edited by B. Gardner and G. Rausser. Amsterdam: Elsevier Science.

Evenson, R., and D. Gollin. 2003. "Assessing the Impact of the Green Revolution, 1960 to 2000." *Science* 300 (5620): 758–62.

Fan, S., and X. Zhang. 2008. "Public Expenditure, Growth, and Poverty Reduction in Rural Uganda." *African Development Review* 20 (3): 466–496.

Fuglie, K. O. 2015. "Accounting for Growth in Global Agriculture." *Bio-based and Applied Economics* 4 (3): 221–54.

Fuglie, K. O., and N. E. Rada. 2013. *Resources, Policies, and Agricultural Productivity in Sub-Saharan Africa.* Economic Research Report 145. Washington, DC: United States Department of Agriculture Economic Research Service.

Ivanic, M., and W. Martin. 2014. "Short-and Long-Run Impacts of Food Price Changes on Poverty." World Bank Policy Research Working Paper 7011, World Bank, Washington, DC.

Jayne, T. S., D. Mather, N. M. Mason, and J. Ricker-Gilbert. 2015. "Rejoinder to the Comment by Andrew Dorward and Ephraim Chirwa on Jayne, T. S., D. Mather, N. Mason, and J. Ricker-Gilbert. 2013. 'How Do Fertilizer Subsidy Programs Affect Total Fertilizer Use in Sub-Saharan Africa? Crowding Out, Diversion, and Benefit/ Cost Assessments.' *Agricultural Economics* 44 (6): 687–703." *Agricultural Economics* 46 (6): 745–55.

López, R., and G. I. Galinato. 2007. "Should Governments Stop Subsidies to Private Goods? Evidence from Rural Latin America." *Journal of Public Economics* 91: 1071–94.

Mogues, T. 2011. "The Bang for the Birr: Public Expenditures and Rural Welfare in Ethiopia." *Journal of Development Studies* 47 (5): 735–52.

Pardey, P., J. James, J. Alston, S. Wood, B. Koo, E, Binenbaum, T. Hurley, and P. Glewwe. 2007. "Science, Technology, and Skills." Background Paper for *World Development Report 2008,* World Bank, Washington, DC.

Sadoulet, E., and A. de Janvry. 1995. *Quantitative Development Policy Analysis*. Baltimore, MD: Johns Hopkins University Press.

Thirtle, C., J. Piesse, and L. Lin. 2003. "The Impact of Research-Led Agricultural Productivity Growth on Poverty Reduction in Africa, Asia and Latin America." *World Development* 31 (12): 1959–75.

Torero, M. 2015. "Alternative Mechanisms to Reduce Food Price Volatility and Price Spikes: Policy Responses at the Global Level." In *Food Price Volatility and Its Implications for Food Security and Policy*, 115–138. Cham, Switzerland: Springer International Publishing.

UN (United Nations). Commodity Trade Statistics (Comtrade) database, New York, NY. http://comtrade.un.org/.

USDA (United States Department of Agriculture). Economic Research Service database, Washington, DC. http://www.ers.usda.gov/.

World Bank. 2013. *Growing Africa: Unlocking the Potential of Agribusiness*. Washington, DC.

———. World Development Indicators database, Washington, DC, http://data.worldbank .org/data-catalog/world-development-indicators.

# Chapter 2

# Agricultural Public Spending in Africa Is Low and Inefficient

We begin the evaluation of public agricultural spending in Africa with a broad overview using metrics of both quantity and quality. This chapter first analyzes the patterns of agricultural public spending, in comparison with other forms of public spending, across different developing regions of the world.[1] While optimal levels of spending will of course depend on characteristics of countries and regions, it is nonetheless informative to see how Africa stacks up to other regions. The chapter also provides evidence on the returns to public spending in the agricultural sector in Sub-Saharan Africa, considering total agriculture spending and agricultural research spending, using data on 34 Sub-Saharan countries from 1980 to 2012. Annex 2A synthesizes evidence on the impacts of different types of agricultural public spending in Africa.

Most of the studies commonly cited in reference to the body of work on the returns to agricultural public spending in Africa were conducted with data prior to 2003. But recent trends in agricultural spending on the continent—especially following the commitment by African leaders in 2003 to increase their annual spending on agriculture to 10 percent of total national spending—are quite different from the trends associated with the periods previously analyzed. Compared with the trends in the 1980s and 1990s, for example, the share of agricultural spending in total spending and the growth of agricultural spending in 2001–10 declined (table 2.1). Therefore, new evidence on the returns to agricultural public spending that accounts for recent trends in spending and productivity is warranted.

The main results for the trends and impacts of different types of agricultural public spending in Africa are in table 2.2. Between 1980 and 2012, total agricultural spending increased at an average of 0.8 percent a year and constituted 4 percent of total spending (far below the Comprehensive Africa Agriculture Development Programme [CAADP] 10 percent target) and 4.7 percent of agricultural value added. Furthermore, a 1 percent increase in total agricultural spending is associated with a 0.1–0.3 percent increase in agricultural output or productivity.

**Table 2.1** Agricultural Public Spending and Productivity in Sub-Saharan Africa, 1971–2010

| Indicator | Years and values | | | |
|---|---|---|---|---|
| | 1971–80 | 1981–90 | 1991–2000 | 2001–10 |
| Agricultural output growth rate (%) | 1.0 | 2.7 | 3.1 | 2.6 |
| Agricultural output per hectare (constant 2004–06 US$) | 163[a] | 182[b] | 192[c] | 219[d] |
| Agricultural spending (% of total spending) | — | 7.1 | 3.3 | 3.1 |
| Agricultural spending (% of agriculture value added) | — | 4.9 | 3.0 | 3.9 |

Source: Benin 2015.
Note: — = not available.
a. Data from 1980.
b. Data from 1990.
c. Data from 2000.
d. Data from 2009.

**Table 2.2** Key Trends in and Impacts of Different Types of Agricultural Public Spending in Africa

| Objective area and indicator | Estimate |
|---|---|
| *Main trends in spending* | |
| Total agriculture spending in constant 2005 PPP$, 1980–2012 | — |
| Annual average growth rate (%) | 0.8 |
| Annual average share in total spending (%) | 4.0 |
| Annual average share in agriculture value added (%) | 4.7 |
| Research spending in constant 2011 PPP$, 1981–2011 | — |
| Annual average growth rate (%) | −0.1 |
| Annual average share in agriculture value added (%) | 1.1 |
| *Estimated impacts of spending* | |
| Total agriculture, elasticity | 0.1–0.3 |
| National and CGIAR research, ROR (%) | 22–55 |
| Irrigation, ROR (%) | 11–22 |
| Extension, ROR (%) | 8–49 |
| Extension, benefit-cost ratio | 6.8–14.2 |
| Rural roads, benefit-cost ratio | 7.2 |

Source: Benin 2015.
Note: CGIAR = Consultative Group on International Agricultural Research; PPP = purchasing power parity; ROR = rate of return. — = not available.

The returns vary for spending on different agricultural functions, 22–55 percent for research, 8–49 percent for extension, and 11–22 percent for irrigation. The new estimates in this chapter show that total agricultural spending yielded an average return of 11 percent, but agricultural research spending yielded an average return of 93 percent.

Overall, the higher returns to agricultural research spending (93 percent) than to total agricultural spending (11 percent) reflect the low and declining research spending intensities in the continent. Because the returns to agricultural research spending take time—typically a decade—to develop, having a stable and sustained agricultural research funding will be critical for maintaining the high returns and, consequently, for accelerating agriculture-led development in the continent. And because agricultural spending encompasses spending on functions (such as research, extension, irrigation, marketing, or subsidies) that are expected to have different productivity effects, the estimated low return to total agricultural spending (which was actually negative in several countries and in some groups of countries) suggests that more disaggregated analysis is needed to better inform priorities for agricultural spending.

## Trends and Composition of Spending

### Sectoral Composition of Total Spending in World Regions

To compare how different developing regions prioritize agricultural public spending, figure 2.1 summarizes the composition of total spending by functional classification in terms of share of total spending over the entire period (box 2.1).[2] Social protection attracted the largest share in the developing regions of Europe and Central Asia and Latin America and the Caribbean. In the other developing regions, education was the top spender (10–17 percent), except in the Middle East and North Africa, where defense was the top spender at 17 percent. For most regions, defense and social spending (education, health, and social protection) ranked second, third, and fourth. Spending on infrastructure (transport and communication) and agriculture attracted the smallest shares at 3–7 percent, with some slight differences. In South Asia, infrastructure and agriculture ranked third and fourth at 9 percent and 7 percent, respectively, whereas in Sub-Saharan Africa infrastructure ranked third with 7 percent.

Overall, the rank of sectoral spending did not change much from 1980 to 2012, especially for the top three spenders (table 2.3). Changes were most notable for the bottom three spenders, with the rank and share of agriculture

**Figure 2.1** Annual Average Agricultural Spending Share in Total Spending, 1980–2012

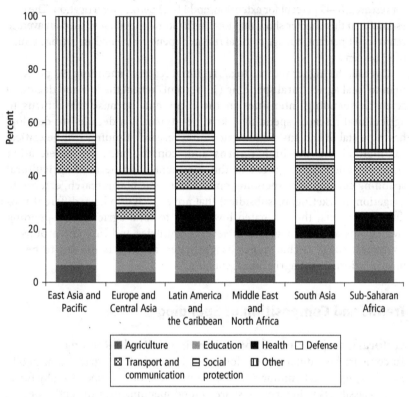

*Source:* IFPRI Statistics on Public Expenditures for Economic Development database.
*Note:* Data for Europe and Central Asia are from 1995 to 2012.

spending faring the worst and declining over time (table 2.4). In Latin America and the Caribbean, agriculture was ranked sixth in 1980–89, 1990–99, and 2000–12, with the annual average share dropping from 3–4 percent in 1980–89 to 2 percent in 2000–12. In Sub-Saharan Africa, the rank of agricultural spending dropped from fourth in 1989 at 7 percent to sixth in 2000–12 at 3 percent. Only in South Asia was agriculture ranked higher than sixth in all the three subperiods, although its share declined over time, ranking third in 1980–89 at 9 percent, fourth in 1990–99 at 7 percent, and fifth in 2000–12 at 5 percent.

## Trends in Total Agricultural Spending

Growth in agriculture spending was erratic in many of the regions (figure 2.2a). East Asia and the Pacific experienced the fastest growth at an annual average of 7.5 percent over 1980–2012, followed by Europe and Central Asia at 6.0 percent,

## BOX 2.1

# Sources of Data

The analysis in this chapter draws on data from three main sources: the Statistics on Public Expenditures for Economic Development (SPEED) database (IFPRI), the Regional Strategic Analysis and Knowledge Support System (ReSAKSS) database (IFPRI), and the Agricultural Science and Technology Indicators (ASTI) database (IFPRI). The SPEED database contains information on government spending in eight sectors (agriculture, transportation and communication, education, health, social security, defense, mining, and fuel and energy) for 147 countries (including 39 from Africa) from 1980 to 2012. The ReSAKSS database contains information on government agricultural spending on African countries only (54 in total) from 1980 to 2014. The ASTI database contains information on governmental and nongovernmental spending in agricultural research for 71 countries (including 42 from Africa) from 1981 to 2012.

To do the comparative analysis of trends in different parts of the world, we follow the standard regional classifications presenting results for six regional groups: East Asia and Pacific, Europe and Central Asia, Latin America and the Caribbean, Middle East and North Africa, South Asia, and Sub-Saharan Africa. We analyze the trends over three subperiods: 1980–89, 1990–99, and 2000–12.

**Table 2.3** Annual Average Sectoral Spending Share in Total Spending, 1980–2012
*Percent*

|  | East Asia and Pacific | Europe and Central Asia | Latin America and the Caribbean | Middle East and North Africa | South Asia | Sub-Saharan Africa |
|---|---|---|---|---|---|---|
| *1980–89* | | | | | | |
| Agriculture | 9 | — | 4 | 4 | 9 | 7 |
| Defense | 13 | — | 9 | 22 | 14 | 14 |
| Education | 17 | — | 15 | 13 | 8 | 15 |
| Health | 6 | — | 10 | 5 | 4 | 6 |
| Social protection | 3 | — | 15 | 8 | 4 | 4 |
| Transport and communication | 12 | — | 8 | 6 | 11 | 10 |
| *1990–99* | | | | | | |
| Agriculture | 6 | 4 | 4 | 3 | 7 | 4 |
| Defense | 13 | 6 | 7 | 20 | 14 | 14 |
| Education | 16 | 8 | 16 | 16 | 10 | 15 |
| Health | 6 | 6 | 9 | 6 | 5 | 6 |
| Social protection | 5 | 7 | 13 | 5 | 4 | 4 |
| Transport and communication | 9 | 3 | 7 | 3 | 9 | 6 |

*(continued next page)*

**Table 2.3** (continued)

| | East Asia and Pacific | Europe and Central Asia | Latin America and the Caribbean | Middle East and North Africa | South Asia | Sub-Saharan Africa |
|---|---|---|---|---|---|---|
| *2000–12* | | | | | | |
| Agriculture | 5 | 4 | 2 | 2 | 5 | 3 |
| Defense | 9 | 7 | 4 | 14 | 12 | 8 |
| Education | 17 | 7 | 17 | 14 | 12 | 14 |
| Health | 7 | 7 | 9 | 6 | 6 | 8 |
| Social protection | 8 | 20 | 16 | 11 | 4 | 6 |
| Transport and communication | 8 | 5 | 5 | 4 | 7 | 6 |

Source: IFPRI Statistics on Public Expenditures for Economic Development database.
Note: Data for Europe and Central Asia are from 1995 to 2012. — = not available.

**Table 2.4** Rank and Share of Agricultural Spending in Total Spending, 1980–2012

| | 1980–89 | | 1990–99 | | 2000–12 | |
|---|---|---|---|---|---|---|
| | Rank | Share (%) | Rank | Share (%) | Rank | Share (%) |
| East Asia and Pacific | 4 | 8.9 | 5 | 6.2 | 6 | 4.6 |
| Europe and Central Asia | — | — | 5 | 4.1 | 6 | 3.9 |
| Latin America and the Caribbean | 6 | 4.1 | 6 | 3.7 | 6 | 2.2 |
| Middle East and North Africa | 6 | 4.1 | 5 | 3.2 | 6 | 2.5 |
| South Asia | 3 | 9.0 | 4 | 6.6 | 5 | 5.1 |
| Sub-Saharan Africa | 4 | 7.4 | 6 | 3.5 | 6 | 3.0 |

Source: IFPRI Statistics on Public Expenditures for Economic Development database.
Note: Data for Europe and Central Asia are from 1995 to 2012. Ranks are from 1 to 6, with 1 being the top rank.
— = not available.

Latin America and the Caribbean at 4.3 percent, South Asia at 4.2 percent, and the Middle East and North Africa at 2.8 percent. Agricultural spending increased at a much slower pace in Sub-Saharan Africa (0.8 percent).

With the rapid growth in agricultural spending in East Asia and the Pacific, spending per capita increased almost fourfold from US$25 in 1980–89 to US$96 in 2000–12 (figure 2.2b).[3] Per capita spending remained stagnant in Latin America and the Caribbean at US$47–US$52, and increased by more than 50 percent in the Middle East and North Africa from US$61 in 1980–89 to US$97 in 2000–12. Sub-Saharan Africa and South Asia experienced the least

**Figure 2.2**  Agricultural Spending, 1980–2012

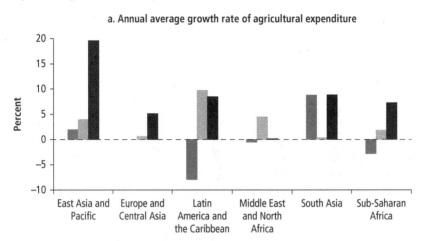

a. Annual average growth rate of agricultural expenditure

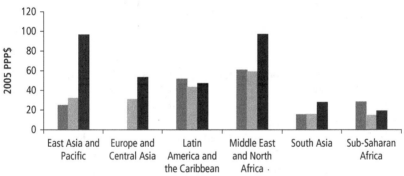

b. Annual average per capita agricultural expenditure

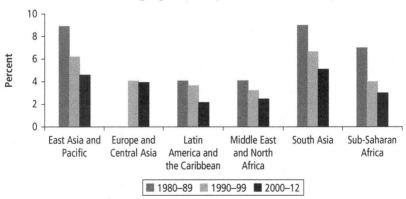

c. Annual average agricultural expenditure share in total expenditure

■ 1980–89  ▨ 1990–99  ■ 2000–12

*(continued next page)*

**Figure 2.2** (continued)

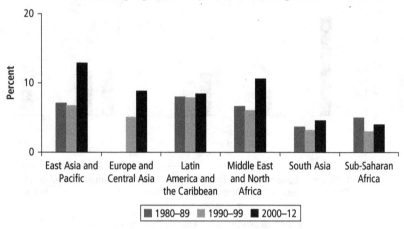

d. Annual average agricultural expenditure share in agricultural value added

*Source:* IFPRI Statistics on Public Expenditures for Economic Development database.
*Note:* Data for Europe and Central Asia are from 1995 to 2012. PPP = purchasing power parity.

per capita spending, although increasing in South Asia from US$15 in 1980–89 to US$28 in 2000–12 but declining in Sub-Saharan Africa from US$28 in 1980–89 to US$19 in 2000–12. This puts Sub-Saharan Africa far behind the other regions in recent years.

In 2000–12, the share of agricultural spending in total spending was around 2–5 percent in East Asia and the Pacific, Europe and Central Asia, Latin America and the Caribbean, and the Middle East and North Africa, but 3–5 percent in South Asia and Sub-Saharan Africa (figure 2.2c). And the share of agricultural spending in agricultural value added was 8–13 percent in East Asia and the Pacific, Europe and Central Asia, Latin America and the Caribbean, and the Middle East and North Africa, but 4–5 percent in South Asia and Sub-Saharan Africa (figure 2.2d).

In the 2003 Maputo Declaration, African heads of state and government agreed that spending on agriculture was inadequate and set a goal of investing 10 percent of their total national spending to agriculture. This goal was reaffirmed in the Malabo Declaration in 2014, and assisting countries to increase the quantity and quality of public agricultural spending has been a major objective of CAADP. There is also an aspirational goal of increasing agricultural annual growth rate to 6 percent for Sub-Saharan countries, though growth is not a policy variable under the direct control of governments the way public spending is.

By volume, public agricultural spending in Africa tends to lag behind other developing regions by several metrics. Agricultural spending as a share of overall public spending is substantially lower than that in other regions, particularly East Asia and the Pacific and South Asia (figure 2.3). In 2014, only Burkina Faso, Malawi, Mozambique, and Zimbabwe had met or surpassed the 10 percent target (Malawi and Mozambique consistently surpassed it), with three countries (Zambia, Niger, and Rwanda) close behind at 9 percent (figure 2.4). By another metric—public spending on agriculture as a share of agricultural GDP—spending is also substantially lower in Africa than in other regions. By yet another metric— spending per capita—Africa also registers the lowest spending by far among regions, and this has declined by around 40 percent between the 1980s and the 2000s (see figure 2.2b).

While almost all countries are spending below the 10 percent target, country conditions and thus spending contexts differ widely across Sub-Saharan Africa. For instance, the spending target is arguably less meaningful for such countries as

**Figure 2.3** Public Agricultural Spending Lags behind Other Regions, 2000–14

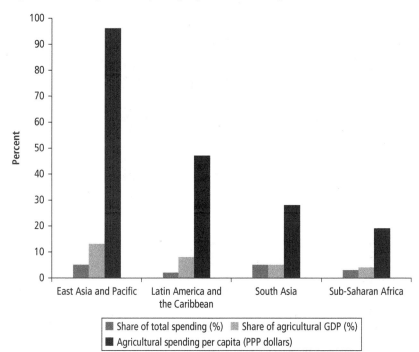

Source: IFPRI Statistics on Public Expenditures for Economic Development database.
Note: The figure represents public agricultural spending across regions. GDP = gross domestic product; PPP = purchasing power parity.

**Figure 2.4** Almost All African Countries Fall Short of 10 Percent Target of Public Spending, 2014

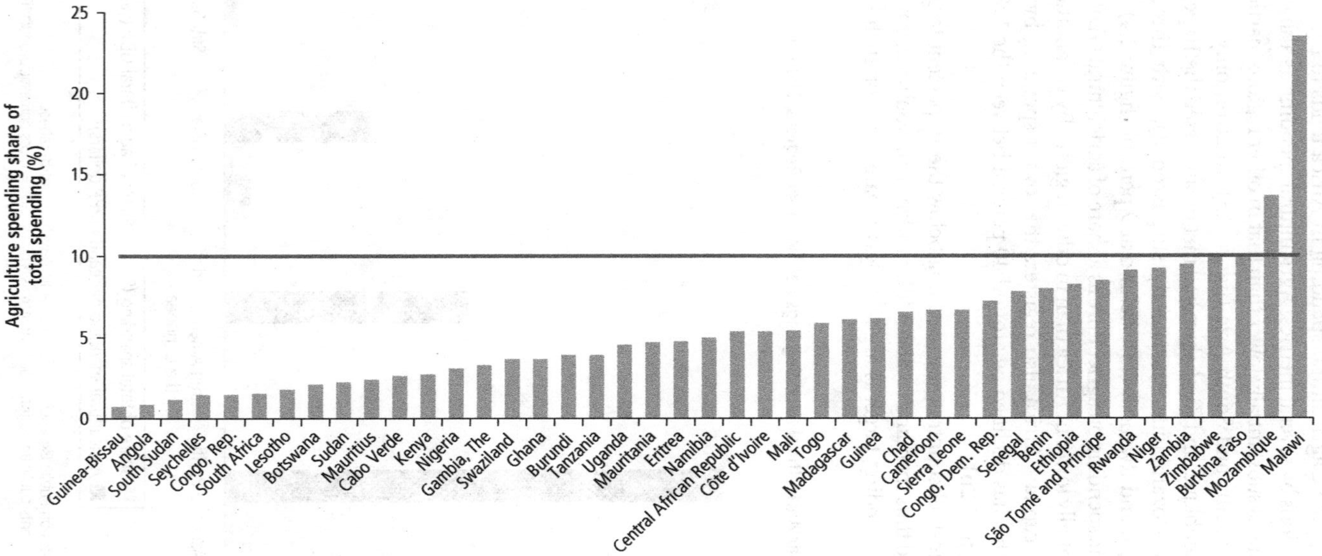

Agriculture spending share of total spending (%)

Malawi
Mozambique
Burkina Faso
Zimbabwe
Zambia
Niger
Rwanda
Sao Tomé and Principe
Ethiopia
Benin
Senegal
Congo, Dem. Rep.
Sierra Leone
Cameroon
Chad
Guinea
Madagascar
Togo
Mali
Côte d'Ivoire
Central African Republic
Namibia
Eritrea
Mauritania
Uganda
Tanzania
Burundi
Ghana
Swaziland
Gambia, The
Nigeria
Kenya
Cabo Verde
Mauritius
Sudan
Botswana
Lesotho
South Africa
Congo, Rep.
Seychelles
South Sudan
Angola
Guinea-Bissau

*Source:* IFPRI Regional Strategic Analysis and Knowledge Support System data.
*Note:* The figure represents public agricultural spending share in Sub-Saharan countries.

South Africa and Botswana, with small agricultural GDP shares in the overall economy. An alternative indicator of public sector budgetary commitment to agriculture is the Agriculture Orientation Index (AOI), defined as agriculture's share of public spending relative to its share in the economy.[4] An AOI value of 1 would indicate that the government spends a share of its budget on agriculture exactly proportionate to agriculture's contribution to gross domestic product (GDP) (figure 2.5).

No country in Africa has an AOI of 1 or more, although some come close. Overall, most African countries spend much smaller proportions of the public budget on agriculture than the sector's share in the economy. Of the 47 countries for which the AOI can be computed, the index in 31 is less than 0.3. There is no reason why expenditure must be allocated exactly in proportion to each sector's contribution to the economy; however, large deviations signal a need for deeper analysis by policy makers.

While the numerical goal of 10 percent is somewhat arbitrary, and the failure to meet this target arguably is not so worrisome, the AOI also appears to demonstrate underspending on the sector in most countries. Even more problematic is the persistent negative trend across three decades in agricultural spending as a share of both agricultural GDP and total public spending in Sub-Saharan Africa (table 2.5).

**Figure 2.5** No Country in Africa Spends as Much on Agriculture as Agriculture Contributes to the Economy, 2014

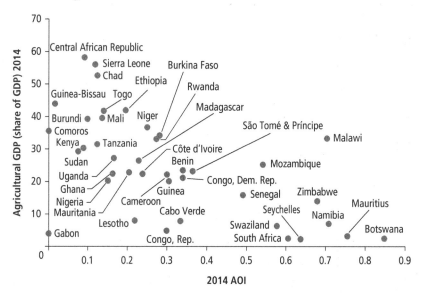

Source: World Bank calculations using SPEED database.
Note: AOI = agriculture orientation index; GDP = gross domestic product.

**Table 2.5** Agricultural Spending Is Low in Almost All Sub-Saharan Countries

| | Agricultural spending | | | | | |
| --- | --- | --- | --- | --- | --- | --- |
| | As a share of total spending (%) | | | As a share of agricultural GDP (%) | | |
| Country | 1980–89 | 1990–99 | 2000–14 | 1980–89 | 1990–99 | 2000–14 |
| **Sub-Saharan Africa** | **9.02** | **6.40** | **5.18** | **11.29** | **9.11** | **8.84** |
| Angola | — | 1.14 | 1.40 | — | 5.02 | 6.83 |
| Benin | — | 8.26 | 6.17 | — | 4.00 | 4.11 |
| Botswana | 9.67 | 5.85 | 3.28 | — | — | — |
| Burkina Faso | 31.30 | 27.14 | 9.99 | 23.33 | 17.46 | 13.43 |
| Burundi | — | 4.90 | 3.42 | — | 2.65 | 2.07 |
| Cameroon | 5.59 | 4.16 | 4.43 | 4.95 | 2.67 | 3.29 |
| Cabo Verde | — | — | 2.91 | — | 5.15 | — |
| Central African Republic | 8.85 | 5.56 | 2.89 | 3.73 | 2.22 | 1.19 |
| Chad | — | — | 5.81 | — | — | 0.56 |
| Congo, Dem. Rep. | — | 5.11 | 2.46 | — | 1.33 | 2.27 |
| Congo, Rep. | — | 0.19 | 1.38 | — | 0.69 | 9.01 |
| Côte d'Ivoire | 2.21 | 3.40 | 3.27 | 3.08 | 3.22 | 2.78 |
| Djibouti | — | — | 1.11 | — | — | 9.27 |
| Equatorial Guinea | — | — | — | — | — | — |
| Eritrea | — | 7.58 | 5.28 | — | 26.59 | 18.81 |
| Ethiopia | 8.40 | 9.22 | 12.28 | 2.86 | 2.94 | 6.14 |
| Gabon | — | — | — | — | — | — |
| The Gambia | 9.58 | 7.57 | 6.23 | 10.38 | 5.04 | 4.80 |
| Ghana | 7.13 | 2.55 | 2.48 | 1.55 | 1.51 | 2.44 |

(continued next page)

**Table 2.5** (continued)

| Country | Agricultural spending | | | | | |
|---|---|---|---|---|---|---|
| | As a share of total spending (%) | | | As a share of agricultural GDP (%) | | |
| | 1980–89 | 1990–99 | 2000–14 | 1980–89 | 1990–99 | 2000–14 |
| Guinea | — | — | 8.09 | — | — | 7.36 |
| Guinea-Bissau | 12.32 | 0.80 | 1.15 | 11.26 | 0.32 | 0.33 |
| Kenya | 9.26 | 6.45 | 4.00 | 8.78 | 5.50 | 3.47 |
| Lesotho | 8.47 | 9.58 | 2.93 | 21.08 | 30.44 | 17.31 |
| Liberia | 6.05 | 2.90 | 4.56 | 5.88 | 3.69 | 0.08 |
| Madagascar | 8.24 | 10.24 | 8.12 | 18.66 | 6.51 | 4.43 |
| Malawi | 12.44 | 8.14 | 12.73 | 9.80 | 7.56 | 12.31 |
| Mali | 6.24 | 12.41 | 9.84 | 3.29 | 7.45 | 7.64 |
| Mauritania | — | — | 5.65 | — | — | 6.50 |
| Mauritius | 7.15 | 5.46 | 2.95 | 14.19 | 14.05 | 18.79 |
| Mozambique | — | — | 5.98 | — | — | 6.19 |
| Namibia | — | 6.49 | 5.02 | — | 23.44 | 18.91 |
| Niger | 14.45 | 23.25 | 13.57 | 7.47 | 10.33 | 8.57 |
| Nigeria | 2.03 | 2.03 | 3.21 | 1.16 | 1.12 | 2.05 |
| Rwanda | — | — | 4.39 | — | — | 3.62 |
| São Tomé and Príncipe | — | — | 6.93 | — | — | 11.15 |
| Senegal | 6.28 | 5.66 | 7.28 | 6.81 | 6.09 | 13.11 |
| Seychelles | — | 1.60 | 1.46 | — | 24.08 | 21.84 |
| Sierra Leone | 4.85 | 1.80 | 3.63 | 2.18 | 0.60 | 2.22 |
| Somalia | — | — | — | — | — | — |

*(continued next page)*

**Table 2.5** (continued)

| | Agricultural spending | | | | | |
| | As a share of total spending (%) | | | As a share of agricultural GDP (%) | | |
| Country | 1980–89 | 1990–99 | 2000–14 | 1980–89 | 1990–99 | 2000–14 |
|---|---|---|---|---|---|---|
| South Africa | — | 0.63 | 1.89 | — | 4.67 | 19.79 |
| South Sudan | — | — | 1.28 | — | — | — |
| Sudan | 11.77 | 12.63 | 5.15 | 5.30 | 0.42 | 3.03 |
| Swaziland | 8.82 | 7.13 | 3.27 | 15.43 | 15.72 | 14.43 |
| Tanzania | 7.04 | 6.16 | 5.72 | — | 2.56 | 3.39 |
| Togo | 8.96 | 3.99 | 5.58 | 9.56 | 2.51 | 3.29 |
| Uganda | 4.57 | 1.74 | 4.14 | 1.20 | 0.53 | 3.21 |
| Zambia | 12.20 | 2.99 | 7.99 | 28.37 | 4.73 | 12.47 |
| Zimbabwe | 9.75 | 5.85 | 11.92 | 27.39 | 28.06 | 7.79 |

*Source:* Benin 2015.
*Note:* GDP = gross domestic product; — = not available.

## Trends in Different Types of Agricultural Spending

Aside from the Agricultural Science and Technology Indicators (ASTI) database on agricultural research spending, there are no similar time series, cross-country comparable databases on the major types of agricultural public spending such as irrigation, extension, marketing infrastructure, and farm support subsidies. The one that offers data most closely suited for the type of analysis desired is the Monitoring African Food and Agricultural Policies (MAFAP) database for a limited set of countries in Sub-Saharan Africa from 2006 to 2013 (FAO). These data, however, do not allow a comprehensive comparative analysis across the different types of spending in all Sub-Saharan Africa countries over as long a time period as we report below for spending on agricultural research.

### Agricultural Research Spending

In the ASTI database, the data measured in 2011 PPP$ are unbalanced in time and country coverage.[5] Thus, although we continue with the same type of comparative analysis, as in previous sections, across the regions, the results should be interpreted with caution. Growth in agricultural spending in Sub-Saharan Africa was negative compared with the growth rates in the other regions (figure 2.6), but it did improve over time, going from an annual average

**Figure 2.6** Public Agricultural Research Spending in Africa Is Low Compared to Other Regions and Declining, 2000–11

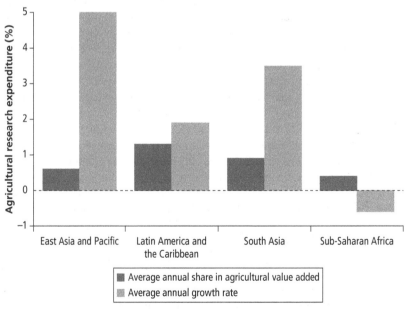

*Source:* IFPRI Agricultural Science and Technology Indicators data.

growth rate of –2.7 percent in 1980–89 to –2.3 in 1990–99 and –0.6 in 2000–11. In 2000–11, East Asia and the Pacific experienced the fastest growth at 5.0 percent a year, compared with South Asia at 3.5 percent, and Latin America and the Caribbean at 1.9 percent. Spending on research constituted about 1.1 percent of agricultural value added in Sub-Saharan Africa in each year in 1980–2011. In the most recent decade of 2000–11, the share was 0.9 in Sub-Saharan Africa compared with 1.3 percent in Latin America and the Caribbean, 0.6 percent in East Asia and the Pacific, and 0.4 percent in South Asia.

Close to 40 percent of the 37 countries covered in Sub-Saharan Africa spent at least 1 percent of the agricultural value added on research, the target set by the African Union's New Partnership for Africa's Development (figure 2.7). Botswana, followed by Mauritius, Namibia, and South Africa, had the highest shares of at least 2 percent per year. Several of the countries with large research spending budgets in absolute terms, including Nigeria, Ethiopia, Tanzania, and Ghana, spent less than 0.7 percent of the equivalent of their agricultural value added each year on average. Unfortunately, in around half of all African countries the absolute volume of spending is either stagnant or falling (figure 2.6).

*Other Types of Agricultural Spending*
The countries in the MAFAP database are Burkina Faso, Ethiopia, Ghana, Kenya, Malawi, Mali, Mozambique, Tanzania, and Uganda, covering different periods from 2006 to 2013. We analyze the data on agriculture-specific spending less subsidies to consumers, and then aggregate into the five main categories of spending: (a) research, (b) irrigation (made up of subsidies on capital for on-farm irrigation and infrastructure and general support to off-farm irrigation), (c) extension (made up of technical assistance, training, and extension and technology transfer), (d) marketing (made up of payments to input suppliers, processors, traders and transporters, and general support to various off-farm services and infrastructure, including inspection, feeder roads, storage, and marketing), and (e) subsidies (made up of payments to producers for inputs and on-farm services).[6]

The original data are in 2011 PPP$ and we analyze the annual average shares of spending on each of the five categories.[7] In the countries with data to compare the composition of spending, input subsidies dominate in the majority of countries, accounting for at least a third of overall agriculture spending (ranging from 30 percent in Kenya to 70 percent in Malawi). Extension and advisory services also generate particularly large shares in some countries, for instance in Ethiopia and Uganda, where they average 35 percent. Research and development (R&D) has a consistently small share. Spending to deliver marketing and irrigation are also crucially neglected. The data are not adequately disaggregated to be able to determine how public agricultural spending is allocated across different functional uses in ways that are reliably comparable across a large number of Sub-Saharan countries. But it is clear that many countries have

**Figure 2.7** Only Six Public Budgets in Sub-Saharan Africa Spend One Percent or More of Agricultural GDP on Research, 2011

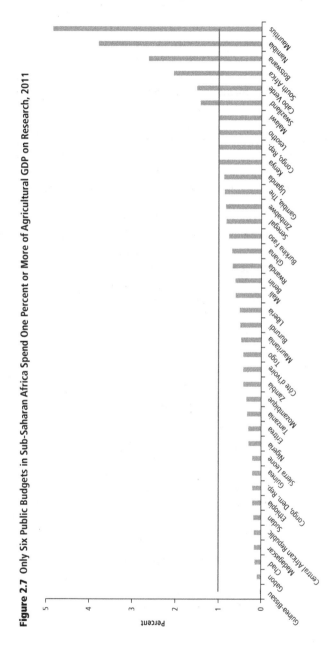

*Source:* IFPRI Agricultural Science and Technology Indicators data.
*Note:* The figure represents agricultural research spending as a share of agricultural GDP. GDP = gross domestic product.

a narrow scope in spending patterns, allocating large shares of their public funds on input subsidy programs, at the expense of high-return investments in core public goods.

Spending on agricultural R&D is worth an especially close look, given the strong evidence that returns to investments in this area are consistently high around the world and in Sub-Saharan Africa. Yet agricultural R&D capacity in Sub-Saharan Africa has remained low by international norms. Over the last decade, spending on agricultural research constituted about 0.4 percent of agricultural GDP in Sub-Saharan Africa, compared with 1.3 percent in Latin America and the Caribbean, 0.6 percent in East Asia and the Pacific, and 0.9 percent in South Asia. And Africa was the only region where agricultural research spending fell on average over this period.

Therefore, it is not surprising that in 2006, in its commitment to implementing an agriculture-led development agenda, the African Union's New Partnership for Africa's Development (NEPAD) set an additional target to increase public spending on agricultural R&D to at least 1 percent of agricultural GDP. This is similar to the level of funding that high-income countries devote to research, and the level of funding to Embrapa, Brazil's highly successful research agency, for example, whose success is attributable to funding and a number of other characteristics and policies (box 2.2). Yet, few African

## BOX 2.2

### Embrapa, a Model of Agricultural Research

Embrapa was created in 1973 as an agricultural research organization under Brazil's Ministry of Agriculture, and has been a major contributor to the remarkable and systematic increases in agricultural productivity that Brazil has enjoyed over the past four decades. In the process, Embrapa has become one of the leading agricultural research organizations in the developing world. Because it has worked effectively on issues important for large commercial agriculture as well as with issues that are crucial for the success of millions of small poor farm enterprises, the Embrapa experience is instructive for agricultural research approaches in Africa.

Some factors in Embrapa's success generate lessons for efforts to strengthen the effectiveness of agricultural research in Africa (Correa and Schmidt 2014; Rada and Valdes 2012).

*Adequate public funding.* Embrapa has been able to secure and sustain a budget of roughly 1 percent of agricultural GDP over the past 25 years. This level of

*(continued next page)*

## Box 2.2 (continued)

sustained investment is necessary to achieve the long-term objectives of agricultural research and could be a reasonable benchmark for Africa, consistent with NEPAD's current target.

*Mix of core and project funding.* Embrapa's core funding has been sufficient to maintain staffing and facilities and cover other fixed expenses—but this has exhausted 90 percent of the core funding, leaving little room for variable operational expenses. Embrapa has consistently raised additional project funding from private sector and development partners to enable its aggressive research and programs. This mix of substantial and stable core funding with significant project funding serves as a good example for similar programs in Africa.

*Independence from bureaucratic impediments.* Embrapa was established as a publicly funded and owned company semiautonomous from the government structure. This has afforded a degree of flexibility (in salaries and planning, for example) that has been essential in building a world-class research staff. This is a model not widely seen in Africa, but would be feasible as an institutional option.

*Independence from political mandates.* This has made it possible for Embrapa to apply disciplined professional focus and professional approaches to its core objectives, relatively unconstrained by short-term political interference. This has greatly facilitated successful achievement of long-term research objectives.

*Independence in dealing with partners.* Embrapa has attained a stature that allows it to work with the private sector, development partners, and the CGIAR system as an equal. As a result, Embrapa has been able to enjoy the benefits of these partnerships even while maintaining focus on its own agenda.

*Sustained investment in human capital.* Embrapa has offered competitive salaries (not bound by the general civil service salary structure), has relentlessly supported advanced training for its staff, and has recruited new staff with advanced degrees. Twenty percent of Embrapa's budget was invested in the education and training of its employees between 1974 and 1982 alone. Currently, three-fourths of Embrapa's 2,000 researchers hold a PhD.

*International collaboration and research excellence.* From the beginning, researchers were drawn from leading universities, setting a high standard of research excellence.

*Intellectual property rights (IPR) consistent with development objectives.* Pursuing an open innovation system and IPR policy in the agricultural sector facilitated technology transfer, diffusion of new cultivars, and the filing of international patents. An IPR policy that favored social well-being rather than benefiting corporations allowed new technology to be disseminated at production costs only. This experience is of particular relevance for improving research impact in Africa—where rules for transfer of new technologies have been rather restrictive to a detrimental effect.

**Figure 2.8** Half the Countries Have Zero or Negative Spending Growth for R&D, 2000–11

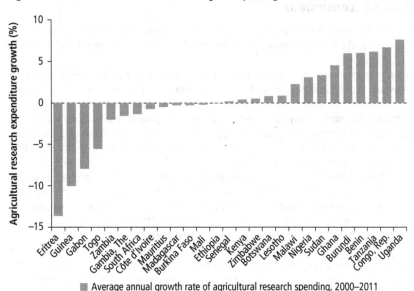

■ Average annual growth rate of agricultural research spending, 2000–2011

Source: IFPRI Agricultural Science and Technology Indicators data.
Note: The figure represents annual growth in agricultural R&D spending. The figure excludes Cabo Verde, the Central African Republic, Chad, the Democratic Republic of Congo, Guinea-Bissau, Liberia, Mauritania, Mozambique, Namibia, Rwanda, Sierra Leone, and Swaziland because time series data did not date back to 2000. R&D = research and development.

countries have hit this target. A closer look at the relative shift in the patterns of spending in agricultural R&D in Sub-Saharan countries over time reveals important cross-country differences and challenges. During 2000–11, half the Sub-Saharan countries experienced near-zero or negative growth in agricultural R&D spending (figure 2.8).

In sum, from several angles there are troubling signs that agricultural research is severely underfunded in Africa. First, there is considerable evidence that a dollar spent on research has a much higher economic return than a dollar spent on other activities, indicating that taking a dollar from elsewhere and putting it into research would raise overall returns (figure 2.9). Second, despite the ostensible political commitment to agriculture R&D in Africa, a minority of Sub-Saharan countries have met the NEPAD target of investing 1 percent of agricultural GDP in this activity. Third, apart from the levels, even the growth in spending on African R&D in many African countries has in recent years been low or even negative.

**Figure 2.9** Returns to R&D Are Uniformly High

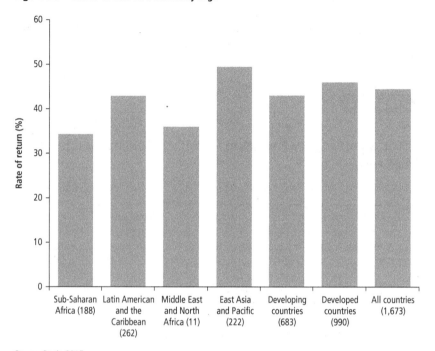

*Source:* Benin 2015.
*Note:* Average rates of return from public spending on agricultural research and development across studies in several regions; numbers of studies that calculated rates of return in each region are in parentheses.

## How Spending Benefits Agriculture

One can conceptually classify the beneficial effects of high-quality public agricultural spending in four channels: advancing technology, enhancing knowledge and skills, reducing transaction costs, and attracting private capital. Each of these channels can be identified with particular classes of programmatic spending to provide goods or services that have the characteristics of "public goods," and public spending in each of them has been empirically demonstrated to be highly productive (see annex 2B for a more comprehensive exposition of the earlier literature on these channels). In addition, agricultural spending can play an important role in confronting challenges of recently emerging issues, which will need to be taken into account when determining spending priorities in the future. These include adaptation to increased risks associated with climate change and lowering emissions from agriculture, the latter of which is an important global public good (box 2.3). In addition, appropriate spending choices in agriculture can help improve the nutritional status of the population (box 2.4).

## BOX 2.3

## Public Spending for Emerging Priorities: Enhancing Climate Resilience

Intergovernmental Panel on Climate Change (IPCC) (2014) projects that without (successful) adaptation, temperatures could increase in excess of 2°C above preindustrial times, potentially reducing food crop yields in parts of Africa between 10 percent and 20 percent. Conclusions of a World Bank (2013) study are even more dire: the world could warm by 4°C (or 7.2°F) above pre-industrial levels by the end of this century if there is not concerted action to reduce greenhouse gases now. For Sub-Saharan Africa, this would mean significant yield decreases in the near term under relatively modest levels of warming. Under 1.5°C–2°C warming, median yield losses of around 5 percent are projected, increasing to median estimates of around –15 percent (range –5 percent to –27 percent) for 2°C–2.5°C warming. Under 3°C–4°C warming, there are indications that yields may decrease by around 15–20 percent across all crops and Sub-Saharan Africa regions. There is also increasing empirical evidence that elevated atmospheric $CO_2$ will lower protein and micronutrient concentrations of cereal grains and thereby reduce the nutritional quality of food and fodder. While agriculture is arguably the sector most heavily impacted by global warming, it is also an important contributor to the problem: it produces 10–12 percent of manmade greenhouse gases, and is the largest producer of non-$CO_2$ greenhouse gases, especially methane. A large part of agriculture's emissions come from land use change, in particular deforestation, and as noted earlier, Africa is the only region where the majority of production increases have come from expanding area, generally at the expense of forests.

In Africa, as around the world, a "climate-smart agriculture" (CSA) approach is needed to achieve the triple win of enhancing agricultural productivity, mitigating emissions of greenhouse gases, and helping farmers adapt to climate change. CSA involves the generation and adoption of locally appropriate technologies, policies, institutions, and investments through the following four kinds of interventions: (a) management of farms, crops, livestock, aquaculture, and capture fisheries to enhance resource management to produce more with less while increasing resilience to climate-related shocks; (b) the restoration of degraded lands for productive agriculture and forestry; (c) ecosystem and landscape management to enhance not only productivity but also ecosystem services that are critical for sustaining resource use efficiency and climate change-resilient productivity; and (d) knowledge, finance, and decision support services for farmers and land managers to enable them to adopt and implement the necessary changes.

*(continued next page)*

## Box 2.3 (continued)

Most of the investments for climate change mitigation (low carbon growth) and adaptation (resilience building) will need to be made by farmers and other private sector agents. But this will require proactive government policies, planning, and investments to provide information, incentives, and an enabling environment to encourage communities, households, and the private sector to change their behaviors, consumption, and investment choices. Many climate resilient investments will not be very different from good investment choices even not taking climate change into account: building resilience has great benefits in any case. But their value is amplified by the changes that will occur with global warming. Policy will rely on a range of policy levers: information, regulation, taxation, and public spending. Public expenditure is an important part of this policy package. Public investments for CSA are essential to ensure (a) the necessary science and technology R&D breakthroughs that will be needed for resilience to the projected climate shocks, (b) the development of cyber data and decision support simulation platforms across multiple and interacting sectors, and (c) creating an appropriate incentive framework for private sector investments and action in CSA and resilient landscapes.

With respect to spending priorities, CSA approaches entail greater investment in (a) managing climate risks, (b) understanding and planning for transitions to newly adapted cropping and livestock systems and livelihood options, and (c) reducing greenhouse gas emissions from fertilizer and livestock practices and from land use change leading to further deforestation and loss of biomass and soil carbon. The successful implementation and scaling up of CSA requires a landscape-scale approach to harness the spatial and time-based synergies of the food, energy, and water subsystems.

There are, however, distinct challenges facing the allocation of public and private investments in CSA: (a) the uncertainty with regard to climate change impacts, because model forecasts are significantly different, especially at local scales; (b) the extended time horizon over which climate change impacts will unfold, which extends far beyond political cycles; (c) the distributional consequences of climate change and disparate incidence of measures to both mitigate and adapt to it, including the fact that the benefits of adaptation are felt locally, while those of mitigating emissions are felt globally; (d) managing the unintended consequences of policies (such as diesel or electricity subsidies for irrigation pumps and insurance subsidies that encourage development in flood-prone areas) and the extent to which international agreements will shape national policy and planning processes; and (e) the need to put in place adequate institutional arrangements.

Climate change has only recently been identified as a specific area of focus for public expenditure reviews (PERs); an extensive review of African country PERs found none related to climate change at the country-specific level. Greater incorporation of climate change considerations into expenditure reviews could help address the challenges of planning expenditures for CSA by identifying opportunities to build flexibility and learning into institutional and policy responses to minimize adverse effects of uncertainty, analyzing trade-offs between short- and long-run measures, quantifying distributional implications of alternative policies and investments, and planning how to take advantage of resource flows in the global climate change architecture.

**BOX 2.4**

## Public Spending for Emerging Priorities: Making Agricultural Spending More Nutrition-Sensitive

Some of the most important policies and public investments for making agriculture more nutrition-sensitive are undertaken not solely—or even primarily—for their positive effects on nutrition, but this may be an important ancillary benefit (Tanimichi Hoberg 2015). The class of intervention with perhaps the strongest empirical link to nutrition is empowering women, which has led to increased production of nutrient-dense foods for household consumption (such as with biofortified crops and homestead gardens). If women had the same access to productive resources as men (by removing legal and customary barriers that bar them from equal access), they could increase yields on their farms by 20–30 percent. This could raise total agricultural output in developing countries by 2.5–4 percent. Investing in women also has high payoffs for nutrition, because women tend to spend more of their discretionary income on factors that positively affect nutritional outcomes, such as education, health care, and food (consumed at home). Among all aspects of women's empowerment, the most relevant for nutrition are increasing women's access to and control over resources—which is particularly important in African agriculture given the significant role played by women in production and marketing.

Policies and investments in many African countries exhibit a strong bias toward staple foods, mainly cereals and root vegetables. These include crop-specific fertilizer subsidies, credit subsidies, grain procurement for food stocks, price supports, and irrigation infrastructure aimed at specific crops (particularly rice). These policies have inadvertently crowded out the production of nonstaple nutrient-rich crops such as fruits, vegetables, and pulses.

In Africa, two-thirds of available food supply is either a cereal or tuber crop, high in dietary energy but typically low in micronutrients and protein (nutrient-light). Only about 20 percent of the food supply is in the nutrient-dense food category (vegetables, fruits, and pulses). This contrasts with non-African countries where the nutrient-light share is less than half (48 percent) and the nutrient-dense share is 35 percent. Shifting the mix requires rethinking strategies that focus budgetary and other support on staple food crops—and going beyond staple grains to crop-neutral strategies. Nonstaples require a different kind of public and private support system such as farmer training, transport systems, cold storage systems, and information systems that allow for better functioning of markets for perishables and development of value chains. Reversing the old policies can also reap great benefits in productive efficiency by encouraging production of products in which the country has a real comparative advantage.

Specific nutrition-focused interventions in the production stage could include:

- Biofortification through plant breeding and agronomic approaches to increase concentrations of key nutrients in staple food crops
- Micronutrient-fortified fertilizers to correct deficiencies of nutrients in order to improve crop yields

*(continued next page)*

---

## Box 2.4 (continued)

- Home production of dairy, fruits and vegetables, and small-scale aquaculture and fisheries (the financial sustainability of these interventions has yet to be tested as these schemes, to date, are largely limited to heavily subsidized interventions)

  Other options involve postharvest interventions:

- Aflatoxin control in the long term through research and more immediately through deployment of aflatoxin management practice

- Food fortification through the addition of micronutrients to processed foods, and consumer education, for example, through consumer guidelines

---

### Advancing Technology

Research creates knowledge, which is both nonexcludable and nonrivalrous. Of course, some knowledge can be embodied in a physical commercial product (such as improved seed varieties) with benefits that are excludable and rivalrous but the knowledge itself is not. Much evidence shows that investments in agricultural R&D have tremendously enhanced agricultural productivity around the world over the past five decades, which in turn has led to higher incomes, lower poverty levels, greater food security, and better nutrition (Alston, Pardey, and Piggott 2006; Evenson and Gollin 2003; World Bank 2008). In Sub-Saharan Africa, numerous studies show that the rates of return to agricultural research are consistently high, in the range of 22–55 percent (Alene et al. 2009; Thirtle, Piesse, and Lin 2003), and the next section reports some new (and improved) estimates of the benefits.

### Improving Knowledge and Skills

Public spending on education, extension, and information services can raise the knowledge and skills of farmers and others engaged in agricultural production. These investments create significant positive externalities through demonstration effects and peer-to-peer learning of benefits from adopting new productivity-enhancing technology. This is important since agricultural production processes are becoming increasingly knowledge-intensive, requiring precise and timely information. Of 375 estimates of returns to extension services reported globally, 44 were in Africa, with a mean return of 43 percent (Evenson 2001). Evidence also points to significant research-extension linkages, and the returns to extension services tend to be higher in a context of rapid technological change (Anderson and Feder 2007). Public spending on farmers' education has a significant positive effect on agricultural productivity and the adoption of improved agriculture technologies (Fan and Zhang 2008; Fuglie and Rada 2013).

The transmission of technologies depends on the rate that new technologies become available, and the productivity gain is limited by the weakest link in this chain. The new technological improvements available on the shelf require effective extension and adaptive research to prosper in local contexts. The balance between R&D and extension has long been an issue, since critics have suggested that many of these workers had nothing to extend owing to weak research and development. In addition, extension has tended to be the poor relation at the bottom of the funding chain (Feder et al. 2010; Thirtle and van Zyl 1994). This has resulted in entire budgets being spent on recurrent items like salaries, even while there were no fuel or parts for vehicles and thus no farm visits.

## Reducing Transaction Costs

Transaction costs are an important determinant of market integration (Sadoulet and de Janvry 1995). Public spending on infrastructure can improve access to input and output markets, reducing the cost of agricultural inputs and technologies. Rural roads are arguably the most critical element of public infrastructure for agricultural growth in developing countries, reducing travel times, transport costs, and in-transit spoilage (Calderón and Servén 2004). This tends to raise the prices farmers receive for their products—and lower the prices they pay for inputs (Dorosh, Dradri, and Haggblade 2009). The value of price information is also high for farmers since it facilitates their access to markets and reduces reliance on intermediaries, getting them better prices for inputs and products (see annex 2B for a more detailed exposition of the literature) (Aker and Mbiti 2010; Deichmann, Goyal, and Mishra 2016; Torero 2015).

## Attracting Private Capital

Public investments raise the productivity of other factors of production, attracting private capital. One example is investing in large irrigation infrastructure, which opens the door to on-farm investments. Public investment in dams and canals for irrigation, for example, increases private investment in irrigation systems, as demonstrated by evidence from India (Fan, Hazell, and Thorat 2000).

The benefits from inspection and quarantine services that prevent public outbreaks of plant, animal, and human diseases lay the foundation for private market development. Many of the other kinds of investments mentioned above can also complement private sector investment. Public R&D have been shown to have significant crowding-in effects on private R&D in Ireland and the United States, with estimated elasticities in the range of 0.10 to 0.28 (Görg and Strobl 2006; Malla and Gray 2005). It is also sometimes argued that spending on programs to subsidize greater use of inputs has the objective of demonstrating to poor farmers the benefits of inputs, thereby encouraging them to continue using inputs and spending their own money after the subsidies end.

## Enhancing Equity

Public spending in agriculture is also often justified on equity grounds, especially salient given the concentration of the poor in rural areas, most of whom rely primarily on agriculture (directly or indirectly) for their livelihoods. One argument for fertilizer subsidies, for example, is that they could help poor farmers break out of a low-productivity poverty trap by raising yields and incomes so they can quit using risk-minimizing but low-productivity techniques (Jayne et al. 2015). The equity justification for spending naturally is stronger for programs that can actually be targeted at the poor, rather than diffusing their benefits, and for programs that demonstrate a high income multiplier effect. In Ethiopia, for example, impacts of spending on extension were found to compare favorably to several kinds of social sector spending with respect to progressivity, and were far superior to spending on subsidies (box 2.5).

## BOX 2.5

## Incidence of Agricultural Expenditure in Ethiopia

Budgetary allocations to the agricultural sector are among the highest in Africa, close to 13 percent on average from the 2003–14 period, almost half of which is spent on extension. The government has devoted significant resources to expanding extension services in Ethiopia, and there is currently one extension agent for every 472 farmers, which is the highest agent-to-farmer ratio in the world (30 percent higher than the next highest ratio in China).

High levels of spending on agriculture appear to have paid off, aiding high rates of inclusive agricultural growth that has driven poverty reduction in rural areas. The extension program has been one of the drivers of the very high levels of agricultural growth that Ethiopia experienced in the 2000s (Bachewe et al. 2015). High levels of agricultural spending are often justified as social spending, but how equitable is on-budget agricultural spending in Ethiopia?

Extension programs are often targeted to better-off, higher-potential farmers with the aim that they will act as model farmers to their less well-off neighbors. In order to capture the spillover effects of extension spending—that is, the benefit that accrues to other households in a village when some members receive extension services— estimates of spillover effects of extension in Ethiopia were taken from Krishnan and Patnam (2013). Krishnan and Patnam examine the impact of extension on technology adoption for farmers in Ethiopia, and the impact of technology adoption on the adoption of neighbors. An additional extension visit increases the probability of technology adoption by 3 percent. Technology adoption increases the adoption of five closest neighbors by 0.1 percent each, a total adoption increase of 0.5 percent. If benefits are accrued proportional to adoption, then 86 percent of spending is directly enjoyed and the remaining 14 percent is enjoyed by others that did not receive extension visits.

*(continued next page)*

## Box 2.5 (continued)

**Figure B2.5.1** The Incidence of Extension Spending

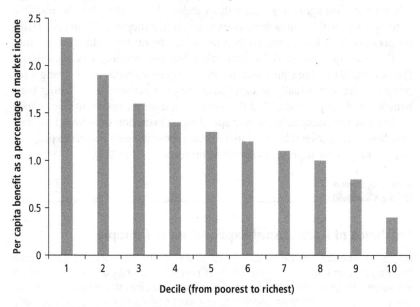

*Source:* Household Consumption Expenditure Survey 2010/11.

Figure B2.5.1 shows the benefits received relative to the income of each decile, showing that spending as a share of market income is highest for the poorest decile. Extension spending comprises over 2 percent of income for the poorest decile. In figure B2.5.2, the progressivity of extension is compared to other government spending on social sectors using the analysis on the incidence of fiscal spending undertaken in Woldehanna et al. (2011). Sectors in which spending is progressive in both absolute and relative terms are those for which the Gini of spending is negative. Sectors in which spending is progressive in relative terms, but not in absolute terms (that is, not pro-poor) are those for which the Gini is positive but less than the Gini of market income. Sectors in which spending is regressive in both absolute and relative terms are those for which the Gini is positive and higher than the Gini of market income. Compared to other social spending, agricultural extension performs quite well. While it is not as progressive as spending on primary education, it is more progressive than spending on secondary education and about the same as spending on health. Subsidies are much less progressive than spending on agricultural extension programs.

*(continued next page)*

## Box 2.5 (continued)

**Figure B2.5.2** Comparison of Spending on Agriculture (Extension) and Other Social Spending

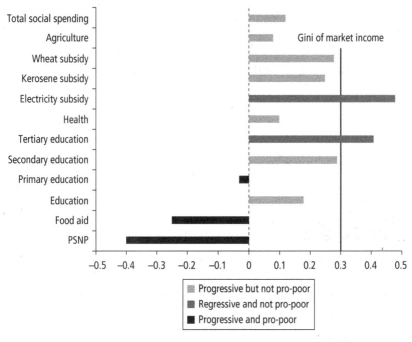

*Note:* PSNP = Productive Safety Net Program.
*Source:* Household Consumption Expenditure Survey 2010/11.

## Public Spending Is Not Always Productive, However

This is a clear implication of the relatively low estimated elasticities, rates of return, and benefit-cost ratios from total agricultural expenditure compared with high benefits of certain categories of agriculture spending (Devarajan, Swaroop, and Zou 1996). In cases where aggregate spending has low or no measurable impact, this is presumably because the positive effects of effective spending are overwhelmed by the negative effects of ineffective spending. Spending can be unproductive or even reduce productivity of other spending for two basic reasons. First, governments sometimes spend on things that are not public goods. Studies that draw a distinction between public spending on public goods versus public spending on private goods, such as subsidies, empirically find the former to be much more productive and more effective in reducing poverty (see chapter 3) (López 2005; López and Galinato 2007). When governments supply private goods, there is a serious risk of displacing the private sector, which would generally be a more efficient provider. Second, even when there are clear failures in particular markets, government spending may not necessarily improve the situation. Inherent characteristics of government interventions can sometimes lead to "government failures," which may exacerbate the original problems caused by the market failure and produce unintended adverse ancillary effects (see chapter 5). We therefore turn below to new evidence on the returns to public spending on agriculture.

# Returns to Agricultural Public Spending in Sub-Saharan Africa

This section provides updated evidence of the impacts of agricultural public spending by estimating the returns to public spending in Sub-Saharan Africa's agriculture sector, considering total agricultural spending versus agricultural research spending (box 2.6). We use data on 34 Sub-Saharan countries from 1980 to 2012. Details of the data, variables, and estimation methods are in annex 2A. As discussed earlier, there are various channels for the productivity effects of public agriculture spending to materialize, the effects are not the same for all types of spending, and the effects often materialize with a lag rather than contemporaneously.

## Key Trends in Underlying Variables

Table 2.6 shows descriptive statistics of the variables used in the estimation, presented separately for the panel used to estimate the impact of total agricultural spending (34 countries from 1996 to 2012) and for the panel used to

---

**BOX 2.6**

## Estimating Elasticities to Estimate Returns

Using a fixed effects (FE) model, we estimate an aggregate agriculture production function of two general forms: one that includes current and lagged values of total agricultural spending per hectare ($gt_t$, $gt_{t-1}$, ..., $gt_{t-5}$), and another that includes current agricultural research spending per hectare ($gr_t$) and capital stock of agricultural research ($sgr_t$, which is derived from lagged values of $gr$). The effect of nonagricultural spending per capita ($ngt$) and other factors $x$ are controlled for. The FE model addresses potential endogeneity of agricultural spending that may derive from unobserved, time-invariant variables, with instrumental variables on governance and political processes. Standard errors are estimated using three types of clusters—each country, different countries within the same agroecological zone, and different countries with the same number of years of participation in CAADP. Various statistical tests are performed to examine robustness, validity of the instruments, and multicollinearity of explanatory variables. The estimated elasticities with respect to spending are used to estimate the rate of return (ROR) for different countries.

**Table 2.6 Summary Statistics, 1996–2012**

| | Panel for analyzing impact of total agricultural spending | | | Panel for analyzing impact of agricultural research spending | | |
|---|---|---|---|---|---|---|
| | 1996–2012 | 1996–2003 | 2004–12 | 1996–2011 | 1996–2003 | 2004–11 |
| Agricultural value added, US$/ha ($y$) | 158.72 | 140.74 | 174.69 | 154.05 | 140.02 | 167.02 |
| Agricultural spending, US$/ha ($gt$) | 6.48 | 4.47 | 8.25 | 6.98 | 4.94 | 8.86 |
| Agricultural research spending, US$/ha ($gr$) | n.e. | n.e. | n.e. | 1.00 | 0.96 | 1.03 |
| Agricultural research capital, US$/ha ($sgr$) | n.e. | n.e. | n.e. | 4.00 | 4.79 | 3.27 |
| Nonagricultural spending, US$/capita ($ngt$) | 257.21 | 224.18 | 286.56 | 289.48 | 254.90 | 321.42 |
| Agricultural labor, number per hectare ($l$) | 0.37 | 0.35 | 0.40 | 0.37 | 0.35 | 0.39 |
| Agricultural capital, US$/ha ($k1$) | 502.18 | 462.05 | 537.83 | 520.03 | 483.31 | 553.96 |
| Fertilizer, kg/ha ($k2$) | 2.79 | 2.59 | 2.97 | 3.52 | 3.48 | 3.55 |
| Animal feed, kg/ha ($k3$) | 59.64 | 48.09 | 69.90 | 67.19 | 57.72 | 75.94 |
| Rainfall, mm ($R$) | 1078.41 | 1074.38 | 1081.99 | 1013.82 | 996.68 | 1029.65 |
| Irrigation, share ($I$) | 0.01 | 0.01 | 0.01 | 0.01 | 0.01 | 0.01 |
| Population density, number per sq km ($P$) | 67.73 | 59.24 | 75.26 | 72.45 | 65.63 | 78.75 |
| *Technology, share (A)* | | | | | | |
| Low | 0.24 | 0.25 | 0.24 | 0.20 | 0.19 | 0.22 |
| Medium-low | 0.27 | 0.27 | 0.27 | 0.28 | 0.31 | 0.26 |
| Medium-high | 0.26 | 0.27 | 0.26 | 0.32 | 0.34 | 0.30 |
| High | 0.23 | 0.22 | 0.24 | 0.19 | 0.16 | 0.22 |

*(continued next page)*

**Table 2.6** (continued)

| Instruments ($Z^c$) | Panel for analyzing impact of total agricultural spending | | | Panel for analyzing impact of agricultural research spending | | |
|---|---|---|---|---|---|---|
| | 1996–2012 | 1996–2003 | 2004–12 | 1996–2011 | 1996–2003 | 2004–11 |
| Voice, –2.5 to 2.5 | –0.67 | –0.74 | –0.61 | –0.51 | –0.57 | –0.45 |
| Law, –2.5 to 2.5 | –0.81 | –0.85 | –0.76 | –0.63 | –0.64 | –0.62 |
| Regulation, –2.5 to 2.5 | –0.66 | –0.67 | –0.64 | –0.50 | –0.49 | –0.51 |
| Stability, –2.5 to 2.5 | –0.73 | –0.82 | –0.64 | –0.59 | –0.63 | –0.55 |
| Effectiveness, –2.5 to 2.5 | –0.77 | –0.76 | –0.77 | –0.63 | –0.61 | –0.65 |
| Corruption, –2.5 to 2.5 | –0.68 | –0.68 | –0.68 | –0.57 | –0.54 | –0.59 |
| Polity, –10 to 10 | 1.55 | 0.78 | 2.22 | 2.33 | 1.48 | 3.12 |
| Durability, years | 8.60 | 6.33 | 10.62 | 8.48 | 6.74 | 10.09 |
| Number of observations | 576 | 576 | 576 | 354 | 354 | 354 |
| Number of countries | 34 | 34 | 34 | 23 | 23 | 23 |

*Source:* Benin 2015.
*Note:* See annex 2B for detailed descriptions of variables. US$ is expressed in 2006 constant prices. n.e. = not estimated, since data were not available for some countries in panel.

**Table 2.7** Determinants of Agricultural Spending in Sub-Saharan Africa, 1996–2012

| | Agricultural spending, US$/ha ($gt$) | | Agricultural research spending, US$/ha ($gr$) | | | |
|---|---|---|---|---|---|---|
| | Model 1 | Model 2 | Model 1 | Model 2 | Model 3 | Model 4 |
| *Lags of agricultural spending* | | | | | | |
| $gt_{t-1}$ | 0.58 *** | 0.57 *** | — | 0.10 *** | — | 0.08 ** |
| $gt_{t-2}$ | 0.01 | 0.01 | — | — | — | — |
| $gt_{t-3}$ | −0.06 | −0.06 | — | — | — | — |
| $gt_{t-4}$ | 0.04 | 0.04 | — | — | — | — |
| $gt_{t-5}$ | −0.07 * | −0.07 * | — | — | — | — |
| Elasticity | 0.49 *** | 0.49 *** | — | — | — | — |
| Agricultural research capital (*sgr*) | — | — | 0.52 *** | 0.49 *** | 0.54 *** | 0.52 *** |
| Nonagricultural spending (*ngt*) | 0.44 *** | 0.44 *** | −0.02 | −0.02 | −0.02 | −0.02 |
| Lag of agricultural valued added ($y_{t-1}$) | — | −0.06 | — | −0.59 *** | −0.59 *** | −0.56 *** |
| *Instruments ($Z^G$)* | | | | | | |
| Stability | 0.15 *** | 0.15 *** | 0.03 | 0.03 | 0.03 | 0.03 |
| Polity | — | — | 0.03 *** | 0.03 *** | 0.03 *** | 0.03 *** |
| *Overall model statistics* | | | | | | |
| R-squared | 0.74 | 0.74 | 0.20 | 0.22 | 0.26 | 0.27 |
| F-statistic | 82.21 *** | 77.57 *** | 5.99 *** | 6.28 *** | 7.98 *** | 7.84 *** |
| *IV tests* | | | | | | |
| Spending is exogenous ($\chi^2$ statistic) | 2.22 | 0.28 | 0 | 0.02 | 0.21 | 0.22 |
| Underidentified ($\chi^2$ statistic) | 15.58 *** | 15.58 *** | 15.90 *** | 16.94 *** | 15.72 *** | 16.51 *** |
| Instrument is weak (*F*-statistic) | 15.53 *** | 16.39 *** | 16.05 *** | 17.10 *** | 15.80 *** | 16.59 *** |

*Source:* Benin 2015.

*Note:* See annex 2B for detailed description of variables. IV tests of the null hypothesis that: spending is exogenous using the Sargan-Hansen $\chi^2$ statistic; underidentified = rank of matrix of first-stage reduced-form coefficients is underidentified, using the Anderson or Kleibergen-Paap Lagrange multiplier test with the $\chi^2$ statistic; and weak = first-stage reduced-form equation is weakly identified using the Cragg-Donald or Kleibergen-Paap Wald test with the *F*-statistic. — = variable omitted from regression. Significance level: * = 10 percent, ** = 5 percent, *** = 1 percent.

estimate the impact of agricultural research spending (23 countries from 1996 to 2011). For all the 34 countries, annual average agricultural value added per hectare (that is, land productivity) was US$159 in 1996–2012, rising by 24 percent from $141 in 1996–2003 (pre-CAADP period) to US$175 in 2004–12 (during CAADP).[8] Agriculture spending per hectare almost doubled from US$4.50 in 1996–2003 to US$8.30 in 2004–12. These represent an increase in the share of agriculture spending in total spending from 2.0 percent to 2.8 percent, respectively, far lower than the 10 percent Maputo Declaration target. Agricultural research spending per hectare remained stagnant at US$1, which represents a decline in the share in total agricultural spending from 19 percent in 1996–2003 to 12 percent in 2004–11.

For spending intensities, agricultural spending as a share of agricultural value added increased from 3.2 percent in 1996–2003 to 4.7 percent in 2004–12, whereas agricultural research spending as a share of agricultural value added declined from 0.7 percent in 1996–2003 to 0.6 percent in 2004–12. For other variables—with the exception of rainfall and irrigation, whose averages remained stagnant over the two subperiods—the data on labor, capital, fertilizer, animal feed, and population density show an increase between 14 percent and 45 percent. For technology, there is little change in the distribution of countries over time.

Table 2.7 shows the determinants of agriculture public spending. The results are consistent in different model specifications, involving exclusion or inclusion of the lag of value added per hectare ($y_{t-1}$) in the estimation of both the impact of total agricultural spending ($gt$) and agricultural research spending ($gr$), and exclusion or inclusion of the lag of total agricultural spending ($gt_{t-1}$) in the estimation of the impact of agricultural research spending ($gr$).

### Sensitivity of Productivity to Agricultural Public Spending

Table 2.8 shows detailed results of the regression estimates, using different model specifications.[9] The model specification that includes the lag of value added per hectare ($y_{t-1}$) gives much higher explanatory power, with $R$-squared values ranging from 0.77 to 0.92 and an $F$-statistic of 89.3, compared with specification without it, with $R$-squared values ranging from 0.57 to 0.71 and an $F$-statistic of 38.27. The total elasticity to agricultural spending per hectare is estimated at 0.04, which is consistently estimated with the specification that includes the lag of value added per hectare and whether the standard errors are clustered. This means that a 1 percent increase in agricultural spending per hectare is associated with a 0.04 percent increase in agricultural value added per hectare. Compared with findings from other cross-country studies, this is lower than the estimated elasticity of 0.08 in Fan, Yu, and Saurkar (2008), for example.

**Table 2.8** Impact of Total Agricultural Spending on Agricultural Value Added per Hectare in Sub-Saharan Africa, 1996–2012

|  | FE model 1 | | | | FE model 2 | | | |
|---|---|---|---|---|---|---|---|---|
| *Agricultural spending* | | | | | | | | |
| $gt_t$ | −0.01 | | | | 0 | | | |
| $gt_{t-1}$ | −0.01 | | | | 0.01 | | | |
| $gt_{t-2}$ | 0.03 | r | c | a | 0.02 | | | a |
| $gt_{t-3}$ | −0.03 | r | c | a | −0.03 | * | r | c | a |
| $gt_{t-4}$ | 0 | | | | 0.01 | | | |
| $gt_{t-5}$ | 0.07 | *** | r | c | a | 0.04 | *** | r | c | a |
| Elasticity | 0.04 | ** | | | 0.04 | ** | r | c | a |
| Nonagricultural spending (*ngt*) | −0.08 | *** | r | c | a | −0.01 | | | |
| Lag of agricultural valued added ($y_{t-1}$) | | | | | 0.65 | *** | r | c | a |
| Intercept | 2.36 | *** | | | 0.36 | | | |
| *Overall model statistics* | | | | | | | | |
| *R*-squared (within) | 0.57 | | | | 0.77 | | | |
| *R*-squared (between) | 0.71 | | | | 0.93 | | | |
| *R*-squared (overall) | 0.70 | | | | 0.92 | | | |
| *F*-statistic | 38.27 | *** | r | | 89.29 | *** | r | |

*Source:* Benin 2015.
*Note:* See annex 2B for detailed description of variables. *R*, *c*, and *a* represent statistical significance at the 10 percent level for clustered standard errors by country (*r*), countries with the same years of participation in CAADP (*c*), and countries within the same agroecological zone (*a*). Significance level for nonclustered standard errors: * = 10 percent, ** = 5 percent, *** = 1 percent.

Table 2.9 shows detailed results of the regression estimates, again for different specifications (exclusion or inclusion of the lag of value added per hectare, $y_{t-1}$) and for clustering the standard errors by different variables. Basically, the model specification that includes the lag of value added per hectare gives much higher explanatory power; including the lag of value added per hectare, however, absorbs the effects of several of the other explanatory variables, particularly capital, fertilizer, rainfall, irrigation, population density, and technology. In addition, exclusion or inclusion of the lag of total agricultural spending ($gt_{t-1}$) has no effect on the estimates.

The total elasticity of land productivity to agricultural research spending per hectare is estimated at 0.09, implying that a 1 percent increase in agricultural research spending per hectare is associated with a 0.09 percent increase in agricultural value added per hectare or land productivity. Compared with other cross-country studies for example, this is lower than the estimated elasticity of 0.17 in Alene and Coulibaly (2009) and 0.36 in Thirtle, Piesse, and Lin (2003), but higher than 0.04 in Fan, Yu, and Saurkar (2008). The estimated elasticities to agricultural public spending are in tables 2.9 and 2.10.

**Table 2.9** Impact of Agricultural Research Spending on Agricultural Value Added per Hectare in Sub-Saharan Africa, 1996–2011

| | FE model 1 | FE model 2 | FE model 3 | FE model 4 |
|---|---|---|---|---|
| Agricultural research spending (*gr*) | −0.06 *** | −0.06 ** | 0.02 | 0.02 |
| Agricultural research capital (*sgr*) | 0.14 *** r c a | 0.15 *** r c a | 0.08 ** r c a | 0.08 ** r c a |
| Total elasticity[a] | 0.08 ** | 0.09 ** | 0.09 *** r c a | 0.09 *** r c a |
| Lag of agricultural spending (*gt_{t-1}*) | — | −0.03 | — | 0 |
| Nonagricultural spending (*ngt*) | 0.01 | 0.01 | 0.01 | 0.01 |
| Lag of agricultural valued added (*v_{t-1}*) | — | — | 0.63 *** r c a | 0.63 *** r c a |
| Intercept | −0.90 | −1.40 a | −0.85 | −0.91 |
| Overall model statistics | | | | |
| R-squared (within) | 0.54 | 0.54 | 0.73 | 0.73 |
| R-squared (between) | 0.83* | 0.84 | 0.97 | 0.97 |
| R-squared (overall) | 0.83 | 0.83 | 0.96 | 0.96 |
| F-statistic | 27.89 *** r | 26.18 *** r | 60.54 *** r | 56.34 *** r |

*Source:* Benin 2015.

*Note:* See annex 2B for detailed description of variables. FE = fixed effects. *R*, *c*, and *a* represent statistical significance at the 10 percent level for clustered standard errors by country (*r*), countries with the same years of participation in CAADP (*c*), and countries within the same agroecological zone (*a*). — = variable omitted from regression. Significance level for nonclustered standard errors: * = 10 percent, ** = 5 percent, *** = 1 percent.

**Table 2.10**  Rates of Return to Total Agricultural Public Spending in Sub-Saharan Africa, 1996–2012

| | Agricultural spending, annual average (US$/ha) | Agricultural value added, annual average (US$/ha) | ROR (%) |
|---|---|---|---|
| Sub-Saharan Africa | 6.48 | 158.72 | 11 |
| *Country* | | | |
| Angola | 3.14 | 45.03 | 1 |
| Benin | 17.44 | 430.19 | 11 |
| Botswana | 5.83 | 10.04 | −25 |
| Burundi | 3.95 | 211.97 | 34 |
| Cameroon | 10.82 | 364.37 | 19 |
| Central African Republic | 1.40 | 136.37 | 65 |
| Chad | 0.27 | 51.68 | 128 |
| Congo, Dem. Rep. | 2.73 | 138.67 | 32 |
| Congo, Rep. | 1.89 | 31.17 | 3 |
| Côte d'Ivoire | 5.47 | 210.79 | 23 |
| Ethiopia | 8.11 | 143.33 | 5 |
| Gambia, The | 12.83 | 265.05 | 8 |
| Ghana | 4.59 | 230.11 | 32 |
| Guinea | 3.18 | 43.46 | 0 |
| Guinea-Bissau | 0.66 | 177.18 | 179 |
| Kenya | 6.39 | 176.93 | 14 |
| Liberia | 0.19 | 148.19 | 507 |
| Madagascar | 1.71 | 32.04 | 6 |
| Malawi | 18.65 | 176.57 | −6 |
| Mali | 3.18 | 46.74 | 1 |
| Mozambique | 1.57 | 33.94 | 9 |
| Namibia | 3.20 | 16.45 | −14 |
| Niger | 2.59 | 32.57 | −1 |
| Nigeria | 8.52 | 413.59 | 31 |
| Rwanda | 12.77 | 525.39 | 25 |
| Senegal | 16.00 | 137.60 | −7 |
| Sierra Leone | 5.39 | 254.55 | 30 |
| South Africa | 11.75 | 73.00 | −11 |
| Sudan | 2.01 | 61.42 | 17 |
| Swaziland | 22.25 | 167.23 | −9 |
| Tanzania | 4.62 | 142.81 | 17 |
| Togo | 6.42 | 226.00 | 20 |
| Uganda | 4.67 | 186.26 | 24 |
| Zambia | 5.47 | 48.73 | −7 |

*Source:* Benin 2015.
*Note:* CAADP = Comprehensive Africa Agriculture Development Programme; ROR = rate of return.

## ROR to Agricultural Public Spending

Based on the estimated elasticities of 0.04 and 0.09 for total agricultural spending and agricultural research spending, respectively, the ROR was calculated for all the countries together, countries with the same number of years of participation in CAADP, countries within the same agroecological zone, and then separately for individual countries. Ideally, the rates of return for the different groups of countries as well as for the individual countries should be based on group-specific and country-specific elasticities, which we are not able to estimate due to data limitations. Because the same estimated elasticities are used for the different groups and individual countries, the main factor driving the differences in the rates of return across the groups and countries are the differences in the ratios of value added to spending (see equation [2B.4] in annex 2B). The estimated rates of return, in addition to the annual average value added and spending, are in table 2.10 for the returns to total agricultural spending and table 2.11 for the returns to agricultural research spending.

**Table 2.11** Rates of Return to Public Spending on Agricultural Research in Sub-Saharan Africa, 1996–2011

|  | Agricultural research spending, annual average (US$/ha) | Agricultural value added, annual average (US$/ha) | ROR (%) |
|---|---|---|---|
| Sub-Saharan Africa | 1.00 | 154.05 | 93 |
| *Country* |  |  |  |
| Benin | 2.09 | 423.45 | 123 |
| Botswana | 0.40 | 9.79 | 9 |
| Burundi | 1.09 | 209.42 | 116 |
| Congo, Rep. | 0.21 | 31.16 | 91 |
| Côte d'Ivoire | 1.08 | 210.13 | 118 |
| Ethiopia | 0.44 | 136.36 | 186 |
| Gambia, The | 2.48 | 264.36 | 64 |
| Ghana | 1.38 | 228.66 | 100 |
| Guinea | 0.14 | 43.35 | 183 |
| Kenya | 2.05 | 172.24 | 50 |
| Madagascar | 0.09 | 31.70 | 225 |
| Malawi | 1.50 | 174.96 | 70 |
| Mali | 0.34 | 45.60 | 81 |
| Namibia | 0.52 | 17.73 | 17 |
| Nigeria | 1.41 | 408.21 | 175 |
| Senegal | 1.34 | 135.86 | 61 |

*(continued next page)*

**Table 2.11** (continued)

|  | Agricultural research spending, annual average (US$/ha) | Agricultural value added, annual average (US$/ha) | ROR (%) |
|---|---|---|---|
| Sierra Leone | 0.58 | 258.94 | 270 |
| South Africa | 1.68 | 73.14 | 24 |
| Sudan | 0.13 | 61.42 | 287 |
| Tanzania | 0.54 | 145.38 | 162 |
| Togo | 1.12 | 221.16 | 119 |
| Uganda | 1.61 | 180.17 | 67 |
| Zambia | 0.29 | 48.06 | 98 |

Source: World Bank calculation based on model results.
Note: CAADP = Comprehensive Africa Agriculture Development Programme; ROR = rate of return.

### Returns to Total Agricultural Spending

The results in table 2.10 show that total agricultural spending in Sub-Saharan Africa has an aggregate ROR of 11 percent, which is generally increasing with the number of years that countries have been participating in CAADP. In general, countries with low or negative rates of return are those with high spending-to-value-added ratios, particularly those with ratios in excess of 10 percent including the group of countries that have yet to sign on to CAADP (ratio of 21 percent), the group of countries in the cool areas (16 percent), Botswana (58 percent), Malawi (16 percent), Namibia (19 percent), Senegal (12 percent), South Africa (16 percent), Swaziland (13 percent), and Zambia (11 percent). Similarly, groups of countries or individual countries with high rates of return are those with low spending-to-value-added ratios, particularly those with ratios of not more than 2 percent, including several countries emerging from civil war such as Liberia, Rwanda, and Sierra Leone.

### Returns to Agricultural Research Spending

The results in table 2.10 show that the returns to agricultural research spending are much higher than the returns to total agricultural spending. The aggregate ROR to agricultural research spending is estimated at 93 percent, which is higher than the estimated ROR of 22 percent in Thirtle, Piesse, and Lin (2003) and 55 percent in Alene and Coulibaly (2009). The calculation of the ROR in Alene and Coulibaly (2009), for example, assumes a period of five years between initiation of research and the beginning of flow of benefits and, thus, imposes the constraint that the first five elasticity coefficients are jointly zero, contrary to what was estimated. Given that the estimated coefficients on all of research spending variables (one current and 1-year through 16-year lags) were statistically significant, the ROR would have been about 600 percent if the constraint was not imposed. Thirtle, Piesse, and Lin (2003) considered only the benefits in the fifth year following the research spending in their calculation of the ROR.

If a cumulative benefit method had been used, the estimated ROR would have been much higher than the 22 percent reported. The returns are also estimated for different groups of countries by the number of years of participation in CAADP and by agroecological zone.

As with the returns to total agricultural spending, groups of countries or individual countries with low rates of return are those with high research spending-to-value-added ratios, particularly those with ratios in excess of 2 percent, including the group of countries that have yet to sign on to CAADP, the group of countries in the cool areas, Botswana, Namibia, and South Africa. Similarly, countries with high rates of return are those with low spending-to-value-added ratios, particularly those with ratios of not more than 0.5 percent, including Ethiopia, Guinea, Madagascar, Nigeria, Sierra Leone, Sudan, and Tanzania.

Overall, the higher returns to agricultural research spending (aggregate ROR of 93 percent) compared with the returns to total agricultural spending (aggregate ROR of 11 percent) reflect the low and declining research spending intensities in the continent. For the 23 countries taken together, agricultural research spending as a share of agricultural value added declined from 0.7 percent in 1996–2003 to 0.6 percent in 2004–2012, which is far from the 1 percent targeted by the African Union's NEPAD. Furthermore, agricultural research spending on the continent, compared with other developing regions, has been highly volatile, due to low government funding and high dependence on short-term and ad hoc donor and other external funding (Stads and Beintema 2015).

## Conclusion

Between 1980 and 2012, total agricultural spending in Africa increased at an average rate of 0.8 percent a year and constituted 4 percent of total spending (far below the CAADP 10 percent spending target) and 4.7 percent of agricultural valued added. The data on different types of agricultural spending, which are limited to nine countries from 2006 to 2013, show that agriculture spending in general had a narrow scope as expenditures on input subsidies and extension seemed to dominate in many countries. In contrast, spending on irrigation and marketing were relatively neglected, and spending on research was the least and accounted for less than 8 percent of the total agricultural spending in these countries.

Earlier evidence on the impact of agricultural spending in Africa showed that in the aggregate, a 1 percent increase in total agricultural spending is associated with a 0.1–0.3 percent increase in agricultural output or productivity. Regarding spending on different agricultural functions, the estimated returns are 22–55 percent for research, 8–49 percent for extension, and 11–22 percent for irrigation. Existing estimates of the returns to spending on agricultural marketing are complicated because public spending is bundled either with private-sector investment or with nonagricultural sector functions. For subsidies, poor targeting of subsidy programs has generally crowded out the use of counterpart commercial inputs and has negatively affected overall returns.

With new evidence on the returns to agricultural public spending in Sub-Saharan Africa, the aggregate return to total agricultural spending in Sub-Saharan Africa is estimated at 11 percent. The aggregate return to agricultural research spending is estimated at 93 percent, but the estimated returns vary substantially across countries and groups of countries. In general, the return to total agricultural spending was increasing with the number of years that countries have been participating in CAADP, with some observed variation by agroecological zones as well. There has been considerable experimentation with research models in Africa, and taking advantage of lessons from this experience can help raise the returns to this kind of investment in the future (box 2.7).

## BOX 2.7

## Lessons of Experience for Advancing Agricultural Research in Africa

Improving productivity growth in Africa will require revitalizing science and technology systems for agriculture. Even within the spending category of research, it is important to put each dollar to its most productive use. Doing this requires understanding the current status of research systems on the continent and identifying useful lessons to move the science and technology agenda forward regionwide.

For now, most investments in agricultural science and technology in Africa come from the public sector—well over 90 percent, as contrasted with a figure that has fallen below 50 percent in Europe and North America. In Africa, most public support for agricultural science and technology is through programs and institutions that belong to ministries of agriculture. Such public agricultural research systems in

*(continued next page)*

## Box 2.7 (continued)

Africa have often stagnated. Since 2000, while investment in public R&D has grown by 20 percent across the region as a whole, the increases are concentrated in just a few countries (mainly Ethiopia, Kenya, Nigeria, and South Africa). Most national public agricultural research institutions and programs across the rest of the continent have declined, and they lack the resources to maintain a broad research portfolio.

Strategic leadership for agricultural research on the continent has been established through the CAADP and the Forum for Agricultural Research in Africa and its associated subregional agricultural research organizations. Among the areas of emphasis from these sources is developing regional collaboration in agricultural research. And research initiatives reflecting regional planning and approaches have expanded from less than 1 percent of all agricultural research activity to nearly 15 percent in the last several years.

The main lessons that are emerging from recent experience include the following:

- *Small national research programs should focus on areas of comparative advantage.* To remain relevant and viable, these smaller country-based research programs are most effective when they focus on and build unique expertise in a selective set of thematic topics that are particularly well-suited for, and are of highest priority, in their locations (bananas and cassava in Uganda, rice in Mali, cocoa in Ghana, and maize in Malawi). Such systems may also focus on adaptation and adoption for a wide variety of crops and livestock.

- *Regional approaches and planning improve efficiency and relevance.* Successful examples are the West Africa Agricultural Productivity Program and the East Africa Agricultural Productivity Program, with coordination from corresponding subregional organizations: West and Central Africa Council for Agricultural Research and Development (CORAF) and the Association for Strengthening Agricultural Research in East and Central Africa (ASARECA).

- *Expanding coordination with CGIAR programs.* Greater participation of African programs in CGIAR planning and priority setting, and greater participation by CGIAR centers in agricultural planning in Africa produces more relevant plans and more synergies in execution, under the CAADP-led Dublin process.

- *Agricultural universities and public agricultural research programs need to be closely linked.* Creating critical mass in staff and equipment enhances the quality of training for graduate students, and reduces the fragmentation of effort. Uganda and South Africa each feature shared research programs, shared laboratories and equipment, and joint appointments—and graduate students do some of their research under the guidance of staff at research organizations.

- *Coordinating public, private, donor-led, and NGO initiatives can enhance coherence and effectiveness.* The Alliance for a Green Revolution in Africa and its support for cocoa and rice research in West Africa show how partnerships can improve strategic

*(continued next page)*

## Box 2.7 (continued)

planning and the implementation of common research and capacity building. Pooled donor funding for core budget support to subregional organizations can also help. Documenting the outcomes and impacts of agricultural research is critical to maintain funding.

- *Close links with agricultural extension systems and farmers are essential to facilitate adoption of research findings and to enhance the relevance of research.* In Ethiopia and Nigeria (and many other places on a small scale), researchers regularly develop and implement applied research programs with farmers in the field. They also work together to evaluate results over time and to plan follow-on research.

# Annex 2A: Synthesis of Impacts of Agricultural Public Spending in Africa

The fundamental notion underlying the productivity effects of public spending is that public and private capital are complements in production, so that an increase in public spending leads to an increase in the public capital stock, which raises the productivity of private capital and other factors in production (Aschauer 1989; Barro 1990). We categorize the productivity effects according to four pathways of impact: technology advancing, human capital enhancing, transaction cost reducing, and private capital crowding. The evidence from past research on these pathways is summarized in table 2A.1.

Technology-advancing productivity effects typically derive from the yield-enhancing technologies of public spending in agricultural R&D.[10] Several studies (for example, Alene and Coulibaly 2009; Alene et al. 2009; Fan, Nyange, and Rao 2012; Fan, Yu, and Saurkar 2008; Fan and Zhang 2008; Fuglie and Rada 2013; Meenakshi et al. 2010; Thirtle, Piesse, and Lin 2003) show that the returns to agricultural research are substantially high in the range of 22–55 percent. As the summary of the studies shows, the bulk of the research on the impact of agricultural spending has focused on research spending.[11] The studies however do vary in many ways, including methodology, country and time series coverage, level and measure of research spending, and outcome indicators on which the impact is estimated.

On the outcome variable, for example, some indicators used include agricultural output, measured at the household level (for example, Fan, Gulati, and Thorat 2008) or national level (Thirtle, Piesse, and Lin 2003), and whether in

**Table 2A.1  Estimated Elasticities, Rates of Return, and Benefit-Cost Ratios for Different Types of Agricultural Spending in Africa**

| Source | Years of spending data | Outcome variable and measure | Type or measure of spending | Elasticity | ROR (%) or BCR | Region or country | Number of countries/units |
|---|---|---|---|---|---|---|---|
| Evenson 2001 | — | Various | Research | n.e. | Mean ROR = 43 | Africa | 44[a] |
| Thirtle, Piesse, and Lin 2003 | 1980–95 | agGDP/ha | Research | 0.36 | ROR = 22 | Sub-Saharan Africa | 22 |
| Fan, Yu, and Saurkar 2008 | 1980–2002 | Agricultural output index | Research | 0.04 | n.e. | Africa | 17 |
| Fan and Zhang 2008 | 1982–99 | Household agricultural output per capita | Research and extension | 0.19 | BCR = 12.4 | Uganda | 1 |
| Alene and Coulibaly 2009 | 1980–2003 | agGDP/ha | National and CGIAR research | 0.38 | ROR = 55 | Sub-Saharan Africa | 27 |
|  |  |  | National research | 0.17 | n.e. |  |  |
|  |  |  | CGIAR research | 0.21 | n.e. |  |  |
| Alene et al. 2009 | 1971–2005 | agGDP | National and CGIAR maize research | n.e. | ROR = 43 | West and Central Africa | 8–12 |
| Meenakshi et al. 2010 | — | DALYs saved | Biofortification research, breeding, maintenance, etc. | n.e. | BCR = 2–66 | Sub-Saharan Africa | 5 |
| Fan, Nyange, and Rao 2012 | 1986–99 | Total household income | Research | n.e. | BCR = 12.5 | Tanzania | 1 |

*(continued next page)*

**Table 2A.1** (continued)

| Source | Years of spending data | Outcome variable and measure | Type or measure of spending | Elasticity | ROR (%) or BCR | Region or country | Number of countries/units |
|---|---|---|---|---|---|---|---|
| Fuglie and Rada 2013 | 1961–2006 | TFP | National research | 0.04 | ROR = 24–29 | Sub-Saharan Africa | 28 |
| | | | CGIAR research | 0.04 | ROR = 55 | | |
| Evenson 2001 | — | Various | Extension | n.e. | Mean ROR = 30 | Africa | 10[a] |
| Benin et al. 2011 | 2001–07 | Household revenue per capita | Extension | n.e. | ROR = 8–49 | Uganda | 1 |
| Wellard et al. 2013 | 2004–08 | Staple crops | Extension | n.e. | BCR = 7.7 | Ghana | 1 |
| | 2002–11 | | | | BCR = 6.8–11.6 | Malawi | 1 |
| | 2004–08 | | | | BCR = 14.2 | Uganda | 1 |
| Fan and Zhang 2008 | 1982–99 | Household agricultural output per capita | Feeder roads | n.e. | BCR = 7.2 | Uganda | 1 |
| Dixie and Tyler 2013 | 1948–97 | Equity value | Agroprocessing | — | ROR > 12 | | 11[b] |
| | | | | | ROR = 0–12 | | 11[b] |
| | | | | | ROR = −25–0 | | 9[b] |
| | | | | | ROR < −25 | | 53[b] |
| Inocencio et al. 2007 | 1967– 2003 | | Irrigation, new | n.e. | ROR = 11 | Sub-Saharan Africa | 45[b] |
| | 1967– 2003 | | Irrigation, rehab | | ROR = 14 | | |

# Table 2A.1 (continued)

| Source | Years of spending data | Outcome variable and measure | Type or measure of spending | Elasticity | ROR (%) or BCR | Region or country | Number of countries/units |
|---|---|---|---|---|---|---|---|
| | 1970s | | Irrigation, rehab | | ROR = 4 | | |
| | 1980s | | Irrigation, rehab | | ROR = 13 | | |
| | 1990s | | Irrigation, rehab | | ROR = 22 | | |
| | 1967– 2003 | | Irrigation, new | | ROR = 14 | North Africa | 39[b] |
| | 1967– 2003 | | Irrigation, rehab | | ROR = 17 | | |
| Fan, Yu, and Saurkar 2008 | 1980–2002 | Agricultural output index | Nonresearch | –0.07 | n.e. | Africa | 17 |
| Fan, Yu, and Saurkar 2008 | 1980–2002 | Agricultural output index | Total agriculture | 0.08 | n.e. | Africa | 17 |
| Mogues 2011 | 1993–2001 | Household consumption spending per capita | Total agriculture | 0.04–0.06 n.s. | n.e. | Ethiopia | 1 |
| Benin et al. 2012 | 2002–06 | Household agricultural output per capita | Total agriculture per capita | 0.22–0.26 | BCR = 3.5–4.2 | Ghana | 1 |

*Source:* World Bank illustration based on cited sources.
*Note:* agGDP = agricultural valued added; BCR = benefit-cost ratio; CGIAR = Consultative Group on International Agricultural Research; DALY = disability-adjusted life year; n.e. = not estimated; n.s. = elasticity not statistically significant; ROR = rate of return; TFP = total factor productivity; — = not available or not applicable.
a. Indicates number of rates of return reported and included in the review.
b. Indicates number of projects included in the review.

level terms (Alene et al. 2009), partial factor productivity (Alene and Coulibaly 2009; Fan and Zhang 2008), or total factor productivity (Fuglie and Rada 2013). Other outcomes include income (Fan, Nyange, and Rao 2012), poverty (Alene and Coulibaly 2009; Thirtle, Piesse, and Lin 2003), and nutrition and health (Meenakshi et al. 2010). On the type and measure of research, most have been on national and international research (for example, Alene and Coulibaly 2009; Fuglie and Rada 2013; Thirtle, Piesse, and Lin 2003). Others have been narrower on specific commodities, such as maize research in the Alene et al. (2009) study, or on the type of research, such as biofortification in the Meenakshi et al. (2010) study.

On methods, most studies cited previously have used ex-post analysis and some have used ex-ante analysis (Meenakshi et al. 2010). Because the productivity effects or impacts of agricultural R&D investments tend to materialize with a long lag and can persist long afterward, different studies have used different approaches. Thirtle, Piesse, and Lin (2003), for example, consider a 5-year lag of agricultural R&D investments whereas Alene et al. (2009) consider a 16-year lag. The choice of the lag length is influenced by the length of the time series data used, with longer lag lengths being used in studies that have longer time series data. Because of these and other differences, each study tends to be unique, which limits their comparability for identifying the specific estimate of the ROR to agricultural research spending. The study by Evenson (2001), for example, reviews several studies on the impacts of research and extension, which show many of the differences discussed earlier. Of the 375 rates of return reported globally that could be classified by region, 44 were in Africa with a mean ROR of 43 percent.[12]

The human capital enhancing productivity effects derive typically from public spending in agricultural education and extension that raises the knowledge and skills of farmers and those engaged in agricultural production. This is important for successful agricultural enterprises because agricultural production tends to be complex and is increasingly becoming knowledge-intensive, considering precision agriculture and the use of information and communications technology, for example. Unfortunately, there are not many new studies estimating rates of return or benefit-cost ratios to extension in Africa.

The bulk of the studies were carried out in the 1980s and 1990s and are reviewed in the studies by Evenson (2001), for example. As with the review of the impacts of research done by Evenson (2001), there were 81 rates of return reported globally that could be classified by region. Ten were in Africa with a mean ROR of 30 percent.[13] The reviews by Evenson (2001) and Alston et al. (2000) highlight concern over data quality and cause-and-effect methodological issues, questioning the reliability of the moderate to high estimated returns to spending on extension. For example, the estimated large positive returns to extension spending in Kenya in the 1980s by Bindlish and Evenson (1997) were later found to be grossly overestimated with careful modeling of the confounding factors, but were included in the estimation by Gautam and Anderson (1999).

Recent studies on the impact of extension in Africa include Benin et al. (2011) on Uganda and Wellard et al. (2013) on Ghana, Mali, and Uganda. The study by Benin et al. (2011) found low to moderate returns, 8–49 percent, to spending on the national agricultural extension program depending on different assumptions of the treatment of the program and other factors. The study by Wellard et al. (2013) looks at the effect of different community-based and farmer-to-farmer extension approaches, with estimated cost-benefit ratios of 7.7 in Ghana, 6.8–11.6 in Malawi, and 14.2 in Uganda. In general, public spending on rural education, health, water, sanitation, and so on, by making the rural labor force more literate and healthier, may increase human capital accumulation in agricultural production (Schultz 1982). This is shown in the study by Fan and Zhang (2008), for example, which finds a significant positive effect of public education spending on agricultural productivity. Similar to agricultural R&D investments, human capital productivity effects materialize with a lag and can persist long afterward. Fan, Yu, and Saurkar (2008), for example, consider a 7-year lag of spending on agricultural extension in Uganda.

The transactions–cost reducing productivity effects are expected to derive from public spending on marketing infrastructure in the agricultural sector (for example, storage facilities, information, processing, and feeder roads) that contributes to improving access to input and output markets, reducing the cost of or increasing the returns to agricultural inputs and technologies, for example. Transactions cost is important, since it drives whether or not markets are integrated, thin, or fail (Sadoulet and de Janvry 1995). By facilitating the movement of goods and services and reducing the cost of doing business, public investment in rural infrastructure (such as roads, bridges, transportation, and energy) may raise the productivity of other forms of capital in agricultural production.

Unfortunately, estimates of the returns to public spending on agricultural marketing infrastructure are complicated, since the public spending is bundled with private-sector investment or with nonagricultural sector functions. For example, Dixie and Tyler (2013) analyze 122 agribusinesses established in Africa at different periods from 1948 to 1997 that were involved mostly with processing for export (especially palm oil, sugar, and tea). They also involved different public-private partnerships with the Commonwealth Development Corporation. There were 84 on which equity returns were assessed, and 22 had some positive ROR, with eleven having an ROR of up to 12 percent and the other 11 having an ROR greater than 12 percent. The remaining 62 had negative returns, with most (53) having losses of more than 25 percent. These estimates are the aggregate or average for the combined public and private investment, and the key to addressing the bundling is isolating the specific public-sector role and related spending and benefits, knowing that the returns to those specific parts may be greater or lower than the average or aggregate estimate.

Regarding the bundling with nonagricultural sector functions, a typical example is the study by Fan and Zhang (2008), which assesses the impact of feeder roads spending on agricultural output in Uganda. It finds that the benefit-cost ratio of investing in feeder roads is 7.2. Because feeder roads or rural roads have nonagricultural sector functions (such as enhancing the provision of education and health services), counting all spending on such roads overestimates the cost, which has similar implications for the returns to the agriculture-specific spending parts as discussed earlier for the agribusinesses.

Several studies assess the productivity or growth impact of infrastructure spending in Africa in general, which has indirect effects on improving markets or reducing transaction costs in the economy. Mogues (2011) and Benin et al. (2012) find significant positive effects of public spending on road infrastructure on agricultural productivity and household consumption spending. Different types of infrastructure have different impacts. The Fan and Zhang (2008) study on Uganda, for example, finds that the return to spending on feeder roads was three to four times higher than the return to spending on laterite, gravel, or tarmac roads. Similarly, different rates of return to different types of economywide infrastructure development in Sub-Saharan Africa have been reported—for example, 5 percent for railway rehabilitation, 17 percent for road upgrade, 24 percent for road rehabilitation, and 17 percent and 139 percent for road maintenance (Foster and Briceño-Garmendia 2010).

The crowding-in productivity effects of agricultural public spending on private capital are a commonly advanced rationale used to advocate for larger public spending on the sector. By raising the productivity of all factors in production, an increase in public spending is expected to cause an increase in private capital to the extent that public and private investment are complements. For example, public investment in dams and canals for irrigation is expected to increase private investment in irrigation systems on the farm, as shown in the study by Fan, Hazell, and Thorat (2000) on India. The importance of irrigation stems from the fact that high-yielding technologies (improved seeds, inorganic fertilizers, pesticides) require specific amounts of water at specific periods of plant growth, development, and flowering, which is risky under rainfed agriculture alone. Excessive irrigation can also be detrimental.

On the returns to public investment in irrigation, Inocencio et al. (2007) review 84 irrigation projects implemented in Africa (45 in Sub-Saharan Africa and 39 in the Middle East and North Africa) from 1967 to 2003 supported by the World Bank, African Development Bank, and International Fund for Agriculture Development. The projects involved different irrigation systems, with river diversion and river lift (or pond or lake) systems being the most common. For the ones in Sub-Saharan Africa, the estimated average ROR is 11 percent for the projects involving new developments and 14 percent for those involving rehabilitation. Those in the Middle East and North Africa had slightly higher returns: 14 percent for the projects involving new developments and 17 percent for those involving rehabilitation. The crowding-in effect is seen through the relative percentage contribution of donors, government, and farmers to the funds for the projects in Sub-Saharan Africa: 49-34-17, respectively, in the 1970s; 69-23-8, respectively, in the 1980s; and 28-15-57, respectively, in the 1990s.

The impact of the public-private partnerships in the agribusinesses discussed above also fits the crowding-in pathway. On the other agricultural functions, for example, Malla and Gray (2005) and Görg and Strobl (2006) find significant crowding-in effects of public R&D on private R&D in the United States and Ireland, with estimated elasticities in the range of 0.10 to 0.28. Typically, these involve the government subsidizing some private sector activities. Similar crowding-in arguments have been made for input subsidies in African agriculture, which involve subsidizing the price of the input sold in the market—especially for chemical fertilizers and mechanical equipment. In many cases, however, public spending on such subsidies have not increased overall use of the input, because poor targeting of the programs has crowded out use of commercial inputs since the bulk of the subsidized inputs has been provided to farmers who would have purchased them regardless (Jayne et al. 2013). Specific estimates of the return to spending on these programs in Africa is lacking.

The broader literature on public investment analysis also shows that not all types of public spending are productive (Devarajan, Swaroop, and Zou 1996). The relatively low estimated elasticities, rates of return, or benefit-cost ratios associated with total agricultural spending (Fan, Yu, and Saurkar 2008; Mogues 2011; Benin et al. 2012) or nonresearch spending (Fan, Yu, and Saurkar 2008)—compared with those for research, irrigation, extension, feeder roads, and so on—supports this (table 2A.1). In fact, the estimated impact of agriculture spending in Mogues (2011) was not statistically significant, but the estimated impact of nonresearch spending in Fan, Yu, and Saurkar (2008) was negative. Much spending is spent on salaries and other recurrent items, suggesting this type of spending may be less productive. For agricultural subsidies, for example, there are indirect price effects that may restrict or encourage production and supply of particular agricultural inputs and commodities. Thus, public spending on such subsidies rarely creates any productive capital, so the link with productivity is often weak. But the high rates of return shown for certain activities that likely involve large current spending as opposed to capital spending, for example, 139 percent for road maintenance (Foster and Briceño-Garmendia 2010), also suggest that not all current spending is unproductive.

Together, these findings of heterogeneous effects of different spending choices point to the need to identify and prioritize high-impact parts of agricultural spending. But this will be difficult to do comprehensively based on evidence assembled so far. This is because the underlying studies vary in many aspects (including methodology, country and time series coverage, and level and measure of spending and impact indicators), which limits their comparability for ranking different spending types, and for understanding how the impacts have evolved. The study by Fan, Gulati, and Thorat (2008) on India provides an example of the nature of evidence that is extremely useful for prioritizing investments (results shown in table 2A.2). It estimates returns in agricultural GDP and poverty reduction to public spending in agricultural R&D, irrigation, and fertilizer and credit subsidies as well as spending in rural roads, education, and power. The returns are estimated for different periods: 1960s–1970s, 1980s, and 1990s.

The results in table 2A.2 thus offer a rich comparative analysis of temporal returns to spending within and across agriculture and nonagriculture sectors, with the intertemporal speaking to the need to consider reprioritization. The results show, for example, that spending on roads, education, and R&D has the largest returns, but spending on fertilizer and power subsidies has the least returns. For subsidies, those on credit outperform those on irrigation, fertilizer, and power. Credit on subsidies is among the top two or three highest ranked within the agriculture spending portfolio, suggesting that some forms of subsidies are indeed favorable.

The analysis was possible by having disaggregated data on spending from 1951 to 1993 for different states in India. Even getting national-level spending data on African countries was challenging. Thus, more effort by governments and donors to invest in similar data collection activities in Africa is critical to generate the necessary evidence to prioritize high-impact parts of spending and agricultural spending in particular.

**Table 2A.2** Returns in Growth and Poverty Reduction to Investments and Subsidies in India

| | Return in agricultural GDP (RPS per RPS spending) | | | | | | | | |
|---|---|---|---|---|---|---|---|---|---|
| | 1960s–1970s | | | 1980s | | | 1990s | | |
| | Return | R1 | R2 | Return | R1 | R2 | Return | R1 | R2 |
| *Agricultural sector* | | | | | | | | | |
| Research and development | 8.65 | 2 | 5 | 7.93 | 1 | 2 | 9.50 | 1 | 1 |
| Irrigation investment | 8.00 | 3 | 6 | 4.71 | 2 | 4 | 4.37 | 2 | 4 |
| Irrigation subsidies | 5.22 | 4 | 7 | 2.25 | 4 | 6 | 2.47 | 4 | 6 |
| Fertilizer subsidies | 1.79 | 5 | 8 | 1.94 | 5 | 8 | 0.85 | 5 | 8 |
| Credit subsidies | 18.77 | 1 | 2 | 3.00 | 3 | 5 | 4.26 | 3 | 5 |
| *Rural sector* | | | | | | | | | |
| Roads | 19.99 | 1 | 1 | 8.89 | 1 | 1 | 7.66 | 1 | 2 |
| Education | 14.66 | 2 | 3 | 7.58 | 2 | 3 | 5.46 | 2 | 3 |
| Power subsidies | 12.06 | 3 | 4 | 2.25 | 3 | 6 | 1.19 | 3 | 7 |

*(continued next page)*

**Table 2A.2** (continued)

| | Return in rural poverty reduction (number of poor reduced per million RPS spending) | | | | | | | | | | | |
|---|---|---|---|---|---|---|---|---|---|---|---|
| | 1960s–1970s | | | 1980s | | | 1990s | | |
| | Return | R1 | R2 | Return | R1 | R2 | Return | R1 | R2 |
| *Agricultural sector* | | | | | | | | | |
| Research and development | 642.69 | 2 | 5 | 409.00 | 1 | 3 | 436.12 | 1 | 2 |
| Irrigation investment | 630.37 | 3 | 6 | 267.01 | 2 | 4 | 193.21 | 3 | 5 |
| Irrigation subsidies | 393.70 | 4 | 7 | 116.05 | 4 | 7 | 113.47 | 4 | 6 |
| Fertilizer subsidies | 90.07 | 5 | 8 | 109.99 | 5 | 8 | 37.41 | 5 | 8 |
| Credit subsidies | 1,448.51 | 1 | 3 | 154.59 | 3 | 5 | 195.66 | 2 | 4 |
| *Rural sector* | | | | | | | | | |
| Roads | 4,124.15 | 1 | 1 | 1,311.64 | 1 | 1 | 881.49 | 1 | 1 |
| Education | 1,955.56 | 2 | 2 | 651.40 | 2 | 2 | 335.86 | 2 | 3 |
| Power subsidies | 998.42 | 3 | 4 | 125.50 | 3 | 6 | 59.15 | 3 | 7 |

*Source:* Based on Fan, Gulati, and Thorat 2008.
*Note:* RPS = retention pricing scheme. R1 = rank of return within sector, where 1 is the highest rank. R2 = rank of return across sectors, where 1 is the highest rank.

## Annex 2B: Conceptual Framework and Description of the Data and Estimation Methods

### Production Function

The aggregate production function for the agricultural sector in year $t$ is modeled as:

$$Y_t = A_t * f\left(L_t, K_t, D_t, G, Z_t\right) + e_t^Y \qquad (2B.1a)$$

$$G_t = h\left(Y_t, Z_t^G\right) + e_t^G \qquad (2B.1b)$$

where $Y$ is the value added of agricultural output; $L$ is labor or the number of agricultural workers; $K$ is the value of private capital and other intermediate inputs; $D$ is agricultural land; $G$ (representing $G_t$, $G_{t-1}$, $G_{t-2}$, ..., $G_{t-N}$) is public agriculture spending with appropriate lag length $q = 1, 2, ..., N$; $Z$ is a vector of other factors affecting agricultural output; and $A$ is a measure of total factor productivity (TFP). Rewrite equation (2B.1) in terms of per unit agricultural land area as follows:[14]

$$y_t = A_t * f\left(l_t, k_t, g, Z_t^y\right) + e_t^y \qquad (2B.2a)$$

$$g_t = h\left(y_t, Z_t^g\right) + e_t^g \qquad (2B.2b)$$

where $y = Y/D$, $l = L/D$, $k = K/D$, and $g = G/D$ to represent value added, labor, capital, and agricultural spending per unit agricultural area, respectively; $Z^y$ and $Z^g$ are used to differentiate the vector of other factors that affect $y$ and $g$, respectively; and $e^y$ and $e^g$ are random error terms in equations (2B.2a) and (2B.2b), respectively.[15]

### Marginal Effects and Elasticities

Ignoring equation (2B.2b) for now, the total elasticity of land productivity with respect to public agriculture spending at any time $t$, which is defined as the ratio of the percentage change in land productivity ($dy/y$) to the percentage change in public agriculture spending ($dg/g$), can be obtained from equation (2B.2a) according to

$$\frac{dy_t / y_t}{dg_t / g_t} = \frac{\partial y_t}{\partial A_t} \sum_{q=0}^{N} \frac{dA_t}{dg_{t-q}} \frac{g_t}{A_t}$$

$$+ \left[\frac{\partial y_t}{\partial l_t} \sum_{q=0}^{N} \frac{dl_t}{dg_{t-q}} + \frac{\partial y_t}{\partial k_t} \sum_{q=0}^{N} \frac{dk_t}{dg_{t-q}} + \sum_{q=0}^{N} \frac{\partial y_t}{\partial g_{t-q}}\right] * \frac{G_t}{f(\cdot)}, \qquad (2B.3)$$

where $\partial$ refers to the partial derivative, so that $\partial y_t / \partial g_{t-q}$, for example, measures the direct marginal effect of public agriculture spending on land productivity at time $t$ and $\partial y_t / \partial k_t * \partial k_t / \partial g_{t-q}$ measures the indirect marginal effect through its effect on capital $k$. Together, the first terms on the right-hand side of equation (2B.3) capture the technology-advancing productivity effect of public agriculture spending. The first parts of the first and second terms in the brackets capture the human capital enhancing and transactions cost reducing productivity effects, but the second parts of the first and second terms in the brackets capture the crowding-in productivity effects. The elasticity of land productivity with respect to public agriculture spending is interpreted as the percentage change in land productivity ($y$) due to a 1 percent change in public agriculture spending per hectare ($g$).

## ROR

Using $\hat{\vartheta}_t^{yG}$ to represent the estimated elasticity, the ROR can be obtained using equation (2B.4) as the discount rate ($r$) that equates the net present value of marginal productivities $\hat{\vartheta}_{t-q}^{yG} * \bar{y}$ over the relevant time periods of lag (that is, $q = 0, 1, \dots , N$) to an initial or one-time public agriculture spending ($g_0$).

$$\sum\nolimits_{q=0}^{N} \frac{\hat{\vartheta}_{t-q}^{yG} * \bar{y}}{\left(1+r\right)^q} = g_0 \tag{2B.4}$$

where $\bar{y}$ is the annual average agricultural value added per hectare and $g_0$ is equivalent to 1 percent of the annual average agricultural spending per hectare (that is, $0.01 * \bar{g}$). We use N = 10 in the actual calculations.

## Data Sources and Empirical Approach

The main data constraint faced in the estimation lies with public spending, which has been compiled from SPEED (IFPRI) and ReSAKSS (IFPRI) for total government spending ($TE$) and total agriculture spending ($GT$) from 1980 to 2014 (table 2B.1). Spending on agricultural research ($GR$) and number of research scientists ($GS$) were obtained from ASTI (IFPRI) for 1980 to 2012. Agricultural production data were compiled from the World Development Indicators (WDI, World Bank) and FAOStat (FAO) as shown in table 2B.1. These include data on agricultural value added ($Y$), agricultural land area ($D$), agricultural labor ($L$), crop and livestock capital, chemical fertilizers, feed ($K$), and irrigation ($I$). Data representing $Z^y$ were obtained

**Table 2B.1** Description of Variables, Data, and Sources Used in Estimating Productivity Effects of Public Agriculture Spending

| Variable | Description/disaggregation | Years available | Data source |
|---|---|---|---|
| Total spending ($TE$) | Total government spending in constant 2006 currency | 1980–2014 | ReSAKSS, SPEED (IFPRI) |
| Agricultural spending ($GT$) | Government spending on agriculture (crops, livestock, forestry, fishery, and research) in constant 2006 US$ | 1980–2014 | ReSAKSS, SPEED (IFPRI) |
| Agricultural research spending ($GR$) | National agricultural research spending, including salary-related expenses, operating and program costs, and capital investments by government, nonprofit, and higher education agencies. Original values in current local currency units (LCUs) were deflated using the ratio of GDP in constant 2006 US$ to GDP in current LCUs. | 1981–2011 | ReSAKSS, SPEED (IFPRI), WDI (World Bank) |
| Agricultural research scientists ($GS$) | National agricultural researchers in full-time equivalent (FTE) | 1981–2011 | ASTI (IFPRI), WDI (World Bank) |
| Agricultural valued added ($Y$) | Net output (gross output less intermediate inputs) in constant 2006 US$. Original values in current LCUs were deflated using the ratio of GDP in constant 2006 US$ to GDP in current LCUs. | 1961–2014 | WDI (World Bank) |
| Agricultural land area ($D$) | Hectares of land, including arable land, land under permanent crops, meadows, pastures, and forests | 1961–2014 | FAOStat (FAO) |
| Agricultural labor ($L$) | Total economically active population engaged in or seeking work in agriculture, hunting, fishing, or forestry | 1961–2012 | Benin and Nin Pratt 2015 based on FAOStat |
| Capital ($K1$) | Sum of gross fixed capital stock in constant 2006 US$<br>• Crop capital: land development, plantain crops, and machinery and equipment<br>• Livestock capital: animal stock, structures for livestock, and milking machines | 1961–2012 | Benin and Nin Pratt 2015 based on FAOStat |
| Fertilizer ($K2$) | Metric tons of nitrogen, phosphorus, and potassium nutrients consumed | 1961–2012 | Benin and Nin Pratt 2015 based on FAOStat |
| Animal feed ($K3$) | Metric tons (maize equivalent) of edible commodities fed to livestock | 1961–2012 | Benin and Nin Pratt 2015 based on FAOStat |

(continued next page)

**Table 2B.1** (continued)

| Variable | Description/disaggregation | Years available | Data source |
|---|---|---|---|
| Rainfall (R) | Total rainfall in mm | 1960–2013 | HarvestChoice |
| Irrigation (I) | Share of agricultural area equipped with irrigation | 1960–2013 | FAOstat (FAO) |
| Population density (P) | Total population divided by the total land area in persons per sq km | 1961–2014 | WDI (World Bank) |
| Agroecology (AEZ) | Dummy variable representing the dominant agroecological zone within the country: 1 = subtropic; 2 = tropic, cool, semiarid or arid; 3 = tropic, cool, semihumid or humid; 4 = tropic, warm, semiarid or arid; 5 = tropic, warm, semihumid or humid; 6 = other | 2015 | HarvestChoice |
| CAADP | Number of years since country signed a CAADP compact, measured in 2012 | 2012 | AU-NEPAD 2015 |
| Technology (A) | Dummy variable representing the level of technology at specific time periods (1961–69, 1970–79, 1980–89, 1990–99, and 2000–12): 1 = low, 2 = medium low, 3 = medium high, 4 = high | 1961–2012 | Benin and Nin Pratt 2015 |
| Instruments (Z⁶) | Governance indicators with range −2.5 to 2.5: | 1996–2013 | WDI (World Bank) |
| • Voice | • Voice and accountability | 1961–2014 | Polity IV Project (CSP) |
| • Stability | • Political stability and absence of violence | | |
| • Effectiveness | • Government effectiveness | | |
| • Regulation | • Regulatory quality | | |
| • Law | • Rule of law | | |
| • Corruption | • Control of corruption | | |
| • Polity | Political regime characteristics: | | |
| • Durability | • Combined polity score, −10 to 10 | | |
| | • Durability of regime, number of years | | |

*Source:* Benin 2015.
*Note:* CAADP = Comprehensive Africa Agriculture Development Programme; FTE = full-time equivalent; GDP = gross domestic product; LCUs = local currency units.

115

from other sources, including precipitation and agroecological zones from HarvestChoice, population density from World Bank (2015), and participation in CAADP from AU-NEPAD (2015).

The level of technology $(A)$ is measured using a time dummy variable representing the level available at specific time periods (1961–69, 1970–79, 1980–89, 1990–99, and 2000–12), based on the total factor productivity (TFP) estimates in Benin and Nin Pratt (2015). We use the quartiles of the TFP estimates as the cutoff points (table 2B.2) to categorize the level of technology, where 1 = low if the estimated TFP is less than the quartile 1 cutoff point; 2 = medium low if the estimated TFP is greater than the quartile 1 cutoff point but less than the quartile 2 cutoff point; 3 = medium high if the estimated TFP is greater than the quartile 2 cutoff point but less than the quartile 3 cutoff point; and 4 = high if the estimated TFP is greater than the quartile 3 cutoff point. Data representing $Z^G$ were obtained from two sources: the Worldwide Governance Indicators project for six dimensions of governance (voice and accountability; political stability and absence of violence; government effectiveness; regulatory quality; rule of law; and control of corruption) from 1996 to 2013 (World Bank); and the Polity IV project on political regime characteristics and transitions for a combined (democracy and autocracy) polity score and durability of regime (CSP).

Although the data were compiled for all countries in Africa on the various indicators for all years available, the actual panel used in the estimation is dictated by data availability on all the relevant indicators for at least 10 consecutive years, with the data on spending and governance indicators the most limiting. Thus, the final data set used is an unbalanced panel on 35 countries on total agricultural spending and 24 countries on agricultural research spending as shown in table 2B.3.

**Table 2B.2** Annual Average TFP in African Agriculture and TFP Quartile Cutoff Points, 1961–2012
*Index, 1961 = 1.00*

| TFP quartile cutoff | 1961–69 | 1970–79 | 1980–89 | 1990–99 | 2000–12 |
|---|---|---|---|---|---|
| 0 (minimum TFP) | 1.00 | 1.00 | 1.00 | 1.00 | 1.01 |
| Cutoff 1 | 1.03 | 1.06 | 1.09 | 1.13 | 1.19 |
| Cutoff 2 | 1.05 | 1.10 | 1.18 | 1.19 | 1.28 |
| Cutoff 3 | 1.08 | 1.18 | 1.24 | 1.39 | 1.47 |
| 4 (maximum TFP) | 1.28 | 1.52 | 1.82 | 2.10 | 2.65 |

*Source:* World Bank calculation based on Benin and Nin Pratt 2015.
*Note:* TFP = total factor productivity.

**Table 2B.3** Coverage of Countries in the Panel Data

| Spending type | Years | Countries |
|---|---|---|
| Total agriculture (*GT*) | 1996–2012 | Benin; Botswana; Burundi; Central African Republic; Chad; Congo, Rep.; Côte d'Ivoire; Ethiopia; Gambia, The; Ghana; Guinea; Guinea-Bissau; Kenya; Liberia; Madagascar; Malawi; Mali; Mauritius; Mozambique; Namibia; Nigeria; Rwanda; Senegal; Sierra Leone; South Africa; Sudan; Swaziland; Tanzania; Togo; Uganda; Zambia |
| | 1997–2012 | Congo, Dem. Rep. |
| Agricultural research (*GR*) | 1996–2011 | Benin; Botswana; Burundi; Congo, Rep.; Côte d'Ivoire; Ethiopia; Gambia, The; Ghana; Guinea; Kenya; Madagascar; Malawi; Mali; Mauritius; Nigeria; Senegal; Sudan; South Africa; Togo; Uganda; Zambia |
| | 2000–11 | Tanzania |
| | 2001–11 | Namibia; Sierra Leone |

*Sources:* World Bank compilation based on ASTI, ReSAKSS, and SPEED (IFPRI), and World Bank 2015.

# Notes

1. Much of this chapter is based on a background paper (Benin 2015).
2. There may be differences in the trends because of differences in the data due to updates and revisions in the spending data as well as other variables such as population, total and agricultural GDP, purchasing power parity (PPP) converters, GDP deflators, and exchange rates used in calculating various spending indicators.
3. All monetary values in this section are in 2005 purchasing power parity dollars (PPP$).
4. AOI = [(Ag PE/Total PE)]/(Ag GDP/GDP)].
5. See Beintema and Stads (2011), Benin and Yu (2013), and Stads and Beintema (2015) for further comparative analysis across different subregions and countries in Africa. There may be differences in the trends presented in those studies and this one due to differences in data.
6. In the MAFAP data, general support to agricultural infrastructure was broken down into feeder roads, off-farm irrigation, and other infrastructure. In Mali however, this disaggregation was not available, and so we assumed 50 percent of the aggregate to off-farm irrigation and 50 percent to other off-farm infrastructure.
7. Similar analysis is presented in Benin, McBride, and Mogues (2016), which uses a previous version of the data set on five countries (Burkina Faso, Kenya, Mali, Tanzania, and Uganda) from 2006 to 2010. As such, there may be differences in the trends presented in that study and this one.
8. All monetary values are expressed in 2005 prices.
9. See Benin (2015) for further discussion on the instrumental results.
10. Technologies may be biological (such as genetically-modified organisms and hybrids), chemical (such as fertilizers and pesticides), mechanical (such as tractors

and implements), or informational (husbandry, value chains, and early-warning systems).

11. See Mogues, Fan, and Benin (2015), a recent review of the evidence on the impacts of different types of public spending in and for agriculture.

12. This was estimated by the sum of product of the share of the rates of return in a category (0.27 in 0–20, 0.27 in 21–40, 0.18 in 41–60, 0.11 in 61–80, 0.11 in 81–100, 0.05 in 100+) and the midpoint of the category (10, 30, 50, 70, 90, 110).

13. This was estimated by the sum of product of the share of the rates of return in a category (0.4 in 0–20, 0.3 in 21–40, 0.2 in 41–60, 0.1 in 61–80) and the midpoint of the category (10, 30, 50, 70).

14. We could have alternatively divided through by $L$ or $K$ to arrive at similar results, though with different interpretations—for example, labor productivity instead of land productivity.

15. To explicitly capture the different pathways of productivity effects of $g$ discussed in annex 2B of this chapter, equations (2B.1a) and (2B.2a) could have been written to make $A$, $l$, and $k$ as functions of $g$, as done in Benin (2015).

# References

Aker, J. C., and I. M. Mbiti. 2010. "Mobile Phones and Economic Development in Africa." Working Paper 211, Center for Global Development, Washington, DC.

Alene, A. D., and O. Coulibaly. 2009. "The Impact of Agricultural Research on Productivity and Poverty in Sub-Saharan Africa." *Food Policy* 34 (2): 198–209.

Alene, A. D., A. Menkir, S. O. Ajala, B. Badu-Apraku, A. S. Olanrewaju, V. M. Manyong, and A. Ndiaye. 2009. "The Economic and Poverty Impacts of Maize Research in West and Central Africa." *Agricultural Economics* 40 (5): 535–50.

Alston, J., M. Marra, P. Pardey, and T. Wyatt. 2000. "Research Returns Redux: A Meta-Analysis of the Returns to Agricultural R&D." *Australian Journal of Agricultural and Resource Economics* 44 (2): 185–215.

Alston, J., P. Pardey, and R. Piggott, eds. 2006. *Agricultural R&D in the Developing World.* Washington, DC: IFPRI.

Anderson, J., and G. Feder. 2007. "Agricultural Extension." In *Handbook of Agricultural Economics*, edited by R. Evenson and P. Pingali. Amsterdam: Elsevier.

Aschauer, D. A. 1989. "Is Public Expenditure Productive?" *Journal of Monetary Economics* 23 (2): 177–200.

AU-NEPAD (African Union; New Partnership for Africa's Development). 2015. "Countries with Compacts/Investment Plans." http://fpdb.nepad.org/resource/count ries-compacts-investment-plans-%E2%80%93-nov-2015.

Bachewe, F. N., G. Berhane, B. Minten, and A. S. Taffese. 2015. "Agricultural Growth in Ethiopia (2004–2014): Evidence and Drivers." International Food Policy Research Institute (IFRPI), Ethiopia Strategy Support Program (ESSP). Background paper prepared for this book, Washington, D.C.

Barro, R. 1990. "Government Spending in a Simple Model of Endogenous Growth." *Journal of Political Economy* 98 (5): 103–25.

Beintema, N. M., and G. J. Stads. 2011. *African Agricultural R&D in the New Millennium: Progress for Some, Challenges for Many*. Food Policy Report. Washington, DC: IFPRI.

Benin, S. 2015. "Returns to Agricultural Public Spending in Africa South of the Sahara." Discussion Paper 01491, IFPRI, Washington, DC.

Benin, S., L. McBride, and T. Mogues. 2016. "Why Do Countries Underinvest in Agricultural R&D?" In *Agricultural Research in Africa: Investing in Future Harvests*, edited by J. Laynam, N. Beintema, J. Roseboom, and O. Badiane. Washington, DC: IFPRI.

Benin, S., T. Mogues, G. Cudjoe, and J. Randriamamonjy. 2012. "Public Expenditures and Agricultural Productivity Growth in Ghana." In *Public Expenditures for Agricultural and Rural Development in Africa*, edited by T. Mogues and S. Benin. London and New York: Routledge, Taylor and Francis Group.

Benin, S., and A. Nin Pratt. 2015. "Inter-Temporal Trends in Agricultural Productivity." In *Agricultural Productivity in Africa: Inter-Temporal Trends, Spatial Patterns, and Determinants*, edited by S. Benin. Washington, DC: IFPRI.

Benin, S., E. Nkonya, G. Okecho, J. Randriamamonjy, E. Kato, G. Lubade, and M. Kyotalimye. 2011. "Returns to Spending on Agricultural Extension: The Case of the National Agricultural Advisory Services (NAADS) Programme of Uganda." *Agricultural Economics* 42 (2): 249–67.

Benin, S., and B. Yu. 2013. *Complying the Maputo Declaration Target: Trends in Public Agricultural Expenditures and Implications for Pursuit of Optimal Allocation of Public Agricultural Spending*. ReSAKSS Annual Trends and Outlook Report 2012. Washington, DC: IFPRI.

Bindlish, V., and R. E. Evenson. 1997. "The Impact of T&V Extension in Africa: The Experience of Kenya and Burkina Faso." *World Bank Research Observer* 12 (2): 183–201.

Calderón, C., and L. Servén. 2004. "The Effects of Infrastructure Development on Growth and Income Distribution." Policy Research Working Paper 270, World Bank, Washington, DC.

Correa, P., and C. Schmidt. 2014. "Public Research Organizations and Agricultural Development in Brazil: How Did Embrapa Get It Right?" *Economic Premise* 145 (June). http://siteresources.worldbank.org/EXTPREMNET/Resources/EP145.pdf.

Cox, G. W., and M. D. McCubbins. 1986. "Electoral Politics as a Redistributive Game." *Journal of Politics* 48 (2): 370–89.

CSP (Center for Systemic Peace). Polity IV Project: Political Regime Characteristics and Transitions, 1800–2013 (database) (accessed September 15, 2015), http://www .systemicpeace.org/polity/polity4.htm.

Deichmann, U., A. Goyal, and D. Mishra. 2016. "Will Digital Technologies Transform Agriculture in Developing Countries?" Policy Research Working Paper 7669, World Bank, Washington, DC.

Devarajan, S., V. Swaroop, and H. F. Zou. 1996. "The Composition of Public Expenditure and Economic Growth." *Journal of Monetary Economics* 37 (2–3): 313–44.

Dixie, G., and G. Tyler. 2013. *Investing in Agribusiness: A Retrospective View of a Development Bank's Investments in Agribusiness in Africa and Southeast Asia and the Pacific*. Washington, DC: World Bank.

Dorosh, P. A., S. Dradri, and S. Haggblade. 2009. "Regional Trade, Government Policy and Food Security: Recent Evidence from Zambia." *Food Policy* 34 (4): 350–66.

Evenson, R. 2001. "Economic Impacts of Agricultural Research and Extension." In Vol. 1A of *Handbook of Agricultural Economics,* edited by B. Gardner and G. Rausser. Amsterdam: Elsevier Science.

Evenson, R., and D. Gollin. 2003. "Assessing the Impact of the Green Revolution, 1960 to 2000." *Science* 300 (5620): 758–62.

Fan, S., ed. 2008. *Public Expenditures, Growth, and Poverty: Lessons from Developing Countries.* Baltimore, MD: Johns Hopkins University Press.

Fan, S., A. Gulati, and S. Thorat. 2008. "Investment, Subsidies, and Pro-Poor Growth in Rural India." *Agricultural Economics* 39 (2): 163–70.

Fan, S., P. Hazell, and S. Thorat. 2000. "Government Spending, Agricultural Growth and Poverty in Rural India." *American Journal of Agricultural Economics* 82 (4): 1038–51.

Fan, S., D. Nyange, and N. Rao. 2012. "Public Investment and Poverty Reduction in Tanzania: Evidence from Household Survey Data." In *Public Expenditures for Agricultural and Rural Development in Africa,* edited by T. Mogues and S. Benin. London and New York: Routledge, Taylor, and Francis Group.

Fan, S., B. Yu, and A. Saurkar. 2008. "Public Spending in Developing Countries: Trends, Determination, and Impact." In *Public Expenditures, Growth, and Poverty: Lessons from Developing Countries,* edited by S. Fan. Washington, DC: IFPRI.

Fan, S., and X. Zhang. 2008. "Public Expenditure, Growth, and Poverty Reduction in Rural Uganda." *African Development Review* 20 (3): 466–96.

FAO (Food and Agriculture Organization). FAOstat: Commodities by Country (database), Rome (accessed April 15, 2014), http://faostat.fao.org/site/339/default.aspx.

———. Monitoring African Food and Agricultural Policies (MAFAP) database, Rome, http://www.fao.org/in-action/mafap/database/en/.

Feder, G., J. Anderson, R. Birner, and K. Deininger. 2010. "Promises and Realities of Community-Based Agricultural Extension." IFPRI Discussion Paper 00959, IFPRI, Washington, DC.

Foster, V., and C. Briceño-Garmendia, eds. 2010. *Africa's Infrastructure: A Time for Transformation.* Washington, DC: World Bank.

Fuglie, K. O., and N. E. Rada. 2013. *Resources, Policies, and Agricultural Productivity in Sub-Saharan Africa.* Economic Research Report 145. Washington, DC: U.S. Department of Agriculture Economic Research Service.

Gautam, M., and R. Anderson. 1999. "Reconsidering the Evidence of Returns to T&V Extension in Kenya." Policy Research Working Paper 2098, World Bank, Washington, DC.

Görg, H., and E. Strobl. 2006. "The Effect of R&D Subsidies on Private R&D." *Economica* 74: 215–34.

Griliches, Z. 1980. "R&D and the Productivity Slowdown." *American Economic Review* 70 (2): 343–48.

HarvestChoice. Long-Term Climate Trends for Sub-Saharan Africa (database) (accessed September 15, 2015), http://harvestchoice.org/tools/long-term-climate-trends-and -variations-sub-saharan-africa.

Holtz-Eakin, D., W. Newey, and S. Rosen. 1988. "Estimating Vector Autoregressions with Panel Data." *Econometrica* 56 (6): 1371–95.

Hsiao, C. 1986. *Analysis of Panel Data.* Cambridge, U.K.: Cambridge University Press.

IFPRI (International Food Policy Research Institute). Agricultural Science and Technology Indicators (ASTI) database, Washington, DC (accessed September 15, 2015), www.asti.cgiar.org/data/.

———. Regional Strategic Analysis and Knowledge Support System (ReSAKSS) database (accessed September 15, 2015), http://www.resakss.org/about.

———. Statistics on Public Expenditures for Economic Development (SPEED) database, Washington, DC (accessed September 15, 2015), http://www.ifpri.org/book-39 /ourwork/programs/priorities-public-investment/speed-database.

Inocencio, A., M. Kikuchi, M. Tonosaki, A. Maruyama, D. Merrey, H. Sally, and I. de Jong. 2007. *Costs and Performance of Irrigation Projects: A Comparison of Sub-Saharan Africa and Other Developing Regions.* (IWMI) Research Report 109. Colombo, Sri Lanka: International Water Management Institute.

IPCC (Intergovernmental Panel on Climate Change). 2014. *Fifth Assessment Report.* Geneva: Intergovernmental Panel on Climate Change.

Jayne, T. S., D. Mather, N. M. Mason, and J. Ricker-Gilbert. 2013. "How Do Fertilizer Subsidy Programs Affect Total Fertilizer Use in Sub-Saharan Africa? Crowding Out, Diversion, and Benefit/Cost Assessments." *Agricultural Economics* 44 (6): 687–703.

Jayne, T. S., D. Mather, N. Mason, and J. Ricker-Gilbert. 2015. "Rejoinder to the Comment by Andrew Dorward and Ephraim Chirwa on Jayne, T. S., D. Mather, N. Mason, and J. Ricker-Gilbert. 2013. 'How Do Fertilizer Subsidy Programs Affect Total Fertilizer Use in Sub-Saharan Africa? Crowding Out, Diversion, and Benefit/ Cost Assessments.' *Agricultural Economics* 44 (6): 687–703." *Agricultural Economics* 46 (6): 745–55.

Kennedy, P. 1985. *A Guide to Econometrics.* Cambridge, MA: MIT Press.

Krishnan, P., and M. Patnam. 2013. "Neighbours and Extension Agents in Ethiopia: Who Matters More for Technology Diffusion?" Working Paper, International Growth Centre, London.

Lindbeck, A., and J. Weibull. 1993. "A Model of Political Equilibrium in a Representative Democracy." *Journal of Public Economics* 51 (2): 195–209.

López, R. 2005. "Under-investing in Public Goods: Evidence, Causes, and Consequences for Agricultural Development, Equity, and the Environment." *Agricultural Economics* 32 (1): 211–24.

López, R., and G. I. Galinato. 2007. "Should Governments Stop Subsidies to Private Goods? Evidence from Rural Latin America." *Journal of Public Economics* 91: 1071–94.

Malla, S., and R. Gray. 2005. "The Crowding Effects of Basic and Applied Research: A Theoretical and Empirical Analysis of an Agricultural Biotech Industry." *American Journal of Agricultural Economics* 87 (2): 423–38.

Meenakshi, J. V., N. Johnson, V. Manyong, H. De Groote, J. Javelosa, D. Yanggen, F. Naher, C. Gonzalez, J. Garcia, and E. Meng. 2010. "How Cost-Effective is Biofortification in Combating Micronutrient Malnutrition? An Ex-Ante Assessment." *World Development* 38 (1): 64–75.

Mogues, T. 2011. "The Bang for the Birr: Public Expenditures and Rural Welfare in Ethiopia." *Journal of Development Studies* 47 (5): 735–52.

Mogues, T., S. Fan, and S. Benin. 2015. "Public Investments in and for Agriculture." *European Journal of Development Research* 27 (3): 337–52.

Rada, N., and C. Valdes. 2012. *Policy Technology and Efficiency in Brazilian Agriculture.* USDA Economic Research Report 137. Washington, DC: U.S. Department of Agriculture.

Sadoulet, E., and A. de Janvry. 1995. *Quantitative Development Policy Analysis.* Baltimore, MD: Johns Hopkins University Press.

Schaffer, M. E. 2010. xtivreg2: Stata Module to Perform Extended IV/2SLS, GMM and AC/HAC, LIML and K-Class Regression for Panel Data Models. http://ideas.repec.org/c/boc/bocode/s456501.html.

Schultz, T. W. 1982. *Investing in People: The Economics of Population Quality.* Berkeley, CA: University of California Press.

Stads, G. J., and Beintema, N. 2015. "Agricultural R&D Expenditure in Africa: An Analysis of Growth and Volatility." *European Journal of Development Research* 27 (3): 391–406.

Tanimichi Hoberg, Y. 2015. "The Nutrition Dimension of Agriculture Policies in Sub-Saharan Africa." Background paper for this book, mimeo.

Thirtle, C., J. Piesse, and L. Lin. 2003. "The Impact of Research-Led Agricultural Productivity Growth on Poverty Reduction in Africa, Asia and Latin America." *World Development* 31 (12): 1959–75.

Thirtle, C., and J. van Zyl. 1994. "Explaining Total Factor Productivity Growth and Returns to Research and Extension in South African Commercial Agriculture, 1947–91." *South African Journal of Agricultural Extension* 23 (1): 21–27.

Torero, M. 2015. "Alternative Mechanisms to Reduce Food Price Volatility and Price Spikes: Policy Responses at the Global Level." In *Food Price Volatility and Its Implications for Food Security and Policy,* 115–38. Cham, Switzerland: Springer International Publishing.

Wellard, K., J. Rafanomezana, M. Nyirenda, M. Okotel, and V. Subbey. 2013. "A Review of Community Extension Approaches to Innovation for Improved Livelihoods in Ghana, Uganda, and Malawi." *Journal of Agricultural Education and Extension* 19 (1): 21–35.

Woldehanna, T., R. Gudisa, Y. Tafere, and A. Pankhurst. 2011. *Understanding Changes in the Lives of Poor Children: Initial Findings from Ethiopia.* Young Lives Round 3 Survey Report. Oxford, U.K.: University of Oxford.

World Bank. 2008. *World Development Report 2008: Agriculture for Development.* Washington, DC: World Bank.

———. 2013. *Growing Africa: Unlocking the Potential of Agribusiness*. Washington, DC: World Bank.

———. World Development Indicators (database). Washington, DC, http://data .worldbank.org/data-catalog/world-development-indicators.

———. Worldwide Governance Indicators (database). Washington, DC, World Bank presentation based on first-stage model results.

# Chapter 3

# Smart Subsidies?

Of the many issues facing agriculture policy makers in Africa, one the most pressing is whether input subsidy programs—which have come to dominate agricultural budgets—are an effective way to raise productivity.[1] The gap is widening between agricultural productivity growth in Africa and the rest of the world. Closing this gap is a sine qua non to improve Africa's competitiveness on international markets and allow it to capture the rapidly growing regional market opportunities. Lagging productivity growth is attributed to the levels of modern input use, and Africa has by far the lowest rate of fertilizer use of any region, a rate that has practically remained the same over the last 40 years, despite considerable efforts by governments and donors to raise it (figure 3.1). The use of other yield-enhancing inputs—such as improved crop varieties, pesticides (herbicides, insecticides, fungicides), water control, and mechanization—is similarly limited. And in the absence of proper management techniques, yields are not sustainable in the long term on currently cultivated lands since soils are depleted of nutrients without proper agronomic practices.

African governments' commitment after the 2006 Abuja African Fertilizer Summit to increase fertilizer use from 8 to 50 kg of nutrients per hectare by 2015 reinforces the importance of inorganic fertilizer for increasing crop productivity and attaining food security in Africa. The impacts of achieving this target, however, will depend greatly on the agronomic efficiency of applied fertilizer. Many African governments' efforts to raise agricultural productivity have focused on programs to increase the volume of fertilizer used. Relatively little effort has been made in recent decades to help African farmers raise the efficiency of their fertilizer use.

Over the past decade, targeted input subsidy programs have been the main tool for many African governments to boost fertilizer use. In many countries, the programs have become the centerpiece of national agricultural development and food security strategies. While these programs have tended to produce important benefits for national food production and food security in the short run, the impacts have been attenuated by poor crop response to fertilizer use and to implementation features that depress the programs' contribution to overall fertilizer use more broadly. These limitations in turn have

**Figure 3.1** Fertilizer Use in Africa Lags behind Other Regions, 1970–2004

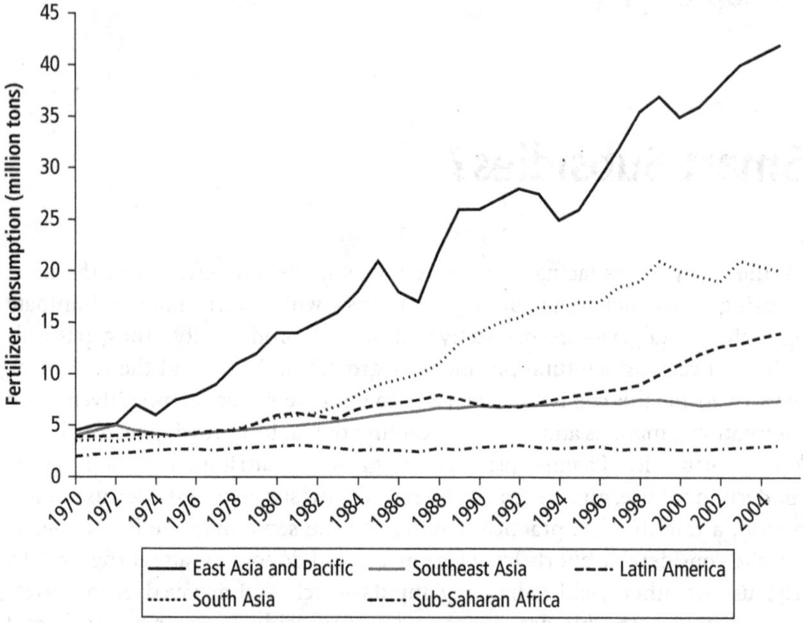

*Source:* FAO, MAFAP database.

diminished the subsidy programs' contribution to poverty reduction and sustainable agricultural productivity growth, and in countries where these programs have been carefully examined, costs exceed benefits on average. Low crop response to fertilizer has also impeded the growth of commercial demand for fertilizer in Africa, and the subsidy programs have further crowded out the development of commercial distribution channels. There is strong evidence, however, that farmers will demand more fertilizer when they are able to obtain higher crop responses to fertilizer and make its use more profitable.

A more systematic strategy for raising smallholder crop productivity—focusing on sustainably raising the efficiency of fertilizer use as well as the quantity of fertilizer used—will more effectively achieve the region's agricultural, food security, and poverty reduction objectives. Such a comprehensive strategy may include input subsidy programs, if they can be implemented according to smart subsidy criteria, which has often proven difficult. Other and probably more important components of such an agricultural productivity strategy will include greater public investment in coordinated systems of agricultural research and development, and water management and extension that emphasize bidirectional learning among farmers of varying resource constraints and agroecologies.

Sub-Saharan agricultural systems are undergoing rapid change in population densities, land scarcity, land degradation, climate variability, and new technologies. Because farming systems are dynamic, yesterday's best agronomic and crop management practices are unlikely to be suitable for today. Effective agricultural science and extension programs are thus necessary to interactively work with farmers to identify best practices to maintain and increase crop productivity in the face of these dynamic changes in the economic and biophysical environments. And because of substantial micro-level variation in these environments, effective crop science and extension systems must be "localized" to properly tailor agronomic best practices to heterogeneous environments.

While African governments' efforts to raise fertilizer use are laudable, spending on input subsidy programs *in most cases* appears to produce substantially smaller impact on national development objectives than their potential, and lower than the alternative ways of spending scarce resources. The gap between existing and potential impacts reflects both informational or knowledge constraints and political economy barriers. The contribution of input subsidy programs (and fertilizer use in general) to sustainable growth could be much greater with strong and sustained government commitment to complementary public goods investments as well as to government redesign of certain aspects of subsidy programs. But it is necessary to take a hard country-by-country assessment of the feasibility of achieving these outcomes in the foreseeable future.

This chapter investigates the extent to which inputs are underused, and attempts to close the knowledge gap on some of the key questions about the overall costs and benefits of input subsidy programs in the context of what is known more broadly about agricultural productivity growth. It identifies design features of these programs that make them cost-effective in meeting their goals. And it synthesizes evidence on the cost-effectiveness of other agricultural expenditures aimed at the same underlying objective as input subsidies—that is, raising productivity. The overall aim is to lay the groundwork for a more solid evidence-based dialogue on the subject.

## Tipping the Balance

Fertilizer subsidy programs are among the most contentiously debated of development issues in Africa. Throughout the 1990s, input subsidy programs (ISPs) were largely phased out in Sub-Saharan Africa, and only two countries (Zambia and Malawi) continued to implement modest input subsidy programs sporadically over this period. Based on evidence from the 1980s and early 1990s, a consensus emerged that fertilizer subsidy programs were largely ineffective in promoting African governments' development goals, contributing little to agricultural productivity growth, food security, or poverty reduction while placing a major fiscal burden on treasuries (Kherallah et al. 2002; Morris et al. 2007; World Bank 2008).

Fertilizer subsidy programs in Africa also tended to have adverse side effects, contributing to corruption and state paternalism, often hindering the development of commercial input distribution systems, and contributing to local supply gluts that put political pressure on governments to implement costly grain purchases and support price policies for farmers. For these reasons, international lenders and bilateral donors tended to discourage African governments from relying on input subsidy programs during this period of aid conditionality.

Starting in 2005, however, the landscape changed quickly and profoundly. Within several years after African governments committed to raise their expenditures on agriculture under the 2003 Maputo Declaration, at least 10 countries had introduced or reintroduced fertilizer subsidy programs costing roughly US$1 billion annually (figures 3.2 and 3.3).[2] Large-scale input subsidy programs often became the centerpiece of governments' agricultural development programs. Skepticism based on the past performance of these programs was swept

**Figure 3.2** The 10 Largest African Programs Spend US$1.2 Billion a Year on Input Subsidies Alone

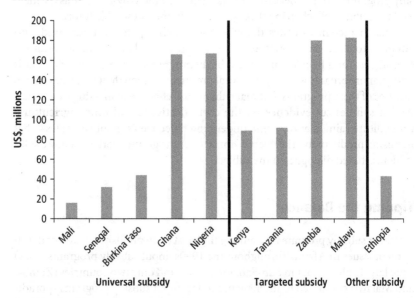

Source: Jayne et al. 2016.

**Figure 3.3** Input Subsidy Program Cost as Share of Agricultural Spending, 2014

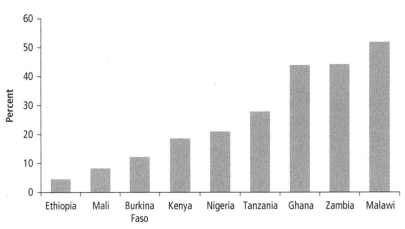

Source: Jayne et al. 2016.

aside by arguments that a new genre of smart subsidy programs could take account of past lessons to maximize the benefits and minimize the problems of prior programs.

How did this sea change occur so quickly? And what have we learned about this recent wave of input subsidy programs in Africa? Despite the proliferation of smart input subsidy programs, there has been limited rigorous evaluation of their impacts to date. Filling these knowledge gaps is the major motivation for this chapter. More specifically, the chapter has two main objectives. The first is to assemble the recent evidence on ISPs in Sub-Saharan Africa and to place this work in the broader literature on agricultural productivity growth. In so doing, we strive to shed light on two major questions:

- To what extent are ISPs evolving toward smart subsidy principles, especially by targeting beneficiaries and involving the private sector?
- What are the economic impacts of ISPs in Africa? Specifically, we address the effects of country-level ISPs on indicators such as total fertilizer use, national food production, the development of commercial input distribution systems, and the general equilibrium effects on food prices, wage rates, and poverty rates. We also assess whether ISPs are generating dynamic and enduring effects that kick-start broader growth processes or sustainable intensification in rural areas.

The chapter's second main objective is to identify ways that ISPs could more effectively achieve national policy objectives, given that many African governments are likely to continue these programs, at least in the near future. This work focuses on potential changes in program design and implementation as well as complementary public expenditures and policies that assist farmers in raising the efficiency of input use. These two objectives are addressed through comprehensive reviews of the micro-level evidence in seven countries where input subsidy programs have featured prominently (Ethiopia, Ghana, Kenya, Malawi, Nigeria, Tanzania, and Zambia).[3] We also draw from recent multicountry assessments of ISPs in Africa (Druilhe and Barreiro-Hurlé 2012; Jayne and Rashid 2013; Wanzala-Mlobela, Fuentes, and Mkumbwa 2013). The annexes are a comprehensive compendium of virtually all recent empirical evidence from research on the impacts of ISPs, organized by major issue.

Given the rapid evolution of ISP design and implementation, many knowledge gaps remain. ISPs in Rwanda, Burundi, and Nigeria, for example, are undergoing design changes to incorporate lessons from prior assessments and overcome weaknesses, leading to continual refinement over the past decade. Efforts in several countries have been made to ensure that ISPs are now "smarter" and more effective than in prior years. Moreover, the evidence base on ISPs and smallholder crop response to fertilizer is expanding rapidly. The growing availability of farm panel survey data—combined with soil sample data, advances in estimation methods, and innovations in survey design methods—have enhanced economists' ability to identify program effects with greater precision. This chapter provides an updated review of evidence over the past decade, but both the continued lack of evidence about program impacts in some areas and the conflicting evidence in others pose challenges for consensus building. Even so, the weight of the empirical studies does point in clear directions on some key points.

## Rationale for Input Subsidy Programs

Most rural African settings suffer from multiple market failures, providing an important entry point for subsidies to address the constraints faced by economic agents, especially poor farmers. Welfare economics has long recognized the potential usefulness of subsidies in situations in which social benefits exceed private benefits (due to market failures or externalities). Subsidies can also be justified under specific circumstances—for example, when there are strong learning-by-doing effects, strategic trade intervention opportunities, or environmental benefits, as well as for equity considerations (Morris et al. 2007; World Bank 2008).

In primarily agrarian economies, low levels of inorganic fertilizer use are associated with low crop yields, low rural incomes, and high poverty rates. Dorward, Hazell, and Poulton (2008) present a conceptual framework that describes African rural economies as being in a productivity-poverty trap, from which risk-averse farm households are unable to extricate themselves. Input use remains low in equilibrium with low productivity, reinforcing staple crop self-sufficiency goal and stifling diversification into other agricultural and nonagricultural activities. The trap impedes rural people's ability to protect themselves from shocks, and hampers wider local and national economic development, resulting in a vicious cycle. Unstable food prices inhibit producers' net investment in staple production, reduce consumers' willingness to rely on the market for staple purchases, and limit consumers' opportunities to escape from low productivity staple cultivation. These in turn inhibit the growth of the nonfarm economy.

Relieving these constraints through input subsidy programs can not only help affected farmers but also potentially unleash strong general equilibrium impacts—boosting agricultural productivity and incomes; lowering food prices; raising real wages, employment, and broader economic growth through forward and backward linkages; and strongly contributing to poverty reduction. Because staple crops account for such a large proportion of total cultivated area in most African countries, smallholder staple crop productivity growth is likely to generate dynamic growth processes that will lead to agricultural diversification and farm-nonfarm growth linkages and employment effects that contribute to economic transformation and poverty reduction.[4]

By raising crop yields dramatically for several years in a row, fertilizer subsidy programs have the potential to kick-start dynamic growth processes that allow households to break out of the trap and move onto a higher productivity and income growth trajectory. Eventually, recipients may generate cash savings that enable them to invest in productive farm equipment and purchase commercial fertilizer. These investments in complementary farm assets and inputs sustain farmers' upward productivity growth trajectory. If millions of small farms experience such growth, it could lower food prices, increase demand for agricultural wage labor, and increase circulation of money in rural areas that generate multiplier effects—all contributing to employment and economic growth. In these ways, fertilizer subsidy programs are argued to be a powerful tool for transforming agrarian societies and kick-starting broader structural transformation processes.

Other motivations for fertilizer subsidy programs in Africa have focused on a "learning effect." Fertilizer use may be inadequate in some areas because farmers have no experience with it. A subsidy on fertilizer could enable farmers to gain valuable information about the benefits of using fertilizer without risking a major capital outlay (Carter, Laajaj, and Yang 2014). After learning about the benefits of using fertilizer, farmers may then continue to purchase it after the subsidy program ends. Such a learning effect would be confined to areas where fertilizer use is uncommon but likely to be profitable.

A frequently articulated argument for input subsidy programs in Africa is that many developed countries have implemented them for decades to build up their agricultural sectors, and there is no reason why countries in Africa should not enjoy the same benefits. This view assumes that input subsidy programs in developed countries actually contributed to those countries' development, or that they were a more effective use of public resources than other public investments such as investments in technological improvements, farmer education, infrastructural development, and irrigation. However, we are not aware of empirical research to support these positions. Studies from Asia, for example, found that fertilizer subsidy programs were quite far down on the rankings of public expenditures with respect to cost-effective impacts on agricultural productivity growth and poverty reduction (EIU 2008; Fan, Gulati, and Thorat 2008). A comprehensive review of these studies is discussed in the previous chapter.

### Reasons for Low Fertilizer Use: Is It Really "Too" Low in Africa?

While there are varied motivations for fertilizer subsidy programs, all are based on the assumption that existing fertilizer use in Africa is "suboptimal." The causes of low fertilizer use are often considered to be related to the following:

- Households' insufficient access to credit to purchase fertilizer in quantities even close to official recommendations, if at all
- Households' lack of information about the benefits of using fertilizer
- Risks of using fertilizer—even if fertilizer use is expected to raise net household income on average, the risk of a loss discourages use
- Weak development of commercial input markets
- Price volatility in output markets, which deters farmers from purchasing inputs to produce a marketable surplus

Of all the reasons for low fertilizer use in Africa, the expected profitability of using fertilizer typically is rarely questioned. Instead, in many areas of Africa, fertilizer is shown to be highly valued by farmers, and studies demonstrate high financial returns to most farmers. However, there appears to be a selection bias in the literature on farmer returns to fertilizer use in Africa. Studies tend to be concentrated in areas where fertilizer use is already common and fairly high. Moreover, prior to 2005, analysts' main source of fertilizer response estimates for African smallholder farmers came from experimental stations or on-farm trials. But on-farm trials tend to be managed by scientists in heavily controlled environments for seed type, planting date, row spacing, seed spacing, weeding, and even the choice of farmer to participate. Few nationally representative smallholder farm panel data sets were available to understand staple crop response to fertilizer on fields that were managed by smallholder farmers and accounting for the various resource constraints that they faced.

While on-farm trials are generally considered to provide accurate estimates of the crop response rates to fertilizer that farmers *may get* under near ideal conditions on well-managed plots, they are often not representative of the response rates that smallholder farmers *do get* when they follow the management practices they often employ given the various resource constraints they face. Farm trials often involve farmers on a nonrandom basis. They tend to be disproportionately "master farmers" who possess better management practices and encounter fewer constraints. Cases of crop damage from drought, flooding, pests, or disease are often dropped from trials, even though these are real possibilities for farmers purchasing inputs in the real world. Trial plots tend to be carefully chosen for suitability and are generally smaller than most farmer-managed plots, providing greater "edge effects" that likely raise crop responses to fertilizer.

For these reasons, it is likely that prior estimates of crop response rates (or nutrient use efficiency, hereafter NUE) from researcher-managed farm trials in Africa provide potentially misleading estimates of fertilizer use profitability. Our understanding of the economics of fertilizer use needs to be updated based on observations from farmer-managed fields. Since roughly 2005, a growing number of studies have begun estimating crop response rates to fertilizer based on increasingly available panel surveys of smallholder farmers. Farm panel surveys are arguably the most accurate source of obtaining estimates of the NUE that farmers obtain in their fields for many reasons:

- Many are nationally representative and are thus more representative of the population than trials, many of which are in high-potential areas.
- They take into account farmers' actual behavior and resource constraints ("farmer managed plots" as opposed to "researcher-managed plots").
- Panel survey data are better able to control for the effects of unobserved time-invariant factors correlated with fertilizer use, which might otherwise bias researchers' estimates of NUE in cross-sectional data.
- From an ex ante framework of the farmer deciding whether to purchase and apply fertilizer to a particular field, survey data that retain cases of crop damage, floods, striga (parasitic weed), and shocks leading to inadequate labor, for example, represent valid cases that need to be included in estimations of on-farm averages for NUE.[5]

The evidence on "researcher-managed" farm trials in East and Southern Africa produced NUE estimates ranging from 18 to 40 kg of maize per kg of nitrogen (Tscharntke et al. 2012; Vanlauwe et al. 2011). Until recently, this was the range of NUE commonly believed to hold for smallholders' own fields using their own management practices. Given prevailing fertilizer and farmgate maize prices in the region, nitrogen use efficiency estimates in the range of 18–40 kg of maize per kg of nitrogen almost always show highly profitable returns to farmers. By contrast, table 3.1 shows our inventory of recent survey-based estimates of NUE from studies based on farmer-managed fields.

The estimates in table 3.1 consistently find response rates in the range of 8–24 kg of maize per kg of nitrogen applied, with a concentration at the lower end around 8–15 kg. These studies suggest that smallholder households obtain levels of crop response that generally are substantially lower than those estimated from researcher-managed on-farm trials.

Indeed, if the cause of low fertilizer use is low profitability, this implies that the net value of output produced from incremental fertilizer use may not exceed the social cost of the additional fertilizer (box 3.1). Under such conditions, it is not clear that increased fertilizer use will enhance economic efficiency or productivity goals until crop response rates to fertilizer use are increased (box 3.2).

### Why Is the Crop Response Rate So Low in Africa?

Both the mean and variance of crop response rates vary greatly between irrigated and rainfed conditions. Water control is a fundamental "game changer" for the economics of fertilizer use. Roughly 45 percent of South Asia's grain crops are under irrigation, which typically affords two to three cropping seasons per year and relatively stable yield responses to fertilizer. Consequently, fertilizer application rates on cereal crops are substantially higher on irrigated fields than on rainfed plots).[6] By contrast, 96 percent of Sub-Saharan Africa's cultivated land is rainfed, much of it in semiarid areas experiencing frequent water stress and with one crop season a year.

Fertilizer application rates on rainfed fields in India are also quite low and not different from application rates in much of rainfed Africa (Rashid 2010). Water control may be an increasingly important determinant of fertilizer use rates in the future, with more variable climate conditions. For these reasons, the economics of fertilizer use in Africa are generally less favorable than in other regions of the world where water control is more common. The water constraint on fertilizer use can be relieved, albeit to a limited extent and only with investments over a significant period.

Soil quality is another massive challenge that African farmers face in raising crop responses to fertilizer. The availability of 17 essential nutrients (or elements) ultimately determines a plant's growth and the yield potential of food crops (Jones et al. 2013).[7] The efficiency of fertilizer use depends on the level of preexisting *available* nutrients stocked in the soil as well as the *availability* of nutrients applied as fertilizer. Part of what determines nutrient availability is the soil characteristics that represent the physical, biological, and chemical properties of soils. There are numerous ways to measure each of them, but common metrics include pH (soil chemistry), soil organic matter (soil biology),[8] and texture (soil physics).

**Table 3.1 Recent Estimates of Fertilizer Application and Response Rates in Sub-Saharan Africa**

| African study areas (sources) | Geographic focus | Maize fields receiving commercial fertilizer use (%) | Application rate for users | Estimated nitrogen use efficiency (kg maize output per kg N) | Estimated value-cost ratio (VCR) |
|---|---|---|---|---|---|
| Sheahan, Black, and Jayne (2013) | 20 districts of Kenya where maize is commonly grown, 5 years of data between 1997 and 2010 | 64 (1997) to 83 (2007) | 26 kg N/ha (1997) to 40 kg N/ha (2010) | AP = 21 kg maize/kg N<br><br>MP = 17 kg maize/kg N | AVCR=1.3 (high-potential maize zone) to 3.7 (eastern lowlands) |
| Marenya and Barrett (2009) | Kenya (Vihiga and S. Nandi districts); relatively high-potential areas | 88 (maize and maize/bean intercrop) | 5.2 kg N/ha | MP = 17.6 kg maize/kg N | MVCR=1.76 (but fertilizer was <1.0 on 30% of plots) |
| Matsumoto, Yamano, and Sserunkuuma (2012) | 100 locations in Western and Central Kenya (2004, 2007) | 74 | 94.7 kg fertilizer product/ha maize | MP = 14.1–19.8 kg hybrid maize/kg N | MVCR=1.05–1.24 for hybrid maize |
| Snapp et al. (2014) | Malawi—nationally representative LSMS survey data | 27 (maize plots) | 62.9 kg/ha maize | 5.33 for monocrop; 8.84 for intercropped maize | MVCR=1.04–1.38<br>AVCR=1.25–1.71 |
| Morris et al. (2007) | W/E/S Africa | — | — | E/S Africa: 14 kgs maize/kg N (median)<br><br>W Africa: 10 kg maize/kg N (median) | E/S Africa: 2.8<br>W Africa: 2.8 |
| Minten, Koru, and Stifel (2013) | Northwestern Ethiopia | 69.1 of maize plots fertilized | 65.3 kg N/ha | MP=12kg maize/kg N for on-time planting; 11 kg maize/kg N for late planting | 1.4–1.0 (varying by degree of remoteness) |
| Pan and Christiaensen (2012) | Kilimanjaro District, Tanzania | — | — | 11.7 kg maize/kg N | — |
| Xu et al. (2009) | AEZ IIa in Zambia (relatively good quality soils/rainfall suitable for maize production) | 56.4 on maize | 61.4 kgs N/ha (among users) | AP = 18.1 (8.5–25.5)<br>MP = 16.2 (6.9–23.4) | Accessible areas=1.88<br>Remote areas=1.65 |

*(continued next page)*

**Table 3.1** (continued)

| African study areas (sources) | Geographic focus | Maize fields receiving commercial fertilizer use (%) | Application rate for users | Estimated nitrogen use efficiency (kg output per kg N) | Estimated value-cost ratio (VCR) |
|---|---|---|---|---|---|
| Burke (2012) | Zambia (nationally representative), 2001, 2004, 2008 | 36–38 of maize fields; 45–50 of maize area | 35.2 N/ha maize | 9.6 kg maize/kg N | 0.3–1.2 depending on soil pH level for 98% of sample |
| Ricker-Gilbert and Jayne (2012) | Malawi national panel data | 59 of maize fields | 47.1 N/ha maize | 8.1kg maize/kg N | 0.6–1.6 |
| Chibwana, Fisher, and Shively (2012) | Malawi farmer-managed field data in Kasumgu and Machinga Districts | — | — | 9.6–12.0 kg maize/kg N | MVCR 1.4–1.8 |
| Chirwa and Dorward (2013) | Malawi national LSMS survey data | — | — | Negative to 9.0 | Below 2.0 |
| Liverpool-Tasie and Takeshima (2015) | Nigeria national LSMS survey data | — | — | 8.0 kg maize/kg N; 8.8 kg rice/kg N | Below 2.0; Below 2.0 |
| Mather et al. (2015) | Tanzania national LSMS-ISA survey data | 15.9 (2009) 20.6 (2011) 17.9 (2013) | 55.6 N/ha maize | 7.8 kg maize/kg N (highlands); 5.7 kg maize/kg N | MVCR 0.94–1.23 (varies by year); MVCR 0.71–1.08 |

*Note:* Given prevailing commercial retail input and output price ratios, we (or the studies' authors) calculate either the expected MP and AP and, subsequently, the expected MVCRs and AVCRs of the following forms:

$$E(MVCR_{fijt}) = \frac{E(p_{yijt}) * E(MP_{xijt})}{w_{fijt}}$$

$$E(AVCR_{fijt}) = \frac{E(p_{yijt}) * E(AP_{xijt})}{w_{fijt}}$$

in which $w_t$ is the price of fertilizer, $p_y$ is the producer price of the crop in question, $i$ indexes individual farms, $j$ indexes their fields and $t$ indexes time, and E indicates average or expected.

AEZ = agroecological zone; AP = average physical products; AVCR = average value-cost ratio; LSMS-ISA = Living Standards Measurement Study—Integrated Surveys on Agriculture; MP = marginal physical products; MVCR = marginal value-cost ratio; VCR = value-cost ratio; W/E/S = West/East/South; — = no estimates.

SMART SUBSIDIES? 137

**BOX 3.1**

## Are Response Rates High Enough to Incentivize Farmers to Increase Fertilizer Use?

An expected average value-cost ratio (AVCR) of greater than 1 suggests that a farmer expects to increase his income as a result of fertilizer use (the average gain per unit). An expected marginal value-cost ratio (MVCR) of greater than one indicates income would be expected to increase with an increase in the rate of fertilizer application. But African smallholder farmers tend to be risk-averse, and the inclusion of a risk premium is important to measure the relationship between the VCRs and farmer adoption behavior (Anderson, Dillon, and Hardaker 1977). Moreover, farmers incur other costs associated with fertilizer use that are unaccounted for in VCR measures, such as increased weeding labor needed on fertilized plots because the fertilizer contributes to weed growth that competes with plants for the nutrients. Farmers may also incur transaction costs of obtaining inputs and selling crops that are not accounted for in $w_f$ and $p_y$.

For these reasons, an AVCR of 2 has been typically used in the literature as the benchmark for reliably profitable adoption (Bationo et al. 1992; Sauer and Tchale 2009; Xu et al. 2009).[a] This dates back to work by the FAO (1975) to better accommodate risk and uncertainty, adjust for the many unobserved costs associated with fertilizer use, and serve as an approximation for the rate at which fertilizer is profitable *enough* for smallholder farmers to want to use it.

The VCR estimates in the far right column of table 3.1 show very few cases over 2.0. Most of the estimates fall between 1.0 and 2.0, signifying marginal or moderate profitability when risk and other unmeasured costs are not taken into account. The growing evidence that low fertilizer use is at least partially driven by low response rates on many African soils suggests that if response rates are not high enough to provide incentives to use inorganic fertilizers, a rational farmer's efficient choice would be to not adopt it.

Another important point is the makeup of the VCR calculations in equations (3.1 and 3.2): using input prices, output prices, and input productivity. Despite the efforts of subsidy programs, the fact remains that the ratio of these prices, while volatile, has been fairly constant on trend. This includes various maize-to-fertilizer price ratios for locations throughout Zambia and Kenya (figure B3.1.1). The majority of trends in these ratios (not shown) are essentially flat and *no ratio trend is statistically positive* (or negative) over time. If the ratio of grain-to-fertilizer prices continues with a zero trend for the foreseeable future, this would indicate that shifts over time in fertilizer profitability must be driven by changes in response rates.

*(continued next page)*

## Box 3.1 (continued)

**Figure B3.1.1** Various Maize-to-Fertilizer Price Ratios for Zambia and Kenya, 1985–2004

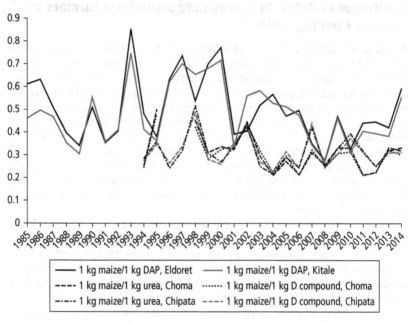

— 1 kg maize/1 kg DAP, Eldoret    — 1 kg maize/1 kg DAP, Kitale

---- 1 kg maize/1 kg urea, Choma    ······ 1 kg maize/1 kg D compound, Choma

-·--· 1 kg maize/1 kg urea, Chipata    ---- 1 kg maize/1 kg D compound, Chipata

*Source:* Jayne et al. 2016.

a. This dates back to work by the FAO (1975) to better accommodate risk and uncertainty, adjust for the many unobserved costs associated with fertilizer use, and serve as an approximation for the rate at which fertilizer is profitable *enough* for smallholder farmers to want to use it. In recent data, it becomes possible to account for some farm-specific costs (such as transportation) in which case the VCRs considered profitable would be lower than 2. By how much is unfortunately still dependent on unobservable factors, so there is no "rule of thumb" for estimates accounting for farmgate pricing; we simply accept that "2" is an increasingly pessimistic choice. It is, however, recommended to discuss the *distribution* of VCR estimates so that readers can make their own assessments as well.

## BOX 3.2

# Welfare Effects of the Malawi Farm Input Subsidy Program

The Malawi Farm Input Subsidy Program (FISP) is perhaps the most publicized of the current generation of smart subsidies in Africa, and the inspiration for many of them. Smart ISPs typically provide farmers with vouchers to purchase small quantities of fertilizers (and sometimes seeds) at a subsidized price less than market value. FISP's impacts have

*(continued next page)*

## Box 3.2 (continued)

**Figure B3.2.1** Four Categories of Farmer Demand for Fertilizer

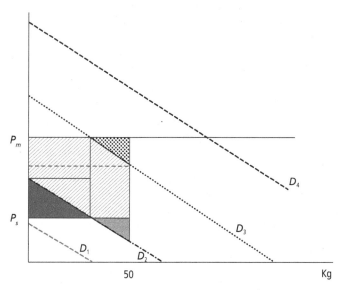

*Source:* Jacoby 2016.

been analyzed in numerous studies, including some that estimate costs and benefits of the program. To our knowledge, however, none of these analyses have explicitly recognized that the aggregate benefits of this kind of program depend on the differing benefits accruing to farmers in terms of consumer surplus. The classes of farmers correspond to the four demand schedules in figure B3.2.1. For each of them, the cost of the subsidy program is the difference between the commercial price (the price paid by the government) and the subsidized price, times the amount of fertilizer purchased by the farmer. The net benefit of the subsidy is the difference between the consumer surplus and the cost. The consumer surplus is different for each class of farmer:

- *Class 1* comprises those with a demand for fertilizer so low that they are not willing to buy fertilizer at the subsidized price even if it is possible to purchase in fractions of 50 kg bags. These farmers get no benefits, but also incur no costs to the program.

- *Class 2* includes those who would not purchase any fertilizer at the commercial market price, but have a demand high enough to make it worthwhile to buy the full 50 kg bag at the subsidized price, even though they would prefer to purchase only a fraction of a bag. The net welfare gain to this class of farmer from the subsidy is represented by the area of the solid darker gray triangle minus the area of the solid light gray triangle.

- *Class 3* encompasses those who would purchase some fertilizer (but not a full bag) at the market price, but would willingly purchase a full bag at the subsidized price. As in

*(continued next page)*

## Box 3.2 (continued)

class 2, the subsidy in class 3 induces the farmer to procure more fertilizer than she otherwise would. But the marginal value of these additional units to the farmer is less than the cost of providing them. This difference is represented by the cross-hatched triangle in the upper right of the figure.

- *Class 4* covers farmers for whom the subsidy is inframarginal—that is, they would buy more than one bag at the full market price. Here, the subsidy does not change farmer behavior at all, so the welfare gain, the entire rectangle (cross-hatched area plus the lower solid dark gray triangle), is equal to the cost of the subsidy.

Using data from the 2013 household survey (Jacoby 2015), which included information on FISP voucher receipts and redemptions, the study estimated demand for each type of fertilizer using data for nonrecipients of vouchers. The demand schedule was conditional on household characteristics and various measures of soil quality, which is a critically important determinant of the value of fertilizer. Using this information, and information on voucher redemptions by households that received them, the study estimated how many farms fall into each of the four classes and the net benefits (consumer surplus minus cost) for each of the households. It turns out that few farmers were predicted to be in class 1 or class 4, and about 73–75 percent (depending on the type of fertilizer) were in class 3.

Benefit-cost ratios were estimated for each household under two assumptions: one was that the household's demand for fertilizer was not constrained by lack of access to credit; the other was that the demand was credit-constrained, in which case the estimated benefit of the subsidy was higher. The unconstrained demand estimate assumed that all households value fertilizer as though they were in the 90th percentile of the per capita expenditure distribution.

The key finding is that benefit-cost ratios are well below 1 (table B3.2.1), the upper bound achieved when all households are inframarginal with respect to the FISP. For the consumer surplus computed based on constrained demand, the national benefit-cost ratio is only 0.41, which means that 59 percent of every kwacha spent on FISP is wasted. The poor account for much more of this deadweight loss than the nonpoor for the simple reason that the poor have a lower demand for fertilizer. Obviously, moving from constrained to unconstrained demand as a basis for computing the consumer surplus attenuates the difference in benefit-cost ratios between the

**Table B3.2.1**  Benefit-Cost Ratios for the Malawi Farm Input Subsidy Program

|  | Constrained demand | Unconstrained demand |
| --- | --- | --- |
| All agricultural households | 0.41 | 0.62 |
| Poor agricultural households | 0.29 | 0.53 |
| Nonpoor agriculture | 0.46 | 0.46 |

*Source:* Jacoby 2016.

*(continued next page)*

## Box 3.2 (continued)

**Figure B3.2.2** Share of Net Benefits According to Expenditure Bracket, Based on Unconstrained Demand

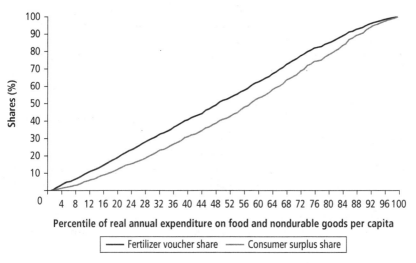

Source: Jacoby 2016.

poor and the nonpoor, although in reality the assumption of credit constraints is likely to be more realistic for the poor.

As a final step, the study estimated benefit incidence curves for the FISP, showing what percentage of the benefits (consumer surplus) accrued to each expenditure bracket percentile. Figure B3.2.2 shows the curve based on unconstrained fertilizer demand. In the figure, the naïve curve is plotted, which is just the share of vouchers that actually went to the bottom $k^{th}$ percentile of the per capita expenditure distribution. Evidently, FISP voucher distribution does not effectively target the poor; indeed, there is no discernible progressivity in the distribution of vouchers. However, when the actual estimated benefit due to the voucher is taken into account, the FISP appears much more regressive, which again is attributable to the low demand for fertilizer among the poor.

Several important points emerge from this analysis. First, notwithstanding the "smart" features of the FISP, the program is not progressive. Second, the program is inefficient, in the sense that its cost is considerably more than its value to recipients. Finally, the results demonstrate a tension between the two objectives often cited for input subsidies for inframarginal farmers: boosting agricultural production and reducing poverty.

Research in the fields of agronomy, soil science, and farming systems ecology is pointing the way to how sustainable intensification will need to occur in rain-fed Sub-Saharan Africa and the role of fertilizer in these systems (Powlson et al. 2011; Snapp and Pound 2011; Vanlauwe et al. 2011). A substantial body of evidence documents how rising rural population density in much of Africa is leading to rising land pressures, reduced fallows, more continuous cultivation, soil degradation, and weaker responses to fertilizer application over time (Drechsel et al. 2001; Roy et al. 2003; Tittonell and Giller 2013). Declining soil fertility is an important factor causing stagnant or declining trends in maize-fertilizer response rates observed over time, even while hybrid seed adoption is on the rise.

Smallholder farmers are largely unable to benefit from the current yield gains offered by plant genetic improvement due to their farming on depleted soils that are nonresponsive to fertilizer application (Giller et al. 2006; Tittonell et al. 2007). The efficiency with which fertilizer nutrients affect crop yield is strongly reduced by soil degradation (nutrient loss, too high or too low pH, or lower soil organic matter).[9] Sustainable intensification efforts can be thought of in relation to three categories of fields: responsive to fertilizer use, nonresponsive but still productive, and nonresponsive and degraded. Rising population pressures and more continuous cropping are shifting the relative proportion of cropped area in much of Africa from the first and second categories to the third, where productivity and crop response to fertilizer are poor (Tittonell and Giller 2013).

Facile comparisons of average fertilizer application rates between Africa and other regions of the world (particularly East and South Asia) tend to be highly misleading. Policy discussions of low fertilizer use in Africa have tended to overemphasize failures in credit markets and underemphasize declining soil fertility associated with rising land pressures and continuous cultivation, poor soil management practices, and rainfed farming conditions in limiting African farmers' ability to use fertilizer profitably. This has led to the widespread but overly simplified view that low fertilizer use in Africa primarily reflects market access problems that can be overcome through input subsidy programs.

A potential consequence is that official fertilizer use recommendations are often based on unrealistic assumptions about smallholders' soil conditions and response rates (often derived from trials and experiments). In some African countries, official fertilizer use recommendations of the national extension systems are uniform throughout the country. For example, Zambia's Ministry of Agriculture advises the "4 by 4" strategy of four 50 kg bags of Compound D and four 50 kg bags of urea per hectare of maize, for a total application rate of 400 kg per hectare. Perhaps not surprisingly, less than 3 percent of Zambian smallholder farmers use fertilizer this intensively on their maize. Similarly, three studies investigating the profitability of fertilizer use in Kenya all found that official recommended use rates are far in excess of the economically optimal level for most farmers (Duflo, Kremer, and Robinson 2008; Marenya and Barrett 2009; Sheahan, Black, and Jayne 2013). The policy challenge of sustainably raising crop response to fertilizer is somewhat like turning a battleship: it is imminently feasible but will take considerable time. The profitability and effective demand for fertilizer in African agriculture in 2030 will depend on the extent to which African governments invest *today* in efforts to educate farmers about agronomic practices to rebuild soil organic matter and take advantage of crop rotations and intercrops capable of restoring soil responsiveness to fertilizer application. Unfortunately, public sector funding to crop science, agronomic management, and extension systems built on appropriate recommendations has remained chronically underprovisioned in many African countries, being much smaller than in any other region of the world. Public agricultural extension systems in many African countries are virtually defunct. In Zambia and Malawi, these expenditures currently account for less than 15 percent of total annual expenditures to agriculture. By contrast, input subsidy programs in these countries accounted for over 60 percent of public agricultural expenditures in recent years. Clearly, the foundation for increased fertilizer use in Sub-Saharan Africa will depend on a more systematic and integrative approach to sustainable agricultural intensification.

## Evolution of Subsidy Programs in Africa

Given the weak evidence that increased fertilizer use would be financially or economically viable, how did ISPs become so widely used? Throughout the 1990s and until 2005, agricultural input subsidy programs had been largely phased out in Sub-Saharan Africa. The discontinuation of fertilizer subsidy programs occurred during this period of structural adjustment, aid conditionality, and strong international lender influence over agricultural policies.[10]

Starting in 2005 the landscape changed quickly and profoundly. Within several years after African governments had committed to raise their spending on agriculture under the 2003 Maputo Declaration, at least 10 countries had introduced or reintroduced fertilizer subsidy programs costing more than US$1 billion annually (table 3.2). Large-scale input subsidy programs became the centerpiece of many African governments' agricultural development programs. Five main factors drove this rapid sea change.

First, many African governments struggled to accept the tenets of structural adjustment and cut ISPs only under duress. Leaders had incentives for attempting to retain input subsidy programs. They were politically popular and often were part of the postindependence "social contracts" between leaders and their constituents to rectify earlier policies that discriminated against smallholder farmers.

Table 3.2 ISP and Broader Agricultural Sector Spending, 2011–14

| Country | Year | ISP cost (US$, millions) Official source | ISP cost (US$, millions) Computed using secondary data (B) | Program fertilizer distributed (MT) (C) | Program cost per MT of program fertilizer distributed (US$/MT) [B/C] (D) | Public agricultural spending (US$, millions) (E) | ISP cost as % share of public agricultural spending [=(B/E)*100] (F) |
|---|---|---|---|---|---|---|---|
| *Universal subsidy* | | | | | | | |
| Burkina Faso | 2011 | — | 39 | 173 | 890 | 213 | 18.1 |
| | 2012 | — | 15 | 65 | 918 | 195 | 7.7 |
| | 2013 | — | 18 | 75 | 947 | 204 | 8.7 |
| | 2014 | — | 16 | 84 | 780 | 199 | 8.3 |
| Ghana | 2011 | — | 22 | 25 | 867 | 291 | 7.5 |
| | 2012 | — | 31 | 36 | 841 | 310 | 9.9 |
| | 2013 | — | 42 | 51 | 819 | 351 | 12.0 |
| | 2014 | — | 44 | 51 | 850 | 358 | 12.2 |
| Mali | 2011 | 122 | 112 | 176 | 634 | 419 | 26.6 |
| | 2012 | 123 | 114 | 176 | 646 | 364 | 31.2 |
| | 2013 | — | 143 | 262 | 545 | 391 | 36.5 |
| | 2014 | — | 166 | 268 | 619 | 378 | 43.9 |
| Senegal | 2011 | — | 42 | 54 | 785 | 182 | 23.3 |
| | 2012 | — | 33 | 41 | 785 | 374 | 8.7 |
| | 2013 | — | 27 | 36 | 764 | 368 | 7.4 |
| | 2014 | — | 32 | 43 | 736 | 390 | 8.2 |

*(continued next page)*

**Table 3.2** (continued)

| Country | Year | ISP cost (US$, millions) | | Program fertilizer distributed (MT) | Program cost per MT of program fertilizer distributed (US$/MT) [B/C] | Public agricultural spending (US$, millions) | ISP cost as % share of public agricultural spending [=(B/E)*100] |
|---|---|---|---|---|---|---|---|
| | | Official source | Computed using secondary data | | | | |
| | | | (B) | (C) | (D) | (E) | (F) |
| Nigeria | 2011 | — | 190 | 264 | 719 | 817 | 23.3 |
| | 2012 | — | 177 | 249 | 711 | 788 | 22.4 |
| | 2013 | — | 187 | 264 | 708 | 802 | 23.3 |
| | 2014 | — | 167 | 256 | 653 | 795 | 21.0 |
| *Targeted subsidy programs* | | | | | | | |
| Kenya | 2011 | 15 | 61 | 57 | 1072 | 356 | 17.2 |
| | 2012 | — | 61 | 68 | 894 | 386 | 15.7 |
| | 2013 | — | 72 | 81 | 896 | 444 | 16.3 |
| | 2014 | — | 89 | 112 | 796 | 479 | 18.6 |
| Malawi | 2011 | 127 | 179 | 149 | 1200 | 345 | 52.0 |
| | 2012 | 151 | 116 | 177 | 654 | 355 | 32.7 |
| | 2013 | 207 | 185 | 213 | 868 | 350 | 52.9 |
| | 2014 | 168 | 183 | 208 | 879 | 352 | 51.9 |
| Tanzania | 2011 | 94 | 134 | 110 | 1223 | 349 | 38.4 |
| | 2012 | 76 | 104 | 126 | 828 | 326 | 32.0 |
| | 2013 | — | 104 | 105 | 989 | 338 | 30.9 |
| | 2014 | — | 92 | 112 | 829 | 332 | 27.9 |

*(continued next page)*

145

# Table 3.2 (continued)

| Country | Year | ISP cost (US$, millions) Official source | ISP cost (US$, millions) Computed using secondary data (B) | Program fertilizer distributed (MT) (C) | Program cost per MT of program fertilizer distributed (US$/MT) [B/C] (D) | Public agricultural spending (US$, millions) (E) | ISP cost as % share of public agricultural spending [=(B/E)*100] (F) |
|---|---|---|---|---|---|---|---|
| Zambia | 2011 | 184 | 239 | 182 | 1010 | 613 | 30.1 |
| | 2012 | 166 | 164 | 184 | 902 | 325 | 50.6 |
| | 2013 | 113 | 173 | 188 | 601 | 376 | 45.9 |
| | 2014 | — | 180 | 208 | 865 | 407 | 44.2 |
| *Ethiopia's program (officially not a "subsidy")* | | | | | | | |
| | 2011 | — | 55 | 551 | 100 | 530 | 10.4 |
| | 2012 | — | 54 | 633 | 86 | 771 | 7.0 |
| | 2013 | — | 38 | 449 | 84 | 850 | 4.5 |
| | 2014 | — | 43 | 597 | 73 | 937 | 4.6 |

*Sources:* Official data are from government sources. Ghana: Ministry of Food and Agriculture, http://mofa.gov.gh; Malawi: NEPAD; Tanzania: World Bank appraisal of the Accelerated Food Security Program; Mali: Ricker-Gilbert et al. 2013; Malawi and Zambia: FAO, MAFAP database; Nigeria: Liverpool-Tasie and Takeshima 2015. Quantities of subsidized fertilizer are obtained from NEPAD for all countries except Ethiopia, Mali, Malawi, and Zambia. Other estimates are from Rashid et al. 2013.

*Note:* Computed costs are weighted average of commercial and fertilizer prices by amount of subsidized fertilizer in each country, and do not include administrative and other programmatic costs (such as import commissions). Prices for all countries except Ethiopia are obtained from the International Fertilizer Development Center. ISP = input subsidy program; — = not available.

Politically influential rural elites benefitted from input subsidy programs and lobbied forcefully for their reemergence when the environment for their reintroduction was more favorable (Bates 1987; van de Walle 2001). Hence, the seeds of strong local support for ISPs were most likely in the policy soil throughout the past several decades but were largely dormant during the structural adjustment period.

Starting around 2000, many African governments experienced a relaxation of the constraints on public budgets associated with the highly indebted poor countries (HIPC) debt forgiveness programs and a shift in international donor support to budget support. With the autonomy afforded governments by the relaxation of public budget constraints, the desire to reinstitute politically popular but expensive programs such as ISPs was revived.

A third factor encouraging the return to ISPs was the emergence of multiparty political systems in Africa starting in the early 2000s. Political parties often sought to outdo one another in terms of the support promised to constituents (Levy 2005), and ISPs were one of the promises that leaders often made (as in Malawi, Nigeria, and Zambia) to garner the rural vote.

The watershed event heralding the reemergence of ISPs in Africa was the "Malawi miracle." Initial but somewhat superficial assessments reported how Malawi's program had turned the country from a food basket case into a grain exporter and dramatically reduced rural poverty rates. While more recent analyses have shown the Malawi program's successes to be debatable in some respects and factually incorrect in others,[11] the Malawi case had an important "primacy effect" on policy discourse on the continent, convincing numerous governments to undertake similar targeted input subsidy programs. By 2010, at least nine other countries accounting for over 60 percent of Sub-Saharan Africa's population[12] had re-instituted input subsidy programs.

The term *smart subsidy* allowed politicians and supporters to argue that even though the prior track record of ISPs in Africa was quite dismal, it was possible to redesign the programs in ways that overcame prior political interference and implementation problems, and to learn from experience so as to increase the benefits of ISPs going forward. Morris et al. (2007) and the World Bank (2008) identified specific criteria for smart subsidy programs to guide African governments. The most important of these criteria were that they (a) promote the development of the private sector; (b) target farmers who were not using fertilizer but who could find it profitable to do so; (c) are one part of a wider strategy that includes complementary inputs and strengthening of markets; (d) promote competition and cost reductions by reducing barriers to entry; and (e) have a clear exit strategy. While these are clearly useful criteria to guide the design of subsidy programs, in hindsight few questions were raised as to how these criteria could be implemented in practice and whether sufficient change had been instituted on the ground to justify expectations that well-known past implementation problems could now be overcome.

The final major factor contributing to the reemergence of ISPs in Africa was the global food price crisis in 2007 and 2008. During this time, panic over the availability of food supplies on world markets convinced many analysts and African leaders to support ISPs to promote national food self-sufficiency. And finally, in response to these concerns, the World Bank also started to support and even finance several countries' ISPs—including those of Ethiopia, Tanzania, Zambia, and Malawi—either directly or through budget support provided to ministries of finance.

Since 2010, other factors contributing to the staying power of ISPs have emerged. A recent study addresses a longstanding concern (only anecdotally addressed) that incumbent political parties are able to use ISPs to their benefit (such as to finance their political campaigns) by granting import licenses to particular fertilizer companies in exchange for receiving funds from overstating the cost of imports (Bigsten and Shimeles 2007).[13] Bigsten and Shimeles (2007) find an inverse correlation between government effectiveness and the gap between world fertilizer prices and retail prices in the country. The study suggests another important incentive that incumbent political parties may have to continue large-scale ISPs. Several institutional recipients of development assistance funds, while not officially supporting ISPs, have also promoted them by offering technical support to African governments in the design and implementation of ISPs.

## Main Findings of Recent Research: What Is the Evidence on the Crucial Issues of ISPs?

Most of the divergent findings in the analysis of fertilizer subsidy programs are due to (a) differing assumptions about crop response rates to fertilizer use, (b) the contribution of subsidy programs to total fertilizer use after accounting for diversion of program fertilizer and crowding out of commercial fertilizer demand, and (c) the strength of multimarket effects on food prices and employment.[14] Fortunately, many studies have been carried out in recent years, and the weight of the evidence has coalesced around some particular findings on crucial questions that most can agree on. The annexes present a more granular and comprehensive discussion of lower-level issues summarized in box 3.3.

### Significant Effects on Food Production
Large-scale input subsidy programs have tended to raise beneficiary households' crop yields and production levels, at least in the year that they receive the subsidy. However, the production effects of subsidy programs tend to be smaller than originally thought because of low crop yield responses to fertilizer on most

**BOX 3.3**

# Summary of Evidence of Targeting and Impacts

Annex 3B has the full exposition of evidence of targeting and the impacts, which are summarized here.

## Targeting

- *Targeting by gender of the household head.* Male- and female-headed households are equally likely to participate in ISPs and receive the same quantity of inputs on average. ISPs generally fail to meet the criterion of favoring female-headed households.

- *Targeting by landholding size.* Households with more land are more likely to receive program inputs or receive a larger quantity of such inputs on average. In Zambia, for instance, the lowest landholding quintile captured only 6 percent of the subsidies, while the highest quintile captured 40 percent (figure B3.3.1). While participation in ISPs is generally higher among households with more land, the extent to which this is the case varies considerably across countries (figure B3.3.2). Households with more land are often both more likely to receive inputs from the programs and receive larger quantities, on average, upon participating. This exacerbates crowding out of commercial input demand by the programs, reduces impacts on total fertilizer use (and hence incremental crop production), and attenuates poverty reduction effects.

**Figure B3.3.1** Share of Subsidized Fertilizer Acquired in ZFISP by Landholding Quintile

**Figure B3.3.2** Share of Households Particpating in MFISP and ZFISP by Landholding Quintile

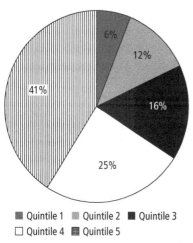

Quintile 1  Quintile 2  Quintile 3
Quintile 4  Quintile 5

*Source:* Jayne et al. 2016.
*Note:* ZFISP = Zambia Farmer Input Support Program.

MFISP  ZFISP

*Source:* Jayne et al. 2016.
*Note:* MFISP = Malawi Farm Input Subsidy Program; ZFISP = Zambia Farmer Input Support Program.

*(continued next page)*

## Box 3.3 (continued)

- *Targeting by assets, wealth, or poverty.* A higher level of farm assets is associated with receiving more ISP fertilizer and seed, but these estimated effects are not statistically significant after controlling for time-constant farmer characteristics. Differences in methodology and the definitions of assets, wealth, or poverty measures likely underlie many of the varying results.

- *Targeting and political factors.* The empirical record shows which groups of voters—core supporters of the incumbent party, swing voters, or core supporters of the opposition—are actually targeted. Overall, there is mounting empirical evidence of the politicization of ISPs in Sub-Saharan Africa, but the nature of the politicization varies across countries as well as within countries over time. The political economy of input subsidies is discussed in more detail in chapter 5 of this volume.

- *Targeting, social capital, and elite capture.* Social capital factors also lead to "elite capture" of ISP benefits. Where this issue has been investigated empirically, there is evidence that social capital factors influence access to subsidized inputs.

## Household-Level Effects of ISPs

- *Fertilizer and improved seed use.* Although a few instances of crowding in exist, most ISPs crowd out commercial demand for subsidized inputs. That is, an additional ton of fertilizer (improved seed) distributed through input subsidy programs raises total fertilizer (improved seed) use, but by less than 1 ton. More recently, crowding out of commercial fertilizer sales may have been substantially underestimated due to fertilizer that has been diverted from subsidy program channels into what can be mistaken for commercial sales. Diverting program fertilizer has important distributional effects, with program implementers receiving a major portion of the program benefits rather than farmers. But there have yet to be any comprehensive studies of the extent to which ISPs encourage or deter private sector investment in input distribution.

- *Crop yields.* ISPs do raise maize yields. But crowding out and late delivery of ISP inputs are likely attenuating these effects, as are poor soil quality and the minimal use of complementary practices to raise crop yield response to fertilizer.

- *Crop production.* ISPs have had modest, positive, ceteris paribus effects on household-level maize production in all countries where this issue has been examined (Kenya, Malawi, and Zambia). In general, ISPs have modest, positive effects on maize production and on net crop income for some segments of the population. But the magnitudes of these effects vary at different points in the distribution of maize production.

- *Food security and nutrition.* Little research has been conducted on this topic.

- *Incomes, assets, and poverty.* ISPs have the potential to raise incomes and reduce poverty severity at the household level but are less likely to decrease the probability that households fall below the poverty line.[a]

*(continued next page)*

## Box 3.3 (continued)

- *Soil fertility management practices, fallow land, and forests.* ISPs can alter incentives for various soil fertility and land management practices, but much remains to be learned about how ISPs affect the adoption of crops and inputs beyond those being promoted. To the extent that the ISPs encourage monocropping or otherwise "crowd out" good soil management practices—as some studies suggest—they exacerbate one of the fundamental causes of the low fertilizer use.

- *Dynamic or enduring effects of ISPs on farm households.* Depending on the outcome variable and context, ISPs may or may not have lasting positive effects on farm households beyond the year of receipt.

### Market and General Equilibrium Effects

- *Aggregate fertilizer use.* Most ISPs partially crowd out demand for commercial fertilizer. However, a substantial share (roughly one third in Malawi and Zambia) of fertilizer intended for ISPs is diverted by program implementers before reaching intended beneficiaries and resold as commercial fertilizer at or near commercial prices. Although ISPs raise total fertilizer use, there are major inefficiencies and diversions by program implementers, representing another form of elite capture of ISP benefits.

- *Aggregate crop production and food self-sufficiency.* The only studies that directly estimate these effects have been conducted for Malawi and take either a partial equilibrium or computable general equilibrium (CGE) modeling approach. They suggest increases in national maize production as a result of the Malawi Farm Input Subsidy Program (MFISP) of 9–23 percent (with even larger percentage increases among targeted households) and increases in net maize exports of 132–188 percent.

- *Food prices.* In general, ISPs reduce food prices—but by substantively small magnitudes.

- *Agricultural labor wage rates and supply/demand.* ISPs could further benefit poor nonbeneficiary households, which often engage in agricultural wage labor, if the programs increase demand for such labor and therefore put upward pressure on agricultural wages.

- *Incomes and poverty.* ISPs could reduce the national poverty rate and, more specifically, notoriously stubborn rural poverty rates. That said, there is little empirical evidence to examine these relationships.

- *Voting patterns and election results.* The conventional wisdom is that scaling back of ISPs is politically damaging, whereas establishing or scaling up ISPs is politically beneficial. But does the empirical record support these claims? The answer depends on the context, both in the political dynamics and in the design and implementation of the ISP.

a. See Awotide et al. (2013) and Carter, Laajaj, and Yang (2014) for randomized controlled trial (RCT) estimates of income and poverty eff ects of a certifi ed rice seed voucher pilot program in Nigeria and the income effects of a government ISP pilot program in Mozambique, respectively. Unlike the studies for Kenya and Zambia, Awotide et al. (2013) find that participation in the seed voucher pilot program in Nigeria does reduce the probability of household income falling below the poverty line.

smallholder-managed fields and because of the tendency of subsidy programs to partially crowd out commercial fertilizer demand. Therefore, the national production response to subsidy programs, while significant, has typically been lower than expected.

### Fertilizer Use Inhibited by Diversion and "Crowding Out"

Recent subsidy programs, even those asserted to conform to smart subsidy criteria, have remained vulnerable to diversion and crowding out of commercial fertilizer demand. Subsidy programs often distribute fertilizer to beneficiaries who consistently purchased commercial fertilizer in the past, which can result in fewer purchases from commercial sources after being given several bags of subsidized or free fertilizer. The magnitude of "crowding out" of commercial fertilizer depends primarily on the characteristics of targeted beneficiary farmers. Crowding out tends to be smallest when beneficiaries have not purchased commercial fertilizer in the past and in areas where commercial fertilizer sales are low or nonexistent. Under such conditions, crowding in of commercial fertilizer purchases may even occur.

### Crop Response Rates of Smallholder Farmers Are Highly Variable and Usually Low

Production impacts of fertilizer subsidy programs tend to be lower than previously envisaged because a large proportion of smallholder farmers do not use fertilizer efficiently. Smallholder farmers tend to obtain marginal and average products of fertilizer that are substantially lower than those obtained from studies of researcher-managed trials and experiment stations. Well-designed extension and service delivery programs could enable farmers to use complementary inputs and management practices that raise their crop response rates to fertilizer application, raising the benefit-cost ratio of ISPs.

### Fertilizer Use in Much of Africa Is Low by International Standards but Not Necessarily Suboptimal

Because of the low efficiency of fertilizer use on the majority of smallholder farms—and based on prevailing input-output price ratios, which have stayed remarkably constant over the past several decades—fertilizer use does not appear to be clearly profitable for many farmers, especially in the semiarid areas with variable rainfall. While Africa is often compared unfavorably with Asia in terms of fertilizer use, high intensity of fertilizer use in areas experiencing their Green Revolutions were confined largely to irrigated areas or areas with significant potential for water control and where the risks of fertilizer use were relatively low but expected returns tended to be higher (Gautam 2015). Areas of dryland Asia also tend to have relatively low fertilizer use rates and application rates comparable to many drought-prone areas of Africa (Jayne and Rashid 2013).

## Relatively Small and Transitory Effects on the Incomes of Beneficiary Households

Recipient households tend to significantly increase their net farm incomes in the year in which they receive subsidized fertilizer, because they pay only a fraction of the cost of the fertilizer and because of the additional output obtained from the fertilizer. However, the lack of persistent yield response and crowding out are directly linked to the relatively small transitory effects of ISP participation on incomes and poverty.

## No Major Effect on Food Prices or Wage Rates

Fertilizer subsidy programs have either insignificant or modest but significant impacts on national maize prices. The factors explaining small food price effects vary by country. Sometimes, the production effect of subsidy programs can be quite large in a few years of the program, as in Malawi, but not large enough to totally displace national cereal imports, such that most of the country remains at import parity price levels both before and during the subsidy program period (Ricker-Gilbert et al. 2013). In other cases, the production effects of subsidy programs are not large enough to even have major effects on local food markets or rural wage rates.

## ISPs Produce Beneficiaries Who Lobby Forcefully for the Continuation of Programs Once Initiated

Evidence from countries where the distribution of subsidies has been documented indicates that most benefits go to farmers who are higher-income or larger landholders (see box 3.2 and table 3.3). There is also mounting statistical evidence that the geographic distribution of fertilizer subsidies reflects the influence of political and election-related motives.

## Limited Evidence That Fertilizer Subsidy Programs Kick-Start Dynamic Growth Processes

While only a few studies exist on the potential enduring effects of fertilizer subsidy programs, the evidence is mixed. Carter, Laajaj, and Yang (2014) find enduring production and income impacts for Mozambican farmers receiving a subsidy two years in a row, but the impacts seem to decay after two years. Another study shows little impact on fertilizer use or crop production even one year after Malawi farmers graduated from the subsidy program following three years of participation (Ricker-Gilbert and Jayne 2015). This question of whether

**Table 3.3** Benefits Are Low in Relation to Costs—and Go to Richer Farmers

| Country | Characteristics of recipient households acquiring subsidized fertilizer | Financial benefit-cost ratio | Economic benefit-cost ratio |
|---|---|---|---|
| Malawi | Households with larger landholding and asset wealth get more | 0.62 | 0.80 |
| Zambia | Households with more land get slightly more | 0.56 | 0.92 |
| Tanzania | Voucher recipients more likely to be nonpoor | n.a. | n.a. |
| Kenya | Households with higher landholding receive more subsidized fertilizer | 0.79 | 1.09 |
| Ghana | Asset wealth greater among beneficiaries than among nonbeneficiaries | n.a. | n.a. |
| Nigeria | Increase in landholding raises subsidized fertilizer received | n.a. | n.a. |

*Sources:* Chirwa and Dorward 2013; Jayne et al. 2015.
*Note:* The table presents summary evidence from farm and household studies on impacts. Ratios are estimated based on five-year estimated response rates. The ratios reported here use baseline calculations, making adjustments to average partial effect of 1 kg of subsidized fertilizer on total smallholder fertilizer use. n.a. = not applicable.

fertilizer subsidies can generate dynamic growth processes that put recipient farmers on a higher long-term income trajectory is an area in which more research is needed.

# Implications for the Design and Implementation of Smarter Subsidy Programs

*Smart subsidy programs* could be more than a slogan. The scope for improving subsidy program impacts could be substantial in the following areas. Assuming that African governments will continue to run ISPs for some time to come, evidence indicates that these programs can more effectively achieve their goals in the following ways:

- Target the subsidies to households that could use fertilizer profitably but could not afford to do so (or whose purchases are well below optimal levels) due to credit constraints.

- Involve the private sector to a greater degree than is currently done in most cases, as through the use of vouchers that are redeemable at any private retail store.

- Confront and tackle the problem of diversion of subsidy program fertilizer by authorities.

## Target Recipients More Effectively

Appropriate target criteria are difficult to define because they depend on program objectives, which tend to be variously articulated in Africa. Many African governments state their ISP objectives in vague and inconsistent terms, making it difficult to identify the extent to which beneficiaries conform to targeting criteria. Ex post assessments show that recipients of vouchers and fertilizers were generally "better off" initially than nonrecipients in terms of farm sizes, asset wealth, and political or social connections, suggesting that ISPs tend to be disproportionately targeted to, or captured by, the better-off members of rural communities. Relatedly, recipients also tend to have already been using fertilizer in prior years compared to nonrecipients, at least partially because they are able to afford it. Targeting areas where fertilizer use is low and yield response potential is sufficiently high (that is, where use is hindered primarily by credit constraints) will more likely contribute to increased fertilizer use and increased production and productivity. Programs that do not exclude households already purchasing commercial fertilizer or that operate in areas where commercial fertilizer use is already high tend to have a diminished positive impact.

## Targeted Versus Untargeted Universal Subsidy Programs?

Decentralized targeting systems have been considered attractive because they reduce the costs of targeting effectively by tapping into local knowledge. However, local political systems have their own political economy challenges, and it is not clear that programs relying on village-level targeting outcomes necessarily improve the distribution of recipients compared to universal subsidy programs through the market or what random allocations of vouchers would have yielded (Pan and Christiaensen 2012). Since many, if not most, studies assessing ISP targeting show regressive targeting *in practice*, it might be asked whether the benefits of ISPs based on targeting (as opposed to nontargeted allocations such as the universal subsidy programs, as in much of Asia) outweigh the significant costs involved in the process of determining recipients.

But universal subsidy programs also have major disadvantages. Past experiences across the world indicate that larger farmers disproportionately benefit from universal subsidies. And it is questionable whether many governments would find a truly universal, unrationed fertilizer subsidy program financially feasible (or desirable given the high opportunity cost and the probability that some portion of the fertilizer would end up in other countries).

## Minimizing "Crowding Out"

As noted in the section dealing with targeting, subsidies generally fail to effectively target poor farmers and farmers who are not already using fertilizer.

As a consequence, empirical analyses show significant displacement of commercial channels of distribution. To minimize the potential for "crowding out" of commercial fertilizer demand, one suggestion would be to avoid areas where the private sector is already highly active. Of course, this would imply focusing on areas of low private sector activity, but one must then consider *why* the private sector has not been active. If the reason is that low response rates render fertilizer use unprofitable at commercial prices, fertilizer subsidies are not a viable tool (at least in the long run) for reducing poverty or increasing production. In such a case, one of the alternative strategies discussed later (investments in technological development and extension) is probably more appropriate. If, by contrast, a high transfer cost is the factor driving down profitability, again, fertilizer subsidies are at best a short-term solution to a long-term problem, and again, an alternative strategy (investments to lower transfer costs) will probably be more effective.

Alternatively, a subsidy program could aim to employ the private sector distribution network, rather than supplant it. The most promising option using this approach is voucher-based ISPs, but this strategy has potential drawbacks as well. First, most pilot voucher programs also remain vulnerable to the problem of diversion (of vouchers instead of bags of fertilizer). Second, relying on the private sector *does* accompany the risk of leaving behind those underserved by the private sector for whatever reason. This brings us back to the question of *why* the private sector is not active in some places, and whether input subsidies are the best (or at least not the only important) strategy for long-term productivity growth.

## Transparency of ISP Costs and Diversion

Many ISPs in Africa seem to suffer from underreporting or hidden program costs. Some governments do not publish the fiscal costs of their ISPs. Others report the budgeted costs but not actual ex post expenditures, which are found to be substantially higher (Mason and Jayne 2013). On top of this is the related problem of potential diversion of public resources associated with fertilizer subsidy programs. Widespread anecdotal reports suggest that governments and fertilizer import companies may collude to overinvoice the cost of delivering fertilizer to designated supply points. Shimeles, Gurara, and Tessema (2015) examine the fertilizer retail-import price gap in 14 African countries between 2002 and 2013. The price differentials between the retail fertilizer price and the world market price are negatively correlated with measures of government effectiveness, suggesting that in environments with poor governance, these programs may be susceptible to this kind of overinvoicing and corruption. In such cases, costs to the treasury and farmer prices could both be driven up. Increased transparency regarding the program costs could go a long way toward reducing the risk of this problem.

## Absence of Complementary Public Sector Actions Reduces The Effectiveness of ISPs

In responding to incentives, farmers are likely to demand more fertilizer if obtaining a higher crop response to fertilizer enables them to use it more profitably. Doing so will require that farmers obtain higher response rates to fertilizer application, which will in turn require greater public investment in effective systems of agricultural research, development, and extension that emphasize bidirectional learning between farmers of varying resource constraints and agroecologies, extension workers, and researchers.

Variations in crop response to fertilizer application are primarily due to variation in soil quality and farmer management practices that affect soil quality and yield. Examples include timeliness of planting, row spacing, seed spacing, intercropping and crop rotations, water control, sufficient weeding, plot drainage, terracing in hilly terrains, and adoption of conservation farming practices such as planting basins, ripping, and mulching. Many of these practices and technologies are promising in some agroecologies and not in others. Some may also not be feasible for resource-constrained farmers, and must be adapted through bidirectional learning between farmers and researchers to fit the conditions of different types of farmers.

There is currently a lack of specific information on the profitability of the different soil-crop-fertilizer combinations that could be employed in most countries' diverse agroecologies and soil types. The lack of location-specific information on crop-fertilizer profitability and the various farmer management factors that can favorably influence response rates means that researchers and extension agents are not in an informed position to provide guidance to farmers about "best practices." Suboptimal farmer practices for soil fertility management increase yield risk, impede farmers' incentives to use fertilizer, and result in forgone agricultural output. Knowledge of soil characteristics and processes regulating nutrient availability is essential to raise productivity per unit of fertilizer.

## Try a Program of Soil Fertility Management

Therefore, the contribution of ISPs—and fertilizer use in general, even in the absence of ISPs—to sustainable growth could be much greater if the soil-related constraints on agricultural productivity were addressed through a broad program of soil fertility management. The general elements of such a program are as follows:

- *Public sector research and development programs* to identify region-specific best practices for amending soil conditions, given the great microvariability in agroecological conditions in each country.

- *Public agricultural extension programs* to disseminate improved technologies and cultivation practices, as well as provide learning opportunities between researchers and farmers to refine practices in light of farmers' experiences in their fields.

- *Input distribution systems* that make available a full range of products and services required by farmers. Input distribution systems for a wider set of soil-enhancing products, such as organic fertilizer, lime, and new lines of inorganic fertilizer (such as deep-placement, slow-release types), will be developed once there is proven effective demand for such products. The point is that commercial input distribution systems do not develop spontaneously; instead, they require public investments to generate effective demand among farmers for new inputs.

- *Ancillary public support services,* such as investments in port, rail, and road infrastructure to reduce costs of delivering fertilizer to rural areas and goods to markets; rural electrification;[15] and small-scale irrigation schemes.

To move from general thrusts to concrete steps, consider the following proposals:

- *Step 1. Provide support to existing research institutions* in countries' diverse agroecologies and regions to develop best practices for crop and soil management in different landscape conditions. Site-specific recommendations on practices require a better understanding of the factors that might constrain productivity. Soil maps need to be updated to reflect soil functional properties (rather than soil taxonomic class) as well as more spatial detail on the variation of these functional soil properties. Affordable techniques are available for wide-scale soil testing and analyses. Building the capacity to conduct soil testing services in rural Africa would provide an important foundation to provide farmers with improved knowledge on how to manage soils and improve returns from farming.

- *Step 2. Conduct extensive testing of the recommended soil management practices* on farmers' fields to allow local research institutes to determine crop response to the various inputs. This would support the formulation of recommended input packages to raise farmers' expected returns to investment. Use of locally available (organic) resources could be considered as part of the solution. This will involve collecting, collating, and analyzing existing secondary and primary data and using appropriate crop and soil fertility models.[16] Local extension services could provide soil management recommendations—such as implementing nutrient management options with other soil amendments for the crops, and using improved varieties, aiming to improve the agronomic efficiencies of the fertilizer use—that would in turn raise demand for fertilizer.

- *Step 3. Conduct monitoring and evaluation of yields* on the fields of farmers who have adopted the recommended practice, allowing for gradual development toward a "best fit" solution that reflects the farmer's socioeconomic situation. Improved information and communications technology (ICT) tools can be used for data collection and enhance collaboration with the research community.

- *Step 4. Implement fertilizer quality regulations to protect farmers.* Ongoing efforts to identify how to reduce potential problems associated with fertilizer quality and product adulteration should be encouraged. For example, West African governments could identify areas that need strengthening in terms of their capacity to adapt the regional regulatory framework signed by the Economic Community of West African States (ECOWAS) in 2012. This will help ensure that farmers access good quality fertilizers with correctly specified nutrient content having implications for crop response rates.

- *Step 5. Review policies affecting fertilizer use and response rates.* Specific government policies may have unintended adverse consequences on governments' efforts to promote fertilizer use. In some countries, fertilizer-importing companies pay multiple fees from different regulatory bodies involved in fertilizer control at the clearing stage. In Tanzania, for example, this includes the Tanzania Fertilizer Regulatory Authority (TFRA), the Weight and Measures Authority, the Radiation Commission and Chief Government Chemist, and the Tanzania Bureau of Standards. As a result, there are multiple fees, which are inevitably passed to farmers through higher prices.

## Other Complementary Measures Are Also Needed

Beyond all these measures to address the soil fertility and crop response rates, perhaps even more important is for the public sector to use policies and investments to make fertilizer use more profitable for farmers and thereby raise effective commercial demand. This would involve identifying how to streamline costs and reduce risks in fertilizer supply chains to lower the price of fertilizer at the farmgate (Jayne et al. 2003). It would also involve supporting reliable and competitive output markets through policies that promote new investment and competition in agri-food value chains (World Bank 2007). And it would involve using research, extension, and education services to promote farmer training and education programs to improve fertilizer efficiency in the context of a more comprehensive soil fertility management program (Dreschel et al. 2001; Tittonell and Giller 2013). Much of the investment comes from the private sector, but public policy can play an important role by removing regulatory barriers and making appropriate investments.

## Annex 3A: Overviews of Specific Input Subsidy Programs in Africa

This annex provides brief overviews of the major government ISPs in Sub-Saharan Africa: Ethiopia, Ghana, Kenya, Malawi, Nigeria, Tanzania, and Zambia. We focus on these countries because each has been the subject of multiple econometric- or simulation-based studies of de facto program targeting or impacts—results that are synthesized in the next section. There are several other government ISPs in Sub-Saharan Africa, including in Burkina Faso, Burundi, Mali, Rwanda, and Senegal. These programs are not covered here because there have been few, if any, analyses of the programs' targeting or impacts.[17] These are major knowledge gaps in need of future research.

We begin with Malawi, which in 1998 was the first country to explicitly implement a major fertilizer subsidy program after the structural adjustment period of the 1980s to mid-1990s.[18] Malawi continues to garner the most attention of all countries implementing ISPs, most likely due to the media attention that it garnered after a front-page New York Times article in 2007 (Dugger 2007). Nigeria began subsidizing fertilizer in 1999 and Zambia established its new Fertilizer Support Program in 2002. After pledges were made at the 2006 Africa Fertilizer Summit, Kenya joined the field in 2007, followed soon after by Ghana, Ethiopia, and Tanzania in 2008 (Druilhe and Barreiro-Hurlé 2012; Jayne and Rashid 2013).[19]

## Ethiopia

Prior to the 1990s the main social safety net in Ethiopia was international food aid. But food aid was understood to be a weak development strategy that had little or no impact on the underlying causes of Ethiopia's poorly functioning food markets, including high transfer costs associated with a lack of market information, infrastructural investment, and storage capacity (Minten, Stifel, and Tamru 2014). Since the 1990s (and earlier under central planning), fertilizer in Ethiopia has been distributed almost exclusively by government agencies. Early on, this was the Agricultural Input Supplies Corporation (AISCO), later called the Agricultural Input Supplies Enterprise (AISE). AISE-led marketing was generally considered inefficient, however, so in 1992 the New Marketing System (NMS) was an effort to introduce the private sector (Rashid et al. 2013). Private companies were slower to respond than policy makers expected and by the late 1990s just four fertilizer companies were active market participants. The next evolution was the growth of companies owned by regional governments and supplying to AISE, and by the early 2000s nongovernment imports had reduced to zero (Rashid et al. 2013). In the mid-2000s farmer organizations became more involved with distribution and allocation. By 2008 roughly 75 percent of all fertilizer used moved through this market. The system was rife with inefficiencies, though, and in recent years government holding companies have been crowded out of the market. All imports come directly through AISE and what is now called the Growth and Transformation Program (GTP) (Rashid et al. 2013).

The amount of fertilizer to be distributed each year is determined through a consultative process between development agents (extension workers) and policy makers at GTP based on planned planting and centrally decided production targets. During the 2000s, fertilizer use increased dramatically, having been applied to 24 percent of all cereal crops in 2011, up from 16 percent in 2004 (Rashid et al. 2013). Total fertilizer use has similarly increased during that time. Throughout the 1970s, for example, fertilizer use was essentially nil, but 550,000 tons were applied in 2010 and 2011 (the most recent data available, figure 3A.1). In addition to subsidizing prices, much of the Ethiopian efforts attempted to address cost buildups in the value chain related to, for example, an inadequate road system. Planned openings of two major breweries were expected to increase fertilizer demand (Rashid et al. 2013), but delays resulted in official openings being pushed to January 2015. It is not possible to know if this has indeed driven input demand.[20] In a country of more than 100 million, it is unlikely that these relatively fortunate smallholders will have much effect at the national level.

**Figure 3A.1** Fertilizer Use in Ethiopia, 2003–12

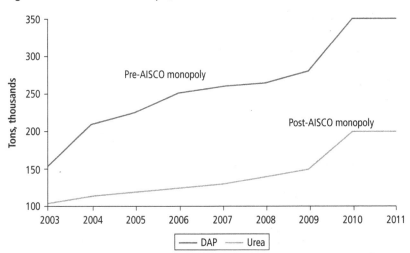

*Source:* Jayne et al. 2016.
*Note:* AISCO = Agricultural Input Supplies Corporation; DAP = diammonium phosphate.

The direct costs of running Ethiopia's subsidy plan average roughly US$40 million. But there are frequent miscalculations made on how much is imported by the government each year. Rashid et al. (2013) reckon the carryover and loss costs have added an additional US$30 million in recent years.

A second Ethiopian safety net program (which is not officially a subsidy, though public sector agencies are involved in input handling and distribution) comes under the umbrella program called the Ethiopia Food Security Program (EFSP). The first component of the EFSP is the Productive Safety Net Program (PSNP), also designed to replace food aid as the main social safety net. The PSNP provides direct support in the form of work-for-food or work-for-pay on public work projects, thus simultaneously addressing social welfare and preexisting market constraints (for example, infrastructure building). Work activities are usually planned to occur from January to June to avoid conflicting with the agricultural season (Hoddinott et al. 2012; Rashid et al. 2013). Some recipients (about 15 percent) receive direct cash transfers if they are deemed very poor, but unable to supply labor (Gilligan, Hoddinott, and Taffesse 2009; Rashid et al. 2013). Work-for-food recipients receive 3 kg of cereal per day. Cash transfers were initially Br 6 per day, which increased with inflation to Br 8 per day in 2008 and Br 10 (roughly US$0.75 per day) in 2010 (Hoddinott et al. 2012).

The second component of the EFSP was first named the Other Food Security Program (OFSP), then revised and renamed the Household Asset Building Program (collectively OFSP/HABP) in 2009. OFSP/HABP activities are meant to include access to regular outreach from extension agents on soil and water conservation, irrigation, and even beekeeping, as well as access to other "modern inputs" including fertilizer and improved seed varieties (Gilligan, Hoddinott, and Taffesse 2009; Hoddinott et al. 2012). While the PSNP was designed as a social safety net, the OFSP/HABP is intended to aid in the growth of smallholders' asset wealth and decrease or eliminate household dependence on government assistance. Early challenges were faced due to a lack of extension agents (Hoddinott et al. 2012). Therefore, after the 2009 reforms, each kebele (a subdivision of woredas, or wards) receiving assistance was assigned three resident development agents specializing in crops, livestock, and natural resource management. Anecdotal evidence from farmer interviews suggests this has improved the situation, but it is also noted that the primary assistance remains highly focused on crops. Partly due to EFSP activities, it has also been noted that the current level of infrastructure development is unprecedented (Minten, Stifel, and Tamru 2014). This too has theoretically improved access to fertilizers, but these effects, to our knowledge, have not been rigorously quantified. That said, Rashid et al. (2013) have noted that the fertilizer value chain in Ethiopia is competitive relative to its neighbors, with fertilizer prices 12–35 percent lower than in neighboring Kenya, Uganda, Rwanda, and Tanzania.

Targeting for the EFSP is done at the administrative level. Initially, 282 woredas considered rural, poor, and food insecure were targeted. The PSNP is said to have delivered support to more than 7 million Ethiopians in 2007, for example (Hoddinott et al. 2012). That said, the definition of the term *poor* and indeed the household targeting criteria have been criticized as unclear, and the characteristics of recipients (gender, wealth, political affiliation, and so on) varies widely across woredas (Rashid et al. 2013).

## Ghana

Ghana's history of subsidizing inputs dates back to the 1970s, where, like many other countries, early versions were characterized by government monopolies for importation and distribution. The fertilizer subsidy rate peaked at 65 percent in the early 1980s. Recognizing that the early program was fiscally unsound and detrimental to Ghana's macroeconomy, and with urging from the World Bank and other donors, the parastatal-led subsidies were phased out during the late 1980s and removed altogether by 1990 (Jebuni and Seini 1992; Resnick and Mather 2015). Thereafter the entire fertilizer supply chain has been managed by the private sector (Resnick and Mather 2015).[21]

Fertilizer subsidies for the country's main cash crop, cocoa, were reintroduced in 2003 and for food crops in 2008. The latter was called the Ghana Fertilizer Subsidy Program (GFSP), and still is, though in 2012 the program expanded to include seed inputs for maize, rice, and soybeans (Resnick and Mather 2015). The GFSP was intended as a temporary program but it has become a perennial (and seemingly permanent) part of Ghana's agricultural budget. The reinvigorated subsidy program came about for several reasons, including encouragement from the private sector, fertilizer and food price increases, political popularity and imminent elections in 2008, and the perception that Ghana faced challenging soil infertility problems and below-average fertilizer use (even among African nations) (Banful 2009; Resnick and Mather 2015).

Unlike Ghana's earlier programs and contemporary programs in other countries, the GFSP was heavily reliant on the private sector. Initially, the government's role was limited to allocating benefits to targeted farmers using paper vouchers. According to several structured interviews summarized by Resnick and Mather (2015), the heavy role for the private sector was motivated by the government's desire to maintain its reputation as business-friendly. Furthermore, donors (including the World Bank) had recently increased funding for Ghana's agricultural budget and strongly advocated for private sector inclusion.

In 2010 still more responsibility was shifted to the private sector as vouchers were abandoned in favor of a "waybill" design. This required approved farmers to acquire subsidized fertilizer from registered agents. GFSP agents were then to submit receipts to government for approval, shifting the bulk of administrative responsibility to the private sector. This revision also loosened constraints on the time of extension agents, many of whom complained that issuing and monitoring vouchers hindered their ability to carry out their intended duties (Resnick and Mather 2015).

In the seven years since the program's beginning, motivation for the GFSP has frequently shifted from increasing productivity as an urgent response to price spikes to providing a social safety net for the poor, to demonstrating the benefits of fertilizer to farmers (Resnick and Mather 2015). Correspondingly, the intended group of beneficiaries has been a moving target. Under the initial voucher system only smallholder food crop producers were intended to receive the subsidy. Banful (2009) and others, however, found that this criteria was often implemented poorly—substantial quantities were being distributed to larger farms or smuggled out of the country and resold. Yawson et al. (2010) also report overwhelming dissatisfaction with the timing of fertilizer availability during the period of the voucher system. In 2010, with the shift to waybill-based distribution, targets were essentially abandoned and, while the total quantity subsidized fertilizer was limited, food crop producers of any size were eligible to receive subsidized prices. In 2013, the target shifted back to smallholders, but with geographic and crop priority going to maize, rice, sorghum, and millet farmers in the savannah. Outgrower schemes and female farmers were also given priority (Resnick and Mather 2015).

Despite (or perhaps because of) many attempts to revise the GFSP, the program has faced considerable criticism. This includes a lack of transparency, poor monitoring and evaluation, delayed payments to suppliers, the aforementioned shifting and sometimes unclear objectives, and regular uncertainty on GFSP's design and rollout. In some years GFSP details have not been announced until very near the beginning of the planting season (Resnick and Mather 2015). Partly for these reasons, but most important because the government lacked funding to pay importers, the GFSP was suspended for the 2014 season. The program was renewed in 2015, but in light of past frustrations at least two of the country's major private importers declined participation (Resnick and Mather 2015). Notably, these are the same companies that advocated for instituting the GFSP less than a decade earlier.

The program supplies four types of fertilizer: NPK (15:15:15), NPK (23:10:05), urea (46:0:0), and ammonium sulfate (21:0:0, plus 24 percent sulfur) (Yawson et al. 2010). The goal during the first two years of the program was to keep subsidized prices consistently at 50 percent of the market price (Yawson et al. 2010). By best estimates, initial subsidies were 30 percent of the fertilizer's market value on average (Wanzala-Mlobela, Fuentes, and Mkumbwa 2013). This steadily increased until 2012 when the peak subsidy rate was 47 percent on average, then declined to 26 percent and 21 percent in 2013 and 2015, respectively. Similarly, the quantity of subsidized fertilizer has climbed steadily from the initial level of 43,000 MT to roughly 170,000 MT on average from 2011 to 2013. After the 2014 hiatus, announced plans were to distribute 180,000 MT in 2015. GFSP share of Ghana's agricultural budget naturally followed suit, increasing from 20 percent to more than 50 percent between 2008 and 2012. When the subsidy rate declined in 2013, the GFSP share of the agricultural budget decreased back to roughly 20 percent, where it is expected to remain in 2015.

In 2008 the government budgeted about US$11 million to the GFSP, but exceeded this target by more than US$3 million. The following year more than US$26 million was allocated and was expected to absorb the program's debt from the previous year. Total spending on the GFSP in 2015 (for fertilizer and seed) is expected to be roughly equivalent to US$23.5 million, which is less than 70 percent of peak spending in 2013 (Resnick and Mather 2015, and government documents referenced therein; Wanzala-Mlobela, Fuentes, and Mkumbwa 2013).

On the effectiveness of fertilizer use, survey data collected in 2012 in various Ghanaian production zones do show noteworthy differences in yield, particularly when fertilizer use is coupled with hybrid seed planting (table 3A.1; Ragassa, Chapoto, and Kolavalli 2014). On average, local maize seed varieties on fertilized fields are about 70 percent more productive than when fertilizer is *not* used. Moreover, fertilized fields planted with hybrid seeds are an additional 60 percent more productive per unit of land than fertilized fields using local varieties. Altogether, based on these data, fields with fertilized hybrid maize seeds are about 175 percent more productive than unfertilized fields using local seed (at least in terms of per unit of land). Some important caveats to these results are that these average comparisons mask a wide variety in the differences in fertilizer use efficiency across regions (and almost certainly across farms within regions); these results are naïve and potentially subject to some of the biases we've outlined and even the most productive group found in these results (hybrid seed and fertilizer using farmers in the Sudanese Sahel) are obtaining yields (about 2.4 MT per ha) that would be considered low by most standards.

**Table 3A.1** Maize Yields by Farming Systems in Ghana, 2012

| Maize system | Transition | Guinea savannah | Sudan savannah |
| --- | --- | --- | --- |
| Local, no fertilizer | 756 | 745 | 547 |
| Fertilized local | 1,208 | 914 | 1,339 |
| Fertilized hybrid | 1,819 | 1,444 | 2,374 |

*Source:* Adapted from Ragassa, Chapoto, and Kolavalli 2014.

# Kenya

Kenya has had two major ISPs since structural adjustment—the National Accelerated Agricultural Inputs Access Program (NAAIAP), which is targeted, and the National Cereals and Produce Board (NCPB), which is universal. We describe each of these.

## National Accelerated Agricultural Inputs Access Program, 2007/08–2013/14

The Kenyan government initiated NAAIAP in the 2007/08 agricultural year, shortly after the 2006 Africa Fertilizer Summit and in the midst of the 2007–08 food, fuel, and fertilizer price crisis. The program ran through 2013/14, after which county-level governments assumed responsibility for ISPs in Kenya. NAAIAP's main goal was "to improve farm input (fertilizer and seeds) access and affordability of smallholder farmers to enhance food security/availability at the household level and generate income from the sale of surplus produce" (KMOA 2007, 7). Additional objectives included raising smallholders' productivity and production, and reducing poverty (KMOA 2007). The ISP portion of NAAIAP, called Kilimo Plus, provided targeted beneficiaries with a voucher redeemable at accredited agro-dealers' shops for 100 kg of fertilizer (50 kg each of basal and top dressing) and 10 kg of improved maize seed.[22] The inputs were fully subsidized; no farmer top-up payment or contribution was required.

The NAAIAP aimed to target "resource-poor" farmers who were unable to afford inputs at market prices, who grew maize, had 1–2.5 acres of land, and who were "vulnerable members of society," with female-headed households given priority (KMOA 2007, 19). Beneficiaries were selected by stakeholder forums, which included farmers, other community members, and representatives from the Ministry of Agriculture, Livestock, and Fisheries (KMOA 2007). The NAAIAP was not implemented in all districts; rather, districts were selected based on their suitability for maize production and poverty level. Over the life of the program, NAAIAP was implemented in 149 districts (of more than 200 districts in Kenya at the time) (KMOA 2013). The scale of NAAIAP varied over time, and the program peaked in 2009/10 at 176,000 intended beneficiaries or about 5 percent of Kenyan smallholder households. See table 3A.2 for a summary of the number of beneficiaries and approximate voucher values from 2007/08 through 2011/12.[23]

## National Cereals and Produce Board Fertilizer Subsidy Program, 2001–Present

The National Cereals and Produce Board (NCPB) is a crop marketing board that has existed since the colonial era; since 2001, it has also distributed subsidized fertilizer to Kenyan farmers. During the program's first seven years, the quantities distributed were small (averaging just 7,625 MT per year). In 2008/09 the program was scaled up dramatically to 52,608 MT (see table 3A.3). The Kenyan government justified this increase, as well as the establishment of NAAIAP, as temporary responses to the 2007–08 price crisis as well as to the post-2007 election violence and associated poor harvest (Ariga and Jayne 2011; Mather and Jayne 2015). According to the NCPB, its vision for the subsidy program is to "take ... inputs closer to the farmer," "provide [a] one-stop point for the farmer's needs," "to supply the farmer with the right quality at the right time and at competitive prices," and to enable the farmer to buy inputs at the same time that s/he sells maize to the NCPB to cut down on transport and transactions costs (NCPB 2013, 6).

NCPB subsidized fertilizer is sold at panterritorial prices at NCPB depots throughout the country. The program is universal in that (in theory) any farmer can access it. The quantity available to a given farmer is determined roughly based on farm size. Subsidy rates have varied but are typically in the range of 30 percent (Jayne et al. 2013).

**Table 3A.2** Key Features of the Kenya National Accelerated Agricultural Inputs Access Program, 2007/08–2011/12

|  | 2007/08 | 2008/09 | 2009/10 | 2010/11 | 2011/12 | Total |
|---|---|---|---|---|---|---|
| Total number of beneficiaries | 36,000 | 92,876 | 175,973 | 125,883 | 63,737 | 494,469 |
| Number of districts covered | 40 | 70 | 131 | 95 | 63 | 149 |
| Voucher value (US$) | 103.67 | 93.95 | 76.03 | 81.25 | 95.69 | — |

*Source:* KMOA 2013.
*Note:* — = not available.

**Table 3A.3** Quantities of Subsidized Fertilizer Distributed through Kenya's National Cereals and Produce Board, 2001/02–2011/12

| Year | MT of subsidized fertilizer distributed |
|---|---|
| 2001/02 | 1,403 |
| 2002/03 | 2,207 |
| 2003/04 | 6,827 |
| 2004/05 | 11,131 |
| 2005/06 | 6,167 |
| 2006/07 | 16,137 |
| 2007/08 | 9,506 |
| 2008/09 | 52,608 |
| 2009/10 | 8,388 |
| 2010/11 | 45,264 |
| 2011/12 | 82,023 |

*Source:* NCPB 2013.
*Note:* More recent data not publicly available.

## Malawi

### Starter Pack, 1998/99–1999/2000

Malawi's initial ISP in the wake of structural adjustment was the Starter Pack program. In place during the 1998/99 and 1999/2000 agricultural seasons, the Starter Pack grew out of the recommendations of the Malawi Maize Productivity Task Force, which had been established to explore policy options for addressing the country's chronic food shortages (Harrigan 2008). The task force identified declining soil fertility and maize productivity as two major contributors to the food shortage problem. The Starter Pack entitled all Malawi smallholder farm households to 15 kg of inorganic fertilizer, 2 kg of hybrid maize seed, and 1 kg of legume seed for free. The maize inputs were sufficient to plant about 0.1 ha of maize (Druilhe and Barreiro-Hurlé 2012; Harrigan 2008). The initial objectives of the program were to raise agricultural productivity by introducing farmers to "best bet" technologies in a risk-free way, to kick-start agricultural development, and to achieve national food self-sufficiency (Harrigan 2008; Levy 2005), not social protection (Dorward and Chirwa 2011).

National maize production increased markedly in Malawi in the years of the Starter Pack (likely due in part, but not entirely, to the program), but the program was unpopular with donors, who highlighted its high fiscal cost, negative effects on the development of private sector input markets, and late delivery, among other challenges (Harrigan 2008). Donor opposition, including pressure from the International Monetary Fund to reduce spending on the Starter Pack, eventually led to its scaling down and transformation into the Targeted Inputs Program (TIP) (Harrigan 2008).[24] Under TIP, the emphasis shifted from raising agricultural productivity and food self-sufficiency to providing a safety net for poor smallholder farm households.[25]

### Targeted Inputs Program, 2000/01–2004/05

TIP was essentially a "targeted version of the Starter Pack" (Druilhe and Barreiro-Hurlé 2012, 18). Its scale varied with 1.5 million free input packs distributed in 2000/01, 1 million in 2001/02, 2.8 million in 2002/03 (following the 2002 food crisis), 1.7 million in 2003/04, and 2 million in 2004/05. This is in contrast to the 2.8 million input packs distributed each year of the Starter Pack (Harrigan 2008). In its last year (2004/05), the TIP input pack size increased to 25 kg of fertilizer, 5 kg of OPV maize seed, and 1 kg of legume seed.[26]

### Agricultural Inputs Subsidy Program and Farm Input Subsidy Program, 2005/06–Present

Malawi's present-day ISP, the MFISP, also referred to as the AISP, was established in 2005/06. The program's core objectives are raising household and national food security, food self-sufficiency, and incomes by improving resource-poor smallholders' access to improved agricultural inputs (Dorward and Chirwa 2011; Kilic, Whitney, and Winters 2015; Lunduka, Ricker-Gilbert, and Fisher 2013).

The number of smallholder farm households that MFISP has aimed to reach has varied over time, but has been 1.5 million per year during the three most recent agricultural years (2012/13 through 2014/15) (Logistics Unit 2015). Other key features of the program, including the total quantities of subsidized inputs distributed, the fertilizer subsidy rate, and program costs, are summarized in table 3A.4. As of 2014/15, beneficiary farmers were to each receive vouchers for fertilizer, maize seed, and legume seed:

- Two fertilizer vouchers: one for a 50 kg bag of NPK as basal dressing, and one for a 50 kg bag of urea as top dressing. When redeeming their vouchers for the fertilizer, farmers had to pay MK 500 per 50 kg bag top-up fee.

- One maize seed voucher for 5 kg of hybrid maize seed or 8 kg of OPV maize seed for free, although seed companies could apply a discretionary top-up fee of MK 100 on the voucher.[27]

- One legume seed voucher for 3 kg of soybean seed or 2 kg of other legume seed (beans, cowpeas, pigeon peas, or groundnuts) for free (Logistics Unit 2015).[28]

In August 2015, the Malawi government announced that the farmer contributions would increase to MK 3,500 per 50 kg bag of fertilizer, and MK 1,000 and MK 500 for the previously mentioned quantities of maize and legume seed, respectively. This is equivalent to a fertilizer subsidy rate of about 70 percent—much lower than the 90–95 percent subsidy rates that had prevailed in recent years (Logistics Unit 2015).

Beneficiary farmers redeem their fertilizer coupons at government-run outlets (Agricultural Development Marketing Corporation [ADMARC] and Smallholder Farmers Fertilizer Revolving Fund of Malawi [SFFRFM] locations) and their seed vouchers at registered, private agro-dealers' shops (Kilic, Whitney, and Winters 2015; Logistics Unit 2015). That is, fertilizer for MFISP is distributed through government, not private sector, channels.[29] Until 2013/14, all MFISP coupons were paper, but an electronic voucher (e-voucher), scratch-card based system was piloted for seed in six extension planning areas (EPAs) in 2013/14 and expanded to 18 EPAs in 2014/15. Fertilizer e-vouchers were piloted in 2014/15 in the six EPAs where seed e-vouchers had been piloted in 2013/14 (Logistics Unit 2015). The fertilizer e-voucher is to be expanded to eight districts and used to distribute 30,000 MT of the 150,000 MT of fertilizer intended for the 2015/16 MFISP.

Table 3A.4 Key Features of the Malawi Farm Input Subsidy Program, 2005/06–2014/15

| Cropping year | 2005/06 | 2006/07 | 2007/08 | 2008/09 | 2009/10 | 2010/11 | 2011/12 | 2012/13 | 2013/14 | 2014/15 |
|---|---|---|---|---|---|---|---|---|---|---|
| Total fertilizer subsidized (MT), planned | 137,006 | 150,000 | 170,000 | 170,000 | 160,000 | 160,000 | 140,000 | 154,440 | 150,000 | 150,000 |
| Total fertilizer subsidized (MT), actual | 131,388 | 174,688 | 216,553 | 202,278 | 161,074 | 160,531 | 139,901 | 153,846 | 149,821 | 149,813 |
| Total maize seed subsidized (MT) | — | 4,524 | 5,541 | 5,365 | 8,652 | 10,650 | 8,244 | 8,582 | 8,268 | 8,434 |
| Total legume seed subsidized (MT) | 0 | 0 | 24 | — | 1,391 | 2,727 | 2,562 | 2,968 | 3,042 | 3,027 |
| Redemption price (MK/50 kg maize fertilizer) | 950 | 950 | 900 | 800 | 500 | 500 | 500 | 500 | 500 | 500 |
| Redemption price (US$/50 kg maize fertilizer) | 8.02 | 6.98 | 6.43 | 5.69 | 3.54 | 3.32 | 3.19 | 2.01 | 1.37 | 1.18 |
| Fertilizer subsidy rate (%) | 64 | 72 | 79 | 91 | 95 | 90 | — | — | — | — |
| Total program cost (US$, millions) | 55.71 | 88.69 | 114.62 | 274.92 | 114.6 | 127.47 | 151.25 | 207.03 | 168.21 | 126.83 |
| Total cost as % of agricultural budget | — | 61 | 61 | 74 | 62 | 61 | 52 | 38 | 53 | 52 |
| Total cost as % of national budget | 5.6 | 8.4 | 8.9 | 16.2 | 8.2 | 6.5 | — | — | — | — |

Sources: Dorward and Chirwa 2011; Logistics Unit 2015; Lunduka, Ricker-Gilbert, and Fisher 2013.
Note: All redemption prices converted from MK to US$ using the official exchange rate per World Development Indicators. For 2011/12 through 2014/15, program costs exclude government operational costs and voucher printing, and do not reflect funds recuperated through farmers' top-up fees. — = not available.

MFISP beneficiary selection and coupon allocations occur as follows (Kilic, Whitney, and Winters 2015; Lunduka, Ricker-Gilbert, and Fisher 2013; Wanzala-Mlobela, Fuentes, and Mkumbwa 2013). First, the Ministry of Agriculture and Food Security (MoAFS) allocates coupons to districts in proportion to their number of farm households. Second, within each district, the district commissioner, district agricultural development officer, traditional authorities, nongovernmental organizations (NGOs), and religious leaders determine how to allocate the district's coupons to EPAs within the district, and to villages within the EPAs. And third, within each village, beneficiary village residents are to be selected through community-based targeting in open forums. In general, MFISP beneficiaries are to be full-time smallholder farmers who cannot afford one or two bags of fertilizer at commercial prices (Dorward et al. 2008). Priority is to be given to resource-poor households (for example, those with elderly, HIV-positive, female, child, orphan, or physically challenged household heads or household heads taking care of elderly or physically challenged individuals) (Kilic, Whitney, and Winters 2015).

# Nigeria

### Federal Market Stabilization Program, 1999–2011

The federal government of Nigeria reintroduced fertilizer subsidies in 1999 with the establishment of the Federal Market Stabilization Program (FMSP), after having abolished fertilizer subsidies in 1997 due to their high fiscal cost (Liverpool-Tasie and Takeshima 2013).[30] Under the program, which ran through 2011, the federal government provided fertilizer to Nigerian state governments at a 25 percent subsidy. See table 3A.5 for the quantities of fertilizer nutrients distributed through the program each year from 2000 through 2008. The goal of the program was to improve farmers' timely access to fertilizer, in both quantity and quality (Wanzala-Mlobela, Fuentes, and Mkumbwa 2013). The FMSP was a universal ISP in that there were no targeting criteria, and in theory any farmer could obtain subsidized fertilizer through the FMSP; moreover, there was no cap on the quantity that an individual farmer could receive. But the quantity of subsidized fertilizer distributed to each state was rationed (Takeshima and Liverpool-Tasie 2015).

To obtain FMSP subsidized fertilizer, each state submitted its total fertilizer request to the federal government based on estimates of the farm area in the state and recommended fertilizer application rates (Takeshima and Nkonya 2014). The federal government then determined the quantity of subsidized fertilizer to allocate to each state. The federal government purchased fertilizer for the FMSP from importers through a tender process (Liverpool-Tasie and

**Table 3A.5** Fertilizer Distributed through Nigeria's Federal Market Stabilization
Program, 2000–08

| Year | Subsidized fertilizer nutrients distributed (MT, thousands) |
|------|-----------------------------------------------------------|
| 2000 | 54 |
| 2001 | 20 |
| 2002 | 52 |
| 2003 | 43 |
| 2004 | 91 |
| 2005 | 66 |
| 2006 | 117 |
| 2007 | 134 |
| 2008 | 255 |

Source: Takeshima and Nkonya 2014, based on information from the Nigeria Federal Department of Fertilizer.

Takeshima 2013). It then delivered and sold the fertilizer to the states at a
25 percent subsidy (Takeshima and Liverpool-Tasie 2015). States and local
government areas could add their own subsidies on top of the federal subsidy,
and use their resources to increase the quantities of subsidized fertilizer
beyond the quantities allocated by the federal government. The typical subsidy
rate by the time the fertilizer reached farmers was approximately 75 percent
(Takeshima and Liverpool-Tasie 2015).

The fertilizer was mainly distributed to farmers through Agricultural
Development Project outlets (a state-level public institution that provided
extension services and inputs to farmers), but also distributed through other
outlets. No vouchers were used in the distribution of FMSP fertilizer, and there
was no seed component to the program. Late delivery and diversion and sale of
fertilizer intended for the FMSP as commercial (unsubsidized) fertilizer were
common, as was leakage, that is, the resale of FMSP fertilizer by subsidy recipients (Liverpool-Tasie and Takeshima 2013; Liverpool-Tasie 2014c).

## Targeted Fertilizer Subsidy Voucher Pilot Programs, 2009–11

In the lead up to its 2010 pronouncement that it aimed to withdraw from
fertilizer procurement by 2012 and instead support the development of private sector agro-dealer networks, in 2009 the federal government of Nigeria
began piloting targeted fertilizer subsidy voucher programs in collaboration
with select state governments. The pilot programs were run in the states of
Kano and Taraba in 2009, with the states of Bauchi and Kwara added in 2010
(Wanzala-Mlobela, Fuentes, and Mkumbwa 2013). The FMSP continued to
be implemented alongside the voucher pilot programs in these states, as well
as in the states without pilot programs. To our knowledge, all of the

empirical evidence on the targeting and impacts of the pilot programs is based on the Kano and Taraba experiences, so we focus on those two programs in the remainder of this subsection.

The federal and state governments partnered with the International Fertilizer Development Center (IFDC), three major private fertilizer suppliers, and more than 150 agro-dealers to implement the Kano and Taraba State pilots (Liverpool-Tasie 2014c). The IFDC and federal and state governments determined what part of the FMSP fertilizer earmarked for each state to distribute through the voucher pilot program, in which selected smallholder farmers were given paper vouchers that they could redeem for a discount on fertilizer at participating agro-dealers' shops. The federal government still procured the fertilizer and delivered it to the states as in the standard FMSP; only the means of distribution to farmers differed (Liverpool-Tasie 2014a). (The rest of FMSP fertilizer earmarked for each state was distributed to farmers through the standard FMSP government distribution system.)

While the Kano and Taraba State pilot programs had these features in common, there were also three important differences between the programs. First, the number of bags of fertilizer and the value of the vouchers allocated to beneficiary farmers in the two states differed. In Kano State, each participating farmer was to get a ₦2,000 (US$13.50) discount on each of two 50 kg bags of NPK and one 50 kg bag of urea, for a total subsidy value of US$40.50 (or about 60 percent and 65 percent off the market price of NPK and urea, respectively) (Liverpool-Tasie 2014c). In Taraba State, participating farmers still got a ₦2,000 discount per bag, but were entitled to two 50 kg bags of NPK and two 50 kg bags of urea, for a total subsidy value of US$54. These represented subsidy rates of about 55 percent for both types of fertilizer, slightly lower than in Kano State (Liverpool-Tasie 2014a). In both states, farmers paid the difference between the voucher value and the fertilizer's market price.

A second set of differences between the two states' programs relate to the eligibility requirements and who received (and redeemed) the vouchers. In Kano State, which had a long history of farmer organizations, beneficiaries were required to be a member of such a group. Only one voucher was given to the entire farmer group. It then entitled every group member to the aforementioned fertilizer discounts. Any farmer group leader (chairperson, treasurer, or secretary) could redeem the voucher on behalf of all group members (Liverpool-Tasie 2014c). But in Taraba State, where farmer organizations were less well established, beneficiaries were only required to be members of some sort of organization or group (be it farmer-related or otherwise) (Liverpool-Tasie 2014b). Moreover, each beneficiary received his or her own vouchers. As will be discussed in the section on empirical evidence related to the targeting of ISP fertilizer, these differences in who received vouchers had important implications for elite capture of the subsidy program benefits (Liverpool-Tasie 2014b).

Finally, the scale of the two pilot programs in 2009 differed. While the Kano State program aimed to reach 140,000 smallholders (Liverpool-Tasie and Salau 2013), the Taraba State program targeted only 76,000 (Liverpool-Tasie 2014b).

## Growth Enhancement Support Scheme, 2012–Present

Drawing on the experiences of and lessons learned from the targeted fertilizer voucher pilot programs of 2009 to 2011, in 2012 the federal government of Nigeria established the Growth Enhancement Support Scheme (GESS), which scaled the pilot programs up to the national level with some important changes (Liverpool-Tasie and Takeshima 2013). First, instead of being paper-based, the GESS delivered vouchers to beneficiary farmers electronically through a mobile phone platform called the e-wallet system; farmers then used the vouchers to obtain subsidized inputs at their assigned redemption center (a selected private agro-dealer's shop).[31] Second, under GESS, the private sector was responsible for the procurement and distribution of the fertilizer (Liverpool-Tasie and Takeshima 2013). Third, the GESS included subsidies for maize and rice seed (Liverpool-Tasie and Takeshima 2013). GESS focused on "resource-constrained" farmers, and its objective was to provide a "series of incentives to encourage the critical actors in the fertilizer value chain to work together to improve productivity, household food security, and income of the farmer."[32]

At its launch in 2012, the GESS aimed to reach 5 million farmers per year for four years, and beneficiary farmers were to receive 25 kg of certified rice seed or 20 kg of certified maize seed for free, and two 50 kg bags of fertilizer at a 50 percent subsidy (Maur and Shepherd 2015). But seed supplies were insufficient to cover these quantities, so the seed quantities were reduced to 12.5 kg (Maur and Shepherd 2015). Another challenge faced by GESS is that many Nigerian smallholders live outside of mobile phone network coverage areas or do not own mobile phones; in response, offline processes are also being developed (IFDC 2014).[33] In 2013, GESS was implemented in all 36 Nigerian states as well as in the Federal Capital Territory, and involved 4.8 million farmers, 500,000 MT of fertilizer, and 23,000 MT of improved seed (IFDC 2013). See IFDC (2013) for more details on how GESS works.

With the transition to the new government of President Muhammadu Buhari in 2015, there have been some challenges with GESS. Agro-dealers participating in the program under former President Goodluck Jonathan have not been paid and the 2015 distribution of subsidized inputs has been delayed (Yusuf 2015).

# Tanzania

Input subsidy programs were reintroduced in 2003/04 in Tanzania, though they were small (no data as yet available on quantities of fertilizer distributed under the program). Private companies tendered for particular areas; winning firms were allocated fertilizer and seed at fixed prices to provide to farmers. The fixed prices at which they purchased fertilizer at regional depots were below market price; transport costs and part of the cost of fertilizer were provided by the government as subsidies. The program ended in 2007/08 based on the conclusion that private traders were not passing along the full subsidy to targeted smallholder farmers. It was difficult for government to monitor this because fertilizer was also selling in rural areas through commercial markets, and hence it was difficult to ascertain whether prices paid by farmers were for commercial or subsidized fertilizer. The lack of transparency and ability to properly monitor the subsidy pass-through to farmers spelled this program's end.

This program was replaced by the National Agricultural Inputs Voucher Scheme (NAIVS), which started in 2008/09 for maize and rice. The program was launched in 56 districts, but because food prices remained high and volatile in the aftermath of the world food price rise, the program was expanded in 2009 to 65 districts for three years, with the aim to reach 2.5 million households in 2012. The program was almost entirely financed by the World Bank, and cost roughly US$80 million to US$100 million a year (World Bank 2014).

The objectives of the NAIVS were to improve farmers' access to modern inputs; to educate farmers on fertilizer's benefits; and to improve crop productivity for the main staple food in the area, mainly maize and rice.

The input package consisted of three vouchers: one for one 50 kg bag of urea; one for a 50 kg bag of diammonium phosphate (DAP) or two 50 kg bags of Minjingu rock phosphate (MRP) with a nitrogen supplement (farmers were supposed to choose); and one for 10 kg of hybrid or open-pollinated maize seeds or 16 kg of rice seeds, sufficient for half a hectare of maize or rice. Vouchers for each input had a face value equivalent to 50 percent of the market price of the respective input. The remaining 50 percent was to be paid by the farmers. Agro-dealers then submitted the vouchers to the district agricultural and livestock development officer for approval and then submitted them to the appointed bank for redemption.

The program targeted smallholder farmers cultivating not more than 1 ha. Priority was given to first-time fertilizer users, female-headed households, and relatively poor farmers (Msolla 2014). Each household was to receive fertilizer for three years only and then graduate from the program, in theory to a higher productivity trajectory.

The number of beneficiaries reached by the NAIVS is reported by Msolla (2014) as follows: 2008/09 (735,000 beneficiaries); 2009/10 (1.5 million); 2010/11 (2 million); 2011/12 (1.8 million); 2012/13 (640,873); and 2013/14 (932,100).

The modalities of fertilizer distribution under the NAIVS are described as follows by Pan and Christiaensen (2012):

> The central government allocates the vouchers to the target regions, which subsequently distribute it to their districts, which in turn distribute it to the villages in their district. At each level of government a special voucher committee is set up to allocate the vouchers to the lower levels based on the expected demand for inputs using historical production data for maize and rice as well as other related information such as the number of smallholder farmers who grow maize and rice and the average land size per farmer. The last step in the distribution is at the village level. First, the village council, in consultation with the village assembly, organizes the election of the village voucher committee (VVC), consisting of three men and three women. Then, the VVC draws up a list of beneficiary farmers for approval by the village assembly. After approval, the VVC issues the vouchers to the approved farmers, who can redeem them with local agro-dealers participating in the program.

According to the guidelines, the VVC selects farmers who are able to cofinance the inputs purchased with the voucher; are literate; and do not cultivate more than 1 ha of maize or rice. Priority is given to female-headed households and households who have used little or no modern inputs on maize or rice over the past five years. As such, these criteria reflect the implicit dual objective of the program: to increase overall maize and rice output (for example, by focusing on noninput using, literate farmers who are more likely to have a higher marginal productivity), and to increase access to modern inputs among poor and vulnerable smallholders (for example, by giving priority to female-headed households).

NAIVS clearly increased fertilizer use and maize and rice production in Tanzania (World Bank 2014). Msolla (2014) reports that maize production rose from 0.5 MT per ha in 2007/08 to 2.0 MT per ha. But official Ministry of Agriculture data show the following annual figures for maize yield and production (figure 3A.2).

Except for the 2013/14 season, Tanzania maize yields have been stagnant over the past decade, even with the NAIVS program operating every year since 2008/09. Area expansion is the main form of production growth. Anecdotally, the small change in yield suggests a low crop response rate to fertilizer given that the program distributed between 100,000 and 200,000 added metric tons of fertilizer each year.

Roughly 3,855 agro-dealers were trained under the program on methods of fertilizer use, which they were to pass along to farmers participating in the program (Msolla 2014; World Bank 2014). Msolla (2014) notes several

**Figure 3A.2** Maize Production in Tanzania, 2005/06–2013/14

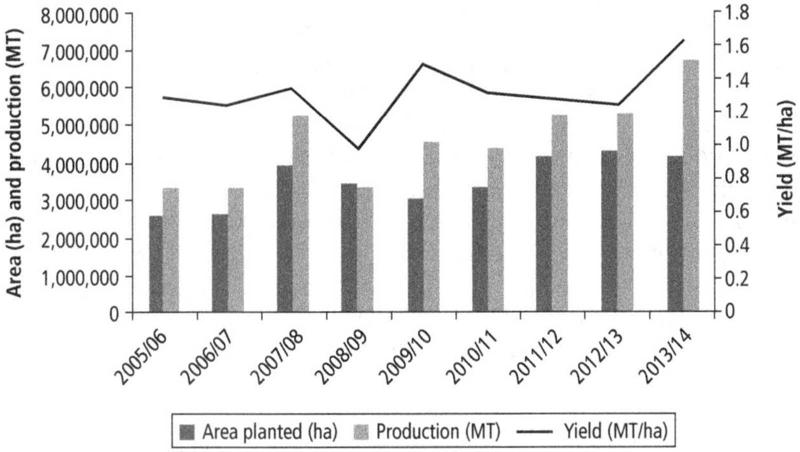

Source: Jayne et al. 2016.

challenges facing the program: input requirements are higher than what the government can afford, indicating that the government is unable to continue a large-scale program without external assistance; vouchers were often distributed late under NAIVS, forcing households to apply fertilizer late and suffer some loss of yield as a result; and payments to input suppliers participating in the program often occurred late, causing friction between private firms and the government. There were also reports of adulteration and low quality of the inputs provided, and maize output markets and trade were restricted at times by the Government of Tanzania, reducing maize prices received by farmers and depressing the value to farmers of the added production due to NAIVS.

## Zambia

Zambia's main ISP since structural adjustment has been the Zambia Farmer Input Support Program (ZFISP), originally called the Fertilizer Support Program. This program has been in place since 2002/03. The ZFISP is implemented by the Zambia Ministry of Agriculture and Livestock (ZMAL). The Ministry of Community Development, Mother, and Child Health has implemented its own, substantially smaller ISP since 2000/01: the Food Security Pack Program. We describe these programs below.

## Farmer Input Support Program, 2002/03–Present

Established in 2002/03 in the wake of a severe drought in southern Africa, the ZFISP was originally envisaged as a temporary program to be phased out after three years (ZMACO, Agricultural Consultative Forum, and FSRP 2002). Instead, it has grown in scale over the last 13 years and has seemingly become a permanent feature of Zambia's agricultural policy landscape. (See table 3A.6 for key features of the ZFISP, including the number of intended beneficiaries, quantities of subsidized inputs distributed, and subsidy rates over time.) The ZFISP is a targeted ISP, with overall objectives "to improve the supply and delivery of agricultural inputs to small-scale farmers through sustainable private sector participation at affordable cost, in order to increase household food security and incomes" (ZMAL 2014, 6). The program is one of Zambia's two major agricultural sector poverty reduction programs, the other being the Food Reserve Agency, a maize marketing board and strategic food reserve.

Fertilizer and seed for maize production have been central to the ZFISP since its inception. In the program's early years (2002/03–2008/09), participating farmers received 400 kg of fertilizer (200 kg each of compound D and urea) and 20 kg of hybrid maize seed at a 50 percent subsidy. The input pack size was halved to 200 kg of fertilizer and 10 kg of hybrid maize seed from 2009/10 onward. Small quantities of rice seed were added to the program in 2010/11, and sorghum, cotton, and groundnut seed were added in 2011/12. In 2014/15 cottonseed was dropped and the groundnut seed quantity increased more than 10-fold (table 3A.6). Subsidy rates have varied over time, ranging from 50 to 79 percent for fertilizer, and 50 to 100 percent for seed (table 3A.6).

Based on the 2014/15 official eligibility criteria, targeted beneficiaries were to be small-scale farmers (that is, cultivating less than 5 ha of land); registered with ZMAL and actively engaged in farming; members of a farmer organization that had been selected to participate in the ZFISP; and not concurrent beneficiaries of the Food Security Pack Program. They also needed to have the financial means to pay the farmer share of the input costs (for example, approximately US$65 total for 200 kg of fertilizer and 10 kg of hybrid maize seed in 2014/15). In previous years of the program, there was also a requirement that beneficiaries have the capacity to cultivate a minimum land area (for example, 1 ha in 2012/13) (ZMAL 2012). Farmers apply to, pay their contributions to, and collect the subsidized inputs from their farmer organization. ZFISP beneficiaries are selected by camp agriculture committees, which include representatives of the local chief, farmer organizations, other community-based organizations; and representatives from public offices other than ZMAL, and for which ZMAL, through the camp extension officer, serves as the secretariat.[34]

**Table 3A.6 Key Features of the Zambia Farmer Input Support Program, 2002/03–2014/15**

| Cropping year | Number of intended beneficiaries | Quantities of subsidized inputs (MT) | | | | | Fertilizer subsidy rate (%) | Seed subsidy rate (%) | Total program cost (US$, millions) | Total cost as % of agricultural spending | Total cost as % of national spending |
|---|---|---|---|---|---|---|---|---|---|---|---|
| | | Fertilizer | Maize seed | Rice seed | Sorghum seed | Groundnut seed | | | | | |
| 2002/03 | 120,000 | 48,000 | 2,400 | 0 | 0 | 0 | 50 | 50 | 4.04 | 10.4 | 0.5 |
| 2003/04 | 150,000 | 60,000 | 3,000 | 0 | 0 | 0 | 50 | 50 | 10.56 | 17.2 | 1.1 |
| 2004/05 | 115,000 | 46,000 | 2,500 | 0 | 0 | 0 | 50 | 50 | 20.52 | 26.8 | 1.6 |
| 2005/06 | 125,000 | 50,000 | 2,500 | 0 | 0 | 0 | 50 | 50 | 31.36 | 26.9 | 1.9 |
| 2006/07 | 210,000 | 84,000 | 4,234 | 0 | 0 | 0 | 60 | 60 | 51.08 | 25.5 | 2.4 |
| 2007/08 | 125,000 | 50,000 | 2,550 | 0 | 0 | 0 | 60 | 60 | 51.10 | 18.0 | 2.2 |
| 2008/09 | 200,000 | 80,000 | 4,000 | 0 | 0 | 0 | 60 | 60 | 131.37 | 37.6 | 3.5 |
| 2009/10 | 500,000 | 100,000 | 5,342 | 0 | 0 | 0 | 75 | 50 | 111.99 | 42.5 | 3.7 |
| 2010/11 | 891,500 | 178,000 | 8,790 | 30 | 0 | 0 | 75 | 50 | 122.78 | 29.9 | 3.4 |
| 2011/12 | 914,670 | 182,454 | 8,985 | 39 | 0 | 0 | 76 | 53 | 184.21 | 30.1 | 4.4 |
| 2012/13 | 877,000 | 183,634 | 8,770 | 143 | 60 | 150 | 79 | — | 165.68 | 50.3 | 3.1 |
| 2013/14 | 900,000 | 188,312 | 9,000 | 159 | 107 | 130 | 50 | 100 | 113.22 | 30.2 | 1.9 |
| 2014/15 | 1,000,000 | 208,236 | 10,000 | 127 | 119 | 1,357 | — | — | — | — | — |

Sources: ZMAL various years; ZMFNP various years.
Note: Input quantities rounded to the nearest metric ton. — = not available.

To date, no vouchers are used in the ZFISP, local agro-dealers are not involved, and inputs for the program are distributed through what is essentially a government system.[35] In recent years, the parastatal Nitrogen Chemicals of Zambia has provided the compound D for the program, and private firms are selected through a tender process to import the urea. Private sector transporters are then selected through a tender process to transport the inputs to main depots in the districts and ultimately to the farmer organizations.

From 2010/11 through 2013/14, the ZFISP aimed to reach about 900,000 beneficiaries per year. Over this period, spending on the program averaged 35 percent of the Zambian government's agricultural sector spending (see table 3A.6).

## Food Security Pack Program, 2000/01–Present

The Food Security Pack Program is intended to target farmers who do not have the resources to pay the ZFISP farmer contribution or, when there was a minimum land requirement for ZFISP participation, farmers who could not meet it. More specifically, the Food Security Pack Program targets "vulnerable but viable" farmers, which it defines as households with less than 1 ha of land, adequate labor, not in gainful employment, and also having at least one of the following characteristics: female-, child/youth-, elderly-, or terminally-ill headed, or caring for orphans or disabled individuals (PAM 2005). In addition, participating farmers are trained in conservation farming techniques and are required to prepare their field(s) using these practices (PAM 2005). Community Welfare Assistance Committees or Area Food Security Committees select program beneficiaries.

The contents of a Food Security Pack vary by agroecological region but generally consist of seed and fertilizer to plant 0.5 ha of cereals (maize, rice, sorghum, or millet), legume seed for 0.25 ha, sweet potato vines or cassava cuttings, and, in areas with acidic soils, 100 kg of lime. Fertilizer quantities are either 50 kg or 100 kg depending on the cereal seed received (PAM 2005). The program's objective is "to empower the targeted vulnerable but viable households to be self-sustaining through improved productivity and household food security and thereby contribute to poverty reduction" (PAM 2005, 1). Beneficiaries are not required to make a cash contribution for the Food Security Pack inputs; rather, they are required to pay in-kind a fraction of the value of the inputs received (for example, 100 kg of maize for those receiving input packs containing maize seed).

The scale of the Food Security Pack Program has been much smaller than that of the ZFISP. While at its peak in 2003/04 it reached 145,000 households— nearly as many as the ZFISP (see table 3A.6), by the late 2000s and early 2010s the Food Security Pack Program received only enough funding to reach about

15,000 households a year (compared to 900,000 under the ZFISP) (Kasanga et al. 2010).

Although small, the Food Security Pack Program has been considerably more innovative than the ZFISP. For example, it has taken a more integrative approach to raising smallholder productivity and incomes by including a significant extension component (training farmers in conservation farming) and by including inputs other than just maize seed and fertilizer. In addition, since 2012/13, it has piloted in three districts an Expanded Food Security Pack Program, which utilizes e-voucher scratch cards redeemable at private agro-dealers' shops for the aforementioned inputs and a *chaka* hoe (a specialized hoe designed for digging planting basins, the hand-hoe variant of conservation tillage promoted in Zambia). The program also includes a social cash transfer component: Each beneficiary household receives ZMW100 (about US$16.25 in 2014) in January, near the peak of the lean season and when school fees are due.[36] The Expanded Food Security Pack Program has been funded by the Royal Norwegian Embassy in Lusaka; the pilot is due to end after the 2015/16 agricultural season, by which time the program hopes to have reached 27,000 households. Discussions are underway to determine if the Ministry of Community Development, Mother, and Child Health will adopt and roll out the Expanded Food Security Pack program model to other districts in Zambia after the pilot ends.

## Annex 3B: Evidence of Targeting and Impacts

In the years since the 2005 sea change and revival of ISPs in Africa, the empirical literature on the targeting and impacts of the programs has been expanding rapidly. In this section we synthesize the findings from econometric- and simulation-based studies that estimate (a) the effects of various household, community, and other characteristics on the probability or level of participation in ISPs in Sub-Saharan Africa; and (b) the effects of participation in a given ISP (measured in various ways) on household- and more aggregate-level outcomes, including fertilizer and improved seed use, crop yields, area planted, production, crop prices, and wage levels.

## Targeting

Eligibility criteria for ISP participation vary markedly across (and sometimes within) countries (table 3B.1). Some programs officially target "resource-poor" households (for example, Kenya's NAAIAP) or those that cannot afford fertilizer at unsubsidized prices (for example, Malawi's MFISP). Other programs officially

**Table 3B.1** Empirical Findings on the Targeting of ISP Inputs

| Country | Empirical findings |
|---|---|
| *By household head gender* | |
| Ethiopia | — |
| Ghana | No differences: A study of smallholder rice farmers in the Ghana's Volta region finds that approximately 25 percent of both beneficiaries and nonbeneficiaries are female, and gender had no significant c.p. impact on the likelihood of participation [G1] |
| Kenya | No FHH-MHH differences in probability of receiving NAAIAP voucher, c.p. [K1] |
| Malawi | No differences: No FHH-MHH differences in probability of receiving [M12, M24, M28], value or number of MFISP vouchers [M7, M28], or kg of MFISP fertilizer or maize seed [M16, M17, M24] received, c.p. HHs with female plot managers equally likely to participate in the MFISP as HHs with only male plot managers, c.p. [M20] |
| | Differences: FHH less likely to receive MFISP fertilizer or seed+fertilizer, c.p. [M8]. FHH receives 12 kg less MFISP fertilizer, c.p. [M3]. Respondents in FHH less likely to receive the MFISP, c.p. [M5] |
| Nigeria | No FHH-MHH differences in quantity of FMSP, KSVP, or TSVP fertilizer acquired, c.p. [N1, N2] |
| Tanzania | MHH significantly more likely to receive vouchers than FHH [T1] |
| Zambia | No FHH-MHH differences in receiving ZFISP fertilizer or hybrid maize seed, c.p. [Z1, Z2, Z3, Z4] |
| *By landholding size* | |
| Ethiopia | — |
| Ghana | Mean plot size for both beneficiary and nonbeneficiary smallholders in Volta is 2 ha, but after controlling for other factors there is a negative and statistically significant correlation between plot size and subsidy participation [G1] |
| | Mean total crop area among beneficiaries is slightly lower in the Northern region (3.7 ha versus 4.2 ha among nonbeneficiaries) [G1] |
| Kenya | HHs with more than 5 ha of land 7–9 p.p. less likely to receive NAAIAP voucher, c.p. [K1]. HHs with more land get slightly more NCPB fertilizer, c.p. (3.1 kg more per 1 ha increase in landholding) [K2] |
| Malawi | Value of MFISP vouchers higher among HHs with more land, c.p. [M7]. Probability of receiving MFISP vouchers increases by 1.3–1.6 p.p. with 1 ha increase in landholding, c.p. [M12]. Probability of participating in the MFISP and number of coupons received increases with HH landholding (at a decreasing rate), and highest among largest land quintile, c.p. HHs in this last group are 18.9 p.p. more likely to get the MFISP than HHs in the smallest landholding quintile [M28] |
| | 1 ha increase in landholding raises FISP fertilizer acquired by 3.3–11.3 kg, c.p. [M3, M16, M17], but has no effect on kg of FISP maize seed [M16] |
| | Probability of MFISP receipt increases with the number of plots cultivated by the HH, c.p. [M20] |
| | Probability of receiving MFISP fertilizer voucher and kg of MFISP fertilizer acquired increases with HH area cultivated, c.p. [M24] |
| Nigeria | No c.p. landholding effects on quantity of FMSP fertilizer acquired [N1]. 1 ha increase in landholding raises fertilizer received through the KSVP and TSVP, c.p. (APE not reported) [N2] |
| Tanzania | No significant relationship between landholding size and HHs receiving vouchers (T1) |
| Zambia | HHs with more land get slightly more ZFISP inputs, c.p. (0.2 kg more hybrid maize seed [Z2] and 2.5 kg more fertilizer [Z5] per 1 ha increase in landholding). No c.p. landholding effect in some studies, for example [Z4] |

*(continued next page)*

**Table 3B.1** (continued)

| Country | Empirical findings |
|---|---|
| *By assets, wealth, or ex ante poverty status* | |
| Ethiopia | — |
| Ghana | Asset wealth was found to be 44 percent greater among beneficiaries compared with those not receiving fertilizer subsidies in the cross-sectional data from the Volta region [G1] |
| Kenya | HHs in highest asset quintile 8–12 p.p. less likely to receive NAAIAP voucher, c.p. [K1]. No c.p. effect of farm assets on quantity of NCPB fertilizer [K2] |
| Malawi | Value of MFISP vouchers received lower among poor HHs, c.p. [M7]; some evidence that poor HHs less likely to receive FISP vouchers, c.p. [M8]. Poor HHs 1.9–2.8 p.p. less likely to receive MFISP vouchers, c.p. [M12]. HHs that consider themselves to be poor less likely to receive MFISP voucher and receive less MFISP fertilizer, c.p. [M24] |
| | [M3] finds that an increase in value of assets raises MFISP fertilizer acquired, c.p. But [M17] and [M24] find no c.p. effects of asset wealth on MFISP fertilizer acquired (or probability [M24]). [M16] find the same for MFISP maize seed, but find that MFISP fertilizer kg acquired is decreasing in asset wealth, c.p. |
| | [M20] find that probability of MFISP participation decreases with a wealth index and access to nonfarm labor income but increases with an agricultural implement access index and access to nonfarm nonlabor income, c.p. |
| | [M28] find that middle three wealth quintiles more likely to participate in the MFISP (by 6–10 p.p.) than poorest and richest wealth quintiles, c.p. No statistically significant difference in participation between poorest and richest wealth quintiles, c.p. But top four wealth quintiles all get significantly more FISP coupons, c.p., with the largest effect in quintile four [M28] |
| | An increase in the district poverty rate increases the percentage of HHs receiving the MFISP in 2007/08, but an increase in the district percentage of HHs reporting a food shortage or famine does not, c.p. [M6] |
| Nigeria | No c.p. asset (livestock) effects on quantity of FMSP (KSVP and TSVP) fertilizer acquired [N1, N2, N6] |
| Tanzania | Voucher recipients more likely to be nonpoor in the prior survey than nonrecipients [T1]. |
| Zambia | Panel data regressions suggest no farm asset effects, c.p. [Z1, Z2, Z4]. Cross-sectional regressions suggest that ZFISP fertilizer and seed recipients have more farm assets, c.p. [Z3, Z10 for five provinces only] |
| *By political factors* | |
| Ethiopia | — |
| Ghana | More vouchers targeted to districts lost by the ruling party in the last presidential election, c.p.; vouchers received increases with the ruling party's margin of loss [G2]. Notably, the incumbent party that initiated the GFSP lost the following presidential election by a slim margin [G3] |
| Kenya | Some evidence that increase (decrease) in constituency-level electoral threat (support for runner-up) in last election reduces (increases) NAAIAP and NCPB fertilizer receipt, but election data questionable [K2] |
| Malawi | [M16] find that HHs in districts won by Bingu wa Mutharika in the 2004 presidential election got 13.2 kg (1.7 kg) more MFISP fertilizer (maize seed) in 2006/07 and 2008/09 than HHs in districts lost by Mutharika, c.p. |

*(continued next page)*

**Table 3B.1** (continued)

| Country | Empirical findings |
|---|---|
| | [M23] finds no evidence that districts with more Mutharika core supporters were favored with MFISP vouchers, c.p., in 2008/09 (just before the 2009 election) relative to earlier and later years. Districts with more swing voters appear to have been allocated more MFISP vouchers in 2008/09, c.p., at the expense of districts with more opposition core supporters, c.p. Also, no evidence that core supporters were rewarded with more MFISP vouchers after the 2009 election, c.p. |
| | More HHs received the MFISP in 2007/08 in districts where the incumbent lost in 2004, c.p., but the winning party in 2004 had no c.p. effect [M6] |
| | [M5] find that respondents' partisan affinities in 2008 had no c.p. effect on their likelihood of receiving the MFISP in 2009 |
| | [M17] find that HHs in communities with a resident MP get 7.5 kg more MFISP fertilizer, c.p., but [M28] find no c.p. of this on probability of participating in MFISP or number of coupons received |
| | HHs in villages with resident or recent visit of MP 2.7 p.p. more (2.5 p.p. less) likely to receive MFISP fertilizer voucher only (fertilizer and maize seed voucher), c.p. [M12] |
| Nigeria | 1 km decrease in distance from LGA to the state governor's district of origin increases the mean FMSP fertilizer acquired by HHs in the LGA by 22–30 kg, c.p. [N6] |
| Tanzania | Vouchers disproportionately targeted to HHs having elected officials and village voucher committee members [T1] |
| Zambia | Through 2010/11, HHs in constituency won by the MMD (ruling party) in the last presidential election got 23.2 kg more ZFISP fertilizer, and 0.5 kg more per p.p. increase in MMD margin of victory, c.p. [Z6] |

*By social capital factors (nonpolitical)*

| | |
|---|---|
| Ethiopia | — |
| Ghana | — |
| Kenya | — |
| Malawi | HHs with heads originating from outside the district 3.0–7.7 p.p. less likely to receive MFISP vouchers, c.p. [M12] |
| | 1-year increase in time HH head has lived in the village raises MFISP fertilizer receipt by 0.09 kg, c.p. [M3] |
| | HHs with village head, VDC, or traditional authority in their networks 13–14 p.p. more likely to participate in the MFISP, c.p. [M28] |
| Nigeria | Relatives of farm group leaders (chairperson, secretary, or treasurer) get more subsidized fertilizer through the KSVP but not TSVP, c.p. [N2, N5] |
| Tanzania | Households more likely to receive vouchers if they participate in public meetings, are members of farmer associations, or talk to government officials at least once a month [T1] |
| Zambia | HHs related to chief/headman get 0.6 kg more ZFISP hybrid maize seed, c.p. [Z4]. No evidence of similar effects on ZFISP fertilizer acquired |

*By select other factors*

| | |
|---|---|
| Ethiopia | — |
| Ghana | Age, experience (years farming), and plot fertility (self-described) are all roughly the same on average, but beneficiaries are 30 percent (1.5 km) closer to the nearest extension agent distributing vouchers. The negative correlation is statistically significant, all else held constant [G1] |

*(continued next page)*

**Table 3B.1** (continued)

| Country | Empirical findings |
| --- | --- |
| Kenya | HHs that did not use fertilizer in previous year(s) 8–12 p.p. less likely to receive NAAIAP voucher, c.p. [K1]. 1 km increase in distance from motorable road reduces NCPB fertilizer by 19 kg, c.p. [K2] |
| Malawi | Value of MFISP vouchers received lower among maize net buyers, c.p. [M7] |
| | 1 km increase in distance from major road increases probability of MFISP voucher receipt by 0.03 p.p., c.p. [M12]. 1 km increase in distance from nearest paved road raises MFISP fertilizer receipt by 0.08 kg, c.p. [M3]. But [M16] and [M17] find no c.p. effects of distance to paved road, district capital, or main market on kg of MFISP fertilizer or maize seed acquired |
| | An increase in soil quality in the HH's area is associated with an increase in the probability of participation in the MFISP and the MFISP coupons received, c.p. [M28] |
| Nigeria | 1-hour increase in travel time to nearest 20k+ town reduces FMSP fertilizer by 0.7 to 1 kg, c.p. [N1]. 1 km increase in distance to main market raises fertilizer received through KSVP, c.p. (APE not reported) [N2] |
| Tanzania | — |
| Zambia | 1 km increase in distance from feeder road reduces ZFISP fertilizer by 1.1–2.5 kg, c.p. [Z1] |

*Note:* Results are APE and statistically significant at the 10 percent level or lower. "No effect" indicates no statistically significant effect at the 10 percent level or lower. Electoral threat is the share of votes won by the runner-up divided by the share of votes won by the presidential winner. See annex 3C for full references for the studies cited here, and for brief overviews of the data and methods used. APE = average partial effects; c.p. = ceteris paribus; FHH = female-headed household; FMSP = Federal Market Stabilization Program; GFSP = Ghana Fertilizer Subsidy Program; HH = head of household; KSVP = Kano State voucher program (in 2009); MHH = male-headed household; LGA = local government area; MFISP = Malawi Farm Input Subsidy Program; MMD = Movement for Multi-Party Democracy; NAAIAP = National Accelerated Agricultural Inputs Access Program; NCPB = National Cereals and Produce Board; p.p. = percentage point; TSVP = Taraba State voucher program (in 2009); VDC = village development committee; ZFISP = Zambia Farmer Input Support Program; — = no analyses to date.

give priority to female-headed households (for example, MFISP and Zambia's Food Security Pack Program). Still others have a minimum or maximum land-holding- or area cultivated-related eligibility criterion (for example, Zambia's ZFISP and NAAIAP). Given this heterogeneity, one approach would be to evaluate each ISP against its stated targeting criteria. In many cases, however, there is little correlation between the official targeting criteria and de facto characteristics of farmers and households receiving input subsidies (Kilic, Whitney, and Winters 2015; Pan and Christiaensen 2012; Ricker-Gilbert, Jayne, and Chirwa 2011; Sheahan et al. 2014).

Despite this disconnect, all programs share the common objective of raising use of the inputs distributed through the ISP. Another approach is to assess targeting performance against this goal. On average and other factors constant, the potential for positive impacts of ISPs on fertilizer use is greatest when they are administered in areas where the private sector has been inactive and among households that cannot afford fertilizer at commercial prices (Jayne et al. 2013; Mason and Jayne 2013; Mather and Jayne 2015; Ricker-Gilbert, Jayne, and

Chirwa 2011; Xu et al. 2009). ISPs are particularly effective at increasing fertilizer use when beneficiaries include female-headed households and relatively
poor households, be it in land, assets, income, or consumption. We therefore
begin this subsection with a synthesis of the empirical record on how these factors affect household participation in ISPs. We then turn to the empirical record
on the politicization and elite capture of ISPs. Table 3B.1 summarizes empirical
findings on the targeting of ISP inputs.

### Targeting by Gender of the Household Head
Looking across the various country ISPs and studies, the evidence suggests that
female-headed households and male-headed households are equally likely to
participate in ISPs and receive the same quantity of inputs on average, other
factors constant (see table 3A.3). This is the case for all reviewed studies: on
Ghana's GFSP [G1]; Kenya's NAAIAP [K1]; Zambia's ZFISP [Z1 to Z4], and
Nigeria's ISPs prior to the Growth Enhancement Support Scheme (GESS)
[N1, N2] (see annex 3C for the full sources, cited here as initials). It is also true
for most studies on Malawi's MFISP. Where there are differences for the latter
program, the findings suggest that female-headed households are less likely to
receive MFISP inputs or receive a smaller quantity of MFISP inputs [M3, M5,
M8]. Thus, ISPs in Sub-Saharan Africa generally fail to meet the criterion of
favoring female-headed households.

### Targeting by Landholding Size
The empirical record suggests that households with more land are more
likely to receive ISP inputs or receive a larger quantity of such inputs on average (see table 3B.1). Of the more than 70 studies reviewed, only one suggests
that households with more land are *less* likely to receive ISP inputs [K1], and
only a handful suggest that an increase in landholding size has no effect on
ISP receipt (see table 3B.1). But despite the consistent findings that households with more land are favored by the programs, the landholding effects
are small: A 1 ha increase in household landholdings is associated with
increases in subsidized fertilizer received of just 2.5–11.3 kg on average
under Kenyan, Malawi, and Zambian programs. With recommended fertilizer application rates of 400 kg per ha in Zambia, for example, these effects
are minimal.

Perhaps more striking are the unconditional probabilities of participation in
ISPs by landholding size. There is a much larger spread across landholding
quintiles in the probability of participation in the ZFISP than in the MFISP.
While only 13 percent of Zambian smallholders in the lowest landholding quintile participated in the ZFISP in 2010/11, 43 percent of their Malawi counter-
parts participated in the MFISP in 2009/10. This is compared with 47 percent
and 62 percent of Zambian and Malawi smallholders, respectively, in the largest

landholding quintile (a 34 percentage point spread for Zambia but only 19 percentage points for Malawi). This may be related to the minimum landholding requirement for the ZFISP (0.5 ha in 2010/11) or the broader coverage of the MFISP (which reached 54 percent of smallholders during the years in question compared with just 30 percent for the ZFISP). While participation in ISPs is higher among households with more land, the extent to which this is the case varies considerably across countries.

But participation rates alone can mask even larger disparities in the share of subsidized inputs received by households in different landholding quintiles. Even in countries where the input pack size is supposedly standardized (for example, 200 kg per household in Zambia in 2010/11 and 100 kg per household in Malawi throughout the duration of the MFISP), the quantities received often vary markedly across beneficiary households. Households with more land are often both more likely to receive inputs from the programs and receive larger quantities, on average, upon participating (Mason and Jayne 2013; Mason and Ricker-Gilbert 2013; Ricker-Gilbert, Jayne, and Chirwa 2011). As shown in annex 3A, Zambian smallholders in the smallest landholding quintile garner just 6 percent of all ZFISP fertilizer distributed, while those in the largest landholding quintile (who are most likely to be able to afford fertilizer at commercial prices) receive 41 percent of it. This exacerbates crowding out of commercial input demand by the programs, reduces impacts on total fertilizer use (and hence incremental maize production), and attenuates poverty reduction effects.

### Targeting by Assets, Wealth, or Ex Ante Poverty Status

After controlling for landholding size and other factors, the empirical evidence on the effects of assets, wealth, and ex ante poverty status on ISP receipt is mixed, especially in Malawi's case (see table 3B.1). While some studies for Malawi suggest that relatively poorer (wealthier) households are less (more) likely to receive MFISP inputs or receive smaller (larger) quantities [M3, M7, M8, M12, M24, M28], some find the opposite [M16, M20], and still others find no wealth effects at all [M16, M17]. In a cross-sectional study of GFSP receipts, it was found that asset wealth in Ghana's Volta region was 44 percent greater among beneficiaries compared with those not receiving fertilizer subsidies [G1]. There is no evidence of wealth-related targeting in Nigeria's pre-GESS ISPs (see table 3A.3). De facto targeting under Kenya's NAAIAP favored households in the bottom four wealth quintiles [K1], while no farm asset effects are found for the country's universal National Cereals and Produce Board (NCPB) fertilizer subsidy program [K2]. Cross-sectional evidence from Zambia suggests that more farm assets are associated with receiving more ISP fertilizer and seed, but these estimated effects are not statistically significant after controlling for time-constant farmer characteristics (see table 3B.1). Differences in methodology and the definitions of assets, wealth, or poverty measures likely underlie many of the varying results from Malawi as well.

In the most detailed study of the targeting of MFISP to date, Kilic, Whitney, and Winters (2015, 29) argue that Malawi's "FISP is not poverty targeted in that it does not exclusively target the poor or the rich at any level of the programme administration ... The multivariate analysis of household programme participation reinforces these findings and reveals that the relatively well off in terms of wealth and landholdings, rather than the poor or the wealthiest ... have a higher likelihood of program participation and, on average, receive a greater number of input coupons." In Zambia, targeting is decidedly not pro-poor, since smallholder households in the lowest income per adult equivalent quintile received just 5 percent of all ZFISP fertilizer in 2010/11, while those in the highest quintile received 42 percent of it (Mason and Tembo 2015), mirroring the landholding distribution.

Overall, the empirical record for most ISPs suggests little or no targeting by assets or wealth, on average, and holding other factors constant. But there is some evidence that the wealthiest households were less likely to receive subsidized inputs under Kenya's NAAIAP, which explicitly sought to reach resource-poor farmers.

## Targeting and Political Factors

It is widely believed that ISPs in Sub-Saharan Africa are politicized. The empirical record shows which groups of voters—core supporters of the incumbent party, swing voters, or core supporters of the opposition—are actually targeted. Based on the findings in table 3B.1, there is considerable evidence of politically motivated targeting of ISP inputs, but the groups targeted vary across countries, and in Malawi's case studies reach different conclusions about which groups are targeted. In both Ghana and Kenya, empirical evidence suggests that areas with more opposition supporters in the last presidential election get significantly more subsidized fertilizer [G2, K2]. But the political logic to such targeting is questionable since the political payoff to targeting opposition (versus swing voter) areas are likely to be small. Notably, for example, the incumbent party that initiated the GFSP lost the following presidential election by a slim margin in 2008 [G3]. In Zambia, by contrast, results based on multiple nationally representative surveys (both panel and cross-sectional) consistently suggest that from the late 1990s through 2010, smallholder households in constituencies won by the ruling party (at that time the Movement for Multi-Party Democracy, or MMD) in the last presidential election received significantly more (23 kg) subsidized fertilizer than those in areas lost by the ruling party. Moreover, the quantity of subsidized fertilizer received increased with the ruling party's margin of victory [Z3, Z6]. The findings from Malawi related to which groups of voters and partisans are targeted are too mixed to draw general conclusions, but the disparate findings are partially driven by differences in data and methods, and in the years under consideration (see table 3A.3). But for Malawi and Nigeria, there is some evidence that communities with resident elected leaders or communities that are geographically closer to the hometown of those leaders (for example, members of parliament in Malawi and state governors in Nigeria) receive significantly more subsidized fertilizer on average, other factors constant [M12, M17]. Overall, there is mounting empirical evidence of the politicization of ISPs in Sub-Saharan Africa, but the politicization varies across countries as well as within countries over time (Chinsinga and Poulton 2014, [M23]).

### Targeting, Social Capital, and Elite Capture

In addition to the consistent findings that households with more land get more ISP inputs and the findings in some countries that wealthier households get more, empirical evidence from several Sub-Saharan African countries suggests that social capital also leads to "elite capture" of ISP benefits. In Tanzania, for example, Pan and Christiaensen (2012) found that 60 percent of the households receiving input vouchers contained a village official as a member. They also found that households with elected officials and voucher committee members were 1.7 and 4 times more likely to receive input vouchers than households without such members. Similarly, evidence from Zambia and Malawi suggests that households with links to traditional authorities are more likely to receive input subsidies [Z4, M28]. In Malawi, "locals" (either because they originate from the village or have lived in the village longer than others) are favored. In Nigeria, relatives of farm group leaders get more subsidized fertilizer under the Kano State voucher pilot program (where a single voucher was given to the farmer group) but not under the Taraba State program (where farmers were each given their own vouchers) [N2, N5]. Thus, in all Sub-Saharan African countries where this issue has been investigated empirically, there is evidence that social capital influences access to subsidized inputs.

## Household-Level Effects of ISPs

### Household-Level Effects on Fertilizer and Improved Seed Use

One of the first sets of ISP impacts to be empirically investigated was the effect of the programs on household demand for fertilizer at commercial (unsubsidized) prices. Originally investigated by Xu et al. (2009, [Z7]), and followed by numerous later studies, empirical assessments of how much subsidized fertilizer "crowds in" or "crowds out" commercial fertilizer demand are based on the following relationship (3B.1):

$$\frac{\partial total}{\partial ISP} = \frac{\partial ISP}{\partial ISP} + \frac{\partial comm}{\partial ISP} = 1 + \frac{\partial comm}{\partial ISP} \qquad (3B.1)$$

in which *total* is the quantity of fertilizer demanded, *ISP* is the quantity of ISP fertilizer acquired, *comm* is the quantity of commercial fertilizer demanded, and δ indicates a partial derivative.[37] The term $\frac{\partial comm}{\partial ISP}$ is estimated by regressing *comm* on *ISP* and other factors, and using econometric techniques to correct for the potential endogeneity of ISP fertilizer to commercial fertilizer demand. A negative (positive) and statistically significant partial effect of *ISP* on *comm* in this regression indicates crowding out (crowding in). When there is crowding out (in), a 1 kg increase in subsidized fertilizer acquired by a household leads to a less (more) than 1 kg increase in total fertilizer demand. Thus understanding the crowding out and in effects of ISPs is critical for understanding the programs' impacts on fertilizer use and thus on the incremental production of the crop(s) to which the fertilizer is applied.

Looking across multiple relevant studies for Sub-Saharan Africa, only two cases show evidence of crowding in: under the Kano state voucher pilot program in Nigeria [N2] and in areas with low private sector commercial retailing activity in Zambia [Z7].[38] All other studies [K2, M2, M3, N1, N7, Z1] suggest crowding out of commercial fertilizer demand by subsidized fertilizer in Kenya, Malawi, Nigeria (under the FMSP), and Zambia, and similarly for improved maize seed in Malawi and Zambia [M16, Z2].[39] In general, the extent to which ISP inputs crowd out commercial demand is lower among female-headed households, households with less land or fewer assets, households that did not previously purchase the inputs, in areas with less private sector fertilizer retailing activity, and in areas that have lower agroecological potential. That adverse effects on the private sector are less common in lower potential areas also raises questions on the long-run potential of ISPs in these areas. Specifically, what is the likelihood of sustaining a commercial market where fertilizer use may be sensible only at subsidized prices?

The crowding out effects vary considerably across countries where it has been found. Estimates suggest that an added 100 kg of ISP fertilizer crowds out 42–51 kg of commercial fertilizer in Kenya [K2], 18 kg in Malawi [M2], 19–35 kg in Nigeria under the FMSP [N7]. The substantially larger crowding out effects in Kenya are likely because the country's private sector fertilizer markets were already well developed and most farmers were already using fertilizer prior to the reintroduction of fertilizer subsidies there [K1, K2].

Thus, though there are a few findings of crowding in, the evidence suggests that most ISPs crowd out commercial demand for subsidized inputs. That is, an additional ton of fertilizer (improved seed) distributed through input subsidy programs raises fertilizer (improved seed) use, but by less than 1 ton.

More recently, some studies have estimated that crowding out of commercial fertilizer sales may have been substantially underestimated due to fertilizer that has been diverted from subsidy program channels into what can be mistaken for commercial sales (Jayne et al. 2013; Mason and Jayne 2013). Both in Malawi and Zambia, comparing the official subsidized fertilizer distribution volumes and the estimated volume of subsidized fertilizer received by farmers according to nationally representative survey data suggests that diversion of 25–35 percent of subsidized fertilizer is common. Diversion of program fertilizer has important income distributional effects, with program implementers receiving a major part of the program benefits rather than farmers (Jayne et al. 2015).

While those studies focus on crowding in and out of commercial *demand*, there have yet to be any overall studies of how much ISPs encourage or deter private sector investment in input distribution.[40] The conventional wisdom is that ISPs distributing inputs through parallel government channels are more likely to crowd out private sector market participation, but ISPs operating through vouchers redeemable at private agro-dealers are more likely to crowd in private sector participation. But little empirical evidence either supports or refutes this claim. A study on this topic is underway in Tanzania, but otherwise the subject remains a large knowledge gap.

## Household-Level Effects on Crop Yields

In addition to raising the use of fertilizer and improved seed, another common ISP goal is to raise the productivity of the crops for which these inputs are intended. Despite this goal's centrality, the econometric evidence on these effects is surprisingly thin (table 3B.2).[41] In the countries where this issue has been examined (Kenya, Malawi, and Zambia), the findings suggest positive ISP effects on maize yields [K3, M7, M13, Z3]. There is also some evidence of positive spillovers of ZFISP fertilizer on the yields of nonmaize crops in Zambia [Z3]. And while participation in Malawi's MFISP raises the value of crop output per hectare [M20], this is not the case for Kenya's NAAIAP, where it appears that positive increases in maize yields are offset by reduced productivity of other crops [K3].

Comparing ISP yield impacts across countries is difficult due to the different ways in which ISP participation is measured, differences in econometric approaches, and the difficulty in computing effect sizes given that many studies do not report standard errors. We can conclude from the available evidence, however, that ISPs do raise maize yields. But crowding out by and

**Table 3B.2** Empirical Findings on the Household-Level Effects of ISPs

| Country | Empirical findings |
|---|---|
| *Fertilizer and improved seed use (accounting for crowding out)* | |
| Ethiopia | Evidence suggests no significant crowding out impact on improved seed or fertilizer use unless HHs were able to participate in both a public works program and OFSP. The probability of such households using improved seeds is estimated at 8.2 percent, roughly 5 p.p. greater than nonparticipants, c.p. The probability of participants in both programs using fertilizer is 27 percent, 11 p.p. higher than nonparticipants, c.p. [E1] |
| Ghana | To the best of our knowledge, no studies account for crowding effects |
| Kenya | Crowding out (fertilizer): 49 (58) kg increase in fertilizer use per 100 kg increase in NAAIAP (NCPB) fertilizer, c.p. [K2]. Crowding out of commercial fertilizer purchases worse in medium to high potential zones, for MHHs, and for HHs in top half of land or assets distribution [K2]. No known analysis for improved seed use |
| Malawi | Crowding out (fertilizer): 78 (82) kg increase in fertilizer use per 100 kg increase in MFISP fertilizer, c.p., based on 2 (3) waves of HH panel survey data [M3, M2]. Crowding out worse among HHs with more assets [M3], in high PSA than low PSA areas [M2], and among HHs in top 50 percent of landholding distribution [M2] |
| | Crowding out (seed): 42 kg increase in improved maize seed use per 100 kg increase in MFISP maize seed received, c.p. [M16]. Simulation results in [M26] consistent with this general finding of seed crowding out |
| | Other: No cross effect of MFISP fertilizer on improved maize seed use. Increase in value of MFISP vouchers received raises maize fertilizer use intensity, c.p. [M7] |
| | In HHs that receive MFISP fertilizer (but do not buy commercial fertilizer), no difference in probability of fertilizer use between male- vs. female-controlled plots, c.p. [M11] |
| | No c.p. effects of MFISP vouchers on adopting modern maize varieties overall (MHH + FHH pooled) but receiving maize seed + fertilizer MFISP voucher increases probability of modern maize variety use on plots in FHHs by 92.4 p.p., c.p. [M12] |
| | [M13] suggest that MFISP fertilizer increases the probability and intensity of fertilizer use, c.p., but [M21] suggest it increases the probability of fertilizer use by 37 p.p. but has no c.p. effect on the kg or kg/ha of fertilizer used |
| | The effect of MFISP participation on fertilizer use is larger on plots managed by women than those managed by men, c.p. [M20] |
| Nigeria | Crowding out: 100 kg increase in FMSP fertilizer reduces probability of commercial fertilizer use by 10–21 p.p., but has no effect on quantity of commercial fertilizer used among users, c.p. Overall effect not reported [N1]. Earlier working paper results suggest overall crowding out effect of 19–35 kg per 100 kg of FMSP fertilizer [N7] |
| | Crowding in: 100 kg increase in KSVP raises commercial fertilizer purchases by 26 kg, total fertilizer acquired by 126 kg [N2], and the probability of using improved maize or rice seed by 8 p.p., c.p. [N3] |
| Tanzania | — |
| Zambia | Crowding out (fertilizer and seed): 87 (51) kg increase in fertilizer (hybrid maize seed) use per 100 kg increase in ZFISP fertilizer (hybrid seed), c.p. [Z1, Z2] |
| | Crowding out (in) of commercial fertilizer purchases by ZFISP in high (low) PSA areas, c.p. [Z7] or worse in high PSA than low PSA areas, and among MHHs and HHs with more than 2 ha of land [Z1] |
| | Other: No cross effect of ZFISP fertilizer on commercial maize seed use [Z2]. 10 kg/ha increase in fertilizer application rate per 100 kg increase in ZFISP fertilizer, c.p. [Z3] |

*(continued next page)*

**Table 3B.2** (continued)

| Country | Empirical findings |
|---|---|
| *Crop yields* | |
| Ethiopia | Estimated yield impacts for maize varies regionally and ranges from 3.8 to 4.5 marginal kg of cereal per kg of fertilizer applied [E2] |
| Ghana | Land productivity is similar between subsidy program recipients and nonrecipients, but labor productivity of participants is lower[a] |
| Kenya | NAAIAP participation raises maize yields by 299–721 kg per acre, c.p. (see source note for caveat) [K3]. No c.p. NAAIAP effects on net crop income per acre [K3]. No analyses to date for NCPB |
| Malawi | Receiving standard MFISP input pack raises maize yields by 447 kg per ha, c.p. [M7] |
| | Access to MFISP fertilizer raises maize yields, c.p. [M13] |
| | MFISP participation raises the value of crop output/ha by 13–17 percent, and there is no differential effect by plot manager gender, c.p. [M20] |
| Nigeria | — |
| Tanzania | — |
| Zambia | 74.3 kg/ha increase in maize yield per 100 kg increase in ZFISP fertilizer, c.p.; small, positive spillovers on yields of other crops [Z3]. Late delivery of ZFISP fertilizer reduces technical efficiency and maize yields by 4.2 percent c.p., resulting in 84,924 MT of foregone maize production in 2010/11 [Z11, cross-section] |
| *Crop area planted* | |
| Ethiopia | — |
| Ghana | — |
| Kenya | No c.p. NAAIAP effects on maize or total area cultivated, or on the number of different field crops grown (a rough proxy for crop diversification) [K3]. No analyses to date for NCPB |
| Malawi | Maize MFISP voucher recipients devote larger shares of land to maize, especially improved varieties, and tobacco, and smaller shares of land to other crops, especially legumes, c.p. [M8] |
| | Some evidence that MFISP access incentivizes maize intensification and reductions in maize area and share of area planted, c.p. [M13]. Similar findings in [M21]—for example, participation in MFISP reduces the share of area planted with maize by 23 p.p. each for improved and traditional varieties, increases share of area planted with legumes and tobacco by 37 and 15 p.p., respectively, and reduces the share of area planted with other crops by 5 p.p. But no c.p. effects on crop diversification [M21] |
| Nigeria | — |
| Tanzania | — |
| Zambia | 0.07 ha increase in maize area planted per 100 kg increase in ZFISP fertilizer, c.p. [Z3]. No c.p. effect on area planted with other crops [Z3], groundnuts [Z8], or cotton [Z12] |
| *Crop production* | |
| Ethiopia | — |
| Ghana | — |
| Kenya | NAAIAP participation (that is, receiving 100 kg of fertilizer and 10 kg of improved maize seed) raises main season maize kg harvested by 187–533 kg (estimates vary by estimator; FE estimate is 361 kg) and raises maize share of value of crop production by 2–5 p.p., c.p. No c.p. effect on net crop income [K3] |

*(continued next page)*

**Table 3B.2** (continued)

| Country | Empirical findings |
|---|---|
| Malawi | 165 kg increase in maize output per 100 kg increase in MFISP fertilizer, c.p. [M17] |
| | 100 kg increase in MFISP fertilizer raises the 10th, 25th, 50th, 75th, and 90th percentiles of maize production by 75 kg, 111 kg, 204 kg, 276 kg, and 261 kg, respectively, c.p. [M18] |
| | HHs receiving MFISP coupons for free had maize production that was 43 percent higher and were less (more) likely to be maize net buyers (net sellers), c.p. [M14] |
| | MFISP fertilizer has small, positive effects on tobacco production and net value of rainy season total crop production, c.p. [M17] |
| Nigeria | — |
| Tanzania | — |
| Zambia | 188 kg (106 kg) increase in maize output per 100 kg increase in ZFISP fertilizer (10 kg increase in ISP hybrid maize seed), c.p.; small, positive effects of ZFISP fertilizer on output of other crops, and on net crop income [Z3, Z4, Z13]. In Gwembe District, 224 kg increase in maize output per 100 kg increase in ZFISP inputs (seed or fertilizer) [Z9] |

*Food security and nutrition*

| | |
|---|---|
| Ethiopia | Results are mixed. Participation in public works and OFSP is associated with 0.4 fewer months of food security over two years, but participants acquire 230 (10 percent) more calories per week than nonparticipants, and both relationships are significant at the 5 percent level or lower, c.p. [E1] |
| Ghana | — |
| Kenya | — |
| Malawi | HH participation in MFISP raises per capita nonfood spending by 125 percent but has no c.p. effect on per capita food consumption or health-related expenditures, or on dietary diversity [M21] |
| | Among HHs with preschool-aged children, participation in MFISP increases weight-for-height by 2.1 standard deviations overall, and 3.1 (1.5) for male (female) children, on average, c.p., suggesting reductions in wasting as a result of MFISP [M21] |
| Nigeria | — |
| Tanzania | — |
| Zambia | No analyses to date, but study in progress |

*Incomes, poverty, and assets*

| | |
|---|---|
| Ethiopia | Public work participants experience roughly 45 percent growth in asset wealth over three-year period, but nonparticipant asset growth is 23 p.p. greater and this difference is significant at the 1 percent level [E1] |
| Ghana | — |
| Kenya | NAAIAP participation has no c.p. effect on total HH income or US$1.25 per day poverty incidence but reduces US$1.25 per day poverty severity by 4–11 p.p. [K3]. See note on [K6] |
| Malawi | Starter Pack participation reduced HH per capita income by 8.2 percent, but receiving full MFISP input pack raises HH per capita income by 8.2 percent, c.p. [M10] |
| | Increase in MFISP fertilizer has no c.p. on HH assets, off-farm income, or total (farm + off-farm) income [M17] |
| Nigeria | — |
| Tanzania | — |

*(continued next page)*

**Table 3B.2** (continued)

| Country | Empirical findings |
|---|---|
| Zambia | 100 kg of ZFISP fertilizer (10 kg of ZFISP hybrid maize seed) raises total HH income by 3.9 percent (1.1 percent) and reduces US$2 per day poverty severity at that HH level by 1.4 (0.7) p.p., c.p. No c.p. ZFISP seed or fertilizer effects on US$2 per day poverty incidence. Similar (and slightly larger impacts on poverty severity) when the US$1.25 per day poverty line is used [Z4, Z13] |

*Soil fertility management practices, fallow land, and forests*

| Country | Empirical findings |
|---|---|
| Ethiopia | — |
| Ghana | No evidence of FSP impact on broadly defined soil and water management after controlling for hired and household labor and other factors. Correlation is positive, but not significant [G1] |
| Kenya | — |
| Malawi | MFISP fertilizer has no c.p. effect on probability or intensity of organic manure use [M13, M15] or on intercropping [M13] |
| | Access to MFISP fertilizer might incentivize planting new trees but cutting down naturally occurring trees, c.p. [M13] |
| | Access to full set of MFISP maize coupons (seed + fertilizer) reduces forest clearing in both total hectares per household and hectares per capita, c.p., but receiving only seed or only fertilizer coupon has no c.p. effect [M9] |
| Nigeria | — |
| Tanzania | — |
| Zambia | An increase in ZFISP fertilizer reduces fallowing [Z3, Z14] and intercropping, increases continuous maize cultivation on the same plot, and has no effect on use of animal manure, c.p. [Z14] |

*Dynamic or enduring effects*

| Country | Empirical findings |
|---|---|
| Ethiopia | — |
| Ghana | — |
| Kenya | — |
| Malawi | Long-run (4-year) c.p. effect of 100 kg increase in MFISP fertilizer on maize production of 481 kg (165 kg contemporaneous + 316 kg lagged/enduring effects) [M17], and on commercial fertilizer demand of 13 kg (−7 kg contemporaneous crowding out + 20 kg lagged/enduring effects) [M28]. But [M28] find no lagged effects on maize production |
| | No contemporaneous or enduring c.p. effects of MFISP fertilizer on HH assets, off-farm, or total (farm + off-farm) income [M17]. Small, positive contemporaneous effect on HH tobacco production and net value of rainy season total crop production but no enduring effects, c.p. [M17] |
| Nigeria | — |
| Tanzania | — |
| Zambia | No analyses to date, but study planned for 2016 |

*Note:* Results are average partial effects and statistically significant at the 10 percent level or lower. See annex 3C for full references for the studies cited here, and for brief overviews of the data and methods used. c.p. = ceteris paribus; FE = fixed effects; FHH = female-headed household; FMSP = Federal Market Stabilization Program; FSP = Fertilizer Subsidy Program; HH = head of household; ISP = input subsidy program; KSVP = Kano State Voucher Program; MFISP = Malawi Farm Input Subsidy Program; MHH = male-headed household; NAAIAP = National Accelerated Agricultural Inputs Access Program; NCPB = National Cereals and Produce Board; OFSP = Other Food Security Program; p.p. = percentage point; PSA = private sector activity (fertilizer retailing); TSVP = Taraba State Voucher Program in 2009; ZFISP = Zambia Farmer Input Support Program; — = no analyses to date.
a. Wiredu, Zeller, and Diagne 2015.

late delivery of ISP inputs [Z7, Z11] are likely attenuating these effects, as are poor soil quality and the minimal use of complementary practices to raise crop yield response to fertilizer (Burke 2012; Jayne and Rashid 2013; Marenya and Barrett 2009).

## Household-Level Effects on Crop Area Planted

The empirical record is mixed whether ISPs induce an expansion of crop area planted or changes in the shares of land planted to different crops (see table 3B.2). In land-scarce Kenya, NAAIAP appeared to have no effect on farmers' area planted to maize or total area planted, on average and other factors constant [K3]. In relatively land-abundant Zambia, the ZFISP incentivizes an expansion of total and maize areas, such that the maize share of total area increases without affecting the area of land (in absolute terms) devoted to other crops [Z3, Z8, Z12]. The results from Malawi are again difficult to generalize. While [M8] suggests that smallholders increase the share of land devoted to maize in response to MFISP, [M13] and [M21]—which draw on different data sets from each other and from [M8]—suggest that MFISP incentivizes maize intensification and a reduction in the maize share of total area planted. We thus conclude that ISPs have heterogeneous effects on the area planted to maize and other crops.

## Household-Level Effects on Crop Production

Raising crop production is another core goal of most ISPs. The empirical findings summarized in table 3B.2 suggest that ISPs have had modest, positive effects on household-level maize production in all countries where this issue has been examined (Kenya, Malawi, and Zambia). Here the effects are somewhat easier to compare across countries, though still not perfectly. In Kenya, participation in NAAIAP raises maize production by 361 kg on average, other factors constant [K3].[42] The increases in Malawi (165 kg of maize per 100 kg of MFISP fertilizer) and Zambia (188 kg of maize per 100 kg of ZFISP fertilizer) are considerably smaller [M17, Z3]. While this could be due to minor methodological differences or because the latter two estimates are for fertilizer only whereas the Kenya-NAAIAP estimate is for fertilizer *and* seed, differences in the design and implementation of the three ISPs might also contribute to the differences in the estimated impacts on maize production. Of the three programs, only Kenya's NAAIAP successfully targeted resource-poor farmers and distributed inputs to farmers through vouchers redeemable at registered agro-dealers' shops. These differences, coupled with ecological differences leading to higher maize yield response to fertilizer in Kenya compared with Zambia and Malawi, may have contributed to the larger impacts of Kenya's ISP on maize production despite the larger crowding out effects there [K3].

Looking beyond the impacts on maize alone, the empirical evidence on the effects of ISPs on net crop income (or net value of crop production) is more variable. Estimates for Kenya's NAAIAP suggest negligible impacts on net crop income overall but increased net crop income among the poor, while evidence from Malawi and Zambia suggests that the MFISP and the ZFISP, respectively, do have small positive effects on net crop income overall [K3, M17, Z13].

Finally, looking "beyond the mean," quantile regression results from Malawi suggest that MFISP fertilizer has larger effects on higher percentiles of the maize production distribution. For example, a 100 kg increase in MFISP fertilizer raises the 10th percentile of the maize production distribution by only 75 kg but it raises the 90th percentile by 261 kg on average [M18].

In general, the empirical record suggests that ISPs have modest, positive effects on maize production and on net crop income for some population segments. But these effects vary at different points in the distribution of maize production.

## Household-Level Effects on Food Security and Nutrition

Improving household food security is another common ISP objective. But, to date, little research has been conducted on this topic (see table 3B.2). The only study we know of [M21] suggests participation in Malawi's MFISP raises per capita nonfood spending by 125 percent on average, other factors constant, but has no effects on food consumption, health-related spending, or dietary diversity. But there is some evidence that MFISP participation increases weight-for-height among preschool-aged children [M21].[43]

Though not technically an ISP, the EFSP also has mixed and limited empirical results on this question. Participation in public works and the OFSP is associated with 0.4 fewer months of food security over two years, but participants acquire 230 (10 percent) more calories per week than nonparticipants on average, all else equal [E1]. Given this topic's dearth of research, it is difficult to know if these results are generalizable.

## Household-Level Effects on Incomes, Poverty, and Assets

Several econometric studies have estimated the effects of ISPs on income, poverty, and asset wealth at the household level (see table 3B.2). Results for Kenya's NAAIAP and Zambia's ZFISP suggest that while these ISPs reduce poverty severity by several percentage points, the programs do not reduce poverty incidence [K3, Z4, Z13]. All else equal, the programs' effects on the income of the poor, on average, are not large enough to move them above the poverty line. The lack of an ISP effect on household-level poverty incidence in Zambia could be due to elite capture of a disproportionate share of ISP benefits.[44]

The results for Malawi, again, are mixed: [M10] suggests that receiving the full MFISP input pack raises per capita incomes by 8.2 percent, but [M17] finds no significant MFISP fertilizer effects on household assets, total income, or off-farm income. Overall, the literature suggests that ISPs have the potential to raise income and reduce poverty severity at the household level, but are less likely to decrease the probability that households fall below the poverty line.[45]

## Household-Level Effects on Soil Fertility Management Practices, Fallow Land, and Forests

In addition to the oft-stated objectives, ISPs could have spillover effects on other outcomes, such as using other soil fertility management practices. Experimental evidence from Mali suggests that access to free fertilizer induces households to increase fertilizer use but also to reoptimize their use of other inputs, such as herbicide or labor (Beaman et al. 2013).

Some studies have examined how much ISPs encourage (or discourage) the use of other soil fertility management practices. [G1] finds no evidence that Ghana's ISP has an impact on soil and water management after controlling for hired and household labor availability and other factors. Both [M13, M15] and [Z3] find that ISP fertilizer does not affect Malawi and Zambian smallholders' organic manure use. But while [Z14] finds some evidence that the ZFISP reduces intercropping in Zambia, [M13] finds no such effects for MFISP. [Z14] also finds that the ZFISP discourages crop rotation and encourages continually planting maize on the same plot. Results from Zambia also suggest that the ZFISP discourages fallowing [Z3, Z14]. High soil acidity and little soil organic matter on many Zambian smallholders' maize fields reduce fertilizer use efficiency but intercropping, crop rotation, and fallowing can improve soil quality. By incentivizing maize monocropping within seasons and by disincentivizing fallowing, the ZFISP may be undermining the effectiveness of inorganic fertilizer distributed through the program. Thus, while ISPs aim to increase soil fertility, there may be unintended negative consequences of the programs on using inputs or management practices complementary to inorganic fertilizer use.

Turning to the effects of ISPs on forest cover and trees (naturally occurring and planted), the empirical record is again mixed. All studies to date on this topic in Sub-Saharan Africa have been for Malawi. [M9] finds that receiving a full set of MFISP coupons (fertilizer plus maize seed) reduces pressure on surrounding forests. Based on a different data set, [M13] finds that MFISP increases both planting new trees and cutting down naturally occurring trees. Key takeaways are that ISPs can alter incentives for various soil fertility and land management practices and much remains to be learned about how ISPs affect adoption of crops and inputs beyond those being promoted.

## The Dynamic or Enduring Effects of ISPs on Farm Households

The studies discussed in the previous sections focus on the contemporaneous effects of ISPs. But a common argument made for ISPs is that by stimulating learning about the inputs, by helping farm households break out of poverty traps, or by building private sector input markets and increasing demand for inputs, ISPs could kick-start dynamic growth processes and have effects beyond their current year (Chirwa and Dorward 2013). Phosphorus in the fertilizers distributed through many ISPs can also continue to have effects on crop productivity for several years after its initial application. Whether there is empirical evidence of dynamic or enduring effects of ISPs depends on the outcome variable and the context.

In Malawi, the evidence suggests the absence of enduring or lagged effects of the MFISP on household maize production, assets, and income (total, farm, and off-farm) [M17, M28], but possible lagged crowding in effects on demand for commercial fertilizer after an initial crowding out period [M28]. In Mozambique, where far fewer households use fertilizer than in Malawi (and potential for learning effects may be greater), Carter, Laajaj, and Yang's (2014) randomized control trial results for a pilot ISP suggest substantial, positive enduring effects on many but not all the outcome variables considered. Some of these dynamic effects in Mozambique might be due to concurrent efforts by IFDC to strengthen agro-dealer networks and fertilizer supply as part of the pilot program. Thus depending on the outcome variable and context, ISPs may or may not have lasting, positive effects on farm households beyond the year of receipt.

## Market-Level and General Equilibrium Effects of ISPs

As demonstrated earlier, ISPs have had positive (though in several cases, relatively small) effects on household fertilizer use, crop yields, production, and incomes. ISPs' effects on these outcomes at more aggregate or national levels, and ISPs' partial- and general equilibrium effects on food prices and labor markets may differ. We examine the literature on these issues in this subsection, and conclude with a discussion of the empirical evidence on how much ISPs affect voting patterns and election results. See table 3B.3 for a summary of the aggregate level effects of ISPs.

**Table 3B.3** Empirical Findings on the Aggregate-Level Effects of ISPs

| Country | Empirical findings |
| --- | --- |
| *Fertilizer use (accounting for crowding out and diversion)* | |
| Ethiopia | — |
| Ghana | — |
| Kenya | 1 MT increase in subsidized fertilizer (NCPB or NAAIAP) raises national fertilizer use by 0.57 MT with no diversion, and 0.51 (0.38) MT with 10 percent (33 percent) diversion, c.p. [K2, K4] |
| Malawi | With 33 percent diversion, 1 MT increase in MFISP fertilizer raises national fertilizer use by 0.55 MT, c.p. [M1, M2] |
| Nigeria | — |
| Tanzania | — |
| Zambia | With 33 percent diversion, 1 MT increase in ZFISP fertilizer raises national fertilizer use by 0.58 MT, c.p. [Z1, Z15, Z16] |
| *Crop production, food self-sufficiency* | |
| Ethiopia | — |
| Ghana | — |
| Kenya | — |
| Malawi | Based on CGE model, 2006/07 MFISP raised national maize production by 174,300–307,300 MT (9–15 percent) and net maize exports by 44,900–122,500 MT (132–188 percent) [M22] |
| | Based on partial equilibrium model of the informal rural economy, [M27] estimate MFISP raises maize production by 11–23 percent per year across all HHs, and 31–39 percent among target (poor) HHs |
| | Based on an administrative area-level cross sectional data set (2008/09), a 1 percent increase in HHs receiving MFISP raises administrative area maize yields by approximately 0.2 percent, c.p. [M26] |
| Nigeria | — |
| Tanzania | US$300 million in NAIVS cost produced 2.5 million added tons of maize and rice over the program's course [T4] |
| Zambia | — |
| *Food price levels* | |
| Ethiopia | — |
| Ghana | — |
| Kenya | — |
| Malawi | Doubling MFISP scale (fertilizer quantity distributed) reduces retail maize prices by 1–3 percent [M4] |
| | Based on CGE model, 2006/07 MFISP reduced real maize prices by 2–4 percent, and reduced food prices by 2–3 percent [M22] |
| | Based on partial equilibrium model of the informal rural economy, [M27] estimate that MFISP raises mean preharvest (postharvest) wage-to-maize price ratios by 5–26 percent (32–73 percent) through both wage-increasing and maize price-reducing effects |
| Nigeria | Increase in scale of FMSP in an LGA (that is, increase in mean kg per HH or share of HHs receiving subsidized fertilizer) has no statistical significance or very weak negative effect on local rice, sorghum, and maize price interseason growth rates, c.p. [N6] |
| Tanzania | — |
| Zambia | Doubling scale of fertilizer ZFISP (quantity distributed) reduces retail maize prices by 2–3 percent [Z17] |

*(continued next page)*

**Table 3B.3** (continued)

| Country | Empirical findings |
|---|---|

*Agricultural labor wage rates and supply and demand*

| Ethiopia | No evidence of any significant positive correlation between EFSP participation and entering labor markets, agricultural or otherwise [E1] |
|---|---|
| Ghana | — |
| Kenya | — |
| Malawi | *Ganyu* (short-term) labor supply: Among ganyu labor supplying smallholders HHs (all smallholder HHs), a 100 kg increase in MFISP fertilizer reduces (has no effect on) the probability of supplying ganyu labor by 2.3 p.p., and reduces the number of days supplied by 10.7 days (2.9 days), c.p. |
| | Ganyu labor demand: A 100 kg increase in MFISP fertilizer has no effect on the days of ganyu labor demanded (both among all HHs and ganyu-demanding HHs), but raises the probability of ganyu labor demand by 1.6 p.p. among all HHs, c.p. [M18] |
| | Agricultural wage rates: A 10 kg increase in the average quantity of MFISP fertilizer acquired by HHs in a community raises the median agricultural wage rate in the community by 1.4 percent, c.p. This is equivalent to an increase in average annual income of about US$1.40–US$1.86 [M18] |
| | Based on CGE model: 2006/07 MFISP increased the average farm wage by 4–7 p.p. (5–8 percent) [M22] |
| | Based on partial equilibrium model of the informal rural economy, [M27] estimate that MFISP raises mean preharvest (postharvest) wage-to-maize price ratios by 5–26 percent (32–73 percent) through both wage-increasing and maize price-reducing effects |
| Nigeria | — |
| Tanzania | — |
| Zambia | — |

*Incomes and poverty*

| Ethiopia | — |
|---|---|
| Ghana | — |
| Kenya | — |
| Malawi | Based on CGE model, 2006/07 MFISP reduced the national poverty rate by 1.6–2.7 p.p., the rural poverty rate by 1.5–2.7 p.p., and the urban poverty rate by 1.5–2.9 p.p. [M22]. Slightly higher reduction in urban poverty rate due to reduction in food prices and increase in wages [M22] |
| | Based on partial equilibrium model of the informal rural economy, [M27] estimate real income increases as a result of MFISP of 3–11 percent per year across all HHs, and 6–31 percent among target (poor) HHs |
| Nigeria | — |
| Tanzania | — |
| Zambia | — |

*Voting patterns and election results*

| Ethiopia | — |
|---|---|
| Ghana | — |
| Kenya | — |

*(continued next page)*

**Table 3B.3** (continued)

| Country | Empirical findings |
|---|---|
| Malawi | MFISP increased support for DPP party, c.p. [M5, M6]. More specifically, [M5] find that respondents whose HH received MFISP in 2009 were 6–7 percent more likely to "feel close to" the DPP in 2010, c.p. |
| | [M6] find that a 1 p.p. increase in the percentage of HHs receiving MFISP raised the DPP's parliamentary electoral margin over their closest rival in the constituency by 2 percent, c.p. |
| Nigeria | — |
| Tanzania | — |
| Zambia | An increase in percentage of smallholder HHs receiving ZFISP, the mean kg of ZFISP fertilizer received per HH, or the total (administrative) allocation of ZFISP fertilizer to the district had no c.p. on the number or share of votes won by the incumbent in the 2006 and 2010 presidential elections [Z6] |

*Note:* Results are average partial effects and statistically significant at the 10 percent level or lower. See annex 3C for full references for the studies cited here, and for brief overviews of the data and methods used. *Ganyu* refers to short-term rural labor relationships. CGE = computable general equilibrium; c.p. = ceteris paribus; DPP = Democratic Progressive Party; EFSP = Ethiopia Food Security Program; FMSP = Federal Market Stabilization Program; HH = head of household; ISP = input support program; LGA = local government area; MFISP = Malawi Farmer Input Support Program; NAAIAP = National Accelerated Agricultural Inputs Access Program; NAIVS = National Agricultural Inputs Voucher Scheme; NCPB = National Cereals and Produce Board; p.p. = percentage point; ZFISP = Zambia Farmer Input Support Program; — = no analyses to date.

## Aggregate Fertilizer Use

Based on the micro-econometric evidence discussed, most ISPs partially crowd out demand for commercial fertilizer. But a substantial share (roughly one-third in Malawi and Zambia) of fertilizer intended for ISPs is diverted by program implementers before reaching intended beneficiaries and resold as commercial fertilizer at or near commercial prices [Z1, Z15, Z16]. Such diversion needs to be taken into account when moving from household estimates of crowding out to national estimates of the impacts of ISPs on total fertilizer use.[46] Based on diversion estimates of 33 percent, 1 MT of ISP fertilizer injected into the system raises total fertilizer use by just 0.38 MT in Kenya, 0.55 MT in Malawi, and 0.58 MT in Zambia (Carter, Laajaj, and Yang 2014; see also table 3B.3). Thus, although ISPs raise total fertilizer use, there are major inefficiencies and diversion by program implementers representing another form of elite capture of ISP benefits.

## Aggregate Crop Production and Food Self-Sufficiency

Many ISPs aim to raise national crop production to achieve food self-sufficiency or increase net crop exports. The only studies that directly estimate these effects have been conducted for Malawi and take either a partial equilibrium or CGE modeling approach [M26 and M27, respectively].[47] These studies suggest increases in national maize production as a result of the

MFISP (for example, in 2006/07) of 9–23 percent (with even larger percentage increases among targeted households), and increases in net maize exports of 132–188 percent.

## Food Price Levels
Though typically not stated as an explicit objective of ISPs, if the programs reduce food prices (by increasing food supply), the programs could benefit urban consumers and net food buyers, including many poor rural households. The effects of ISPs on food prices have been estimated for Malawi [M4, M22, M27], Nigeria [N6], and Zambia [Z17]. Though using different approaches, [M4, M22, Z17] suggest modest reductions in retail maize prices as a result of Malawi's MFISP and Zambia's ZFISP of about 1–4 percent. [M22] also suggests that the MFISP reduced overall food prices (that is, maize and other food items) by 2–3 percent. Though not directly comparable, [M27]'s findings suggest a decrease in the maize-to-wage price ratio as a result of the MFISP due to both reductions in maize prices and increases in wages. Only for Nigeria is there little evidence of ISP effects on food prices [N6] (see table 3B.3). Thus, the empirical evidence suggests that ISPs in Sub-Saharan Africa reduce food prices but by small amounts.

## Agricultural Labor Wage Rates and Supply and Demand
ISPs could further benefit poor nonbeneficiary households—which often engage in agricultural wage labor—if the programs increase demand for such labor and thus put upward pressure on agricultural wages. Only for Malawi is there empirical evidence on the effects of ISPs on agricultural wages or supply and demand. Collectively, the results suggest that the MFISP does raise agricultural wages, but the effects vary across studies (see table 3B.3). CGE model results suggest increases in average farm wages of 5–8 percent because of the MFISP [M22], but micro-econometric estimates suggest increases of 1 percent [M18]. The MFISP also seems to result in small increases (decreases) in labor demand (supply) [M18].

## Incomes and Poverty
Apart from the household-level poverty impacts discussed above, ISPs could reduce the national poverty rate and, more specifically, notoriously stubborn rural poverty rates. That said, there is little empirical evidence to examine these relationships. CGE modeling work from Malawi [M22] suggests that the 2006/07 MFISP reduced the national poverty rate by 1.6–2.7 percentage points and that poverty reductions in rural and urban areas were similar, if not slightly greater, in urban areas (see table 3B.3).

## Voting Patterns and Election Results

Once established, ISPs often become entrenched features of countries' agricultural sector policies. The conventional wisdom is that scaling back ISPs is politically damaging, but establishing or scaling up ISPs is politically beneficial. But does the empirical record support these claims? Again, the answer depends on the context, both in the political dynamics and the design and implementation of the ISP. Evidence from Malawi suggests that the MFISP substantially increased support for Bingu Wa Mutharika and his Democratic Progressive Party (DPP) in the 2009 election [M5, M6]. But in Zambia, [Z6] find no evidence that the ZFISP affected the number or share of votes won by the incumbent in the 2006 and 2011 presidential elections, on average and other factors constant.

There are several reasons ISPs may have affected voting patterns in Malawi but not in Zambia. First, the run-up to the 2009 election in Malawi was unique. After being elected in 2004, President Mutharika left his former party, the United Democratic Front (UDF), and started his own party (the DPP) in 2005. His old party controlled parliament, so Mutharika needed a large-scale and highly publicized policy initiative to garner support for reelection in 2009 ([M5, M6], Chinsinga and Poulton 2014). There was no such seismic political imperative in Zambia. Second, the MFISP reaches a much larger share of Malawi smallholders than the ZFISP does in Zambia (table 3A.4). Third, the benefits of the ZFISP are much more highly concentrated in the hands of relatively better-off farmers than are the benefits of the MFISP (table 3B.3). Together, these differences in the Malawi and Zambian contexts could explain the different effects of ISPs on voting patterns in the two countries. It would be useful to test whether the MFISP played a similarly important role in elections in Malawi after 2009, when Mutharika's DPP was well established.

## Annex 3C: References for Annexes 3A and 3B and Basic Information on Data Sources and Methods

### Ethiopia

[E1] Gilligan, D. O., J. Hoddinott, and A. S. Taffesse. 2009. "The Impact of Ethiopia's Productive Safety Net Programme and Its Linkages." *Journal of Development Studies* 45 (10): 1684–1706. (Sample of 3,700 households representing the four regions principally served by the Productive Safety Net Programme [Tigray, Amhara, Oromiya, and Southern Nations, Nationalities, and People's Region].)

[E2] Rashid, S., N. Tefera, N. Minot, and G. Ayele. 2013. "Can Modern Input Use Be Promoted without Subsidies? An Analysis of Fertilizer in Ethiopia." *Agricultural Economics* 44 (6): 595–611. (Estimates based on 2008 Ethiopian Development Research Institute–International Food Policy Research Institute [IFPRI] household survey.)

## Ghana

[G1] Vondolia, G. K., H. Eggert, and J. Stage. 2012. "Nudging Boserup? The Impact of Fertilizer Subsidies on Investment in Soil and Water Conservation." Discussion Paper 12-08, Environment for Development and Resources for the Future, Washington, DC. (Cross-sectional data from 460 rice farmers in the Afife irrigation project in Ghana's Volta region.)

[G2] Banful, A. B. 2009. "Old Problems in the New Solutions? Politically Motivated Allocation of Program Benefits and the 'New' Fertilizer Subsidies." *World Development* 39 (7): 1166–76.

[G3] Resnick, D., and D. Mather. 2015. "Agricultural Inputs Policy under Macroeconomic Uncertainty: Applying the Kaleidoscope Model to Ghana's Fertilizer Subsidy Program (2008–2015)." Draft working paper, IFPRI and Michigan State University, Washington, DC, and East Lansing, MI.

## Kenya

[K1] Sheahan, M., J. Olwande, L. Kirimi, and T. S. Jayne. 2014. "Targeting of Subsidized Fertilizer under Kenya's National Accelerated Agricultural Input Access Program (NAAIAP)." Working Paper 52, Tegemeo Institute of Agricultural Policy and Development, Nairobi, Kenya. (Two waves of nation-wide household panel survey data; NAAIAP receipt only captured in second [2010] wave; probit models using NAAIAP receipt as of second wave as dependent variable; and head of household (HH) to village characteristics as of first [2007] wave.)

[K2] Mather, D., and T. S. Jayne. 2015. "Fertilizer Subsidies and the Role of Targeting in Crowding Out: An Assessment of Smallholder Fertilizer Demand in Kenya." Selected paper prepared for the 29th International Conference of Agricultural Economists, Milan, Italy, August 8–14. (Four waves of nation-wide HH panel survey data; NAAIAP/National Cereals and Produce Board receipt captured only in fourth [2010] wave; targeting results based on correlated random effects [CRE] Tobit regressions; crowding out/total fertilizer use effects based on truncated normal hurdle model with CRE and control function [CF].)

[K3] Mason, N. M., A. Wineman, L. Kirimi, and D. Mather. 2015. "The Effects of Kenya's 'Smarter' Input Subsidy Program on Smallholder Behavior and Incomes: Do Different Quasi-Experimental Approaches Lead to the Same Conclusions?" Working Paper, Tegemeo Institute of Agricultural Policy and Development, Nairobi, Kenya. (Three waves of nationwide household panel survey data; NAAIAP receipt captured only in third [2010] wave; range of impact estimates due to range of econometric approaches used—that is, difference-in-differences [DID], fixed effects [FE], propensity score weighting-DID, and propensity score matching-DID with associated Rosenbaum bounds. "Maize yield" is kilogram of maize harvested per acre planted with maize, be it mono- or intercropped. Not feasible to apportion intercropped area to constituent crops with these data.)

[K4] Jayne, T. S., D. Mather, N. M. Mason, J. Ricker-Gilbert, and E. Crawford. 2015. "Rejoinder to the Comment by Andrew Dorward and Ephraim Chirwa on Jayne, T. S, D. Mather, N. Mason, and J. Ricker-Gilbert. 2013. 'How Do Fertilizer Subsidy Programs Affect Total Fertilizer Use in Sub-Saharan Africa? Crowding Out, Diversion, and Benefit/Cost Assessments.' *Agricultural Economics* 44 (6): 687–703." *Agricultural Economics* 46 (6): 745–55.

[K5] Jayne, T. S., D. Mather, N. M. Mason, and J. Ricker-Gilbert. 2013. "How Do Fertilizer Subsidy Programs Affect Total Fertilizer Use in Sub-Saharan Africa? Crowding Out, Diversion, and Benefit/Cost Assessments." *Agricultural Economics* 44 (6): 687–703. (Kenya analysis same as [K2] above.)

[K6] Ochola, R. O., and F. Nie. 2015. "Evaluating the Effects of Fertilizer Subsidy Programmes on Vulnerable Farmers in Kenya." *Journal of Agricultural Extension and Rural Development* 7 (6): 192–201. (Despite the article's title and although it focuses on NAAIAP, it does not estimate the effects of NAAIAP participation on household incomes or other outcomes; the sample includes only NAAIAP beneficiaries.)

## Malawi

[M1] Jayne, T. S., D. Mather, N. M. Mason, J. Ricker-Gilbert, and E. Crawford. 2015. "Rejoinder to the Comment by Andrew Dorward and Ephraim Chirwa on Jayne, T. S, D. Mather, N. Mason, and J. Ricker-Gilbert. 2013. 'How Do Fertilizer Subsidy Programs Affect Total Fertilizer Use in Sub-Saharan Africa? Crowding Out, Diversion, and Benefit/Cost Assessments.' *Agricultural Economics* 44 (6): 687–703." *Agricultural Economics* 46 (6): 745–55.

[M2] Jayne, T. S., D. Mather, N. M. Mason, and J. Ricker-Gilbert. 2013. "How Do Fertilizer Subsidy Programs Affect Total Fertilizer Use in Sub-Saharan Africa? Crowding Out, Diversion, and Benefit/Cost Assessments." *Agricultural Economics* 44 (6): 687–703. (Three waves of nationally representative HH survey data: Integrated Household Survey II [IHS2], Agricultural Input Subsidy Survey 1 [AISS1], and Agricultural Input Subsidy Survey 2 [AISS2]; truncated normal hurdle model with CRE and CF approach.)

[M3] Ricker-Gilbert, J., T. S. Jayne, and E. Chirwa. 2011. "Subsidies and Crowding Out: A Double-Hurdle Model of Fertilizer Demand in Malawi." *American Journal of Agricultural Economics* 93 (1): 26–42. (Two waves of nationally representative household survey data [IHS2 covers 2002/03 and 2003/04, and AISS1 covers 2006/07]; truncated normal hurdle model with CRE and CF approach.)

[M4] Ricker-Gilbert, J., N. M. Mason, F. A. Darko, and S. T. Tembo. 2013. "What Are the Effects of Input Subsidy Programs on Maize Prices? Evidence from Malawi and Zambia." *Agricultural Economics* 44 (6): 671–86. (Malawi analysis based on 12 years of biannual data from 72 markets in 26 districts; Arellano-Bond dynamic panel data models.)

[M5] Dionne, K. Y., and J. Horowitz. 2013. "The Political Effects of Anti-Poverty Initiatives: An Analysis of Malawi's Agricultural Input Subsidy Program." Paper presented at the Midwest Group in African Political Economy meeting, Indiana University, Bloomington, IN, October 17–18. (Data from three districts on Farm Input Subsidy Program [FISP] participation in 2009, and respondent-level panel data from 2008 and 2010 on partisan leanings, and other respondent and HH characteristics; logit models for receipt of FISP; logit, matching, and Rosenbaum bounds sensitivity analysis for effects of FISP receipt in 2009 on partisanship in 2010.)

[M6] Brazys, S., P. Heaney, and P. P. Walsh. 2015. "Fertilizer and Votes: Does Strategic Economic Policy Explain the 2009 Malawi Election?" *Electoral Studies* 39: 39–55. (Various data sources including the 2008 Malawi Welfare Monitoring Survey, the 2004/05 Malawi Integrated Household Survey, AidData, Afrobarometer Round 3 [2005], Malawi Electoral Commission, and others—please see the article for details; constituency and district-level data and two-step procedure/IV approach [district-level regressions] to correct for endogeneity of FISP to election outcomes.)

[M7] Chibwana, C., G. Shively, M. Fisher, and C. Jumbe. 2014. "Measuring the Impacts of Malawi's Farm Input Subsidy Programme." *African Journal of Agriculture and Resource Economics* 9 (2): 132–47. (Two- and three-year household panel survey data set from 375 and 176 total smallholder households, respectively, in two districts—Kasungu and Machinga; IV approach; panel data used to create lagged variables but panel data methods not used.)

[M8] Chibwana, C., M. Fisher, and G. Shively. 2012. "Cropland Allocation Effects of Agricultural Input Subsidies in Malawi." *World Development* 40 (1): 124–33. (Same data as [M7] but used only most recent wave, 2008/09, as cross-section; multinomial logit and probit regressions for targeting; Tobit regressions for share of land devoted to various crops; two-step/IV approach.)

[M9] Chibwana, C., C. Jumbe, and G. Shively. 2012. "Agricultural Subsidies and Forest Clearing in Malawi." *Environmental Conservation* 40 (1): 60–70. (Cross-sectional data from 380 HHs near forest reserves in two districts in Malawi; two-step/IV approach with multinomial logit regression for targeting, and Tobit regression for the extent of forest clearing.)

[M10] Chirwa, T. G. 2010. "Program Evaluation of Agricultural Input Subsidies in Malawi Using Treatment Effects: Methods and Practicability Based on Propensity Scores." Munich Personal Research Papers in Economics Archive Paper 21236, Ludwig-Maximilians-Universität München, Munich, Germany. http://mpra.ub.uni-muenchen.de/21236/1/MPRA_paper_21236.pdf. (Panel data from the nationally representative IHS2 and AISS1; PSM and IV approaches; panel data methods not employed.)

[M11] Chirwa, E. W., P. M. Mvula, A. Dorward, and M. Matita. 2011. "Gender and Intra-Household Use of Fertilizers in the Malawi Farm Input Subsidy Programme." Working Paper 028, Future Agricultures Consortium, Brighton, U.K. (Cross-sectional data from the nationally representative AISS2 survey, which covers the 2008/09 agricultural season; probit regressions; no correction for endogeneity of FISP participation.)

[M12] Fisher, M., and V. Kandiwa. 2014. "Can Agricultural Input Subsidies Reduce the Gender Gap in Modern Maize Adoption? Evidence from Malawi." *Food Policy* 45 (May): 101–11. (Cross-sectional data from the nationally representative IHS3, which covers the 2008/09 agricultural season; multinomial logit for targeting analysis, and logit model for factors affecting adoption of modern maize varieties; two-step/IV approach.)

[M13] Holden, S. T., and R. Lunduka. 2010. *Too Poor to be Efficient? Impacts of the Targeted Fertilizer Subsidy Programme in Malawi on Farm Plot Level Input Use, Crop Choice, and Land Productivity*. Noragric Report 55. Ås, Norway: Department of International Environment and Development Studies, Norwegian University of Life Sciences. (Three-wave panel survey of 450 HHs (378 in balanced panel) in six districts in Malawi; random effects, fixed effects, panel probit, and bivariate probit models; IV approach also tried but authors note that "no good instruments were available for predicting each of the input variables" [5].)

[M14] Holden, S. T., and R. W. Lunduka. 2013. "Who Benefit from Malawi's Targeted Farm Input Subsidy Program?" *Forum for Development Studies* 40 (1): 1–25. (Data same as last two waves in [M13]; ordered probit for maize market position [net buyer, autarkic, net seller], ordinary least squares [OLS] for maize production; lagged dependent variables included in regressions; panel data methods and instrumental variables not employed.)

[M15] Holden, S. T., and R. Lunduka. 2012. "Do Fertilizer Subsidies Crowd Out Organic Manures? The Case of Malawi." *Agricultural Economics* 43 (3): 303–14. (Same data as [M13]; probit and Tobit models with CRE and CF approach.)

[M16] Mason, N. M., and J. Ricker-Gilbert. 2013. "Disrupting Demand for Commercial Seed: Input Subsidies in Malawi and Zambia." *World Development* 45 (May): 75–91. (Two waves of nationally representative household panel survey data—AISSI and AISS2; Tobit models with CRE and CF.)

[M17] Ricker-Gilbert, J., and T. S. Jayne. 2011. "What Are the Enduring Effects of Fertilizer Subsidy Programs on Recipient Farm Households: Evidence from Malawi." Staff Paper 2011–09, Department of Agricultural, Food, and Resource Economics, Michigan State University, East Lansing, MI. (Three-waves of nationally representative HH panel survey data—IHS2, AISS1, AISS2; first-difference estimator and log-normal hurdle model with CRE, both with CF approach.)

[M18] Ricker-Gilbert, J., and T. S. Jayne. 2012. "Do Fertilizer Subsidies Boost Staple Crop Production and Reduce Poverty Across the Distribution of Smallholders in Africa? Quantile Regression Results from Malawi." Selected paper prepared for presentation at the International Association of Agricultural Economists Triennial Conference, Foz do Iguaçu, Brazil, August 18–24. (Same data as [M17]; quantile regression model with CRE.)

[M19] Ricker-Gilbert, J. 2014. "Wage and Employment Effects of Malawi's Fertilizer Subsidy Program." *Agricultural Economics* 45 (3): 337–53. (Same as [M17]; fixed effects and CRE Tobit regressions.)

[M20] Karamba, R. W., and P. C. Winters. 2015. "Gender and Agricultural Productivity: Implications of the Farm Input Subsidy Program in Malawi." *Agricultural Economics* 46 (3): 357–74. (Same data as [M12]; probit model for FISP participation, and OLS, propensity score weighting [PSW], and PSW with spatial fixed effects for yield effects of FISP.)

[M21] Karamba, R. W. 2013. "Input Subsidies and Their Effect on Cropland Allocation, Agricultural Productivity, and Child Nutrition: Evidence from Malawi." PhD dissertation, American University, Washington, DC. (Same data as [M12]; probit and IV models for if used fertilizer on plot, OLS and IV for kg and kg per hectare of fertilizer applied, and crop diversity, OLS and three-stage least squares for cropland allocation decisions. OLS and IV for per capita value of food consumption, nonfood consumption, and health expenditures, dietary diversity, and weight-for-height Z-score for preschool children [6–59 months].)

[M22] Arndt, C., K. Pauw, and J. Thurlow. 2015. "The Economywide Impacts and Risks of Malawi's Farm Input Subsidy Programme." WIDER Working Paper 2014/099, United Nations University, World Institute for Development Economics Research, Helsinki, Finland. (Study of the 2006/07 FISP, which aimed to distribute 150,000 MT of fertilizer for use on maize, along with improved seed (60 percent of which was hybrid, and 40 percent of which was composite); assumed these inputs were used on 500,000 ha of land; CGE model of the Malawi economy based on 2003 Social Accounting Matrix; CGE model linked to a poverty module based on household survey data (IHS2) to estimate impacts of FISP on consumption poverty. "Observed consumption changes in the model are then applied proportionally to survey households, each with a unique consumption pattern. A post-simulation consumption value can then be calculated and compared against an absolute poverty threshold to determine if a household's poverty status has changed from the base." [5].)

[M23] Westberg, N. B. 2015. "Exchanging Fertilizer for Votes?" Working Paper 12/2015, Norwegian University of Life Sciences School of Economics and Business, Ås, Norway. (Main data sources are district-level FISP allocations from the Malawi Logistics Unit, population data from the National Statistical Office, and election data from the Sustainable Development Network Programme and Malawi Electoral Commission; six years of district-level panel data covering all 28 districts in Malawi; district-level fixed effects model of number of FISP vouchers allocated to district regressed on past election results and other controls.)

[M24] Chirwa, E. W., M. Matita, and A. Dorward. 2010. "Targeting Agricultural Input Subsidy Coupons in Malawi." Working Paper, School of Oriental and African Studies, University of London, London, U.K. (Cross-sectional data from the nationally representative AISS2 survey, which covers the 2008/09 agricultural season; probit and Tobit models for factors affecting receipt of FISP fertilizer coupons and kilograms, of subsidized fertilizer acquired, respectively.)

[M25] Holden, S. 2013. "Input Subsidies and Demand for Improved Maize: Relative Prices and Household Heterogeneity Matter!" Centre for Land Tenure Studies Working Paper 06/13, Norwegian University of Life Sciences, Ås, Norway. (Simulations based on nonseparable agricultural household models, with rural Malawi households classified into six households groups based on region [South vs. Central], sex of the HH, and land availability ["land-poor" vs. "land-rich"]. Models calibrated to 2005/06 survey data from six districts.)

[M26] Mkwara, B., and D. Marsh. 2011. "Effects of Maize Fertilizer Subsidies on Food Security in Malawi." Working Paper in Economics 14/11, Department of Economics, University of Waikato, Hamilton, New Zealand. (Cross-sectional, nationwide administrative area data from the 2008/09 Annual National Census of Agriculture. OLS and OLS controlling for spatial autocorrelation regressions of administrative area maize yield on the percentage of HHs receiving FISP and other controls. No correction for potential endogeneity of FISP to maize yields.)

[M27] Dorward, A., and E. Chirwa. 2013. "Impacts of the Farm Input Subsidy Programme in Malawi: Informal Rural Modeling." Working Paper 067, Future Agricultures Consortium, Brighton, U.K. (Partial equilibrium model of the impacts of FISP on smallholder livelihoods in two livelihood zones for 2005/06 through 2010/11. IHS2 data used to develop household/livelihood zone classification scheme. Household livelihood models developed for Kasungu Lilongwe Plain and Shire Highlands for each household type per the classification scheme [see paper for details]; model results then aggregated by livelihood zone to obtain an "informal rural economy" model. "With subsidy" scenario modeled in two ways: (a) universal 50 kg fertilizer + 2 kg hybrid maize seed, and (b) targeted distribution of 100 kg of fertilizer + 2 kg hybrid maize seed to their "poor male-headed household" and "poor female-headed household" types. Per the authors, "An average taken across [the two scenarios] is likely to be closer to distribution patterns actually achieved. However, it should be recognized that this is likely to overestimate access by poorer households." [7].)

[M28] Kilic, T., E. Whitney, and P. Winters. 2015. "Decentralised Beneficiary Targeting in Large-Scale Development Programmes: Insights from the Malawi Farm Input Subsidy Programme." *Journal of African Economies* 24 (1): 26–56. (Cross-sectional, nationally representative HH survey data from IHS3 used to analyze the decentralized targeting of FISP during the 2009/10 agricultural season. Decomposes targeting coefficients into interdistrict, intradistrict intercommunity, and intradistrict intracommunity components. IHS3 rural HHs classified as poor [FISP eligible] or not based on annual rural household consumption per capita predicted as a function of nonmonetary explanatory variables, the IHS2 2004/05 poverty line, and a survey-to-survey imputation approach using the IHS2 data to estimate the relationship between these explanatory variables and per capita consumption. *Poor* defined in this way used as a proxy for *resource poor*, a key FISP eligibility criterion. Household assets and landholding size used as alternative proxies for *resource poor*. Probit [order probit] model for factors affecting household-level participation in FISP [number of FISP coupons received], with controls for district and agroecological zone fixed effects.)

[M29] Ricker-Gilbert, J., and T. S. Jayne. 2015. "What Are the Dynamic Effects of Fertilizer Subsidies on Commercial Fertilizer Demand and Maize Production? Panel Evidence from Malawi." Paper prepared for presentation at the symposium on "Using Smart Subsidies to Support Small Scale Farmers in Africa," International Conference of Agricultural Economists, Milan, Italy, August 18. (Four waves of panel data on 462 farm households in Malawi; panel data techniques to correct for the potential endogeneity of subsidized fertilizer to household commercial fertilizer demand and maize production.)

## Nigeria

[N1] Takeshima, H., and E. Nkonya. 2014. "Government Fertilizer Subsidy and Commercial Sector Fertilizer Demand: Evidence from the Federal Market Stabilization Program in Nigeria." *Food Policy* 47 (August): 1–12. (Two different data sets analyzed: a two-year, nationwide local government area (LGA)-level pseudo-panel data set of export crop growers, and a nationally representative cross-sectional survey of agricultural households; double-hurdle version of simultaneous Tobit model with IV [and LGA-level CRE for pseudo-panel analysis] [Nelson and Olson 1978]).

[N2] Liverpool-Tasie, L. S. O. 2014c. "Fertilizer Subsidies and Private Market Participation: The Case of Kano State, Nigeria." *Agricultural Economics* 45 (6): 663–78. (Cross-sectional data set from Kano State; truncated normal hurdle model with CF approach.)

[N3] Liverpool-Tasie, L. S. O., and S. Salau. 2013. "Spillover Effects of Targeted Subsidies: An Assessment of Fertilizer and Improved Seed Use in Nigeria." Discussion Paper 01260, Development Strategy and Governance Division, IFPRI, Washington, DC. (Same data set and approach as [N2], except probit model instead of truncated normal hurdle model.)

[N4] Liverpool-Tasie, L. S. O. 2014a. "Do Vouchers Improve Government Fertilizer Distribution? Evidence from Nigeria." *Agricultural Economics* 45 (4): 393–407. (Same data as [N2] and [N3] plus cross-sectional data set from Taraba State; PSM and Rosenbaum bounds.)

[N5] Liverpool-Tasie, L. S. O. 2014b. "Farmer Groups and Input Access: When Membership Is Not Enough." *Food Policy* 46 (June): 37–49. (Same data as [N4]; generalized Tobit and lognormal hurdle models.)

[N6] Takeshima, H., and L. S. O. Liverpool-Tasie. 2015. "Fertilizer Subsidies, Political Influence and Local Food Prices in Sub-Saharan Africa: Evidence from Nigeria." *Food Policy* 54 (July): 11–24. (Enumeration area [EA] local rice, maize, and sorghum prices for 187 EAs, and LGA-level subsidized fertilizer quantities; multiple EAs per LGA; prices measured at post-harvest and post-planting in one year; EA-level, two-season panel; three-stage least squares models for growth rate in crop price.)

[N7] Takeshima, H., E. Nkonya, and S. Deb. 2012. "Impact of Fertilizer Subsidies on the Commercial Fertilizer Sector in Nigeria: Evidence from Previous Fertilizer Subsidy Schemes." Working Paper 23, IFPRI Nigeria Strategy Support Program II, Abuja, Nigeria. (Same data as [N1], endogenous Tobit model with both data sets, and combined with CRE in analysis of the pseudo-panel data.)

## Tanzania

[T1] Pan, L., and L. Christiaensen. 2012. "Who Is Vouching for the Input Voucher? Decentralized Targeting and Elite Capture in Tanzania." *World Development* 40 (8): 1619–33.

[T2] Msolla, M. M. 2014. "Effects of the Subsidy Voucher Program on Fertilizer Markets: Example from Tanzania." Paper presented at the International Fertilizer Development Center Training on Fertilizer Value Chain-Supply System Management and Servicing Farmers' Needs, Accra, Ghana, April 14–18.

[T3] Mather, D., B. Waized, D. Ndyetabula, A. Temu, I. Minde, and D. Nyange. 2015. "The Role of Relative Prices, Agro-Ecological Factors, and Household Soil and Crop Management Practices in Explaining Smallholder Profitability of Fertilizer Use on Maize in Tanzania." Michigan State University, East Lansing, MI.

[T4] World Bank. 2014. *Tanzania Public Expenditure Review: National Agricultural Input Voucher Scheme (NAIVS). Strengthening National Comprehensive Agricultural Public Expenditure in Sub-Saharan Africa.* Washington, DC: World Bank. www.worldbank.org/afr/agperprogram.

## Zambia

[Z1] Mason, N. M., and T. S. Jayne. 2015. "Fertilizer Subsidies and Smallholder Commercial Fertilizer Purchases: Crowding Out, Leakage and Policy Implications for Zambia." *Journal of Agricultural Economics* 64 (3): 558–82. (Three waves of nationally representative household panel survey data; Tobit and truncated normal hurdle models with CRE and CF approach.)

[Z2] Mason, N. M., and J. Ricker-Gilbert. 2013. "Disrupting Demand for Commercial Seed: Input Subsidies in Malawi and Zambia." *World Development* 45 (May): 75–91. (Two waves of nationally representative household panel survey data; Tobit models with CRE and CF.)

[Z3] Mason, N. M., T. S. Jayne, and R. Mofya-Mukuka. 2013. "Zambia's Input Subsidy Programs." *Agricultural Economics* 44 (6): 613–28. (Most results based on three waves of nationally representative household panel survey data; targeting results also reported from a more recent nationally representative cross-section; various econometric models combined with CRE and CF.)

[Z4] Mason, N. M., and M. Smale. 2013. "Impacts of Subsidized Hybrid Seed on Indicators of Economic Well-Being Among Smallholder Maize Growers in Zambia." *Agricultural Economics* 44 (6): 659–70. (Two waves of nationally representative household panel survey data; various econometric models with CRE and CF.)

[Z5] Mason, N. M., T. S. Jayne, and R. J. Myers. 2015. "Smallholder Supply Response to Marketing Board Activities in a Dual Channel Marketing System: The Case of Zambia." *Journal of Agricultural Economics* 66 (1): 36–65. (Three waves of nationally representative household panel survey data; various econometric models with CRE and CF.)

[Z6] Mason, N. M., T. S. Jayne, and N. van de Walle. 2013. "Fertilizer Subsidies and Voting Patterns: Political Economy Dimensions of Input Subsidy Programs." Selected paper presented at the Agricultural and Applied Economics Association's (AAEA) and Canadian Agricultural Economics Society Joint Annual Meeting, Washington, DC, August 4–6. (Three waves of nationally representative household panel survey data and Tobit models with CRE for targeting analysis; two waves of district-level panel data and fractional response models with CRE and CF for impacts of input subsidy program on voting patterns.)

[Z7] Xu, Z., W. J. Burke, T. S. Jayne, and J. Govereh. 2009. "Do Input Subsidy Programs 'Crowd In' or 'Crowd Out' Commercial Market Development? Modeling Fertilizer Demand in a Two-Channel Marketing System." *Agricultural Economics* 40 (1): 79–94. (Two waves of nationally representative household panel survey data with truncated normal hurdle models and CRE.)

[Z8] Zulu, P., T. Kalinda, and G. Tembo. 2014. "Effects of the Maize Input Subsidy Program on Groundnuts Production in Zambia." *Journal of Agricultural Science* 6 (7): 253–64. (Three waves of nationally representative household panel survey data; truncated normal hurdle model with CRE and CF.)

[Z9] Sianjase, A., and V. Seshamani. 2013. "Impacts of Farmer Inputs Support Program on Beneficiaries in Gwembe District in Zambia." *Journal of*

*Environmental Issues and Agriculture in Developing Countries* 50 (1): 40–50. (Four waves of panel data from Gwembe District; quantile regression with CRE.)

[Z10] Smale, M., E. Birol, and D. Asare-Marfo. 2014. "Smallholder Demand for Maize Hybrids in Zambia: How Far Do Seed Subsidies Reach?" *Journal of Agricultural Economics* 65 (2): 349–67. (Cross-sectional data from Central, Copperbelt, Eastern, Lusaka, Northern, and Southern provinces; IV and CF approaches.)

[Z11] Namonje-Kapembwa, T., T. S. Jayne, and R. Black. 2015. "Does Late Delivery of Subsidized Fertilizer Affect Smallholder Maize Productivity and Production?" Selected paper presented at the Agricultural and Applied Economics Association and Western Agricultural Economics Association Annual Meeting, San Francisco, CA, July 26–28. (Nationally representative cross-section; stochastic frontier model with CF.)

[Z12] Goeb, J. 2011. "Impacts of Government Maize Supports on Smallholder Cotton Production in Zambia." Master's Thesis, Michigan State University, Lansing, MI. (Three waves of nationally representative household panel survey data and two waves of enumeration area-level panel data; CRE Tobit and truncated normal hurdle models.)

[Z13] Mason, N. M., and S. T. Tembo. 2015. "Do Input Subsidy Programs Raise Incomes and Reduce Poverty among Smallholder Farm Households? Evidence from Zambia." Working Paper 92, Indaba Agricultural Policy Research Institute, Lusaka, Zambia. (Two waves of nationally representative household panel survey data; various econometric models with CRE and CF.)

[Z14] Levine, N. K. 2015. "Do Input Subsidies Crowd In or Crowd Out Other Soil Fertility Management Practices? Evidence from Zambia." Michigan State University, Lansing, MI. (Two waves of nationally representative household panel survey data; FE and FE-IV models.)

[Z15] Jayne, T. S., D. Mather, N. M. Mason, J. Ricker-Gilbert, and E. Crawford. 2015. "Rejoinder to the Comment by Andrew Dorward and Ephraim Chirwa on Jayne, T. S., D. Mather, N. Mason, and J. Ricker-Gilbert. 2013. 'How Do Fertilizer Subsidy Programs Affect Total Fertilizer Use in Sub-Saharan Africa? Crowding Out, Diversion, and Benefit/Cost Assessments,' *Agricultural Economics* 44 (6): 687–703." *Agricultural Economics* 46 (6): 745–55.

[Z16] Jayne, T. S., D. Mather, N. M. Mason, and J. Ricker-Gilbert. 2013. "How Do Fertilizer Subsidy Programs Affect Total Fertilizer Use in Sub-Saharan Africa? Crowding Out, Diversion, and Benefit/Cost Assessments." *Agricultural Economics* 44 (6): 687–703. (Zambia analysis based on three waves of nationally representative household panel survey data; truncated normal hurdle models with CRE and CF.)

[Z17] Ricker-Gilbert, J., N. M. Mason, F. A. Darko, and S. T. Tembo. 2013. "What Are the Effects of Input Subsidy Programs on Maize Prices? Evidence from Malawi and Zambia." *Agricultural Economics* 44 (6): 671–86. (Zambia analysis based on 12 years of biannual data from 50 districts; Arellano-Bond dynamic panel data models.)

# Notes

1. This chapter is based mainly on a background paper (Jayne et al. 2016).
2. As shown in table 3.1, 10 countries with largest ISPs spent US$1.02 billion in 2014.
3. The Government of Ethiopia officially states that it does not have an input subsidy program, yet fertilizer is typically made available to farmers at prices roughly 20–25 percent lower than the price at which commercial distributors sell fertilizer in other countries of the region. Instead of using targeted input vouchers, the Ethiopian government has been promoting fertilizer use through subsidizing the operations of farmers' organizations.
4. See Johnston and Kilby (1975), Mellor (1976), Lipton (2006), and Christiaensen, Demery, and Kuhl (2010) for Africa and worldwide evidence.
5. In many cases, the objectives of on-farm research trials are not to estimate the response rates that farmers are actually getting on their own fields, but to demonstrate the differences in yield or NUE that could be achieved if specific management practices or soil-augmenting investments were made. For these reasons, we believe that NUE estimates derived from researcher-managed trials are generally inappropriate for use in studies estimating the impacts of nationwide input subsidy programs.
6. Irrigated cereal fields in Pakistan, Bangladesh, and India received 43 percent, 84 percent, and 186 percent more fertilizer nutrient per hectare than corresponding nonirrigated fields, respectively (see Rashid et al. 2013).
7. Much of the information on soils in this report is prevalent throughout agronomic literature. Unless otherwise specified, the discussion summarized here and further details can be found in Jones et al. (2013). Also see Burke et al. (2015).
8. Related measurements are organic carbon content or soil carbon content. These measures are highly correlated, and can effectively be thought of as rebased measures of each other.
9. The process of soil nutrient depletion may partially explain why Yanggen et al.'s (1998) crop response rates from the 1980s and early 1990s are generally higher than those recorded recently even in spite of an increased proportion of cereal area under improved varieties.
10. See annex 3A for a summary of ISP implementation modalities in selected African countries.
11. For evidence of this, see Lunduka, Ricker-Gilbert, and Fisher (2013).
12. This figure excludes South Africa because of its fundamentally different agricultural system.

13. Sources in the fertilizer industry in Nigeria provide an illustrative example that has been repeated by other fertilizer sources in other countries: government officials and a chosen firm may agree that the firm will invoice the government for US$800 per ton even though the actual costs associated with delivering the fertilizer to inland markets is only US$600, an excess of US$200 per ton over the landed cost of importing fertilizer. The treasury pays the firm US$700, allowing it to earn monopoly profits of US$100 over its costs plus normal profits, while the party receives US$100 per ton imported to finance its political campaigns or other off-the-books expenses.

14. See, for example, the widely divergent findings of Ricker-Gilbert, Jayne, and Chirwa (2011) on the one hand, and Arndt, Pauw, and Thurlow (2015) on the other regarding the Malawi Farm Input Subsidy Program.

15. Muraoka (2015) links rural electrification to improved livestock breeding and increased availability and application rates of organic matter on crops.

16. Promoting local community awareness campaigns to develop and implement strategies to prevent bush fires that are a major contributor to the current low levels of soil organic matter in parts of Africa will also be important. Community-level strategies in Northern Ghana, for instance, have been successful at enforcing rules to reduce rates of bush fire.

17. See annexes 3A and 3B for overviews of Burundi's and Rwanda's ISPs, respectively. For information on programs not covered in this study, see Wanzala-Mlobela, Fuentes, and Mkumbwa (2013) for Burkina Faso and Senegal; Druilhe and Barreiro-Hurlé (2012) for Burkina Faso, Mali, and Senegal; Fuentes, Bumb, and Johnson (2012) for Mali and Senegal; and Chirwa and Dorward (2013) for Mali and Senegal.

18. Malawi implemented various fertilizer subsidy programs in most years since its independence, but through the 1990s these were generally small. The Zambian government initiated various fertilizer-on-credit schemes for farmers in several years during the 1990s, with fertilizer obtained through the program sold at or near market prices. But default rates on the fertilizer loans were high (for example, 35 percent in 1999/2000), so a large percentage of program participants received the fertilizer at an implicit subsidy rate of approximately 90 percent, having paid only the 10 percent down payment for the fertilizer (Mason, Jayne, and van de Walle 2013; ZMACO, Agricultural Consultative Forum, and FSRP 2002).

19. Kenya actually started distributing subsidized fertilizer through its National Cereals and Produce Board in 2001, but the quantities were small (Mather and Jayne 2015; NCPB 2013). We use 2007 to mark the return of major ISPs to Kenya as this is the year in which it first implemented a large-scale targeted ISP, the National Accelerated Agricultural Inputs Access Program. Both programs are discussed further below. Also, as noted in Jayne and Rashid (2013), though the Ethiopian government subsidizes the retail price of fertilizer in various ways, it does not refer to this as a fertilizer subsidy program.

20. See also Heineken's website, heinekencompany.com/media/media-releases/press-releases/2015/01/1887644.

21. Key features of the Ghana Fertilizer Subsidy Program are discussed here, but for a more thorough review, please see Resnick and Mather (2015).

22. There was also a subsidized credit component to NAAIAP called Kilimo Biashara, which targeted credit-constrained farmers who were relatively better off and

ineligible for Kilimo Plus. Throughout the remainder of the discussion we use the term NAAIAP to refer to the Kilimo Plus part of the program.

23. These are the only years for which data are publicly available.
24. See Levy (2005) and Harrigan (2008) for further details on the Starter Pack.
25. According to Harrigan (2008, 245), "These objections [to the Starter Pack] coincided with an evolution of donor food security policies toward a more holistic livelihoods approach as well as an elevation of the social safety net programme in Malawi. Hence, donors were willing to endorse a scaled down free inputs programme and to recast it in the light, not of a production enhancing technological transfer, but as one of many targeted social safety nets, albeit not necessarily the most effective."
26. See Levy (2005) for a discussion of the other key differences between the 2004/05 program and previous years.
27. Maize seed quantities have varied over time. For example, in the early years of the program, seed coupons were for 2 kg of hybrid seed or 4–5 kg of OPV seed (Lunduka, Ricker-Gilbert, and Fisher 2013).
28. As discussed in Dorward and Chirwa (2011), in the early years of the program MFISP included maize and tobacco fertilizers and OPV maize seed (but no hybrid or legume seed). Hybrid maize seed was added in 2006/07; legume seed as well as cotton seed and chemicals were added in 2007/08; and fertilizers for tea and coffee, and storage chemicals for maize were added in 2008/09. Tobacco, cotton, tea, and coffee inputs were subsequently phased out. See Dorward and Chirwa (2011) for a summary of other program changes from 2006/07 through 2008/09.
29. In 2005/06, both fertilizer and seed vouchers had to be redeemed at ADMARC and SFFRFM outlets. In 2006/07 and 2007/08, seed vouchers were redeemable at private seed retailers while fertilizer vouchers were redeemable at private fertilizer retailers and ADMARC/SFFRFM. But since 2008/09, fertilizer vouchers are only redeemable at ADMARC/SFFRFM (Dorward and Chirwa 2011; Logistics Unit 2015). Government selects, through a tender process, companies to import and deliver fertilizer to SFFRFM and ADMARC locations (Wanzala-Mlobela, Fuentes, and Mkumbwa 2013).
30. See Liverpool-Tasie and Takeshima (2013) for a summary of Nigeria's ISPs from the 1940s to 2013.
31. Note that the e-wallet system is different from the e-vouchers piloted to date in Malawi and Zambia. The latter are electronic on the agro-dealer end but paper scratch cards (similar to cellphone talk time scratch cards) on the farmer end.
32. Nigeria Federal Ministry of Agriculture and Rural Development (NFMARD)'s website, (accessed July 2015), http://www.fmard.gov.ng/Growth-Enhancement-Scheme.
33. See IFDC (2013) for a discussion of other challenges with GES in 2013.
34. Camps are the most disaggregated spatial unit in ZMAL's system.
35. Preparations are underway to pilot an electronic voucher system for the ZFISP in 2015/16 in 13 districts.
36. H. P. Melby, personal communication with authors, February 2015.
37. This relationship has also been used to study the effects of ISP improved maize seed on total improved maize seed demand (Mason and Ricker-Gilbert 2013; [Z2, M16]).

38. In addition, subsidized fertilizer acquired through the Kano State voucher pilot program, which did not distribute subsidized seed, had positive spillover effects on the probability that households used improved maize or rice seed [N3]. No such cross-input effects have been found for Malawi and Zambia, whose ISPs distribute both subsidized fertilizer and improved maize seed [M16, Z2].

39. [Z1] revisits fertilizer crowding out in Zambia using an additional wave of panel data beyond the two waves used by [Z7] and with additional corrections for endogeneity.

40. Note that private sector activity can be either commercial or noncommercial, where firms act as distribution agents for government subsidy programs. Hence it is possible that an ISP program could attract new private sector investment in input distribution at the same time that it crowds out commercial fertilizer sales to farmers.

41. Not only is the evidence base thin on yield effects, but there has also been virtually no research done on the effects of ISPs on labor productivity or total factor productivity.

42. Receipt of 100 kg of fertilizer and 10 kg of improved maize seed if a household obtains a full input pack.

43. Research on the effects of Zambia's ZFISP on household food security and children's nutritional status is underway but results are not yet available. The study by Ward and Santos (2010) has only been released in draft form and explicitly states that the results should not be cited.

44. Poverty severity is equal to zero for households with income at or above the poverty line, and equal to the squared proportion difference between household income and the poverty line for households with incomes below the poverty line (Foster, Greer, and Thorbecke 1984).

45. See also Awotide et al. (2013) and Carter, Laajaj, and Yang (2014) for randomized controlled trial (RCT) based estimates of the income and poverty effects of a small certified rice seed voucher pilot program in Nigeria and the income (and other) effects of a government ISP pilot program in Mozambique, respectively. Unlike the above studies for Kenya and Zambia, Awotide et al. (2013) find that participation in the seed voucher pilot program in Nigeria does reduce the probability of household income falling below the poverty line.

46. We contend that failure to take account of diversion of program fertilizer, as in Mason and Jayne (2013) and Jayne et al. (2013, 2015), is one reason for the divergence in conclusions between these studies and that of Arndt, Pauw, and Thurlow (2015). When Arndt, Pauw, and Thurlow (2015) do take account of crowding out (not diversion), their assessment of the Malawi program becomes less favorable, but these factors were not part of their baseline results on which their main conclusions rest.

47. [Z15 and Z16] also estimate the effects of ISPs on national maize production for Kenya, Malawi, and Zambia but do so indirectly by multiplying the total ISP fertilizer injected into the system by the estimated changes in total fertilizer use per the previous subsection, and further multiplying this quantity by the country-specific estimated maize yield response to fertilizer.

# References

AGRA (Alliance for a Green Revolution in Africa). 2009. *Developing Rural Agricultural Input Supply Systems for Farmers in Africa*. Nairobi, Kenya: AGRA.

Anderson, J., J. Dillon, and J. E. Hardaker. 1977. "Agricultural Decision Analysis." Ames, IA: Iowa State University Press.

Ariga, J. and T.S. Jayne. 2011. "Fertilizer in Kenya: Factors Driving the Increase in Usage by Smallholder Farmers." In *Yes, Africa Can: Success Stories from a Dynamic Continent*, edited by P. Chuhan-Pole and M. Angwafo. Washington, DC: World Bank.

Arndt, C., K. Pauw, and J. Thurlow. 2015. "The Economy-wide Impacts and Risks of Malawi's Farm Input Subsidy Program." *American Journal of Agricultural Economics* 98 (3): 962–80.

Awotide, B. A., A. Karimov, A. Diagne, and T. Nakelse. 2013. "The Impact of Seed Vouchers on Poverty Reduction among Smallholder Rice Farmers in Nigeria." *Agricultural Economics* 44 (6): 647–58.

Banful, A. B. 2009. "Old Problems in the New Solutions? Politically Motivated Allocation of Program Benefits and the 'New' Fertilizer Subsidies." *World Development* 39 (7): 1166–76.

Bates, R.H. 1987. *Essays on the Political Economy of Rural Africa*. Berkeley, CA: University of California Press.

Bationo, A., C. B. Christianson, W. E. Baethgen, and A. U. Mokwunye. 1992. "A Farm-Level Level Evaluation of Nitrogen and Phosphorus Fertilizer Use and Planting Density for Pearl Millet Production in Niger." *Fertilizer Research* 31 (2): 175–84.

Beaman, L., D. Karlan, B. Thuysbaert, and C. R. Udry. 2013. "Profitability of Fertilizer: Experimental Evidence from Female Rice Farmers in Mali." Working Paper 18878, NBER, Cambridge, MA.

Bigsten, A., and A. Shimeles. 2007. "Can Africa Reduce Poverty by Half by 2015?" *Development Policy Review* 25 (2): 147–166.

Brazys, S., P. Heaney, and P. P. Walsh. 2015. "Fertilizer and Votes: Does Strategic Economic Policy Explain the 2009 Malawi Election?" *Electoral Studies* 39: 39–55.

Burke, W. J. 2012. "Determinants of Maize Yield Response to Fertilizer Application in Zambia: Implications for Strategies to Promote Smallholder Productivity." PhD dissertation, Michigan State University, East Lansing, MI.

Burke, W. J., E. Frossard, S. Kabwe, and T. S. Jayne. 2015. "Understanding Fertilizer Effectiveness and Adoption in Zambia." Working Paper, Indaba Agricultural Policy Research Institute, Lusaka, Zambia.

Carter, M. R., R. Laajaj, and D. Yang. 2014. "Subsidies and the Persistence of Technology Adoption: Field Experimental Evidence from Mozambique." Working Paper 20465, NBER, Cambridge, MA.

Chibwana, C., M. Fisher, and G. Shively. 2012. "Cropland Allocation Effects of Agricultural Input Subsidies in Malawi." *World Development* 40 (1): 124–33.

Chibwana, C., C. Jumbe, and G. Shively. 2012. "Agricultural Subsidies and Forest Clearing in Malawi." *Environmental Conservation* 40 (1): 60–70.

Chibwana, C., G. Shively, M. Fisher, and C. Jumbe. 2014. "Measuring the Impacts of Malawi's Farm Input Subsidy Programme." *African Journal of Agriculture and Resource Economics* 9 (2): 132–47.

Chikowo, R., S. Zingore, S. Snapp, and A. Johnston. 2014. "Farm Typologies, Soil Fertility Variability and Nutrient Management in Smallholder Farming in Sub-Saharan Africa." *Nutrient Cycling in Agroecosystems* 100 (1): 1–18.

Chinsinga, B., and C. Poulton. 2014. "Beyond Technocratic Debates: The Significance and Transience of Political Incentives in the Malawi Farm Input Subsidy Programme." *Development Policy Review* 32 (S2): 123–50.

Chirwa, E., and A. Dorward. 2013. *Agricultural Input Subsidies: The Recent Malawi Experience*. Oxford, U.K.: Oxford University Press.

Chirwa, E. W., M. Matita, and A. Dorward. 2010. "Targeting Agricultural Input Subsidy Coupons in Malawi." Working Paper, School of Oriental and African Studies, University of London, London, U.K.

Chirwa, E. W., P. M. Mvula, A. Dorward, and M. Matita. 2011. "Gender and Intra-Household Use of Fertilizers in the Malawi Farm Input Subsidy Programme." Working Paper 028, Future Agricultures Consortium, Brighton, U.K.

Chirwa, T. G. 2010. "Program Evaluation of Agricultural Input Subsidies in Malawi Using Treatment Effects: Methods and Practicability Based on Propensity Scores." Munich Personal Research Papers in Economics Archive Paper 21236, Ludwig-Maximilians-Universität München, Munich, Germany. http://mpra.ub.uni-muenchen .de/21236/1/MPRA_paper_21236.pdf.

Christiaensen, L., L. Demery, and J. Kuhl. 2010. "The (Evolving) Role of Agriculture in Poverty Reduction." Working Paper 2010/36, United Nations University, World Institute for Development Economics Research, Helsinki, Finland.

Dionne, K. Y., and J. Horowitz. 2013. "The Political Effects of Anti-Poverty Initiatives: An Analysis of Malawi's Agricultural Input Subsidy Program." Paper presented at the Midwest Group in African Political Economy meeting, Indiana University, Bloomington, IN, October 17–18.

Dorward, A., and E. Chirwa. 2011. "The Malawi Agricultural Input Subsidy Programme: 2005/2006 to 2008/2009." *International Journal of Agriculture Sustainability* 16: 232–47.

———. 2013. "Impacts of the Farm Input Subsidy Programme in Malawi: Informal Rural Modeling." Working Paper 067, Future Agricultures Consortium, Brighton, U.K.

Dorward, A., E. Chirwa, V. Kelly, T. S. Jayne, and R. Slater. 2008. *Evaluation of the 2006/07 Agricultural Input Subsidy Programme, Malawi*. Lilongwe, Malawi: Ministry of Agriculture and Food Security.

Dorward, A., P. Hazell, and C. Poulton. 2008. "Rethinking Agricultural Input Subsidies in Poor Rural Economies." Policy Brief, Future Agricultures Consortium at the Institute of Development Studies at the University of Sussex, Brighton, U.K.

Drechsel, P., L. Gyiele, D. Kunze, and O. Cofie. 2001. "Population Density, Soil Nutrient Depletion, and Economic Growth in Sub-Saharan Africa." *Ecological Economics* 38 (2): 251–58.

Druilhe, Z., and J. Barreiro-Hurlé. 2012. "Fertilizer Subsidies in Sub-Saharan Africa." ESA Working Paper 12-04, Agricultural Development Economics Division, FAO, Rome, Italy.

Duflo, E., M. Kremer, J. Robinson. 2008. "How High Are Rates of Return to Fertilizer? Evidence from Field Experiments in Kenya." *American Economic Review: Papers and Proceedings* 98 (2): 482–88.

Dugger, C. 2007. "Ending Famine, Simply by Ignoring Experts." *New York Times*, 2 December.

EIU (Economist Intelligence Unit). 2008. *Lifting African and Asian Farmers Out of Poverty: Assessing the Investment Needs.* Research Report. Seattle, WA: Bill and Melinda Gates Foundation.

Fan, S., A. Gulati, and S. Thorat. 2008. "Investment, Subsidies, and Pro-poor Growth in Rural India." *Agricultural Economics* 39 (2): 163–70.

FAO (Food and Agriculture Organization). 1975. *Planning and Organization of Fertilizer Use Development in Africa.* Rome, Italy: FAO.

——. Monitoring African Food and Agricultural Policies (MAFAP) database, Rome, Italy (accessed December 10, 2015), http://www.fao.org/in-action/mafap/database/en/.

Fisher, M., and V. Kandiwa. 2014. "Can Agricultural Input Subsidies Reduce the Gender Gap in Modern Maize Adoption? Evidence from Malawi." *Food Policy* 45 (May): 101–11.

Foster, J., J. Greer, and E. Thorbecke. 1984. "A Class of Decomposable Poverty Measures." *Econometrica* 52 (3): 761–66.

Fuentes, P. A., B. L. Bumb, and M. Johnson. 2012. *Improving Fertilizer Markets in West Africa: The Fertilizer Supply Chain in Mali.* Muscle Shoals, AL: IFDC and IFPRI. http://citeseerx.ist.psu.edu/viewdoc/download;jsessionid=E87A6046004F1F492018 DA0A40CD45E5?doi=10.1.1.590.1554&rep=rep1&type=pdf.

Gautam, M. 2015. "Agricultural Subsidies: Resurging Interest in a Perennial Debate." Keynote address at the 74th Annual Conference of Indian Society of Agricultural Economics, Dr. Babasaheb Ambedkar Marathwada University, Aurangabad, India, December 18.

Giller, K., E. Rowe, N. de Ridder, H. van Keulen. 2006. "Resource Use Dynamics and Interactions in the Tropics: Scaling Up in Space and Time." *Agricultural Systems* 88: 8–27.

Gilligan, D. O., J. Hoddinott, and A. S. Taffesse. 2009. "The Impact of Ethiopia's Productive Safety Net Programme and Its Linkages." *Journal of Development Studies* 45 (10): 1684–1706.

Goeb, J. 2011. "Impacts of Government Maize Supports on Smallholder Cotton Production in Zambia." Master's Thesis, Michigan State University, Lansing, MI.

Harrigan, J. 2008. "Food Insecurity, Poverty and the Malawian Starter Pack: Fresh Start or False Start?" *Food Policy* 33 (3): 237–49.

Hoddinott, J., G. Berhane, D. Gilligan, N. Kumar, and A. Seyoum Taffesse. 2012. "The Impact of Ethiopia's Productive Safety Net Programme and Related Transfers on Agricultural Productivity." *Journal of African Economies* 21 (5): 761–86. http://doi .org/10.1093/jae/ejs023.

Holden, S. 2013. "Input Subsidies and Demand for Improved Maize: Relative Prices and Household Heterogeneity Matter!" Centre for Land Tenure Studies Working Paper 06/13, Norwegian University of Life Sciences, Ås, Norway.

Holden, S. T., and R. Lunduka. 2010. *Too Poor to be Efficient? Impacts of the Targeted Fertilizer Subsidy Programme in Malawi on Farm Plot Level Input Use, Crop Choice, and Land Productivity.* Noragric Report 55. Ås, Norway: Department of International Environment and Development Studies, Norwegian University of Life Sciences.

———. 2012. "Do Fertilizer Subsidies Crowd Out Organic Manures? The Case of Malawi." *Agricultural Economics* 43 (3): 303–14.

———. 2013. "Who Benefit from Malawi's Targeted Farm Input Subsidy Program?" *Forum for Development Studies* 40 (1): 1–25.

IFDC (International Fertilizer Development Center). 2013. *Growth Enhancement Support Scheme 2013: Lessons Learned.* Abuja, Nigeria. Muscle Shoals, AL: IFDC.

———. 2014. "GES-TAP (Growth Enhancement Support Touch-and-Pay) Final Report." Muscle Shoals, AL: IFDC.

Jacoby, H. 2015. "Smart Subsidy? Welfare and Distributional Consequences of Malawi's FISP." Background paper for this study, World Bank, Washington, DC.

Jayne, T. S., J. Govereh, M. Wanzala-Mlobela, and M. Demeke. 2003. "Fertilizer Market Development: A Comparative Analysis of Ethiopia, Kenya, and Zambia." *Food Policy* 28 (4): 293–316.

Jayne, T. S., N. M. Mason, W. J. Burke, and J. Ariga. 2016. "Agricultural Input Subsidy Programs in Africa: An Assessment of Recent Evidence." International Development Working Paper 145, Michigan State University, East Lansing, MI.

Jayne, T. S., D. Mather, N. Mason, and J. Ricker-Gilbert. 2013. "How Do Fertilizer Subsidy Programs Affect Total Fertilizer Use in Sub-Saharan Africa? Crowding Out, Diversion, and Benefit/Cost Assessments." *Agricultural Economics* 44 (6): 687–703.

Jayne, T. S., D. Mather, N. M. Mason, J. Ricker-Gilbert, and E. Crawford. 2015. "Rejoinder to the Comment by Andrew Dorward and Ephraim Chirwa on Jayne, T. S., D. Mather, N. Mason, and J. Ricker-Gilbert. 2013. 'How Do Fertilizer Subsidy Programs Affect Total Fertilizer Use in Sub-Saharan Africa? Crowding Out, Diversion, and Benefit/Cost Assessments.' *Agricultural Economics* 44 (6): 687–703." *Agricultural Economics* 46 (6): 745–55.

Jayne, T. S., and S. Rashid. 2013. "Input Subsidy Programmes in Sub-Saharan Africa: A Synthesis of Recent Evidence." *Agricultural Economics* 44 (6): 547–62.

Jebuni, C., and W. Seini. 1992. "Agricultural Input Policies under Structural Adjustment: Their Distributional Implications." Cornell Food and Nutrition Policy Program Working Paper 31, Ithaca, NY.

Johnston, B., and P. Kilby. 1975. *Agriculture and Structural Transformation: Economic Strategies in Late-Developing Countries.* Oxford, U.K.: Oxford University Press.

Jones, A., H. Breuning-Madsen, M. Brossard, A. Dampha, J. Deckers, O. Dewitte, T. Gallali, S. Hallett, R. Jones, M. Kilasara, P. Le Roux, E. Micheli, L. Montanarella, O. Spaargaren, L. Thiombiano, E. Van Ranst, M. Yemefack, and R. Zougmore. 2013. *Soil Atlas of Africa.* European Commission, Luxembourg: Publications Office of the European Union.

Karamba, R. W. 2013. "Input Subsidies and Their Effect on Cropland Allocation, Agricultural Productivity, and Child Nutrition: Evidence from Malawi." PhD dissertation, American University, Washington, DC.

Karamba, R. W., and P. C. Winters. 2015. "Gender and Agricultural Productivity: Implications of the Farm Input Subsidy Program in Malawi." *Agricultural Economics* 46 (3): 357–74.

Kasanga, J., O. Daka, J. Chanda, and A. Undi. 2010. "Model and Implementation Plan for the Expanded Food Security Pack Programme." Lusaka, Zambia: IMCS Limited.

Kherallah, M., C. Delgado, E. Gabre-Madhin, N. Minot, M. Johnson. 2002. *Reforming Agricultural Markets in Africa: Achievements and Challenges.* Washington, DC: IFPRI.

Kilic, T., E. Whitney, and P. Winters. 2015. "Decentralised Beneficiary Targeting in Large-Scale Development Programmes: Insights from the Malawi Farm Input Subsidy Programme." *Journal of African Economies* 24 (1): 26–56.

KMOA (Kenya Ministry of Agriculture). 2007. *The National Accelerated Agricultural Inputs Access Program (NAAIAP): Program Design and Implementation Framework.* Nairobi, Kenya: KMOA.

————. 2013. "Unpublished Data Files for Nakuru Fertilizer Prices." Nairobi, Kenya: Ministry of Agriculture, Market Information Bureau for Maize Prices.

Levine, N. K. 2015. "Do Input Subsidies Crowd In or Crowd Out Other Soil Fertility Management Practices? Evidence from Zambia." Master's thesis paper, Michigan State University, Lansing, MI.

Levy, S. (ed.). 2005. *Starter Packs: A Strategy to Fight Hunger in Developing and Transition Countries? Lessons from the Malawi Experience, 1998–2003.* Wallingford, U.K.: Centre for Agriculture and Bioscience International.

Lipton, M. 2006. "Can Small Farmers Survive, Prosper, or Be the Key Channel to Cut Mass Poverty?" *Electronic Journal of Agricultural and Development Economics* 3 (1): 58–85.

Liverpool-Tasie, L. S. O. 2014a. "Do Vouchers Improve Government Fertilizer Distribution? Evidence from Nigeria." *Agricultural Economics* 45 (4): 393–407.

————. 2014b. "Farmer Groups and Input Access: When Membership Is Not Enough." *Food Policy* 46 (June): 37–49.

————. 2014c. "Fertilizer Subsidies and Private Market Participation: The Case of Kano State, Nigeria." *Agricultural Economics* 45 (6): 663–78.

Liverpool-Tasie, L., and S. Salau. 2013. "Spillover Effects of Targeted Subsidies: An Assessment of Fertilizer and Improved Seed Use in Nigeria." Discussion Paper 01260, Development Strategy and Governance Division, IFPRI, Washington, DC.

Liverpool-Tasie, L., and H. Takeshima. 2013. "Input Promotion Within a Complex Subsector: Fertilizer in Nigeria." *Agricultural Economics* 44 (6): 581–94.

————. 2015. "Fertilizer Subsidies, Political Influence and Local Food Prices in Sub-Saharan Africa: Evidence from Nigeria." *Food Policy* 54: 11–24.

Logistics Unit. 2015. *Final Report on the Implementation of the Agricultural Inputs Subsidy Programme, 2014–15.* Lilongwe, Malawi: Logistics Unit.

Lunduka, R., J. Ricker-Gilbert, and M. Fisher. 2013. "What Are the Farm-Level Impacts of Malawi's Farm Input Subsidy Program? A Critical Review." *Agricultural Economics* 44 (6): 563–79.

Marenya, P., and C. Barrett. 2009. "State-Conditional Fertilizer Yield Response on Western Kenyan Farms." *American Journal of Agricultural Economics* 91 (4): 991–1006.

Mason, N., and T. S. Jayne. 2013. "Fertilizer Subsidies and Smallholder Commercial Fertilizer Purchases: Crowding Out, Leakage, and Policy Implications for Zambia." *Journal of Agricultural Economics* 64 (3): 558–82.

———. 2015. "Fertilizer Subsidies and Smallholder Commercial Fertilizer Purchases: Crowding Out, Leakage and Policy Implications for Zambia." *Journal of Agricultural Economics* 64 (3): 558–82.

Mason, N. M., T. S. Jayne, and R. Mofya-Mukuka. 2013. "Zambia's Input Subsidy Programs." *Agricultural Economics* 44 (6): 613–28.

Mason, N. M., T. S. Jayne, and R. J. Myers. 2015. "Smallholder Supply Response to Marketing Board Activities in a Dual Channel Marketing System: The Case of Zambia." *Journal of Agricultural Economics* 66 (1): 36–65.

Mason, N. M., T. S. Jayne, and N. van de Walle. 2013. "Fertilizer Subsidies and Voting Patterns: Political Economy Dimensions of Input Subsidy Programs." Selected paper presented at the Agricultural and Applied Economics Association's (AAEA) and Canadian Agricultural Economics Society Joint Annual Meeting, Washington, DC, August 4–6.

Mason, N., and J. Ricker-Gilbert. 2013. "Disrupting Demand for Commercial Seed: Input Subsidies in Malawi and Zambia." *World Development* 45 (May): 75–91.

Mason, N. M., and M. Smale. 2013. "Impacts of Subsidized Hybrid Seed on Indicators of Economic Well-Being Among Smallholder Maize Growers in Zambia." *Agricultural Economics* 44 (6): 659–70.

Mason, N., and S. Tembo. 2015. "Do Input Subsidy Programs Raise Incomes and Reduce Poverty among Smallholder Farm Households? Evidence from Zambia." Working Paper 92, Indaba Agricultural Policy Research Institute, Lusaka, Zambia.

Mason, N. M., A. Wineman, L. Kirimi, and D. Mather. 2015. "The Effects of Kenya's 'Smarter' Input Subsidy Program on Smallholder Behavior and Incomes: Do Different Quasi-Experimental Approaches Lead to the Same Conclusions?" Working Paper, Tegemeo Institute of Agricultural Policy and Development, Nairobi, Kenya.

Mather, D., and T. S. Jayne. 2015. "Fertilizer Subsidies and the Role of Targeting in Crowding Out: An Assessment of Smallholder Fertilizer Demand in Kenya." Selected paper prepared for the International Conference of Agricultural Economics, Milan, Italy, August 9–14.

Mather, D., B. Waized, D. Ndyetabula, A. Temu, I. Minde, and D. Nyange. 2015. "The Role of Relative Prices, Agro-Ecological Factors, and Household Soil and Crop Management Practices in Explaining Smallholder Profitability of Fertilizer Use on Maize in Tanzania." MSU working paper, Michigan State University, East Lansing, MI.

Matsumoto, T., T. Yamano, and D. Sserunkuuma. 2012. "Technology Adoption in Agriculture: Evidence from Experimental Intervention in Maize." In *An African Green Revolution: Finding Ways to Boost Productivity on Small Farms.* The Netherlands: Springer.

Maur, J. C., and B. Shepherd. 2015. *Connecting Food Staples and Input Markets in West Africa: A Regional Trade Agency for ECOWAS Countries.* Washington, DC: World Bank.

Mellor, J. 1976. *New Economics of Growth.* New York: Cornell University Press.

Minten, B., B. Koru, and D. Stifel. 2013. "The Last Mile(s) in Modern Input Distribution: Pricing, Profitability, and Adoption." *Agricultural Economics* 44 (6): 629–46.

Minten, B., D. Stifel, and S. Tamru. 2014. "Structural Transformation of Cereal Markets in Ethiopia Structural Transformation of Cereal Markets." *Journal of Development Studies* 50 (5): 611–29. http://doi.org/10.1080/00220388.2014.887686.

Mkwara, B., and D. Marsh. 2011. "Effects of Maize Fertilizer Subsidies on Food Security in Malawi." Working Paper in Economics 14/11, Department of Economics, University of Waikato, Hamilton, New Zealand.

Morris, M., V. Kelly, R. Kopicki, and D. Byerlee. 2007. *Fertilizer Use in African Agriculture: Lessons Learned and Good Practice Guidelines.* Washington, DC: World Bank.

Msolla, M. M. 2014. "Effects of the Subsidy Voucher Program on Fertilizer Markets: Example from Tanzania." Paper presented at the International Fertilizer Development Center Training on Fertilizer Value Chain-Supply System Management and Servicing Farmers' Needs, Accra, Ghana, April 14–18.

Muraoka, R. 2015. "Three Essays on Land and an Intensive Farming System in Sub-Saharan Africa: Evidence from Kenya." Unpublished PhD dissertation, Michigan State University, East Lansing, MI. ISBN: 9781321736038.

Namonje-Kapembwa, T., T. S. Jayne, and R. Black. 2015. "Does Late Delivery of Subsidized Fertilizer Affect Smallholder Maize Productivity and Production?" Selected paper presented at the Agricultural and Applied Economics Association and Western Agricultural Economics Association Annual Meeting, San Francisco, CA, July 26–28.

NCPB (National Cereals and Produce Board). 2013. "NCPB Fertilizer Business Portfolio." PowerPoint presentation by NCPB official, NCPB, Nairobi, Kenya.

Nelson, F., and L. Olson. 1978. "Specification and Estimation of a Simultaneous-Equation Model with Limited Dependent Variables." *International Economic Review* 19 (3): 695–709.

Ochola, R. O., and F. Nie. 2015. "Evaluating the Effects of Fertilizer Subsidy Programmes on Vulnerable Farmers in Kenya." *Journal of Agricultural Extension and Rural Development* 7 (6): 192–201.

PAM (Programme Against Malnutrition). 2005. *The Targeted Food Security Pack for Vulnerable but Viable Farmers: Programme Implementation Guidelines for the 2005/2006 Agricultural Season.* Lusaka, Zambia: PAM.

Pan, L., and L. Christiaensen. 2012. "Who Is Vouching for the Input Voucher? Decentralized Targeting and Elite Capture in Tanzania." *World Development* 40 (8): 1619–33.

Powlson, D., P. Gregory, W. Whalley, J. Quinton, D. Hopkins, A. Whitmore, P. Hirsch, and K. Goulding. 2011. "Soil Management in Regional to Sustainable Agriculture and Ecosystem Services." *Food Policy* 36: 72–87.

Ragassa, Catherine, Antony Chapoto, and Shashi Kolavalli. 2014. *Maize Productivity in Ghana.* GSSP Policy Note 5. Washington, DC: IFPRI. http://ebrary.ifpri.org/cdm/ref /collection/p15738coll2/id/128263.

Rashid, A. 2010. "Agro-Economic Feasibility of Fertilizer Use for Wheat Cultivation in Rainfed Regions of Pakistan." *Journal of Agricultural Research* 48 (3): 353–59.

Rashid, S., P. Dorosh, M. Malek, and S. Lemma. 2013. "Modern Input Promotion in Sub-Saharan Africa: Insights from Asian Green Revolution." *Agricultural Economics* 44: 705–21.

Resnick, D., and D. Mather. 2015. "Agricultural Inputs Policy under Macroeconomic Uncertainty: Applying the Kaleidoscope Model to Ghana's Fertilizer Subsidy Program (2008–2015). Draft working paper. IFPRI/Michigan State University, Washington, DC, and East Lansing, MI.

Ricker-Gilbert, J. 2014. "Wage and Employment Effects of Malawi's Fertilizer Subsidy Program." *Agricultural Economics* 45 (3): 337–53.

Ricker-Gilbert, J., and T. S. Jayne. 2011. "What Are the Enduring Effects of Fertilizer Subsidy Programs on Recipient Farm Households: Evidence from Malawi." Staff Paper 2011–09, Department of Agricultural, Food, and Resource Economics, Michigan State University, East Lansing, MI.

———. 2012. "Do Fertilizer Subsidies Boost Staple Crop Production and Reduce Poverty Across the Distribution of Smallholders in Africa? Quantile Regression Results from Malawi." Selected Paper for the Triennial Meeting of the International Association of Agricultural Economists, Foz Do Iguacu, Brazil, August 18–24.

———. 2015. "What Are the Dynamic Effects of Fertilizer Subsidies on Commercial Fertilizer Demand and Maize Production? Panel Evidence from Malawi." Paper prepared for presentation at the symposium on "Using Smart Subsidies to Support Small Scale Farmers in Africa," International Conference of Agricultural Economists, Milan, Italy, August 18.

Ricker-Gilbert, J., T. S. Jayne, and E. Chirwa. 2011. "Subsidies and Crowding Out: A Double-Hurdle Model of Fertilizer Demand in Malawi." *American Journal of Agricultural Economics* 93 (1): 26–42.

Ricker-Gilbert, J. N. Mason, F. Darko, and S. Tembo. 2013. "What Are the Effects of Input Subsidy Programs on Maize Prices? Evidence from Malawi and Zambia." *Agricultural Economics* 44 (6): 671–86.

Roy, R., R. Misra, J. Lesschen, and E. Smaling. 2003. "Assessment of Soil Nutrient Balance: Approaches and Methodologies." *Fertilizer and Plant Nutrition Bulletin* 14.

Sauer, J., and H. Tchale. 2009. "The Economics of Soil Fertility Management in Malawi." *Review of Agricultural Economics* 31(3): 535–60.

Sheahan, M., R. Black, and T. S. Jayne. 2013. "Are Kenyan Farmers Under-Utilizing Fertilizer? Implications for Input Intensification Strategies and Research." *Food Policy* 41: 39–52.

Sheahan, M., J. Olwande, L. Kirimi, and T. S. Jayne. 2014. "Targeting of Subsidized Fertilizer under Kenya's National Accelerated Agricultural Input Access Program (NAAIAP)." Working Paper 52, Tegemeo Institute of Agricultural Policy and Development, Nairobi, Kenya.

Shimeles, A., D. Z. Gurara, and D. B. Tessema. 2015. "Market Distortions and Political Rent: The Case of Fertilizer Price Divergence in Africa." Institute for the Study of Labor. Discussion Paper 8998, Institute for the Study of Labor, Bonn, Germany.

Sianjase, A., and V. Seshamani. 2013. "Impacts of Farmer Inputs Support Program on Beneficiaries in Gwembe District in Zambia." *Journal of Environmental Issues and Agriculture in Developing Countries* 50 (1): 40–50.

Smale, M., E. Birol, and D. Asare-Marfo. 2014. "Smallholder Demand for Maize Hybrids in Zambia: How Far Do Seed Subsidies Reach?" *Journal of Agricultural Economics* 65 (2): 349–67.

Snapp, S., T. S. Jayne, W. Mhango, T. Benson, and J. Ricker-Gilbert. 2014. "Maize-Nitrogen Response in Malawi's Smallholder Production Systems." Paper presented at National Symposium on Eight Years of FISP—Impact and What Next? Lilongwe, Malawi, July 14–15.

Snapp, S., and B. Pound, eds. 2011. *Agricultural Systems: Agroecology and Rural Innovation for Development.* Cambridge, MA: Academic Press.

Takeshima, H., and L. Liverpool-Tasie. 2015. "Fertilizer Subsidies, Political Influence, and Local Food Prices in Sub-Saharan Africa: Evidence from Nigeria." *Food Policy* 54: 11–24.

Takeshima, H., and E. Nkonya. 2014. "Government Fertilizer Subsidy and Commercial Sector Fertilizer Demand: Evidence from the Federal Market Stabilization Program in Nigeria." *Food Policy* 47 (August): 1–12.

Takeshima, H., E. Nkonya, and S. Deb. 2012. "Impact of Fertilizer Subsidies on the Commercial Fertilizer Sector in Nigeria: Evidence from Previous Fertilizer Subsidy Schemes." Working Paper 23, IFPRI Nigeria Strategy Support Program II, Abuja, Nigeria.

Tittonell, P., and K. Giller. 2013. "When Yield Gaps Are Poverty Traps: The Paradigm of Ecological Intensification in African Smallholder Agriculture." *Field Crops Research* 143: 76–90.

Tittonell, P., B. Vanlauwe, N. de Ridder, and K. Giller. 2007. "Nutrient Use Efficiencies and Crop Responses to N, P, and Manure Applications in Zimbabwean Soils: Exploring Management Strategies Across Soil Fertility Gradients." *Field Crop Research* 100: 348–68.

Tscharntke, T., Y. Clough, T. Wanger, L. Jackson, I. Motzke, I. Perfecto, J. Vandermeer, and A. Whitbread. 2012. "Global Food Security, Biodiversity Conservation and the Future of Agricultural Intensification." *Biological Conservation* 151(1): 53–59.

van de Walle, N. 2001. *African Economies and the Politics of Permanent Crisis, 1979–1999.* Cambridge, U.K.: Cambridge University Press.

Vanlauwe, B., J. Kihara, P. Chivenge, P. Pypers, R. Coe, and J. Six. 2011. "Agronomic Use Efficiency of N Fertilizer in Maize-Based Systems in Sub-Saharan Africa Within the Context of Integrated Soil Fertility Management." *Plant and Soil* 339 (1–2): 35–50.

Vondolia, G. K., H. Eggert, and J. Stage. 2012. "Nudging Boserup? The Impact of Fertilizer Subsidies on Investment in Soil and Water Conservation." Discussion Paper 12-08, Environment for Development and Resources for the Future, Washington, DC.

Wanzala-Mlobela, M., P. Fuentes, and S. Mkumbwa. 2013. "NEPAD Policy Study: Practices and Policy Options for the Improved Design and Implementation of Fertilizer Subsidy Programs in Sub-Saharan Africa." Midrand, South Africa: NEPAD Planning and Coordinating Agency.

Ward, M., and P. Santos. 2010. "Looking beyond the Plot: The Nutritional Impact of Fertilizer Policy." Selected paper prepared for presentation at the Agricultural and Applied Economics Association (AAEA), Canadian Agricultural Economics Society, and Western Agricultural Economics Association Joint Annual Meeting, Denver, Colorado, July 25–27.

Westberg, N. B. 2015. "Exchanging Fertilizer for Votes?" Working Paper 12/2015, Norwegian University of Life Sciences School of Economics and Business, Ås, Norway.

Wiredu, A., M. Zeller, and A. Diagne. 2015. "What Determines Adoption of Fertilizers among Rice-Producing Households in Northern Ghana?" *Quarterly Journal of International Agriculture* 54 (3): 263.

World Bank. 2007. *World Bank Assistance to Agriculture in Sub-Saharan Africa: An IEG Review.* Independent Evaluation Group. Washington, DC: World Bank.

———. 2008. *World Development Report 2008: Agriculture for Development.* Washington, DC: World Bank.

———. 2014. *Tanzania Public Expenditure Review: National Agricultural Input Voucher Scheme (NAIVS).* Washington, DC: World Bank.

Xu, Z., W. J. Burke, T. S. Jayne, and J. Govereh. 2009. "Do Input Subsidy Programs 'Crowd In' or 'Crowd Out' Commercial Market Development? Modeling Fertilizer Demand in a Two-Channel Marketing System." *Agricultural Economics* 40 (1): 79–94.

Yanggen, D., V. Kelly, T. Reardon, and A. Naseem. 1998. "Incentives for Fertilizer Use in Sub-Saharan Africa: A Review of Empirical Evidence on Fertilizer Response and Profitability." International Development Working Paper 70, Michigan State University, East Lansing, MI.

Yawson, D. O., F. Armah, E. K. Afrifa, and S. K. N. Dadzie. 2010. "Ghana's Fertilizer Subsidy Policy: Early Field Lessons from Farmers in Central Region." *Journal of Sustainable Development: Africa* 12 (3): 191–203.

Yusuf, Vincent. 2015. "Agro Dealers Stop Farm Inputs Supply over N38bn Debt." *Daily Trust,* July 30. http://www.dailytrust.com.ng/daily/index.php/agriculture/61217-agro -dealers-stop-farm-inputs-supply-over-n38bn-debt.

ZMACO (Zambia Ministry of Agriculture and Cooperatives), Agricultural Consultative Forum, and FSRP (Food Security Research Project). 2002. "Developments in Fertilizer Marketing in Zambia: Commercial Trading, Government Programs, and the Smallholder Farmer." Food Security Research Project Working Paper 4, FSRP, ZMAC, Lusaka, Zambia. http://aec.msu.edu/fs2/zambia/wp4zambia.

ZMAL (Zambia Ministry of Agriculture and Livestock). 2012. *Farmer Input Support Programme Implementation Manual, 2012/2013 Agricultural Season.* Lusaka, Zambia: ZMAL.

———. 2014. *Farmer Input Support Programme Implementation Manual.* Lusaka, Zambia: ZMAL.

ZMFNP (Zambia Ministry of Finance and National Planning). Various years. Estimates of Revenue and Expenditure: Activity Based Budget. Lusaka, Zambia.

Zulu, P., T. Kalinda, and G. Tembo. 2014. "Effects of the Maize Input Subsidy Program on Groundnuts Production in Zambia." *Journal of Agricultural Science* 6 (7): 253–64.

# Chapter 4

# Planning, Implementing, and Rebalancing Budgets

Getting the most for the money requires not only making the right policy choices in allocating resources among programs (research, irrigation, subsidies, and so on) but also having an efficient budget process.[1] The variance in budget process capacity in African countries is considerable, but there undoubtedly is scope for continuing improvement. This needs to start from a stronger foundation of periodic sector strategies with detailed and quantitative translation into expected spending priorities and adjustments from the most recent implementation period, accompanied by a monitorable results framework. Annual budget planning can be improved through joint planning of recurrent and capital budgets and cleaning up recurrent spending "hidden" in investment project budgets. Shortcomings also need to be addressed in monitoring and evaluating the outputs and outcomes of spending.

Forward budget planning in almost all countries studied for this book is limited to formulating national investment plans and annual budgets. Recurrent budget planning typically adjusts to prior year levels incrementally. Yet significant policy shifts, such as expanding reliance on private markets for input provision, do not appear to be accompanied by funding for the new recurrent functions required, for example, regulatory capacity for input quality in markets. Such strategic recurrent activities are often difficult to discern in recurrent budgets, but their underfunding risks negative outcomes that could be outsized in relation to the fairly small budget costs of providing public goods.

Budget information systems appear to be improving with the expansion of computerized systems by finance ministries. But there is still more to be done in extending to geographically remote sector agencies and institutes and establishing sector ministries' budget analysis capacities for monitoring and adjustment in the budget year. Ministries of finance also need budget information systems that capture the off-budget finance (usually from external development partners) of projects delivering public goods and services. As long as such spending remains off-budget, the coordination and accountability of activities undertaken with this finance will remain inadequate.

Improving budget execution rates needs to be part of making the case that the agriculture sector can make good use of additional public resources. Narrowing the gap between planned and actual spending involves numerous partners in budget management, and so will need consensual agendas to make real progress. Particular attention needs to focus on improving capital spending, especially where this involves external partner finance and fiduciary systems. Also needed is improving the predictability of releases from ministries of finance, strengthening agriculture ministry procurement planning and implementation, and improving budget information management systems to inform within-year budget implementation so that resources are used effectively.

Two other aspects of budget processes are likely to grow in priority but require attention over several years to build the capacity for higher quality budget outcomes. The first is a shift to program budgeting for the government budget, as some countries have committed to do. Backward-looking reconfiguration of sector public spending by program categories to provide the recent history of composition and trends must benchmark the programs and the specifics of their spending. The second aspect is decentralizing the administration and fiscal management of government functions. It is critical that budget information systems—and information sharing—across the levels of government enable budget planning that leverages potential synergies and avoids duplication in spending.

Unfortunately, it is not possible to firmly link the spending performance with sector outcomes. In part, this is due to a lack of monitoring and evaluation (M&E) data and analysis in sector ministries, the relatively short-time frames of analysis, and the methodological difficulty of discerning public sector activity impacts when they remain small in relation to those from private sector activity. External factors, such as weather and world markets, also complicate linking spending performance with outcomes. These are the main messages from the 20 agriculture public expenditure reviews (AgPERs) conducted as part of the World Bank Strengthening National Comprehensive Agriculture Public Expenditure in Sub-Saharan Africa program.[2]

## Public Expenditure Reviews in 20 Countries

Most of the studies completed under this program are basic diagnostic analyses of individual country expenditure performance. Through compiling of expenditure data on a common methodological basis, consistent with the Comprehensive Africa Agriculture Development Programme (CAADP) guidance, the studies aimed to establish recent trends in spending and in the effectiveness of implementation (see annex 4A). While the studies cover the most recent 10-year period with available expenditure data, the end point differs across the completed studies, with the most recent generally covering periods through 2012 or 2013. Much was learned about conducting AgPERs, since they were implemented progressively over almost five years. Refinements were introduced along the way, though not all issues were resolved in time to have an entirely consistent application across all the studies. Many of the lessons have enriched technical discussions among practitioners in workshops during 2014 and 2015, and are being adopted into a revised CAADP guidance note for public agriculture expenditure analysis and a guidance note on how to conduct an "AgPER Lite."[3]

## Characteristics of the Countries

The 20 countries covered in this chapter present the diverse circumstances of agriculture sector public expenditure management in Africa.[4] They account for about 70 percent of agricultural value added in Sub-Saharan Africa. And they illustrate the differing contexts that public sector agencies are grappling with to achieve better outcomes in planning and deploying resources for public programs in the agriculture sector. Three dimensions of this diversity are useful to bear in mind.

*Political stability.* In the period covered by most of the country studies, a number of the countries went through bouts of internal instability and armed conflict that had direct ramifications for the functioning of public expenditure programs. Facing such circumstances were Côte d'Ivoire, Guinea, Liberia, and Sierra Leone. Protracted conflict typically has impacts on public spending in agriculture. There is often a falloff in the pace of implementation and expenditure in externally funded projects, and in approvals of new projects. As a result, these periods often bring a sharp decline in capital expenditure, which is more dependent on external finance sources, skewing overall expenditure to personnel and core recurrent spending. Territorial insecurity can also impede implementing agricultural programs that are spatially spread out, such as extension, agronomic research, and livestock health campaigns. Political instability can thus be accompanied by significant declines in overall expenditure in the agricultural sector, and substantial changes in composition, which recover only with a return to improved internal political stability.

*Agricultural diversity.* Countries have agricultural sectors with substantially different agronomic and natural resource contexts. Some are predominantly semiarid, with cropping often limited to a single crop per year and a heavier reliance on livestock. Coastal countries typically have larger artisanal fishing opportunities, with this subsector more important in rural economies than for landlocked countries. Greater rainfall is also often related with larger forest endowments, and in these countries, forestry may take on greater importance in public expenditure programs than in countries with more limited national forests. Country expenditures may naturally and reasonably reflect these endowment differences.

*Agriculture's size in national economies.* Public spending on agriculture would not be expected to be as large a part of overall public budgets in countries where the sector is a small part of the national economy. A small agricultural share of national gross domestic product (GDP) could result from economic growth and diversification, or it might result from a country having substantial mining or petroleum sectors. Countries covered in this study that have this latter characteristic are Botswana, South Africa, and to a lesser extent Nigeria—and others, such as Ghana, are moving in this direction due to rapidly developing extractive industry sectors. Where the agricultural sector is small relative to the national economy, but the share of the rural population remains substantial, the dimensions of public spending on agriculture may be quite different from other countries—large in terms of the sector economic importance, but small as a share of the national budget.

*Decentralization.* Countries in Sub-Saharan Africa have made differing commitments to decentralizing public budget management. Nigeria, with a federal structure, has placed significant responsibility for some agricultural public functions with the states rather than the central government. Other countries operate a unitary government, with the government activities at the smallest administrative unit functionally integrated into the hierarchy of central government ministries. For this study, public expenditure to be tracked and assessed is in principle that of consolidated government—all levels of decentralized budget management combined. In practice, though, public expenditure tracking information systems in Sub-Saharan Africa do not yet have the capacity to encompass the expenditure on the sector by autonomous subnational levels of decentralized governments. Chapter 5 of this volume considers the political economy of this decentralization trend; in the current chapter, we look at the implications for budget planning and management.

Annex 4A lists the country studies for this chapter and—along with the devolution of spending authority—indicates the years of coverage and characteristics of the 20 studies, including the scope of agriculture covered, whether off-budget resources were estimated and included, and whether the countries had an updated strategy that affected expenditure.

# Planning and Implementing Budgets

Most of the countries acknowledge the shortcomings of budgets presented as activity or project listings, and the benefits of moving to a program budget approach. The latter present budgets organized by objectives and programs to attain these objectives, and is better articulated with sector strategies. Shifting to program budgets is a significant reform, though, and must be spearheaded by ministries of finance with capacity building to enable roll-out across line ministries and accompanied by overhauls of budget information systems.

Despite the complexity of the transition to program budgeting, some countries are gradually moving. The most ambitious of such reforms is the one across West African Economic and Monetary Union (WAEMU) countries, with the guidance of its Framework for Multiyear Programming and Program Budgets. Passed in 2009, this framework has resulted in guidance and support for implementation of program budgets at the national level, with the transition to be completed by 2017. To facilitate forward planning based on past realizations, the Burkina Faso public expenditure study organized the historical budget data on agricultural expenditure into program categories consistent with the anticipated program budget structure.

Countries need to give adequate attention to capacity for coordination across the ministries and authorities engaged in budget processes in the agricultural sector. The apex structures, whether committees or other institutions, need processes and incentives to manage the budgetary interfaces so their activities will have more impact through better coordination. There are too many examples of problems stemming from failure to coordinate plans, such as a water storage reservoir being completed by a ministry of water resources with no activity yet underway for completing the associated irrigation infrastructure under a ministry of agriculture.

## Planning and Budgeting Context

Government processes for preparing and implementing public budgets in the agricultural sector reveal common areas where improvements could increase the impact of expenditures. This chapter reviews these findings grouped by three levels in the hierarchy of budget making and implementation. The first level is the establishment of sector strategies and the general budgetary context for the government as a whole, usually managed by the ministry of finance. The second level is the annual preparation and approval of the sector budget and the presentation features of this budget. The third level is the actual implementation of the annual budget, including the monitoring and evaluation activities that potentially feed back into planning and budget preparation.

As will be evident throughout this chapter, the agricultural sector ministries are heavily dependent on the core economic management ministries, particularly the ministry of finance, and a ministry of planning if such exists, throughout this budget process. Shortcomings in outcomes may have their causes within the sector administration, but a set of constraints at the ministry of finance or plan level leads to unsatisfactory results, and indicates the need for jointly established and pursued agendas for improvement involving both the core and sector ministries.

Many country studies were accompanied, sometimes as separate documents, by draft action plans to follow up on the recommendations of the reports. These draft action plans were taken into technical validation workshops, where they were worked on further with the expectation that national authorities would take on board the finalization of the action plans. Portions of the action plans often required verification and further consultation with other critical partners, such as ministries of finance, since implementation would need their collaboration. In this way the AgPERs aimed to facilitate the articulation of practical agendas for ministries of agriculture to work on with other partners. But assessing the progress toward the desired outcomes of these action plans was not in the scope of this synthesis.

*Guidance provided by sector strategies on spending.* Almost all countries established or updated a broad agricultural sector strategy. Such strategies establish priorities for action, but those under review lacked key elements and sufficient details to guide subsequent budget planning to implement the public expenditure components of the strategies. Ideally, the sector strategy document would have clear objectives, presented in a specific, measurable, achievable, reasonable, and time-bound way. These elements provide the objectives and indicators needed for a results framework that would later inform the activities for monitoring and evaluation. Good practice for the sector strategy is to translate the objectives into broad programmatic areas for action—with indicative, multiyear, public expenditure targets—and to indicate the main differences against the expenditure outcomes of the most recent implementation period.

Most sector strategy documents fall well short of this ideal. The better cases, such as Ghana's agricultural strategy, accompany the forward-looking program area description and priorities with expenditure targets—and a results framework with identification of measurable indicators and quantified targets. The majority, though, remain at the qualitatively defined description of priorities, lacking expenditure targets and results frameworks. Sector strategies with these latter shortcomings provide almost no guidance to preparing annual budgets and monitoring progress.

As a result of these shortcomings of sector strategies, only a few of the country expenditure reviews could marshal evidence on whether there had been any expenditure shifts from before to after the establishment of the new sector strategies. Only three of the country studies—Côte d'Ivoire, Ghana, and Togo—presented such assessments of expenditures before and after establishing a sector plan (see annex 4A). Seven could provide some assessment, if only qualitative, of whether the expenditure pattern, in the period after establishing a sector strategy, appeared consistent with the priorities in these strategies. This outcome reinforces the observation that sector strategies need to be substantially more specific on spending implications and results frameworks if they are to be concrete and assessable guides to public spending in the sector.

*Sector MTEFs and national agriculture investment plans.* Sub-Saharan countries frequently prepare medium-term expenditure frameworks (MTEFs). This multiyear expenditure planning is limited to the macroeconomic level and led by the ministry of finance, which provides only an aggregate budget allocation to each sector ministry for subsequent disaggregation into a proposed annual budget. A few countries also accompany the macro MTEF with a set of sectoral MTEFs, which further disaggregate the multiyear budget planning to this level. Only a few countries routinely prepare sector MTEFs for agriculture on a rolling, multiyear basis—and use them to translate sector strategies into detailed annual budget proposals. Some countries attempted a decade or more ago to prepare both macro and sectoral MTEFs, but foundered on big divergences in outcomes at the macro level (such as own revenues, exchange rate, donor fund mobilization) that rendered the sectoral MTEFs inoperable. Sector ministry appetites for participating in the administratively demanding sector MTEFs are usually slim unless the macro MTEF has stabilized into a platform that is accurate, predictable, and implementable under the direction of the ministry of finance.

Most agricultural sector ministries have relied instead on national agriculture investment plans (NAIPs) to translate sector strategies into detailed spending targets for the strategy's prioritized programs. These NAIPs provide second-best guidance to annual budget preparation and have two important shortcomings. First, they typically focus on investment, providing no guidance on recurrent expenditure requirements, despite key sector public goods and services being more dependent on the recurrent expenditures than the investment budget. Second, NAIPs are to a significant extent motivated by a fund mobilization objective keyed to scaled-up sector activity. As a result, their investment projections usually come with unrealistic jumps in investment from the most recent realized budget performance to the first NAIP target year, and significant funding gaps grow larger for more future years. Presented with a target annual budget envelope by their ministry of finance that falls short of the NAIP aspirations—and needing to cover both recurrent expenditures and investment—the sector ministry confronts difficult allocation trade-offs, and the sector strategy and NAIP provide little concrete guidance.

*Legislative budget authorization.* Another important element of the general budget context is the expeditiousness of legislative branch deliberations and approvals of the annual budget the executive branch proposes. Delays in budget approval can arise in this inherently political process, which can push budget resource availability months into the implementation year. There is quite a range of experience on this dimension—not only across countries but also over time, depending on mixtures of political synchrony among executive, legislative, and administrative discipline and tradition. The budget implementation by agricultural sector ministries obviously derives from these larger forces, and may reflect the line ministries only beginning to get releases of annual budget resources well into the budget year, making it difficult to use them in the months remaining.

## Off-Budget Funding and "Extraordinary" Budget Transfers

The aggregate public spending on agriculture includes a category of "off-budget" spending that is not captured in the budget information systems of the government ministries responsible for fiscal affairs.[5] The most common manifestation of off-budget expenditure results from external partner finance for development projects that provide public-type investments in goods and services for agricultural sector development. This is under the authorization of the government, but the resource commitment and spending is not captured in the annual national budget management system. Instead, the spending occurs separately through a project management unit with separate procurement and accounting systems. From domestic resources, off-budget spending can occur if resource flows or accounts available to government authorities—as sometimes occurs through special initiatives managed through the presidency—are not included in the normal planning, authorization, and implementation of annual budgets.

Nearly half the countries reviewed had off-budget resources that financed public-type activities in the agricultural sector, mostly from externally funded projects. For some countries, these resources dominated overall public spending on agriculture (table 4.1). They were highest for Liberia, at about two-thirds of public spending in the agricultural sector, and also important for Malawi (one-third) and Burkina Faso (one-fifth). Several countries emerging from periods of national strife such as Guinea and Togo have managed to reduce the importance of off-budget expenditure as a result of strengthening domestic resource mobilization and budgetary processes. Also note that the other half of countries included externally funded projects in their national budget processes and information systems.

In addition to crowding out the private sector, state-owned enterprises (SOEs) have sometimes required large and highly variable "extraordinary" funding, reducing transparency and predictability. SOEs can run up off-budget

**Table 4.1** Off-Budget Funding of Agricultural Spending Can Be a Big Part of Agriculture Budgets

| Country | 2005 | 2009 | 2011 |
|---|---|---|---|
| Burkina Faso (US$, millions) | 23 | 49 | 55 |
| Share of agriculture budget (%) | 18 | 20 | 20 |
| Côte d'Ivoire (US$, millions) | 14 | 54 | — |
| Share of agriculture budget (%) | 19 | 40 | — |
| Guinea (US$, millions) | — | — | — |
| Share of agriculture budget (%) | 46 | 29 | 11 |
| Liberia (US$, millions) | — | 28 | 47 |
| Share of agriculture budget (%) | — | 62 | 72 |
| Malawi (US$, millions) | — | — | — |
| Share of agriculture budget (%) | — | 39 | 35 |

Source: Mink 2016 from individual AgPERs.
Note: AgPERs = agriculture public expenditure reviews; — = not available.

debt on their own account, and when this reaches an unsustainable level, they require an infusion of funds for recapitalization. For example, the Togolese Cotton Company (SOTOCO) in 2007 required a transfer equivalent to 52 percent of the Ministry of Agriculture's budget to pay off its debt. SOTOCO was liquidated and replaced by a public-private enterprise, which required another "extraordinary" transfer to cover the government's share of the capitalization. It is noteworthy that most countries in West Africa now use Organization for the Harmonization of Business Laws in Africa (OHADA)[6] accounting rules, which limit the use of such practices that make expenditures nontransparent and unpredictable.

There are pros and cons to including such off-budget resources in expenditure analysis. The logic for their inclusion is that they are part of the aggregate resources available for realizing governmental efforts to develop the nation's agricultural sector, and therefore useful to include for evaluating aggregate resources available for the sector. An argument against their inclusion is that it weakens the accountability framework for budget expenditure, since the agriculture ministries can rightly argue that their ministries of finance cannot hold them responsible for outcomes of externally funded activities whose finance and implementation do not come to the ministries as part of budget processes and information systems.

Two considerations weigh against inclusion of such off-budget resources in expenditure analysis. First, despite the potential control that negotiation over project legal agreements provides to governments, external partners may simply withdraw the offer of money if they are not permitted to impose their own fiduciary systems on its use. Second, measuring off-budget spending is quite difficult for the agricultural sector, let alone for public sector activity across sectors.

Gathering this information is a time-consuming task of collecting information from each external partner, based on disparate documents, with different formats for presenting information. In any event, total public spending does *not* include off-budget expenditure for the countries covered in this chapter.

The best but also most difficult solution is for the country's core economic management ministry to work with external development partners to integrate information on such resources into budget planning and information systems. If this is not forthcoming, more ad hoc solutions can still be valuable, such as parallel information gathering and partial integration into budget planning and monitoring (that is, charge a unit in the agricultural or finance ministry to do this). This enables moving toward a stronger and more comprehensive mutual accountability system on budgets.

## Overly Ambitious Calendars

Annual budget planning can also be weighed down by overly ambitious investment project and program preparation calendars. Sector ministry planning staff are often short-handed and overburdened, with capacity constraints in getting new projects to an adequate stage of readiness in relation to an annual budget cycle and to political commitments. A consequence is that new investment projects may be inscribed in the annual budget and allocated startup funds despite not being ready for timely startup. Apart from the inefficiencies of an undercoordinated start of components, there are also the costs of slow startups, unused budgeted resources, and lowered budget execution rates. Overcoming such problems will involve action both through strengthening project preparation capacity in ministries—through adequate recruitment and recurrent budgets—and through greater discipline within sector ministries to apply project readiness criteria before inscription in annual budgets.

## Improve Budget Information Systems for Greater Technical Efficiency

Better budget information systems are needed to support course corrections and adjustments at the sector ministry during the budget year. For real-time budget management by agricultural sector ministries, most countries are now operating systems put in place on computerized platforms by ministries of finance. The systems have the capacity for—and in some cases already provide—real-time online access to budget information in sector ministries. Most countries still need to generalize access to such capacity, improve the quality of the data, and strengthen analysis for time management.

Expanding the coverage of these improved systems—to include agencies and institutions under the central ministry but outside the capital—must advance consistent with investments in communications infrastructure information technology (IT) capacity, and this takes time. In Nigeria, for example, from the time that the central Agriculture Ministry departments were brought into the online budget information system, it took another three years to integrate most of the more than 40 agencies and institutes reporting to the Ministry. And these entities accounted for nearly half the Ministry's recurrent budget.

Ministries of agriculture should try to work with ministries of finance to make the budget information systems sufficiently flexible, and to give them authority sufficiently defined to enable sector ministries to add their own identifier parameters to the budget information system. This collaboration would allow additional parameters to be associated with budget lines (apart from the core system designed and controlled by the ministry of finance)—such as crop, subsector, and administrative or agroecological region—to enable expenditure monitoring and analysis disaggregated by such characteristics.

### Reform National Procurement Systems

Most countries made progress in reforming and strengthening national procurement systems. This usually entailed variants on updating the public procurement law to meet international standards, reinforcing central and deconcentrated public procurement authorities as procurement capacity in line ministries, and revising a procurement manual. In some countries, thresholds for procurement types—comparison prices, domestic competitive bidding, and international competitive bidding—are being adjusted to gain the cost benefits of more transparent competition and the time benefits of greater delegation of procurement steps to decentralized units. Some countries are also increasing transparency by establishing a publicly accessible online interface for public procurement.

Agriculture ministries are not in the driver's seat for these national procurement system reforms, but they can take the initiative to participate as early pilot ministries in phased rollouts of implementation. More under the line ministries' control is adequate planning in advance of the annual budget cycle of ministry procurement plans. Ministries in the sector can prepare procurement plans at the same time as the annual budget. And they can aim to have tender documents available at the start of the budget year so that tenders can be issued as soon as the budget is approved, releases start, and bid evaluation committees are constituted. Progress at the national level on overall procurement process strengthening, and at the sector ministry level in implementation and timeliness, are key to drive engagement with donors to channel their development finance support on-budget for implementation under national procedures.

Improving budget execution rates to reduce the gap between planned and actual expenditure is needed as a part of improving the quality of outcomes of budgeted activities. As seen earlier, there usually are many reasons for poor execution rates, and because these involve numerous partners in budget management, they will need consensus agendas to overcome finger-pointing and make real progress. Countries need to focus on capital spending, especially when externally financed, to improve the predictability of releases from ministries of finance and to strengthen procurement planning and implementation.

## Numerous Project Implementation Units

Many countries are struggling with numerous project implementation units (PIUs) outside sector ministry civil service and administrative structures. Each operates within a restrictive horizon of responsibility for a particular, usually externally funded, investment project. A PIU is often established at the insistence of an external funder for fiduciary accountability to the funder, for rapid capacity creation so that the project can proceed quickly, and to bypass cumbersome national institutional processes and limited capacities.

Among the drawbacks are that PIUs may operate outside national treasury systems and off-budget. They may entail separate procurement policies that have their own complexity. They may fail to contribute to the core investment management capacity building that is needed within the sector ministries. In addition, they may have spheres of policy involvement that overlap but inadequately coordinate with other PIUs and national policies. Some countries, such as Sierra Leone, are changing their stance on PIUs and consolidating their numbers or integrating their project management into line ministry functions. While this institutional reform is underway, there will undoubtedly be a mix of results and impacts on implementing spending. But it is a necessary step toward integrated budget management and coherent expenditure accountability across the full set of public sector activity. The issue is more one of pace than of principle.

## Reduce the Plethora of Separate Accounts

Two other public fiscal management reforms can improve technical efficiency of expenditure management. One is a treasury single account (TSA) system; the other is a centralized civil service information system. A TSA aims to rationalize the chaotic situation that characterizes a number of countries where ministries have been permitted to establish a plethora of separate accounts for different agencies, projects, and functions. The TSA reform, driven from a ministry of finance and accountant general, reduces the number of these accounts, applies a common accounting framework to the remaining consolidated accounts, and captures all of them in a single integrated information system. This reform aims to considerably improve efficiency of resource management, transparency of account management, and effectiveness of auditing.

Vested interests in parts of the public administration may resist this. But where the political momentum is favorable, the participation in the reform by agricultural sector ministries will strengthen the link between budget resource mobilization and spending impact.

## Rationalize Management Systems

Civil service management in many Sub-Saharan countries is emerging from an era of manual personnel management information systems. Those systems suffered from inaccuracies, costs of inscribed ghost workers, cumbersome extraction of information useful for human resource planning, and weakness in supporting individual personnel actions. Rationalizing civil service management systems can improve the accuracy of information and its availability for timely personnel system management within a clear hierarchy of decision-making on civil service matters. Such reform is typically managed out of the national civil service commission. The interest to agricultural sector ministries comes when phased rollouts involve pilot ministries, in which the early participation of agricultural sector ministries will bring earlier gains for the effectiveness of human resources and spending.

## Build Capacity for Monitoring and Evaluation

Monitoring and evaluation (M&E) capacity is weak and fails to provide decision makers with information that will strengthen the evidence-based foundations for expenditure management. M&E systems provide information on the links of expenditure to sector outcomes, but at the level of budget implementation, better M&E systems are needed as well. Partly this is being addressed in some countries by strengthening computerized information systems that provide real-time access to budget information and simplify updating of standard analytical tables to better inform midcourse resource and activity adjustments. There is also a clear need for more human capacity in agricultural ministry budget departments for analytical use of budget information: to identify in a timely way when budget implementation is getting off-course and which solutions need to be prioritized during the budget year.

Bolstering capacity for M&E is an important piece of improving execution rates, but it can also contribute to improved budget analysis that underpins and justifies sector ministries' budget proposals for the coming year. Moreover, where budget information systems have not yet fully integrated off-budget resources, M&E can be strengthened to improve information on donor-financed projects and financial status. That would improve the accountability of donors to meet financing commitments—and the accountability of ministers of agriculture to encompass these projects in coherent management of the overall resources for the provision of public goods, services, and investments.

## Striking the Right Balance among Expenditure Categories

A basic question is whether budgets are structured to spend resources on the right things. The "right" things will be defined in a country's sectoral strategy, and will usually be guided by a combination of sector growth; distributed impact on populations engaged in crops, livestock, fisheries, and forestry; and often a contribution to national food security goals. For this study, three expenditure composition dimensions are explored: allocation by (a) recurrent and capital budget element (economic composition), (b) agriculture subsector (also known as functional composition), and (c) subnational spatial unit (typically government or administrative units, at which data are more likely to be available).

### Recurrent Versus Investment Categories

Recurrent budgets consist of wage (plus other personnel benefits) and nonwage (such as goods and services for operations and maintenance). Typically, these are financed from domestic sources of revenue generation (table 4.2). Payment of public servant wages can take on particular political significance (such as contract negotiations or promptness of payment under stress from fiscal constraints), and governments prefer not to be reliant on external sources of

**Table 4.2** Domestic Finance of Agricultural Expenditure
*Percent of total*

| Country | 2005 | 2009 | 2011 |
|---|---|---|---|
| Burkina Faso | 24 | 37 | 48 |
| Cameroon | 94 | 91 | 92 |
| Chad | 40 | 38 | 43 |
| Côte d'Ivoire | — | 62 | — |
| Ghana[a] | 73 | 61 | 63 |
| Guinea | 41 | 35 | 48 |
| Liberia | — | 21 | 38 |
| Madagascar | — | 40 (2008) | — |
| Malawi | — | 51 | 39 |
| Mozambique | 33 | 33 (2007) | — |
| | | 49 (2009 budget plan) | |
| Senegal[a] | 45 | 41 | |
| Sierra Leone | 54 | 20 | 26 |
| Togo | — | 64 | — |

*Source:* Mink 2016 from individual AgPERs.
*Note:* Countries in the 20-country sample for which the data required are not available are not listed in table. AgPERs = agriculture public expenditure reviews; — = data missing for this year.
a. Off-budget expenditure not included.

funding to manage them, just as external partners are reluctant to finance other countries' civil servants. In usual circumstances, governments will do their utmost to ensure that civil servants are paid and that execution rates on the wage component are higher than any other component—typically above 90 percent (table 4.3). Nonwage recurrent expenditure is another matter. The expenditure items in this category are less visible and more easily deferrable if budget resources become tight over the implementation year.[7]

The investment budget has different characteristics than the recurrent budget, which influences governments' ability to spend up to planned levels. Looking first at the investment budget in aggregate, the planning and implementation of investment activities are usually more complicated and harder to manage than that of recurrent expenditure, particularly if significant scaling up of effort is underway. Investment projects may be inscribed in budgets for approval by the legislative branch before full implementation readiness, such that the actual onset of spending is delayed despite the resource having been inscribed. Procurement plans may not be done until budgets are made available, leading to delays late into the budget year of contract finalization and the start of expenditure.

Execution rates for investment budgets are also discernibly different depending on whether the source of finance for the investment is domestic or external. Externally funded investment projects, as alluded to in the earlier discussion on off-budget expenditure, often apply donor fiduciary and management requirements through project management units. These can add complexity of rules and additional layers of decision making compared to domestically financed investments that follow government procedures. This complexity leads to implementation slowness and expenditure delays, visible in table 4.3 as lower execution rates of investment with external funding compared to those with domestic funding.

Countries pursuing the CAADP objective of scaled-up support for their agricultural sectors thus have a balancing act to manage in mobilizing finance to fund sector activities, particularly investment activities. Reliance can be placed on funding more ambitious investment plans from domestic resources, which are more easily managed, but are scarce. Or greater efforts can be made to mobilize external resources, but these are more difficult to manage. What is apparent from table 4.2, which shows the domestically financed share of public agricultural spending, is that finding the appropriate balance remains a relevant budget management preoccupation. The majority of the countries remain reliant on external finance for over half of their aggregate expenditures on agriculture, which is the source of finance that is shown in table 4.3 to be the most difficult to manage to achieve reasonable execution rate outcomes. Some countries, such as Burkina Faso, appear to be on longer-term paths moving to greater reliance on domestic finance as part of expenditure growth trajectories.

**Table 4.3** Execution Rates of Agricultural Expenditure

*Percent*

| | Wages | Nonwage recurrent | Internally funded investment/ capital | Donor-funded investment/ capital | Investment, all funding sources | Total agricultural expenditure |
|---|---|---|---|---|---|---|
| Botswana (2012) | 95 | 101 | — | — | 83 | — |
| (2013) | — | — | — | — | 110 | — |
| Burkina Faso (2004–11) | 90 | 72 | 84 | 59 | — | — |
| Chad (2012) | — | — | — | — | — | 85 |
| (2003–12) | — | — | — | — | — | 92 |
| Côte d'Ivoire (1999–2010) | 90 | 62 | 35 | 23 | — | — |
| Congo, Dem. Rep. (2008–10) | — | — | — | — | — | 70 |
| (2011–13) | — | — | — | — | — | 34 |
| Madagascar (2007) | 93 | 84 | 69 | 20 | 27 | 37 |
| Malawi (2009/10–2011/12) | 87 | 76 | 82 | 44 | — | 73 |
| Nigeria[a] (2008–12) | — | — | — | — | 104 | 98 |
| Senegal (2005–10) | 100 | 94 | 89 | — | — | — |
| Sierra Leone (2012) | — | — | 68 | — | — | 70 |
| Togo (2002–10) | 104 | 71 | 69 | 23 | — | — |

*Source:* Mink 2016 from individual AgPERs.

*Note:* In Mozambique, the country report presented no quantitative analysis due to data shortcomings. AgPERs = agriculture public expenditure reviews; — = data not available for this year.

a. Federal expenditure only.

But others, such as Sierra Leone, are grappling with kick-starting sector scale-ups of investment through greater reliance on external finance. The scope for improving budgeting of recurrent and capital expenditures is considerable in most countries, with two aspects warranting special attention. First is to address the cost accounting weaknesses and incentives issues that lead to recurrent expenditure improperly included in the capital budget. Second is better integrating the planning of recurrent and capital spending. Few countries appear to have budgeting processes that link the two categories, and in some sector ministries, there are even separate units that independently put forward budget proposals for the two budget components. Integrated planning of an appropriate balance between recurrent expenditures and investment and improving the cost accounting of the two categories would minimize cases of investments lacking funds for operations and maintenance and underfunded recurrent public goods and services.

*More attention is required for an appropriate level of and balance within the recurrent budget.* Total public expenditure on agriculture is useful to analyze based on the disaggregation into economic components, that is, its recurrent and investment parts. Recurrent expenditure can be further split into personnel costs and other recurrent costs that usually comprise goods, services, and transfers. Each of these components, and the balance among them, will be discussed in the following paragraphs.

The share of aggregate recurrent expenditure in total agricultural expenditure is shown across countries in table 4.4. The CAADP focus on national agricultural investment plans indicates a preoccupation with increasing the level and quality of investment as the basis for improved sector outcomes, but as will be discussed later, there are pitfalls to underattention to budgeting for recurrent activities, which can undercut progress toward such sector objectives.

There are measurement inconsistencies across countries that are difficult to fully correct so as to clarify cross-country comparisons, notably the embedding of recurrent costs in investment project budgets and the improper categorization in national budget reporting of input subsidies as capital rather than in the recurrent (transfer) category (as in Nigeria) (table 4.4). This measurement issue on personnel compensation and nonwage recurrent budgets leads in most cases to underrecording actual levels in overall sector resource availability. This is because significant recurrent activities are embedded in development projects, with associated expenditure captured in the capital rather than recurrent budget information systems. For instance, an external-donor supported project to strengthen public extension services may result in hiring of additional extension agents and expanding extension activities during an institutional capacity building investment phase, with an expectation that some or all of this expansion will continue on the government's own resources after the project's completion. In the

**Table 4.4** Agriculture Recurrent Expenditure, Share of Total Agriculture Spending
*Percent*

| Country | 2005 | 2009 | 2011 | Latest year(s) |
|---|---|---|---|---|
| Botswana | 91 | 60 | 70 | 57 (2014) |
| Burkina Faso | — | 20–25 | — | — |
| Chad | — | — | — | 34 (2003–12)ᶜ |
| Côte d'Ivoire | — | 66 | — | — |
| Congo, Dem. Rep | — | 26 | 50 | 70 (2013) |
| Ghanaᵃ | 58 | 60 | 40 | — |
| Guinea | 35 | — | — | 42 (2003–12) |
| Liberia | 68 | 83 | 79 | — |
| Madagascar | — | 26 | 38 | 61 (2012) |
| Malawi | — | 84 | 90 | — |
| Mozambique | 24 | 27 (2007) | — | — |
| | — | 25 (2009 budget plan) | — | — |
| Nigeriaᵇ | — | 13 | 23 | 30 (2012) |
| Rwanda | — | 35 | — | 10 (2009/10) |
| Senegalᵃ | 39 | 39 | — | — |
| Sierra Leone | 94 | 91 | 78 | 80 (2012) |
| South Africa | 68 | 71 | 84 | 77 (2013) |
| Togo | — | 73 | — | — |
| Uganda | 74 | 75 | — | — |

*Source:* Mink 2016 from individual country AgPERs.
*Note:* Countries in the 20-country sample for which the data required are not available are not listed in table.
AgPERs = agriculture public expenditure reviews; — = data not available for this year.
a. Off-budget expenditure not included.
b. Federal expenditure only.
c. Wage, debt, transfers, other recurrent.

country's budget information systems, though, this expenditure during the project phase is recorded as a development rather than a recurrent expenditure.

Several of the country studies attempted to quantify the extent of this measurement issue through a thorough analysis of representative samples of projects (table 4.4). In Burkina Faso, the actual share of current expenditures (personnel and operations) in the total budget of the three ministries involved in the agricultural sector was estimated at 20–25 percent, with two-thirds of this funded by projects not in the official budgets of the ministries. In Malawi over the 2000/01–2011/12 period, the noncapital element in development expenditures was estimated in the country study at 63 percent (of which 4 percent was salaries, and 59 percent, other recurrent expenditures), leaving only 37 percent of the development budget for real capital expenditure. For Cameroon, an estimated 20 percent of the investment budget was actually funding operational expenses rather than capital asset creation.

This common occurrence of recurrent expenditure being embedded in the development budget raises two fundamental problems. First, this situation does not allow the ministries concerned to effectively manage their current expenditures because they have only few levers with which to control them. Second, this situation emphasizes the issue of the sustainability of interventions. What becomes of the provisions required to supervise and maintain investments carried out after the project that supported them comes to an end? In a number of the countries reviewed in this synthesis, accounting for recurrent costs for investment maintenance is one of the weak links in the budget planning of ministries involved in the agricultural sector that lack a systematic mechanism for addressing this issue.

These measurement issues notwithstanding, the expenditure interest of governments and their external donors under CAADP and national agricultural development programs has been much more on ramping up capital expenditure than the appropriateness of recurrent expenditure. There are risks if this leads to the neglect of adequate recurrent expenditure. Some of the country studies began to identify these risks, though more in qualitative than quantitative terms. Two examples of public functions that appear from many of the country studies to be underfunded are core budget planning and implementation (including M&E), and sector regulatory functions. Underfunding of budget planning and M&E capacity in ministries negatively affects the quality and impact of public spending on agriculture in a number of ways.

On the capital budget, underprepared projects can be rushed onto the budget for implementation because of inadequate staffing, and result in delayed startup, underutilization of budgeted resources, and diminished impacts on the ground. Inadequate support for central and technical department staff to undertake project and program M&E results in reduced ability to track results and make adjustments to improve impacts or reorient approaches. While it is understandable that politically attuned ministers are reluctant to divert budget resources from front-line activities that directly benefit constituencies to unglamorous back-office functions, the country studies generally reveal that despite a significant scale-up of public expenditure on the sector, there has been little or no increase in these core administrative functions that provide essential information to steer the endeavor.

Recurrent core public regulatory functions seem underfunded at a time when the need for them is growing because of evolving sector strategies that are spreading through many countries in Sub-Saharan Africa. Examples of this, related to the expanding roles that are being promoted for private sector supply to farmers of fertilizer and seed, are the regulatory capacities to ensure good quality and fair labeling of these products in the input market chains. There can be debate over the appropriate balance of public regulation and private sector self-regulation, which may evolve as the market chains mature, but a core capacity for regulatory oversight in the private sector will be essential while the market chains are new and quickly evolving. Much of this capacity, in budget terms, is recurrent, including inspectors, mobility on the ground to reach retail markets (for fertilizer) and seed production fields, payment for laboratory tests, and communications campaigns to inform farmers and input market participants. The budgets for adequate provision of these regulatory functions are relatively small in the context of most countries' overall sector budgets, and not a single recurrent budget line item that would be simple for public expenditure analysis to pick up. Nonetheless, while not quantified in the available country studies, where the issue has been examined in more detail (as in Nigeria), it is clear that the potentially positive impact of expanded access by farmers to fertilizer and seeds because of government-funded activities risks dilution through some portion of this expansion consisting of poor quality inputs.

Funding an appropriate level and balance of recurrent and capital expenditure is a dynamic context of choices and trade-offs. Public sector employees, when adequately accompanied by operational budgets, provide core services and goods to the agricultural sector, but can also be a potent lobbying group seeking higher compensation to the detriment of funding of other sector priorities. Operational budgets, which are essential for agricultural agent mobility and service provision such as extension and animal vaccination campaigns, are vulnerable to underfunding and lack a robust constituency in times of fiscal tightening. Capital expenditure on such things as public infrastructure and institutional capacity provides assets for longer-term growth, the maintenance of which creates the need for larger operations and maintenance budgets in the future. Decisions on these levels and balances are difficult, if only for the strategic and political complexities involved. For the countries reviewed in this synthesis, an additional constraint to informed management of these choices is the weakness and incompleteness of coverage for budget information systems on which decision makers in the relevant ministries must rely.

The share of personnel compensation (wages and benefits) in agricultural sector budgets is quite diverse across the countries but reveals several things (table 4.5). First, the two countries for which the agricultural sector size is the smallest in relation to the overall economy—Botswana and South Africa—devote the largest share of total public agricultural spending to personnel costs. This is most likely because of their stage of overall economic transition, and the recognition that delivery of recurrent public services to the agricultural sector is more important than commitment of significant public resources into investment. The majority of other countries have personnel costs that are roughly a quarter or less of overall public spending on agriculture. There is no evidence of a broad trend of declining personnel cost shares across countries, and the countries with an increase, such as Madagascar, were maintaining civil servants on payrolls while social strife drained external finances for investment activities in the sector.

**Table 4.5** Agriculture Public Wage Spending, Share of Total Agriculture Spending

| Country | 2005 | 2009 | 2011 | Latest year(s) |
|---|---|---|---|---|
| Botswana | 39 | 45 | 45 | 36 (2014) |
| Burkina Faso | — | 10–15 | — | — |
| Chad | — | — | — | 12 (2003–12) |
| Côte d'Ivoire | — | 36 | — | — |
| Congo, Dem. Rep. | — | 25 | 41 | 33 (2013) |
| Ghana[a] | 27 | 22 | 27 | — |
| Guinea | 23 | 26 | 22 | 28 (2003–12) |
| Liberia | 35 | 48 | 27 | — |
| Madagascar | — | 17 | 23 | 44 (2012) |
| Nigeria[b] | — | 11 | 20 | 27 (2012) |
| Rwanda | — | 30 | — | 30 (2009/10) |
| Senegal[a] | 7 | 6 | — | — |
| Sierra Leone | 43 | 35 | 40 | 42 (2012) |
| South Africa | 38 | 43 | 53 | 52 (2013) |
| Togo | 29 | 17 | 9 | — |
| Uganda | 10 | 10 | — | — |

Source: Mink 2016 from individual AgPERs.
Note: Countries in the 20-country sample for which the data required are not available are not listed in table.
AgPERs = agriculture public expenditure reviews; — = data unavailable for this year.
a. Off-budget expenditure not included.
b. Federal expenditure only.

The majority of countries in this review have increased public investment expenditure in value terms and as a share of overall public sector budgets. There are exceptions, and investment levels actually declined over the country studies' review periods for Chad, Côte d'Ivoire, and Madagascar, related to the difficulty of mobilizing external finance for investment during prolonged periods of civil strife. In the more frequent case of countries increasing investment over time, the resulting investment shares nonetheless differ markedly across countries.

Where the effort to increase public investment in agriculture has been successful, an emerging concern is whether recurrent expenditure has grown commensurately to ensure that the operations and maintenance of the assets created are adequate and that the investments are sustainable. A simple way to examine this is to look at the balance between nonwage recurrent expenditure and investment spending, particularly in countries achieving strong investment level growth. This balance is shown in table 4.6 for both the start and end of the periods covered in the country studies. This shows that, with the exception of Guinea, all the other countries achieving growth in investment spending did not have matching growth in nonwage

**Table 4.6** Change in Relation of Nonwage Recurrent (Goods and Services) Spending to Investment Spending

| | Ratio of nonwage recurrent to investment expenditure | | Investment change, end/start, current values |
|---|---|---|---|
| | Start of period | End of period | |
| Chad (2004–11) | 0.03 | 0.02 | 0.94 |
| Côte d'Ivoire (2000–10) | 0.52 | 4.51 | 0.46 |
| Congo, Dem. Rep. (2007–13) | 0.12 | 0.29 | 0.96 |
| **Ghana (2004–11)** | **0.85** | **0.43** | **1.61** |
| Guinea (2004–12)[a] | 0.04 | 0.05 | 1.61 |
| Madagascar (2007–12)[a] | 0.14 | 0.35 | 0.19 |
| **Mozambique (2002–07)[a]** | **0.04** | **0.03** | **2.95** |
| Nigeria (2008–12)[b] | 0.02 | 0.04 | 0.71 |
| **Sierra Leone (2004–12)** | **16.13** | **5.13** | **7.33** |
| **Togo (2002–10)** | **0.19** | **0.12** | **5.09** |

*Source:* Mink 2016 from individual country AgPERs.
*Note:* Bold denotes countries with both growth in investment (change > 1) and a decline in the ratio of nonwage recurrent to investment expenditure of the period. Countries in the 20-country sample for which the data required are not available are not listed in table. AgPERs = agriculture public expenditure reviews.
a. Indicates country studies for which the nonwage recurrent expenditure is equivalent to goods and services. For other countries, current transfer expenditure may also be included in the nonwage recurrent figures.
b. Federal expenditure only.

recurrent expenditure (the ratio declined over time). In Botswana, Ghana, and Sierra Leone, the ratio of nonwage recurrent to investment expenditure declined by half or more.

While these declines signal a potentially worrisome imbalance in economic composition of budgets and investments vulnerable to inadequate maintenance and nonsustainability, this issue requires more detailed examination than was undertaken in the country studies. For one thing, what constitutes an appropriate ratio is not clear. Moreover, the appropriate level may differ from country to country depending on the composition of their investment, which may be less operation and maintenance (O&M) intensive in some countries than others. The range of ratios is striking in table 4.7. Sierra Leone may be an outlier, emerging from a long period of internal strife during which agricultural investment dried up, but Guinea faced similar internal strife yet apparently prioritized investment with relatively few budget resources going to nonwage recurrent expenditure. While it seems reasonable to conclude that the three countries that have kept their nonwage recurrent spending at less than 5 percent of investment expenditure are likely to face sustainability issues, a more disaggregate analysis by different types of investments would help disentangle what nonwage recurrent budgets would be required as the investment effort grows.

**Table 4.7** Ratio of Nonwage Recurrent (Goods and Services) Spending to Investment Spending, Select Years

| Country | 2005 | 2009 | 2011 | Latest year(s) |
|---|---|---|---|---|
| Botswana | 5.7 | 0.38 | 0.83 | 0.49 (2014) |
| Burkina Faso | — | 0.129 | — | — |
| Chad | — | — | — | 0.33 (2003–12) |
| Côte d'Ivoire | — | 0.882 | — | — |
| Congo, Dem. Rep. | — | 0.02 | 0.19 | 0.29 (2013) |
| Ghana[a] | 0.738 | 0.95 | 0.216 | — |
| Guinea | 0.184 | — | — | 0.228 (2003–12) |
| Liberia | 1.03 | 2.05 | 2.47 | — |
| Madagascar | — | 0.122 | 0.240 | 0.455 (2012) |
| Nigeria[b] | — | 0.017 | 0.03 | 0.042 (2012) |
| Rwanda | — | 0.384 | — | 0.041 (2009/10) |
| Senegal[a] | 0.78 | 0.80 | — | — |
| Sierra Leone | 8.50 | 6.22 | 1.72 | 1.9 (2012) |
| South Africa | 0.937 | 0.965 | 1.93 | 1.08 (2013) |
| Togo | — | 2.07 | — | — |
| Uganda | 2.41 | 2.67 | — | — |

Source: Mink 2016 from individual country AgPERs.
Note: Countries in the 20-country sample for which the data required are not available are not listed in table. AgPERs = agriculture public expenditure reviews; — = data not available for this year.
a. Off-budget expenditure not included.
b. Federal expenditure only.

## Central Versus Local Categories

Agriculture in almost all African countries is practiced across diverse agro-ecological conditions by a multitude of farmers with enterprises of various sizes (but predominantly small-scale). To provide public goods and services to this diverse clientele, it is generally accepted that the decision making on—and administration of—public expenditure should be devolved to the appropriate level of government authority, leading to better outcomes from the expenditure on public goods and services committed to the agricultural sector.

Also affecting the budgeting of investment maintenance is the division of roles and means between central government and local councils—and between public authorities and beneficiaries. Often these roles are not planned in advance or agreed to by parties. Problems arise when responsibility for funding maintenance is assigned without that party having adequate financial means to fund the activity. Avoiding such problems—and the consequent rapid depreciation of completed investments—must start with adequate preparation and agreement early in the investment planning.

Several countries have decentralized governments with significant amounts of public spending for agriculture under the responsibility of local authorities. Other countries committed to decentralization are in the early stages of implementation. For them, the impact of consolidated public expenditure on agriculture across central and local governments will vary depending on the extent of budgeting coordination and cooperation. Budget information systems at the different levels that allow a consolidated view of public activities, budget plans, and their results can help make better use of scarce budget resources. Such budget information would provide a foundation for greater synergies and less waste.

Countries take different decisions on how to pursue such devolution of authority, influenced by the governance decisions beyond agriculture alone, which are in turn impacted by many sectoral, political, and administrative considerations. One approach retains an integrated and hierarchical political structure, in which national and subnational administrative units (such as provinces and districts) operate a single budget for which size and allocative decisions are taken centrally. In these systems with centralized budget authority, implementation may still be *deconcentrated*, with efforts made to get sector ministry and agency staffing located closer to farmers, and procurement and expenditure management put under the responsibility of staff located outside of the central ministry except for the largest of initiatives.

The other main approach is *decentralization* of both fiscal (revenue mobilization and allocation) and administrative (implementation) authority. This decentralization usually specifies that selected functions are to be in the hands of subnational authorities, who are accountable to local populations through elections. These local authorities are responsible for planning revenue sources and expenditure activities. The breadth of decentralized functions is often specified constitutionally, may depend on administrative capacity at the subnational level, and varies over time in the course of nation building. In agriculture sectors, decentralized functions often include extension, training, and animal disease and plant pest management.

The country studies varied widely in their ability to assess public expenditure on agriculture across the deconcentration and decentralization dimension. Data constraints proved to be the main limitation, such as when major portions of expenditure could not be disaggregated, or were simply not available, at levels below central government. Budget information systems often did not have the capacity to disaggregate external funding by subnational spending unit, and only a couple of the studies undertook the laborious ad hoc process of constructing the data set to do this by manually collecting the needed information from individual donor institutions. In decentralized systems there were two main constraints. Some decentralized countries collected information centrally on subnational budgets and spending, but only in aggregate and with insufficient detail to isolate what was being done in agriculture. In other countries, there was simply no centralized data system that captured public spending by local authorities. Several study teams (such as Nigeria) selected and analyzed a few subnational regions' spending on agriculture, but these limited samples were insufficient for robust extrapolation to national aggregates.

Despite these limitations, broad characteristics and observations can be gleaned from the country studies. For the studies with sufficient information, table 4.8 identifies the countries by deconcentration or decentralization, and the extent under each to which budget making or implementation are happening subnationally. Of the 12 countries, information is available for seven on deconcentrated expenditure, while the remaining five are decentralized systems. For countries where subnational spending information was available, it is also possible to use this to draw inferences regarding prioritization of equity versus efficiency goals (box 4.1).

The countries' managing unified budget systems remain largely concentrated. Over 80 percent of public expenditure on agriculture in most of these countries is managed by the ministries' central departments, and is over 95 percent for three (Chad, Liberia, and Togo). The main exception is Ghana. Ghana has locally elected district authorities that manage budgets, but these are not significant in aggregate agriculture public spending, as shown in table 4.8. Over the decade covered by the Ghana country study, 73 percent of spending was managed by central ministry and agency staff while the balance of 27 percent of spending was managed by ministry staff in regional and district offices.

**Table 4.8** Devolution of Agricultural Spending, Regional and Local Authorities, Shares of Total

| | Burkina Faso[a] | Chad[b] | Ghana | Liberia | Mozambique | Togo | Zambia |
|---|---|---|---|---|---|---|---|
| *Deconcentration* | | | | | | | |
| Regional and local authorities | 83 | 4 | 27 | 0 | 19 | 2 | 14 |

| | Cameroon[c] | Nigeria | Rwanda | Sierra Leone | South Africa |
|---|---|---|---|---|---|
| *Decentralization* | | | | | |
| Regional and local authorities | 15 | 47 | 5 | 19 | 57 |

*Source:* Mink 2016 from individual country AgPERs.
*Note:* Countries in the 20-country sample for which the data required are not available are not listed in table. AgPERs = agriculture public expenditure reviews.
a. Burkina Faso shows the location of expenditure, but from the country study the authority over this expenditure is not identifiable as central or subnational.
b. Recurrent budget only.
c. Cameroon is investment budget only.

**BOX 4.1**

## Geographic Distribution of Expenditures—Targeting by Efficiency or Equity?

Some of the country studies were able to disaggregate public agricultural spending by subnational regions, and this allows exploring the extent to which the expenditure appears to serve efficiency or equity objectives. Giving priority to agricultural growth would suggest concentrating public expenditure on regions of the country with better resource endowments (rains, soils), larger agricultural sectors, and favorable growth opportunities. A higher priority for equity outcomes could suggest concentrating public agriculture expenditures on regions with higher poverty (headcount or proportion) in rural farming communities (Mink 2016).[a]

In Burkina Faso, the geographic distribution of expenditures appears to be guided more by criteria of efficiency than by equity. Expenditure data representing 93 percent of the total over 2007–11 could be disaggregated to the regional level. Comparison with the contributions of each region to the value of total crop production reveals that the regions with high agricultural potential (the Western and Southwestern regions of the country—Boucle du Mouhoun, Hauts-Bassins, Cascades, and Sud-Ouest) also receive the largest share of public support. These regions generated 46 percent of crop production over 2002–06 and received 47 percent of public agricultural expenditures over the period 2007–11. However, the distribution of agricultural expenditures in relation to the number of the poor by region shows an unequal allocation of public resources. Although 32 percent of the poor lived in the regions of Centre-Nord, Centre-Sud, Nord, and Plateau Central in 2003, these regions received only 17 percent of public agricultural expenditures from 2007 to 2011. Yet while only 11 percent of the poor lived in Cascades and Hauts-Bassins, these regions received 28 percent of agricultural investments.

For Ghana, geographic distribution of expenditure can only be attributed for the Ministry of Agriculture's expenditure channeled through its regional and district offices; budgets administered by the Ministry's core and technical departments, which come to nearly three-fourths of its expenditure over 2001–11, could not be regionally disaggregated. The disaggregatable expenditure shows a significant bias toward the Greater Accra region, which on a per capita or land area basis, receives more than twice the expenditure resources of the next highest region. In terms of equity orientation, there is only a mildly positive correlation between regions' poverty incidence and their level of expenditure. The poverty incidence is highest in the north's three regions (Upper East, Northern, Upper West), and while the Upper East follows Greater Accra in expenditure levels, the other two northern regions are in the bottom tier of the ten regions' expenditure distribution. It may be that large projects and other activities for which the expenditure is managed under the Ministry's core and technical departments' budgets are more targeted on the poorer regions, but during this period, the RADU/DADU expenditures were not achieving a pro-poor purpose.

*(continued next page)*

## Box 4.1 (continued)

For Sierra Leone, only the 19 percent of sector expenditure made through the agricultural budgets of the districts provides the disaggregation needed for an assessment of the geographic dimension to expenditure. Data on district-level budget allocations and poverty rates reveal a moderately strong relationship linking allocations to the poverty rates for rural districts (Koinadugu District is an outlier). The data show only a modest relationship between food insecurity rate (percent of household food insecure) and agriculture sector budget allocations granted to local councils.

For Togo, a geographic analysis of expenditure must be limited due to data constraints to provisional and implemented capital expenditure budgets for the 2002–10 period. This accounts for 75 percent of total public agriculture expenditure. The expenditure bias is strongly in favor of the region closest to Lomé, the Maritime region, which absorbed almost half of the investment resources, though it accounts for 28 percent of the rural population, 27 percent of rural poverty, and 15 percent of the country's food crop production. The Plateaux region, by contrast, accounts for 29 percent of the rural population, 23 percent of rural poverty, and provides 36 percent of the national food crop production, yet it benefited from only 16 percent of capital expenditures.

The Cameroon country study assessed the allocation to its 10 regions of investment expenditure for the two main ministries engaged in the agriculture sector for crops and livestock over the 2006–12 period. Regions with the highest rates of poverty do not receive additional investment resources, which hampers attempts to reduce poverty. There is a heavy bias favoring the North-West Region, which received an average allocation of 19 percent of investment funds, whereas the region's share of domestic crop production and rural population was 7 percent and 12 percent, respectively, while its 51 percent incidence of rural poverty is below the country's poorest, northern regions. In addition, the West and South-West Regions received investment allocations far exceeding their contribution to domestic crop production and their share of the rural population. In contrast, the Far North Region accounts for 27 percent of the country's rural population, 10 percent of crop production, and a rural poverty incidence of 65.9 percent, yet received only 15 percent of allocations.

*Note:* AgPER = agriculture public expenditure review.
a. As part of national strategy, however, poverty alleviation activities would include people shifting out of agriculture over time through fostering of economic growth in other sectors and urban economic activity. Note that this box contains information from individual country AgPERs (Mink 2016).

The countries with more long-standing decentralized political systems have higher decentralization of public spending in agriculture. In South Africa, the provinces account for 57 percent of the total, and in Nigeria the states are thought to account for about half of total public spending on the sector. Sierra Leone, which instituted a decentralized political system with elected district authorities beginning in 2002, has cautiously extended budgetary decentralization in the agricultural sector to reach 19 percent of aggregate public expenditure. Rwanda introduced a decentralized political authority in 2007, experienced some initial capacity constraints for local administration and budget management, and had only reached 5 percent of aggregate budget expenditure on agriculture managed by these new structures by 2010.

Cameroon began implementing decentralization at the fiscal level with the 2010 budget. These powers were transferred gradually, however, and over the period of the country study, only the responsibility for the development of rural infrastructure has been transferred to the ministry of agriculture; the establishment and management of infrastructure and equipment for animal husbandry to the Ministry of Fisheries and Animal Industries (MINEPIA); and the management of communal forests, financial resources collected from royalties for communal forests, and royalties payable to neighboring communities to the Ministry of Forestry (MINREF). By 2012, about 15 percent of the capital budget was managed in a decentralized manner.

Trends over time in the value of devolved expenditure are shown in table 4.9 for the limited number of countries for which data permit exploring this dimension. These show increases in all cases, thus confirming the momentum, if slow, toward devolution of expenditure in many of the countries covered in the synthesis. The rapid increase in a number of countries flags the importance of building expenditure implementation capacity at the local level, and in the case of decentralization, of expenditure planning capacity as well.

**Table 4.9** Evolution of Devolved Spending, Select Countries

| Country | 2005 | 2009 | 2011 | % change |
|---|---|---|---|---|
| Burkina Faso (CFAF, billions) | — | 101 | 105 | 4 |
| Cameroon (CFAF, billions) | — | — | 15 (2002, investment) | — |
| Côte d'Ivoire (CFAF, billions) | 72 | 133 | — | 85 |
| Rwanda (RF, millions) | — | 949 | — | — |
| Sierra Leone (Le, billions) | 2 (2007) | 6 | 13 | 650 |
| Togo (CFAF, billions) | 15 | 37 | 66 | 352 |
| Zambia (K, billions) | 73 | 103 (2008) | — | 41 |

Source: Mink 2016 from individual country AgPERs.
Note: AgPERs = agriculture public expenditure reviews; — = data not available for this year.

## Using Cross-Country Experience and External Support to Improve Agricultural Public Expenditure Reviews in the Future

Are AgPERs resulting in better budget management? It is not possible to point to concrete follow-up actions based on the analysis and recommendations of every country study. But an inventory of examples shows what is possible in terms of better strategy planning and monitoring, stronger budget processes for expenditure management, improved communications and accountability, and effective mobilization of external funding resources. As the studies progressed and gained experience, it became more routine for the teams to develop a draft action plan that was improved during the study's technical validation workshop, and that was then turned over to the sector authorities for further formalization and use. Assessing the political and economic contexts for driving recommendations into actions also elicited much interest and experience sharing among participants in several cross-country workshops.

To assist governments in quantitatively estimating what are sufficient recurrent budgets to sustain completed investments, it would be valuable to develop cost norms (ranges) for M&E requirements for typical investment categories. To provide essential public goods and services based on a short list of items that are typically recurrent, more granular recurrent budget analysis will be needed to establish common practices across a range of countries, as well as to establish some norms.

Coordinating central and decentralized expenditure authority requires budget information systems. Experience and practice regarding such information systems from regions outside of Africa could be helpful to learn from. Also important would be to bring case study material to Sub-Saharan Africa countries embarking on decentralization, to draw attention to the political economy of budget cooperation across decentralized government levels, with a specific agricultural sector focus. To link expenditures to sector outcomes, further assessment among practitioners is needed on whether country-specific public agricultural spending reviews are the appropriate type of study to analyze these links. The completed public agricultural expenditure studies already provide a solid basis for identifying specific types of information that M&E capacity could focus on to better inform expenditure decisions.

How can public agricultural expenditure analysis be carried out more effectively in support of the African Union's (AU) CAADP objectives? Once a baseline analysis has been established with a core diagnostic review, countries could anticipate more routinely (annually, if possible) updating the basic analysis, in the form of a simplified AgPER, or "AgPER Lite," for which a guidance note could be established. The routine updating needs to be built into the national dialogue on sector expenditure priorities. The analysis could feed into annual budget preparation, into deliberations of the legislative branch committee responsible for the sector, and into the multistakeholder joint sector reviews, such as the ones CAADP supports and promotes. And the M&E improvements for better public agricultural expenditure analysis must be coordinated with the broader sector M&E strengthening supported in some countries through Strategic Analysis and Knowledge Support System (SAKSS) programs.

# Annex 4A: Summary of Country Agricultural Public Expenditure Review Findings

**Table 4A.1** Summary of Country Agricultural Public Expenditure Review Findings

| Country | Years covered | Sector expenditure scope | Off-budget inclusion? | Decentralization or deconcentration | Sector plan, year approved | Analysis before and after expenditure? | Consistency with plan analysis? |
|---|---|---|---|---|---|---|---|
| Botswana | 2000–13 | Fisheries and commercial forestry not included, but insignificant | — | Deconcentration to 26 district offices | National development plans | No | No |
| Burkina Faso | 2004–11 | Follows COFOG | Yes | Decentralization (2004, 2006) and deconcentration | SCADD | No | Yes |
| Cameroon | 2003–12 | COFOG | Yes | Decentralization (from 2009) | Rural Sector Development Strategy (revised 2006) | No | No |
| Chad | 2003–12 | COFOG | Yes | Deconcentration, limited | SDA (2006–15) Plan Quinquennal Agricole (2013–18) CAADP Compact (2013) Programme National d'Investissement dans le Secteur Rural (2014) | No | No |
| Côte d'Ivoire | 1999–2012 | COFOG | Yes | Deconcentration, but minimally | Programme National d'Investissement en Agriculture (2010) | Yes | No |

*(continued next page)*

**Table 4A.1** (continued)

| Country | Years covered | Sector expenditure scope | Off-budget inclusion? | Decentralization or deconcentration | Sector plan, year approved | Analysis before and after expenditure? | Consistency with plan analysis? |
|---|---|---|---|---|---|---|---|
| Congo, Dem. Rep. | 2007–13 | COFOG | Partially, as aggregate commitments over the period | Decentralized to provinces | Note de Politique Agricole et du Développement Rural (2009) | No | No |
| Ghana[a] | 2001–11 | COFOG | | Deconcentration to region units and district units | METASIP, 2011 | Yes | — |
| Guinea | 2003–12 | COFOG | Yes | Deconcentration | Politique Nationale de Développement de l'Agriculture Vision (2007, 2015) PNIASA (2011) | No | No |
| Liberia | 2006/07–2011/12 | COFOG | Integration of expenditure from donor-financed projects began in 2012 | 15 counties, but autonomous expenditure is limited | FAPS (2009) Associated investment plan (2010) | No | No |
| Madagascar[b] | 2007–12 | COFOG | Yes | Decentralization Law (2004), implementation still in transition Deconcentration of Agriculture Ministry to 22 regions and Livestock Ministry to 16 regions | Programme Sectoriel Agricole, 2007 | No | — |

*(continued next page)*

**Table 4A.1** (continued)

| Country | Years covered | Sector expenditure scope | Off-budget inclusion? | Decentralization or deconcentration | Sector plan, year approved | Analysis before and after expenditure? | Consistency with plan analysis? |
|---|---|---|---|---|---|---|---|
| Malawi | 2000/01–2012/13 | COFOG, but forestry data unavailable | Yes, data available for 2007/08–2011/12 | Decentralization, but district councils are responsible for only about 1% of total sector expenditure | Agricultural sectorwide approach (2010) | No | Yes |
| Mozambique | 2001–07 | COFOG | Off-budget is minimal | Decentralization, from 2007, with 50% of OIIL investment transfer to districts assumed used for agriculture | — | No | No |
| Nigeria | 2008–12 | COFOG less forestry | Off-budget is minimal | Decentralized | Agriculture Transformation Agenda (2011) | No | Yes |
| Rwanda | | Ministry of Agriculture central, some agencies, district earmarked transfers, external funding | Exists (USAID), but not included | Ministry of Agriculture budget included, but not districts | PTSA I (2004) PTSA II (2009) | No | Yes, qualitative |
| Senegal | 2005–09 | COFOG | Off-budget expenditure exists, but not included in the analysis | Deconcentration | GOANA (2008) La Grande muraille verte (2008) | No | No |
| Sierra Leone | 2004–12 | COFOG | Exists, and mostly taken into account in aggregates | Decentralization, with 13 rural district councils | National Sustainable Agriculture Development Plan (2010) | No | No |

*(continued next page)*

**Table 4A.1** (continued)

| Country | Years covered | Sector expenditure scope | Off-budget inclusion? | Decentralization or deconcentration | Sector plan, year approved | Analysis before and after expenditure? | Consistency with plan analysis? |
|---|---|---|---|---|---|---|---|
| South Africa | 2002/03–2013/14 | COFOG | No | Decentralization, 9 provinces | Strategic Plan for South African Agriculture (2001); Comprehensive Agricultural Support Programme (2004) | No | No |
| Togo | 2002–11 | COFOG | Yes | Deconcentration | PNIASA (2010) | Yes | Yes |
| Uganda[c] | 2001/02–2008/09 | COFOG for expenditure aggregates | Partial (two external partners only) | Decentralization | Ministry of Agriculture Development Strategy and Investment Plan (2006) | No | Yes |
| Zambia[d] | 2000–08 actuals; 2009–10 budgets | Not COFOG; covers Ministry of Agriculture and co-ops only | | | | | |

*Note:* CAADP = Comprehensive Africa Agriculture Development Programme; COFOG = Classification of Functions of Government (United Nations); FAPS = Food and Agricultural Policy and Strategy; GOANA = Grande Offensive Agricole pour la Nourriture et l'Abondance; ISPs = input subsidy programs; PNIASA = National Program for Agricultural Investment and Food; PTSA = Strategic Plan for Transformation of Agriculture; SCADD = Strategy for Accelerated Growth and Sustainable Development; SDA = Schéma Directeur Agricole; USAID = United States Agency for International Development; — = information not available for this year.

a. Decentralized district expenditure not analyzed.

b. Neither AgPER reflected in budget analysis of the country study. Lack of workers is a constraint at deconcentrated level.

c. Disaggregated analysis does not include COFOG components of forestry, water for production, and activities related to agricultural land.

d. Scope excludes ISPs and Food Reserve Agency except for aggregates.

# Notes

1. This chapter is based mainly on a background paper (Mink 2016).
2. Funded over 2010–16 by the Bill and Melinda Gates Foundation and the Comprehensive Africa Agriculture Development Programme (CAADP) Multi-Donor Trust Fund, this program was administered by the World Bank and coordinated with guidance from the New Partnership for Africa's Development (NEPAD) Planning and Coordinating Agency with CAAPD.
3. The guidance note is available for use by any AU member state and is posted on the Regional Strategic Analysis and Knowledge Support System (ReSAKSS) web page where the AgPER reports are maintained.
4. Countries with basic diagnostic expenditure reviews covered in the study are Botswana, Burkina Faso, Cameroon, Chad, the Democratic Republic of Congo, Côte d'Ivoire, Ghana, Guinea, Liberia, Nigeria, Senegal, Sierra Leone, South Africa, and Togo. Tanzania completed a program impact assessment on its input subsidy implementation, and Togo completed a Medium-Term Expenditure Framework. Studies in Madagascar, Mozambique, Rwanda, Uganda, and Zambia are also incorporated; these were carried out under different support programs.
5. This is usually the ministry of finance, though in some governmental configurations the planning of the annual investment budget is by the ministry of planning.
6. "Organisation pour l'Harmonisation en Afrique du Droit des Affaires," which translates into English as "Organization for the Harmonization of Business Law in Africa."
7. In this category, for example, are utility bill payments for government departments, maintenance on public buildings, and government vehicle transport and repair costs.

# Reference

Mink, S. 2016. "Findings across Agricultural Public Expenditure Reviews in African Countries." Discussion Paper 1522, IFPRI, Washington, DC.

# Chapter 5

# Managing the Political Economy of Pro-Poor Agricultural Spending

Some categories of spending that have significant positive effects on productivity and welfare are often underfunded, and others that generally show unfavorable results often capture large shares of the budget. Explaining such discrepancies between impact and prominence in the public budget requires understanding how the public resource allocation process is shaped by agents' incentive structures, the characteristics of the investments, and the broader governance environment in which agents operate. Budget decisions will always be politically influenced, but understanding the sources of bias that are likely to drive inefficient or ineffective policies can help avoid those outcomes.[1]

Many African countries have long pursued policies of implicit or explicit agricultural taxation, creating a pro-urban, anti-agricultural bias (Anderson 2009; Krueger, Schiff, and Valdes 1988). One explanation is that rural populations exhibit greater difficulty of organizing collective action among dispersed populations that lack easy means of communication (Olson 1985). But if the difficulty of organizing collective action can be overcome, there is strength in numbers (Acemoğlu and Robinson 2001). One way to at least partially offset this natural disadvantage of rural populations is to improve the information base of key actors so that they better understand the effects of alternative policy choices. Policy processes exhibit a status quo bias, such that policies that have outlived their usefulness are often not discontinued. Governments may favor the status quo because those who benefit from the current state are usually the ones with the power to have ensured enactment of those policies in the first place. And their political support for current policies is increased by those who have altered their behavior to become beneficiaries after policies were put in place (Coate and Morris 1999).

Different classes of spending influence how politically attractive they are. Types of spending with highly visible results that are easily attributable are attractive. Visible infrastructure investments and direct cash or in-kind transfers are more easily connected to the efforts and spending decisions of public officials. These can even be conveniently advertised—for example, through labels on the fertilizer voucher ticket indicating who is responsible for subsidizing the fertilizer—thus serving as an effective tool for patronage. In contrast, if a farmer observes that the quality of information provided by a new agricultural extension officer has improved, it may be difficult for her to ascertain whether that is because the agricultural ministry has done a better job in selecting, training, and incentivizing extension officers. The greater visibility (and therefore attributability) of large-scale irrigation schemes has also made them more attractive than small schemes, despite the weaker agricultural performance of the large (Chinsinga 2011; Keefer and Khemani 2005).

Goods and services with a long lag between the time when resources are allocated and the time when the benefits become available are less politically attractive for several reasons. A longer lag tends to break the perceptible link between politicians' decisions and public officials' resource allocations, and politicians may have a short time horizon for their tenure in office. And given the substantial time lag between investing in research and reaping its rewards—usually decades, not years—agricultural research requires a long-term commitment for sufficient sustained funding. Long research cycles rarely coincide with short-term election cycles, shifting political agendas, and changes in government budget allocations. The inability to extract short-term political credit may act as a disincentive for policy makers to commit to long-term agricultural research and development (R&D) investments, thereby jeopardizing future research planning and outputs.

Given low investments by governments, agricultural research in many Sub-Saharan countries is highly dependent on donor funding, which by nature is mostly short-term and ad hoc, and often causes major fluctuations in a country's yearly agricultural investments. In contrast to the long gestation period to realize benefits of investing in research, public spending to subsidize agricultural inputs usually requires a span of only a few months from the time of the investment until the subsidized fertilizer reaches farmers. In Malawi, the time span from the spending being incurred to the fertilizers being received by farmers ranged from one to six months (Chirwa, Matita, and Dorward 2010), and in Ghana, the equivalent time span was about four months (Banful 2011). This is clearly one factor behind the bias toward subsidies in the current policy mix.

The prevalence of corruption tends to increase the share of large capital investment spending in overall spending. Areas of public spending involving large infrastructure or other capital investments create opportunities for public officials to improve the chances of a private agent winning contracts, or to loosen regulatory burdens on the agent, in return for private payments to the official.

For example, incentives for technical staff to properly maintain structures are severely weakened without side payments, given the rents that can be extracted in a context of insecurity about access to functioning irrigation systems (Wade 1982; Walter and Wolff 2002).

Institutional mechanisms to make spending more pro-poor have a mixed record and vary in their strengths and vulnerabilities. In some African countries, the potential benefits of participatory budgeting have been vitiated because the process has been top down and closely managed by the party in power, as in Mozambique (Nylen 2014). The benefit has also been constrained by earmarking transfers from the federal government, as in Kenya and Uganda (Ranis 2012), or high administrative and maintenance costs, as in Uganda (Francis and James 2003). Where spending decisions are decentralized, mechanisms to strengthen electoral accountability need to be put in place, with the objective of prioritizing responsiveness to the needs of individuals over those of elite groups. This must be matched by building local officials' public management capacity and improving citizens' information base on the actions as well as the performance of local governments. The inefficiencies and poor targeting of subsidies can be at least reduced through operational features that improve the clarity and reduce the ambiguity of eligibility criteria, paired with an increase of transparency and information about which localities, and within localities which households, are eligible to receive the transfers.

In Africa, external actors—particularly donors—play a large role in resource provision and potentially in decisions on how to spend the resources. Consultations or negotiations between governments and international partners not only on outcomes and domestic policies but also on aggregate (donor and domestic) public spending in agriculture can be included in packages of assistance. This needs to be accompanied by the continued generation of knowledge and good quality data and tracking of public spending in the sector in a given country, irrespective of the revenue source. Agricultural public spending reviews, increasingly common, can support this. Making commitments to external agents can help governments overcome the problem of policy reforms possibly lacking credibility and therefore not inducing the intended response from the private sector. Such commitments can be made not only—or even primarily—to donors. Commitments to African institutions such as the Comprehensive Africa Agriculture Development Programme (CAADP), through the process of developing national agricultural investment programs and carrying out joint sector reviews, can play this role as well.

Profound reforms, including in resource spending decisions to support agriculture, will of course face political resistance because of an inherent bias toward the status quo, and the difficulty of governments in making credible commitments. Lessons related to the tools that can be useful in counteracting these forces emerge from the political economy literature, including improving the knowledge base of the affected parties on the distributional effects of policies, and making use of commitments to external agents. International experience with large-scale reforms in spending programs also offers lessons. Severe budgetary constraints associated with fiscal pressures often disturb the existing political equilibrium and offer windows of opportunity for reforms. On a practical level, reformers need to be ready with evidence and a plan to support reforms should such a circumstance arise. Another lesson is that resistance to reducing inefficient forms of spending can be reduced by some compensation of losers with "spoonfuls of sugar." This was a crucial component of agriculture reform programs in Mexico, Romania, and Turkey, for instance.

## Framework for Analysis and Summary of Key Findings

This chapter is concerned with political economy determinants of agricultural public spending allocation. It does not examine determinants of total public spending or budgets (often used as a proxy for the size of government, and as such a different topic). It is also "partial equilibrium" in that it is mainly focused on the expenditure side of public finance—for example, it acknowledges that even when public spending on agriculture is relatively high, there may be net taxation of the sector. But the primary interest remains in the determinants on the spending side of public sector activity. It is, however, outside the scope of this chapter to explore the range of drivers of public spending allocation that are not directly related to political economy factors, such as public resource allocation in agriculture based on agroclimatic factors, public spending in reaction to macroeconomic phenomena, or the influence of private investment on public investment.[2]

This survey of theory and evidence on this topic structures the discussion into three thematic areas (figure 5.1). The first area is agent-centric, analyzing agents' incentive structure, constraints, and interface with each other. The second area is investment-centric, analyzing the features of publicly provided goods and services and how these features make it more or less likely that these goods and services would be invested in. The third area is the broader governance environment, analyzing the countrywide political and economic governance environment for agents to allocate public resources to goods and services. In sum, then, the first examination is of political economy factors—organized into the three elements of agent-centric, investment-centric, and broad governance-related determinants—that can affect how public resources are allocated.

**Figure 5.1** Framework for Political Economy Determinants of Agricultural Public Spending

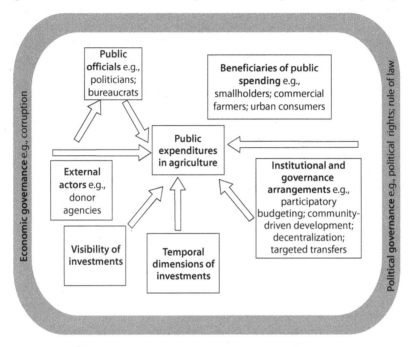

*Source:* Mogues and Erman 2016.

Within the broader discussion of governance, this chapter considers institutional arrangements for distributing publicly provided resources that are intended to make public spending more pro-poor. The evidence is laid out on the extent of success—or failure—in these arrangements' ability to achieve the goal of improving the way spending is allocated. In particular, we assess the extent to which public resources and the goods, services, and infrastructure they produce have become more oriented to benefit the livelihoods and economic potential of the poor. The four prominent ones are participatory budgeting, community-driven development programs, decentralization, and targeted transfers.

Clearly, the framework for this review is highly simplified. For example, there are multiple types of actors within each broad actor category that we discuss, and the channels that represent or influence public spending are diverse. The elements of the framework are also not in reality always sharply delineated—for example, characteristics of investments can matter through the way they interface with actors' incentives. And the institutional reforms and types of interventions discussed are not always designed with political economy and governance factors in mind; for example, transfers targeted to households can in some contexts be devised without attention to the ways that local power dynamics thwart the objectives of channeling the transfers to the poor. The illustration instead simply serves to frame the literature in broad strokes, with the particularities discussed in the subsequent sections.

Table 5.1 focuses on the political economy determinants of public spending compositions and allocations, and table 5.2 on the institutional arrangements to make public spending more pro-poor. As the first summary shows, direct decision makers in resource allocation are strongly driven by a range of incentives in making spending decisions, and how funds are spent is often an equilibrium result of the interactions between diverse types of decision makers—for example, politicians and bureaucrats—with their respective and

**Table 5.1** Evidence on Political Economy Determinants of Public Spending

| Elements of the framework | Selected key findings from the literature |
|---|---|
| *Agents' incentives and constraints* | |
| **Direct decision makers in resource allocation** | Model of unencumbered, benevolent social planner may not be a realistic view of resource allocation process |
| | Decision makers' direct economic incentives, as well as their political incentives, are dominant forces in their spending behavior |
| | Divergent maximization problems of politicians vs. bureaucrats can lead to different public good provision equilibria |
| **Beneficiaries of resource allocation** | Collective action is facilitated by small group size, effective information and education endowment, access to transport and communication infrastructure, and financial endowment. Collective action enables effective advocacy for public spending favorable to the group |
| | Groups in some cases invest in the information endowment of their membership, both for better evaluating merits of alternative investments, and to influence politicians' knowledge |
| | Large group size can be an advantage in attracting investments to benefit the group, if the high coordination costs inherent in larger groups are outweighed by factors that create "strength in numbers" |
| | Status quo bias, favoring continued pursuit of existing spending patterns, is driven by preexisting political clout of the beneficiaries of these patterns, as well as their growth over time as behavior changes to take advantage of opportunities created by policy |
| **External actors** | Donor-supported adjustment policies have led to a decline in public spending shares, while productivity-centered investments have not fallen or even increased. But within the latter category, agricultural spending's share fell |
| | But influence of international development assistance on public spending is checked by significant cases of aid fungibility, especially in the case of aid for agriculture |

*(continued next page)*

**Table 5.1** (continued)

| Elements of the framework | Selected key findings from the literature |
|---|---|
| *Investment characteristics* | |
| **Visibility of investments** | The greater the ease with which citizens can attribute a type of public investment to the effort and actions of the policy makers who were responsible for it, the greater the likelihood that this type of investment will be undertaken |
| | The visibility of publicly provided goods and services greatly increases this attributability. But since the most visible goods are not necessarily the most beneficial ones, this phenomenon may lead to a distortion of resource allocation |
| **Temporal and distributional characteristics** | Longer time lags between when spending takes place and the goods or services funded materialize, the less likely that these investments will be undertaken |
| | This is because a longer lag will make the attributability problem worse, increase the chance that the politician will no longer be in office when the provided services materialize, and increase uncertainty about the returns to the investment |
| | Inefficient forms of spending can prevail over less inefficient ones, such that entrenched interests in support of more inefficient subsidies grow larger and more powerful over time |
| *Governance environment* | |
| **Corruption's impact on resource allocation** | Corruption-prone environments induce policy makers to undertake more capital spending that may lend itself more easily to extraction of bribes than does recurrent spending |
| | This holds more in poor countries than in higher-income countries: in the latter, in settings that are more corruption-prone, capital spending goes down, precisely to ward off opportunities for leakages to take place |
| **Regime type and political contestation** | Results are mixed: some cross-country analysis finds no effect of broader political governance on spending allocation, while other work shows that younger democracies spend more on targeted goods than more mature democracies |
| | Country-level analysis gives more unambiguous evidence that political contestation improves the quality of public goods provision |
| | In the context of agriculture, there is consistent evidence of a nonlinear relationship between political governance and support to agriculture: improvements in political rights from a low level initially increase support to agriculture. But further political governance improvements do not affect or can lead to a mild decrease in agricultural support |

often differing incentives. Beneficiaries of publicly provided goods and services can, even if they are not direct decision makers, have significant influence on how public spending is allocated, while donor agencies' influence can be compromised due to the fungibility of funds, especially prevalent in agriculture. The characteristics of different public investments themselves, as well as the overall governance environment, determine the likelihood of these investments taking place.

**Table 5.2 Summary of the Impact of Four Institutional Arrangements**
*Ordered from most to least explicit design focus on participation of the poor*

| | Level of intervention | Political targeting | From intermediate to further-reaching outcomes | | Responsiveness of public spending/ services to needs of the poor |
| --- | --- | --- | --- | --- | --- |
| | | | Corruption | Local capture | |
| **Participatory budgeting** | Local administrative unit | Prevalent when civil society is weak; important in African context | Assumed benefit— more research needed | Some evidence suggesting overrepresentation of local elites in PB | Increased responsiveness when civil society is strong |
| **Community-driven development** | Communities/groups of individuals | Important in African context | Assumed benefit— more research needed | Especially in unequal societies | Especially in Africa |
| **Decentralization** | Local administrative unit (for example, district) | Splitting subnational units for political gain | Effect of decreasing corruption | Especially in unequal societies | Sensitive to local context |
| **Targeted transfers** | Individuals/households | Vote-buying Rewarding supporters | Can be targeted Substantial in agricultural transfers | Both when targeting administration is centralized and decentralized | Depending on the nature of the transfer |

*Note:* PB = participatory budgeting.

As table 5.2 shows, the success of various institutional arrangements that seek to improve the responsiveness of public spending to the needs of the poor population is mixed. Targeting of spending based on the political affiliation of beneficiaries has been identified as an important determinant of spending in governance arrangements. Spending programs in more unequal societies are particularly vulnerable to capture. Elite capture and political targeting were identified in almost all analyzed agricultural input transfer programs in Africa. Mechanisms such as participatory budgeting and CDD are assumed to make spending more transparent; but evidence is not conclusive in this case. In actual effects on responsiveness and pro-poor resource allocation, evidence is scarce but cautiously optimistic about participatory budgeting, CDD, and decentralization.

## Agents' Incentives and Constraints

### Direct Decision Makers in Public Spending Allocation

Public decision makers' incentives influence public spending allocation process.[3] For example, Besley, Pande, and Rao (2012) detect greater public resource allocation of the *gram panchayats* (GP) in India (an administrative unit that is a collection of villages) to the village from where the GP head originates compared with other villages in the GP.[4] This is a variant of the elite capture literature, one in which the local elite is not merely a socially or economically higher-status person, but also carries the function of a public official. Allocation of public money has been examined as an outcome of the interaction between politicians and the bureaucracy. Bureaucrats have been modeled as "professionals" who evaluate public spending proposals based on their technical quality or merits (Ting 2012), as budget maximizers who seek to have public goods supplied in large quantity (Niskanen 1971), or as agents who seek to maximize the difference between the quantity of public goods claimed to have been provided and that actually have, retaining this difference as private income (Blackburn, Bose, and Haque 2011).

Analysis has identified spatial and temporal resource allocation outcomes that emerge from interaction among politicians, and has compared the choices of different types of hypothetical decision makers (social planner versus politician). For example, extensive research continues to be undertaken to model in detail the spatial allocation outcomes as a result of legislative bargaining approaches taking place under different political systems, such as the many variations on parliamentary and presidential systems. Usually, these studies would consider specific systems of particular countries, typically from among those with advanced democracies, even in cases of theoretical analysis (see Persson and Tabellini [2000] for a review).

Spatial allocation is more often the subject of study than temporal allocation. But there are interesting examples of the latter, such as recent theoretical modeling of intergenerational conflict over how much to spend, save, and invest over time. This study concludes, seemingly counterintuitively, that a social planner whose aim is to make resource allocation decisions so as to maximize the discounted utility of all generations would produce outcomes economically worse in the aggregate and long run than fiscal decisions of agents subject to short-term electoral calculus (Song, Storesletten, and Zilibotti 2012). This analysis is based on a model of small open economies, each consisting of young citizens (who supply labor), and old citizens (who live off their savings), and public goods provision (that can be financed by debt through borrowing from other countries or by domestic taxes on labor). Under conditions of sufficiently low borrowing interest rates, the social planner, who seeks to maximize citizens' welfare, discounting future citizens' utility, may overtax the labor of the young to supply public goods benefiting the old, in a manner that leads to long-run declines in aggregate welfare. In contrast, under the same conditions, an agent facing political constraints from both young and old citizens will provide fewer public goods to the old and incur lower debt, to the benefit of younger generations and of aggregate, intertemporal welfare.

## Beneficiaries of Public Resource Allocations

While agricultural protection policies have consistently been applied in developed nations, several developing countries have pursued policies of agricultural taxation (Bale and Lutz 1981; De Gorter and Swinnen 2002; Krueger, Schiff, and Valdes 1988; Lindert 1991). A rich body of evidence has also pointed to the ways in which agricultural policies in developing countries have favored larger-scale farmers, few in number, even when these policies were intended to specifically target the masses of smallholders. There are similarly many instances in developing countries in which public investments and other measures have benefited urban populations at the expense of rural dwellers—and in particular agricultural households.

These phenomena have been explained as an outcome of the way the characteristics of interest groups—here, this means individuals or producers sharing similar livelihoods or economic interests—affect their ability to press for public policies, including investments, subsidies, and other public interventions that are favorable to them (Becker 1983). Interest groups can supply an adequate quantity of the local (or group-specific) public good of advocating on behalf of the public resource decisions preferred by their members if they can avoid the collective action problems in large groups well known in public goods provision (Anderson and Hayami 1986; Bates 1987).

One factor facilitating collective action is the spatial concentration of group members, enabling coordination and mutual monitoring of actions

(Olson 1985). Agriculture is strongly characterized by spatial dispersion of farmers, in contrast to the relative physical proximity of urban citizens to each other. Similarly, access to transportation and communication infrastructure facilitates intragroup coordination and organization, inferior in rural as compared with urban areas in developing regions.

Third, a critical element in collective action is group size. For any level of spatial concentration and access to transport and communication infrastructure, it is harder to coordinate among larger than among smaller groups. In most developing countries, the agricultural and rural populations are substantially larger than urban populations, resulting in another inherent disadvantage among the former in organizing to appeal for pro-agriculture policies. Group size also matters in a second respect: the same resources allocated to a purpose preferred by a large group versus that preferred by a small group will invariably result in greater gains for individual members of the small group than of the large group. This situation often results in greater incentives for members of a smaller group to engage in (and incur the costs of) lobbying for their preferred spending policies.

Later research highlights, implicitly, the way an inverse relationship between group size and group effectiveness in influencing resource allocation directly hinges on the coordination cost argument. This research suggests that if the effectiveness of collective action is held constant, as well as per capita characteristics such as member incomes, larger groups may be able to wield more political clout (for example, through their greater aggregate income resources and their greater combined voting power) (Acemoğlu and Robinson 2001). Implicit is the argument that collective action failures in large groups often more than offset other potential benefits of "strength in numbers."

Explanations of the patterns of public investment in economies such as China; the Republic of Korea; Malaysia; and Taiwan, China lean on another potential advantage held by large groups at the lower economic levels. These Asian countries undertook expansive public investments in smallholder agriculture and other rural services benefiting small farmers, as well as extensive land reforms, because of the looming threat of unrest among the rural masses fueled by economic neglect, which had brought down regimes in neighboring countries (Doner, Ritchie, and Slater 2005).

Such reaction of public investments to a possible threat from rural areas has been less prevalent in Africa. Leaders' goals for agricultural or agroindustrial production could simply not be met by antismallholder policies, causing leaders to recognize that working with small farmers' incentives is the more successful path to achieving their agricultural strategy objectives. Examples of this go back to when colonial authorities abandoned forced agricultural labor in Burkina Faso's cotton sector: instead, they promoted high-yielding cotton varieties to more effectively obtain the production levels required for exporting the crop for processing in the French textile industry (Bassett 2001).

In many cases, however, postcolonial African countries structured their public investments to support an "agricultural modernization" strategy, which typically meant the promotion of and investments in large state farms. Even where there was a serious debate between such state farm-led production versus significant investments to strengthen smallholder farming, the types of investments made were often inappropriate to the needs of small farmers. An example is Zambia, where smallholder supportive policy took the form of cooperative mechanization for maize. But the tractors promoted were not the suitable technology given farmers' small land sizes, and the resultant levels of maize output were disappointing, leading to an abandonment of policies to support smallholder production (Bowman 2011).

Aside from factors that facilitate collective action among group members, members' financial endowments affect groups' abilities to exert influence on behalf of policies benefiting them—for example, through expending resources for favorable policy outcomes. This is another area where smallholder agricultural populations will usually be at a disadvantage. Similarly, a group with greater educational endowments and access to information can more accurately assess the consequences and relative merits of different policies—for example, the provision of fertilizer subsidies versus investments in rural roads—and thus is better equipped to push for those policies that make its members better off (Binswanger and Deininger 1997). Access to information and transparency about the actions of policy makers not only provides a strong basis for citizens and groups to advocate on behalf of policies that would improve their welfare, but also strengthens political institutions and governance more broadly (Khemani et al. 2016).

The ability to discern the outcomes of alternative public investments and other policies may be used not only by an interest group to inform itself and its members but also to provide knowledge to policy makers, who often operate in an environment of imperfect information about the welfare and distributional outcomes of their policies. The effectiveness of interest groups in undertaking such informational lobbying is based on whether such information provision is costless ("cheap talk") or costly; on the intensity with which the group holds a preference over the policy the effects of which it seeks to provide information on; and on the presence or absence of multiple interest groups, either on the same or opposite side of the policy position (Grossman and Helpman 2001).

An interesting phenomenon in policy processes is a seeming status quo bias among policy makers, such that policies that have outlived their usefulness often fail to be discontinued. Dynamics of policy persistence are quite familiar in agriculture. For example, agricultural input subsidies are not removed even after they have begun to outlive their initial efficiency-enhancing objectives, or after they have served, or have been observed to have failed to serve, equity and poverty reduction goals. Those who benefit from the current state are usually the ones with the requisite power to have ensured policy enactment in the first place. Thus, the constituency for the maintenance of the existing policy is likely to be more powerful and influential than the constituency that prefers an alternative (not yet enacted) policy (Fernandez and Rodrik 1991).

The aggregate willingness to advocate for the continuation of an existing policy is greater than the willingness to pressure politicians to institute the policy before its enactment, because once a policy is in existence, agents undertake actions that position them to benefit from these policies (Coate and Morris 1999). As a consequence, the total constituency (or overall intensity of preference) for an existing policy is larger than that for the same policy before its enactment. Examples in African agriculture of this phenomenon abound. In Uganda, as the fisheries sector experienced a fast growth in the early 2000s, with it grew the number of fishermen, who made investments in boats and gear that were illegal (Kjaer 2015). Fishermen enlisted army officers to protect them in the process of lucrative smuggling of fisheries products into neighboring countries. When the government wanted to take action against both illegal fishing and smuggling, the constituencies that benefited from these actions had grown in both numbers and importance, leading to a failure to enact policies to control the fishing process, and with it the government's ability to meet international standards for export fish.

An analytical tool that seeks to summarize how the workings of various interest groups result in a set of policies, and in a particular distribution of public resources, is the political preference function (PPF) (Bullock 1994). The PPF has some similarities to the well-established social welfare function in welfare economics, in that it expresses a policy maker's utility function over different entities' welfare—with weights placed on different types of agents, and with the policy maker choosing policies to maximize the value of the function. But unlike in the individualistic social welfare function, the elements of which are individuals, the PPF contains as elements different groups within society, such as smallholders, large farmers, urban consumers, and taxpayers.

The PPF is used, for example, to explain the effects of specific agricultural policies on groups. A study in India examines the determinants of wheat and rice policies, and estimates the size of the weights in the PPF that are associated with the various pressure groups (Abler and Sukhatme 1998). The results suggest that agricultural policies are designed to significantly favor consumers of wheat and rice in urban areas, and policy preferences indicate that wheat producers enjoy more power than rice producers.[5]

## External Actors—Donors Allocating Resources and Influencing Others' Allocations

Beyond the domestic interest groups of a developing country (whether decision makers or beneficiaries of public spending allocations), there is also a strong influence that lies outside a country's borders: the external agencies that provide aid to enable public spending for development. The importance of donor assistance in developing countries' economies can be overwhelmingly large, especially in small economies or in countries in or emerging from conflict. For example, in 2008/09, net development assistance as a percentage of gross national income reached as high as 78 percent in Liberia, 46 percent in Afghanistan, and 41 percent in Burundi (World Bank 2015). In large, fast-growing, and mineral- or oil-rich developing countries, the share of development aid in income can be dwindlingly low, constituting, for example, less than one-third of 1 percent in Brazil, China, Islamic Republic of Iran, Mexico, and República Bolivariana de Venezuela.

There have been several cases of developing country governments, breaking with the external development community to avoid external scrutiny and accountability of public resource allocation. But there are also a few interesting and prominent examples of poor countries that extricated themselves from aid dependence because of the latter's detrimental effect on sustained food security. For example, when the grain harvests of 1966 and 1967 failed in India and the government was forced to rely on food aid from the United States to avoid famine, a turning point was reached. Thanks to research and innovation on agricultural development undertaken in the public and private sectors during this time, high-yield varieties of rice and wheat were introduced in the 1970s. These varieties, coupled with irrigation systems and fertilizer use, enabled India to dramatically increase its output of cereals over the subsequent decades. And with this increase in productivity, India was able to reduce the influence not only of food aid but also of external development aid more generally.

When it comes to the impact of external development aid on public spending in developing countries, another long-standing concern has not been that it directs spending policy too much toward donor preferences, but that those preferences have too little impact. Simply put, governments can bypass donors' wishes that their aid increase investments in specific sectors, since donors are not able to tell whether a given amount of investment in a sector, program, or project would have been made (or partially made) in the absence of the aid.

The empirical evidence on how much development aid, including aid geared toward the agricultural sector, displaces other public spending in the same sector is not encouraging. Analysis on the Dominican Republic, for example, identifies agriculture as among the sectors with pronounced aid fungibility (Pack and Pack 1993). Based on estimates of the influence of sector-specific aid flows on public spending in the various sectors, the study finds that although on average one-third of sector-specific development assistance to the country is intended for agriculture, the increase in agricultural spending resulting from this agricultural aid is only 1.5 percent. Pack and Pack (1990) employ a similar methodology for Indonesia, but do not find aid fungibility in this context, including in the agriculture and irrigation category. The cross-country panel analysis by Feyzioglu, Swaroop, and Zhu (1998) estimates a fungibility parameter that can identify the fiscal response of different sectorial spending to sectorial aid as having full, partial, or no fungibility. The results show that agriculture is the only examined sector with full fungibility (when considering both total agricultural spending and just agricultural capital spending separately).

Strong fungibility in aid is also found in a country contrasting starkly with the Dominican Republic in size—namely, India. Swaroop, Jha, and Rajkumar (2000) examine central government spending behavior as a consequence of aid flows, in the context of India's federal structure. When government spending is categorized into development uses (such as health, education, agriculture) and nondevelopment uses (for example, general administration, defense, and interest and principal payments of debt), an estimation of the impact of development assistance on both finds that it increases nondevelopment spending by a statistically significant amount, while not affecting aggregate development-related government spending. The rise in the former is primarily due to shifts of public resources into general administration uses. Development aid's lack of impact on development-related spending holds also when disaggregating this category. Aid does not lead to an increase in public spending on agriculture, irrigation, energy, or other sectors, with the only exception being public spending on social sector expenditures (which respond positively and in a statistically significant manner to increases in aid).

Starting from the premise that donors are likely to want to see a substantial share of their funds go toward capital formation (whether in social, infrastructure, or other sectors), Feeny and McGillivray (2010) explore in Papua New Guinea the extent to which aid instead triggers increases in consumption spending. They find that high shares of aid (directly or indirectly) finance government consumption. For example, 90 percent of increases in aid loans, three-quarters of increases in aid in the form of grants, and 70 percent of additional budget all finance recurrent spending. The general qualitative features of these findings are consistent with cross-country evidence. In the analysis by Feyzioglu, Swaroop, and Zhu (1998), based on panel data of selected developing countries, a US$1 increase in overall official development assistance (ODA) results in an increase of recurrent spending by $0.72 and $1.22, respectively. In contrast, the equivalent increase in capital spending is only $0.29 and $0.27, respectively. The impact of concessionary loans on recurrent spending suggests that this form of aid may, in fact, be leveraging additional recurrent spending from other external or domestic revenue sources.

## Features of Public Spending and the Goods and Services It Creates

Even for a given configuration of actors and their characteristics, particular attributes of different types of public spending—and of the public and private goods and assets they create—can influence how much weight these spending types are given in resource allocation decisions, and how they are substituted or complemented with other spending. One of the salient features considered here is attributability—the ease or difficulty with which citizens can assess to what extent a policy maker was responsible for an investment, and for its outcomes. Another defining feature of spending is the temporal lag between the time when an outlay is incurred and the time when intermediate outputs or final outcomes are realized. A third feature concerns the benefit incidence, or distributional properties, of public spending. We discuss how these features affect the incentives of policy makers to embark on a given investment, subsidy, or transfer.

### Visibility of Public Investments

The previous section elaborated on the value of access to information and of the ability of beneficiaries of spending to undertake the necessary analysis to understand how different policies translate into outcomes. The informational challenge, however, may exist further up the policy chain. Even if citizens know which policies and investments would be best for their welfare, it is often difficult to attribute to policy makers' actions the creation or improvement of certain services. Various factors may result in improved services, only one of which may be the efforts or spending undertaken by politicians. For example, if a farmer observes that the quality of information provided to her by a new agricultural extension officer has improved, it may be difficult for her to ascertain whether that is because the new extensionist is simply more motivated by nature, or whether the agricultural ministry has done a better job in selecting, training, or incentivizing extension officers.

Incorrect or imperfect attribution dampens policy makers' incentives to work to improve services and infrastructure, and influences which investments are prioritized. This stems from the basic phenomenon that public officials will want to maximize credit for improvements and increases in investments (especially those popular with residents), minimize attribution for inappropriate or deteriorating services, and give less weight to services for which they are unable to effectively signal their contribution toward providing these services. The attribution challenge is affected by various characteristics of public investments and services. Visible infrastructure investments and direct cash or in-kind transfers (such as fertilizer vouchers) are relatively more easily connected to the efforts and spending decisions of public officials, and thus can serve as an effective tool for patronage. In fact, these can also be conveniently advertised, indicating who is responsible for subsidizing the fertilizer. In contrast, in the example given previously, the quality improvement in agricultural extension is harder to claim in this way. The greater visibility (and therefore attributability) of large-scale irrigation schemes have made them more attractive than small schemes for public officials to invest in, despite the weaker agricultural performance of the former (Mogues and do Rosario 2015). The positive impact of visibility of a good or service on public spending to provide it increases with increasing levels of democracy from a low base, but only up to an intermediate level of democratic development (Mani and Mukand 2007).

## Temporal and Distributional Features of Public Investments

Another characteristic that affects the ease of correct attribution is the extent to which there is a lag between the time when resources are allocated to provide a good or service, and the time when the good or service is created. The longer this temporal gap, the harder it is to trace the service back to decisions made by politicians.

Investments in agricultural research are known for at least two characteristics. A wide range of studies has pointed to the substantial agricultural productivity and broader welfare benefits derived from investment in agricultural research in developing countries. But another well-known attribute of agricultural research is that there is a long temporal lag between these public investments and welfare outcomes, or even intermediate outcomes such as developing and adopting new agricultural technology. We will thus address the issues arising from lag times by using agricultural research as an example.

A long lag might make it less attractive for public officials to undertake an investment than if the time span between investment and outcomes were shorter. This is so for three reasons. First, a long lag further breaks the perceptible link between politicians' decisions and public officials' resource allocations, as mentioned above in the discussion of attribution of services to politicians' efforts.[6] Second, even if the attribution problem did not exist, in systems where political decision makers do not have reason to believe that they will stay in power for a prolonged period of time, they perceive the probability that they will be able to gain politically from beneficial investments in agricultural research and development to be small, and thus have lowered incentives to undertake these investments. This is especially because they will come at the expense of other public provisions that may have a shorter turnaround time in welfare effects for the population.

Third, a long span of time from the initiation of an investment until the gains materialize also opens up opportunities for things to go wrong. For example, relevant agricultural technologies may be developed through others' investments, such as international research organizations or those of other countries, rendering the incurred costs less valuable, to the extent that technologies developed by others can be copied or adapted. Or prices for crops for which the R&D investments are undertaken may see a medium- or long-term drop that was not anticipated when the research activities began.

The temporal element of the policy process, in particular the effects of the limited longevity of politicians in office, also comes into play in a somewhat different way to determine which types of policies are chosen for implementation. Groups may have a clear preference for certain types of public financial support over others. For example, agricultural interests in developed countries may prefer government spending to subsidize them through price and output controls, rather than through forms of direct income transfer of equivalent size, although the former may be a more inefficient form of subsidy.

The government's bargaining position in relation to the interest groups receiving the subsidies or transfers is stronger when the form of provision is subsidies rather than transfers (Drazen and Limão 2008). The government can demand more lobby goods (provisions the interest groups make to the government in return for receiving subsidies or transfers) for the same amount of public spending for the groups' benefit when these resources are in the form of inefficient subsidies (rather than in the form of more efficient transfers). With both the interest groups and the policy makers understanding this, the interest groups appreciate that the government will need to be paid more highly for incurring the (political) cost of making a more inefficient form of subsidy. Thus, in a first stage, and before engaging the interest groups, the policy-making entity imposes constraints (for example, legislative restrictions) on its ability to undertake transfers using the less inefficient instrument. Then in the second stage, with mostly or only inefficient options available, it has gained a stronger bargaining position in relation to the interest groups than if it had not imposed the restriction in the first stage.

But particular features of public and private goods may also explain why spending on one can bring about more spending on the other, rendering them complementary. Agricultural research benefits agriculture as well as nonagriculture, but the benefits for one sector may be larger than those accruing to the other. This may induce greater subsidy spending by governments seeking to maximize political support, since this spending counteracts the distributional effect of agricultural research investments and thus mitigates potential political opposition to the research investments.

# Broader Economic and Political Governance Environment

After a discussion on the way various actors' incentives and interactions shape the resource allocation process, and on how salient attributes of different types of public spending (and the assets and public and private goods they create) determine the allocation of this spending, this section explores the governance environment's influence on resource allocation decisions. It first considers a particular aspect of economic and political governance—corruption. There seems to be relatively broad consensus that the prevalence of corruption increases the share of capital investment spending in overall spending. The other governance consideration—the wider political governance environment—shows much less uniformity in its effects or other capital investments are undertaken lend themselves to rent-seeking by public officials. Since these investments commonly involve large, discrete contracts, they create opportunities for public officials to improve the chances of a private agent winning contracts, or to loosen regulatory burdens on the agent, in return for private payments to the official. In contrast, public spending on activities that involve mostly salary payments to service providers—and contain a relatively small share of outlays on capital creation or procurement—provide fewer openings for rent seeking.[7]

The maturity of democracies also has consequences for resource allocation. Public investment spending and expenditures on the central government wage bill—proxies of targeted spending—tend to be lower in younger democracies than in older ones, given that in the former, it is harder for politicians to make credible promises of spending to the population as a whole rather than targeted groups of citizens.[8]

Power contests affect the composition of public spending. In China, the presence of electoral mechanisms to freely choose village leaders leads to a higher share of public investment in the total public spending of village governments, compared with villages where the leader is appointed (Zhang et al. 2004). And in Kenya, democratic governance can eliminate the detrimental effects of ethnic favoritism on public infrastructure spending and the creation of the infrastructure itself (Burgess et al. 2015). In India, local leaders of villages who have clientelistic arrangements are less likely to allocate resources to pro-poor programs (Anderson, Francois, and Kotwal 2015).

Political governance can affect whether citizens who are not already supporters of the ruling party are more likely to be punished by withholding public funds, or wooed with more public spending. In Tanzania, government channels funds to areas giving it the greatest electoral support (Weinstein 2011). In Uganda, the government invested heavily in the dairy sector by, among other things, rehabilitating cooling facilities, maintaining roads in areas where dairy production was concentrated (in the southwest of the

country), and establishing milk collection centers. These actions were motivated by the ruling party's need to win the population's support in the south-
west area, which had in the past supported the leader of a different political
party (Kjaer 2015).

Features of political institutions may exercise different levels of influence
on the extent to which governments enact policies that favor the agricultural
sector through subsidies, investments, and nonfiscal policies. One feature is
the degree of political accountability to which politicians are exposed. The
relationship between political governance and government support for agricultural producers can be complex and nonlinear. In a highly autocratic
system with political control centralized in one individual or a narrow elite,
there may be no scope for agricultural producer groups to press for subsidies
or investments that would benefit the sector. Thus, a moderate political
change from a strongly autocratic to a milder form of authoritarianism
somewhat opens up the political space for agricultural groups to exert influence on public policy. But when considering a further, more dramatic change
toward a democratic system with effective governance institutions, policy
makers must consider that the options for seeking protection through subsidies geared to one sector are checked by accountability systems and by
interest groups with diverse policy priorities.

A recent study takes another angle on political governance factors, exploring the effects not of the locus of a country on the democracy-autocracy
spectrum in cross-country samples, but rather of the effects of transitions to
democracy or to autocracy in individual countries over time. Here, Olper,
Falkowski, and Swinnen (2014) find that transitions to democracy increase
the protection and decrease the taxation of the agricultural sector. These
cross-country results are influenced by the developing countries, which have
a greater prevalence of farmers among the poor population, and thus experienced more political transitions, than the developed countries. Therefore,
the results, while not a direct test of the median-voter model, are consistent
with it.[9]

One may, in a refinement, also distinguish between the quality of the
political climate in general, and the quality of specific institutions that
would be expected to affect the ability of agricultural and other interest
groups to lobby for public spending and investments to benefit their sector.
As discussed previously, the extent to which interest groups are able to participate in the political process, but also the extent to which their power to
influence public policy is checked through governance systems. But other
elements may be just as pertinent to the ability of agricultural producers
(and other economic groups) to lobby for investments and subsidies to benefit their sector. These elements include the extent to which property rights
are protected, contractual rights honored, and public goods delivered in a

relatively efficient manner, which depends on a reasonably well-functioning bureaucracy. While measures of political rights and pluralism may affect the ability of agricultural producers to participate in the political process and influence policy, property rights and bureaucratic functioning may affect the transaction costs of doing so. And these governance attributes may mildly correlate with, but are not very well defined by, indexes that proxy for political freedom (box 5.1).

## BOX 5.1

## Areas for Future Research

The political economy of the CAADP process in general, and how it affected funding flows to agriculture in Africa in particular, deserves closer analytical scrutiny. Another area is the use of appropriate analytical tools to understand how resource allocation may be distorted between the point of budget establishment and the stage at which public resources reach the ground. The public expenditure tracking survey (PETS) methodology has so far been employed almost exclusively to analyze public spending allocations in the education and health sectors. To the best of our knowledge, there exists no rigorous analysis using PETS in the agricultural sector, and only one such work in general (World Bank 2010). But PETS could be an invaluable analytical tool for the agricultural sector. For example, it can be used for tracking the allocation of spending for agricultural R&D. Irrigation may be an investment activity requiring even greater analytical attention through spending tracking, due to the pervasive problems with resources being siphoned off, as alluded to in this chapter.

Quantitative (micro) analysis could shed light on how the choices in spending on agricultural public goods and services manifest themselves in concrete, locally realized ways, directly linking this to behavioral predictions about public agents. Moreover, a strong complement to observational data-based enquiries on how political economy phenomena shape outcomes on public spending configurations would be field experimental evidence. Promising new endeavors to examine how political governance shapes economic phenomena (reviewed by Moehler 2010) can provide guidance on applications to public spending in and for the agricultural sector.

Finally, theoretical work that seeks to explain public spending allocation is motivated and developed around institutional phenomena most relevant to advanced democratic economies. For many developing countries, with either highly imperfect democratic arrangements or some form of authoritarian political decision making, many well-established models from political science are not pertinent, and have much room to develop.

## Institutional Arrangements to Make Public Spending Pro-Poor

To what extent have institutional reforms, programs, interventions, and projects been cognizant of these political economy dynamics that can influence public resource allocation? More specifically, what institutions have been designed with these dynamics to orient the composition of public spending toward the poor? And how have such arrangements affected spending flows to the agricultural sector? These are broad questions, and there are many interventions that, to a greater or lesser extent do—or at least attempt—the above. We focus here on four reforms and intervention types that have been widespread in development, and have particular relevance for agriculture, on which there is research evidence on how they affected the direction of publicly provided goods and services.

The institutional arrangements we focus on are (a) participatory budgeting; (b) community-driven development; (c) decentralization; and (d) targeted transfers (table 5.3). This review synthesizes the existing knowledge on the extent to which it has successfully made public spending more favorable to the poor, on how agricultural spending has been influenced in the context of these arrangements, and how able these institutions have been in overcoming political economy pitfalls in the quality of public spending in agriculture and other sectors. As will be shown, there are both encouraging indications of success in achieving these goals, as well as, unfortunately, several examples of an inability of the design of these institutions to mitigate capture of resources by the better-off or more politically connected.

### Participatory Budgeting

A review of participatory budgeting experiences in Sub-Saharan African countries includes seven countries that have both institutionalized and noninstitutionalized processes (table 5.4) (Shall 2007). In Mozambique and Zambia, there are no formal mechanisms of participatory budgeting. But in both countries

**Table 5.3** Institutional Arrangements to Make Public Spending More Pro-Poor, and Key Mediating Factors

| Institutional arrangements | Factors affecting spending under different arrangements | Outcome |
|---|---|---|
| • Participatory budgeting | • Political targeting | Responsiveness of public spending and services to needs of the poor |
| • Community-driven development | • Corruption | |
| • Decentralization | • Local capture | |
| • Targeted transfers | | |

**Table 5.4** Participatory Budgeting in Sub-Saharan Africa

| Kenya | Participation is used as a condition to receive funds from LATF |
|---|---|
| Mozambique | No formal mechanism in place (but some initiatives exist) |
| South Africa | Both on-the-ground initiatives and broad institutional PB |
| Tanzania | PB required for annual public and planning processes |
| Uganda | Several mechanisms are in place |
| Zambia | No formal mechanism in place (but some initiatives exist) |
| Zimbabwe | Several mechanisms are in place |

*Source:* Mogues and Erman 2016, elaboration of Shall 2007.
*Note:* LATF = local authority transfer fund; PB = participatory budgeting.

there is independent implementation of participatory budgeting by local officials. Participatory budgeting has been institutionalized in other African countries in a number of ways. For example, in Tanzania, it is a required element of
the local governmental planning process, and in Kenya, it is used as a condition
to obtain funds from the local authority transfer fund (LATF) meant to incen-
tivize local authorities to improve service delivery and strengthen financial
management.

While country case studies provide valuable lessons on where participatory
budgeting has worked, cross-country evidence may tell us more about the conditions under which it works. In a cross-country study, Bräutigam (2004) identified two complementary factors needed for participatory budgeting to have a
pro-poor effect on public spending: the presence of a committed left-leaning
party or social movement supporting pro-poor spending, and an informed and
active civil society.

Bräutigam's (2004) finding turns out to be particularly useful for understanding the outcome of cases of participatory budgeting in Africa. In Maputo,
Mozambique, participatory budgeting was introduced as a top-down initiative
by the ruling party in a context of intraparty competition. The process was
used as an instrument for the local governor to connect to majority party
neighborhoods and their leaders to build and maintain alliances. Every step of
the participatory process was designed to keep the process confined to party
members; from the partisan micro-institutions in charge of neighborhood-
level recruitment, to the administrative and supervising teams. Opposition
parties, nongovernmental organizations (NGOs), and civil society were virtually absent from the process (Nylen 2014). A similar story played out in
Morocco, where the participatory process was introduced and sustained
mainly as an arena for state control (Bergh 2010).

In addition, the potential of participatory budgeting in many developing
countries is undermined by the large degree of earmarking of intergovernmental transfers to local government in developing countries. In Uganda,

about 85 percent of transfers received by local governments are earmarked (conditioned); in Kenya, about 92 percent (Ranis 2012). Conditional transfer systems limit the resources that can be subject to participatory budgeting, since these transfers can be spent only within a predetermined and often rigid framework. In Uganda, where participation is a mandatory part of local decision making, most funds allocated to participatory budgeting get absorbed by the administrative and maintenance costs of the process itself. Participatory budgeting is locally seen as an obligation imposed by the central government rather than a tool for civic engagement (Francis and James 2003).

## Community-Driven Development Programs

In rural CDD projects, agricultural services play an important role. Seed multiplication and communal farming were the most represented in CDD projects in Sierra Leone, for instance, making up 26 percent of all investments selected by communities (Casey, Glennerster, and Miguel 2012). Evidence on the impact of CDD investments showed that in Senegal, villages that chose relatively more income-generating agricultural projects had a significantly larger reduction of poverty than other villages (Arcand and Bassole 2007). An assessment of the focus of activities of community-based organizations (CBO) in Burkina Faso and Senegal found that government-supported CBOs tended to be more focused on agriculture than CBOs sponsored by donors or private actors (Arcand and Fafchamps 2012).

Unless properly designed and implemented, the CDD approach can be sensitive to elite capture. If local individuals with elevated socioeconomic status are more able to take part in the participatory process due to better access to information, time, and influence, they may skew the project selection to better reflect their interests at the expense of pro-poor spending. Evidence of elite capture was found in Jamaica, where the participatory social fund implemented was highly elite-driven and spending showed few linkages with expressed demands (Rao and Ibanez 2005). The risk of capture seems to be more prominent in contexts of high inequality. Evidence from Ecuador found that higher community inequality made project selection less likely to benefit the poor (Araujo et al. 2008). Community inequality was found to be associated with less democratic forms of group decision-making in Tanzania (La Ferrara 2002). In contrast, no evidence of elite capture in CDD programs was found in Indonesia (Dasgupta and Beard 2007) or in the Philippines (Labonne and Chase 2009).

In Africa, political affiliation rather than belonging to an economic higher status group seems to be a stronger determinant of resource allocation in CDD projects. Political patronage was identified in the evaluation of pro-poor spending of CDD projects in Senegal, Tanzania, and Zambia.

In Senegal, having a member of the majority party of the rural council resid-
ing in the village increased the probability for a village to receive funds for
projects (Arcand and Bassole 2007). In Tanzania, the political affiliation of
participatory council representatives affected the chances of receiving funds
(Wong 2012). In Zambia, the households and villages targeted in the CDD
project, while being among the poorest, were also more likely to be politically active and affiliated with the incumbent politician. Projects were
exchanged for political support and vice versa (De Janvry, Nakagawa, and
Sadoulet 2009).

## Decentralization

Experiences of decentralization in Africa vary across countries. During the
latest decentralization trend in Africa, large federal states such as Ethiopia,
Nigeria, and South Africa were the first to introduce reforms in the mid-1990s.
Other countries followed suit. The pace and extent of the decentralization process differ substantially between countries. Table 5.5 compares decentralization
data from Kenya and Uganda. While local governments spend 30 percent of all
government spending in Uganda, they spend only about 5 percent of
government budget in Kenya. Decentralization in developing countries is characterized by a system of delegation where new responsibilities are accompanied
by fiscal transfers from central to local governments. Local governments in
Kenya finance most of their relatively low level of spending with local taxes,
whereas in Uganda they are highly dependent on intergovernmental transfers
to finance service delivery (Ranis 2012).

The trend toward decentralization has had important implications for the
agriculture sector in Africa. In Ethiopia, decentralization reforms were used,
among other purposes, to increase coverage of extension services with the goal of
increasing input use and agricultural production. Consequently, in four regions
in Ethiopia, districts were given the responsibility to provide rural services,
including extension services and drinking water. In Ghana, extension service
management was decentralized to district agricultural offices who answer to

**Table 5.5** Decentralization in Kenya and Uganda

| Year | Expenditure decentralization ratio | | Financial autonomy ratio | |
|---|---|---|---|---|
| | Kenya | Uganda | Kenya | Uganda |
| 2003/04 | 0.04 | 0.3 | 0.94 | 0.1 |
| 2004/05 | 0.05 | 0.3 | 0.64 | 0.1 |
| 2005/06 | 0.04 | 0.3 | 0.67 | 0 |
| 2006/07 | 0.05 | 0.3 | 0.61 | 0 |

*Source:* Ranis 2012.

regional units of the Ministry of Food and Agriculture. Research and Extension Linkage Committees have also been set up at the regional level to promote exchanges between extension services and agricultural research.

Uganda illustrates some challenges related to decentralization of agricultural service delivery, especially in intergovernmental coordination. While social sectors such as education and health benefited from decentralization, confusion among different tiers of government on responsibilities over management and operation funding of agricultural services led to underprioritization of resource allocation to local governments (Bashaasha, Najjingo Mangheni, and Nkonya 2011). A review of selected district budgets from 2003 found that the part of resources dedicated to production and marketing (including agricultural services) was between 1 and 3.5 percent (Francis and James 2003). In the absence of proper management, extension agents were left without guidance or supervision and the population complained about service quality. In Nigeria, one of the main challenges identified in agricultural service delivery and decentralization is related to the lack of clearly defined roles and responsibilities (that is, financial, provisional, or standard-setting of each government tier in service delivery) (Mogues et al. 2012).

The trade-off between local accountability and elite capture results in a net effect of decentralization on outcomes for the "nonelites" that is presumptively ambiguous depending on the institutional context. The hypothesis of greater elite capture in a context of decentralization relies on the notion that higher status individuals in a given locality are more empowered to influence local politicians than national politicians. Capture of public resources on the part of well-off groups can be found throughout government, but larger competition among elites and other interest groups at the central level will decrease the relative influence of any given elite interest and mitigate the risk of capture.

Where elite groups are marginalized within a district, it is likely that such groups want to create their own subnational government to gain more control over public funds. The division of subnational entities into smaller units is becoming an increasingly common phenomenon in Africa. Half of the countries in Sub-Saharan Africa increased their number of administrative units by more than 20 percent since the mid-1990s. While seemingly in line with the process and objectives of decentralization—bringing people closer to their political authorities—local government proliferation is largely politically motivated. It can hurt pro-poor spending by diverting funds that could have been used for service provision toward the fixed costs associated with the establishment and maintenance of new local governments. In addition, allowing for the creation of smaller units can lead to a recentralization of responsibilities, since smaller subnational units have less capacity and are more dependent on support from the central government.

## Targeted Transfers

Given the resurgence of input subsidy programs (Isps) in recent years (chapter 3), it is important to understand the factors affecting quality of targeting, and thus the extent to which the subsidies are pro-poor in their distribution. Better-off households gained more from the Isps than the poor in virtually all countries. On average, relatively large farmers receive more inputs, even though the objectives of the input programs are to support the "productive poor" in Malawi and the "vulnerable but viable" smallholder farmers in Zambia, to name a few examples (Lunduka, Ricker-Gilbert, and Fisher 2013; Mason and Jayne 2013). In Zambia, households with 2 to 5 hectares of land are 21 percent of the country's poor smallholders. Yet they received 41 percent of the fertilizer distributed through the program. Households with 0.5 to 1 hectare, by contrast, received only 13 percent of the subsidies, despite being 26 percent of the country's poor smallholders and making up 24 percent of all households.

For decentralization and even participatory budgeting, another prominent factor in resource allocation is targeting based on political affiliation. This is a recurring phenomenon in weak democracies and affects pro-poor allocations. Political factors were significant determinants in the distribution of input subsidies in five country cases, but had various effects on spending. In Malawi, Zambia, Nigeria, and Ethiopia, findings indicate that political rewarding or punishment strategies were observed. For example, targeting was biased toward districts where the ruling party had political support (Mason and Ricker-Gilbert 2013), toward individuals who lived closer to the locality of origin of political leaders (Takeshima and Liverpool-Tasie 2015), or against individuals suspected of having voted for the opposition party (Adem 2012).

There are also cases in which incumbent leaders direct transfers to areas where they received less support to secure their position in the next election. In such cases, politicians try to buy votes by using transfers to selectively "win over" households in areas where political support is weak. This tendency was found in Kenya—distribution of transfers to districts was positively related to the support that the opposition received in the previous election. A similar tendency was found in Ghana, where vouchers of a fertilizer subsidy program were targeted to districts that the ruling party had lost in the previous election. The larger the ruling party's loss, the more the vouchers targeted the district (Banful 2011).

These factors are important because political targeting may undermine pro-poor prioritization in public spending and reduce the efficiency of the program. In places where specific targeting of services or transfers in exchange for political support (vote buying) is more likely to be reported, the provision of broader public service that caters to mostly poor people is less likely to be prioritized.

Whether decentralizing the administration of the targeting could make allocation of these transfers more pro-poor is not encouraging. In Tanzania, the decentralized input voucher transfer program failed to target the intended group. Of the selected beneficiaries, 60 percent were families with members in the village council in charge of determining eligibility of families. This significantly reduced the program's targeting performance. This effect was stronger in unequal and relatively distant districts (Pan and Christiaensen 2012). Maybe not too surprisingly, the local socioeconomic and political context plays a key role for the outcome of decentralizing the targeting process.

Another important factor affecting how targeted transfers are directed is corruption, which could lead to the diversion of resources before the benefits reach the targeted or nontargeted groups. As discussed in chapter 3, corruption is a widespread problem in ISPs in African countries. Diversion, measured as the difference between what was supposed to be allocated and what was received by the targeted population, is estimated at between 25 and 42 percent in Malawi (Lunduka, Ricker-Gilbert, and Fisher 2013), about 38 percent in Zambia (Mason and Jayne 2013), and up to 50 percent in Nigeria (Liverpool-Tasie and Takeshima 2013). The leaked subsidies primarily end up being sold on commercial markets. Since the targeted groups of these transfers are small-scale farmers, this level of corruption has a huge impact on aggregate pro-poor spending as well as pro-agriculture spending, when compared with the counterfactual of these targeted transfers without significant corruption nor elite capture.

## Overcoming the Inertia in Policy Making

Too often, countries fail to adopt and implement policies that are known to be necessary for sustained economic development. In addition, for reasons described earlier, there is significant inertia in policy making. How, then, can change occur?

### Be Ready to Take Advantage of Opportunities for Reform
Major reform programs in the past have been necessitated by the realization that more of the same is not fiscally sustainable. External (that is, oil and other commodity) price shocks and debt crises have exposed inefficient and unsustainable policies (World Bank 2008). Much of the restructuring and privatizing of marketing boards in Africa came about when they became fiscally unsustainable, partially because of movements in the international prices of the commodities (Akiyama et al. 2001). Severe budgetary constraints have often disturbed the political equilibria that had supported those policies and

opened space for reforms, often with the strategic and financial support of external actors such as international financial institutions. These reforms involved profound changes in agricultural policies, including major shifts in public spending programs. Among them was a reduction in input subsidies, common in the 1980s and 1990s. Nevertheless, after the crises subsided and economic recovery progressed, some of the same programs and policies (including input subsidies) reemerged, albeit in improved versions, because they remained politically attractive (Jayne et al. 2015). The lesson here is not that reforms must always await the advent of shocks, but rather that reformers ought to be ready with a plan and evidence to influence reforms and alert for opportunities that may arise.

## Notes

1. Much of this chapter is based on Mogues and Erman (2016) and Mogues (2015).
2. The extent to which private and public investment in agriculture act as complements or substitutes is discussed in Mogues, Fan, and Benin (2015).
3. Other distinct branches have developed within this rational choice literature, including those that depart from the notion of an unencumbered policy maker. Tridimas (2001) presents a blended model of the benevolent social planner maximizing a social welfare function, but also maximizing electoral support by factoring in voters' preferences over different types of public spending.
4. This study does not capture actual public spending, but creates a composite index from information about the presence or absence of various public goods and services outputs such as electricity and irrigation facilities.
5. The PPF does have its limits, partly because it is a reduced-form approach and assumes that policy makers maximize a PPF. Von Cramon-Taubadel (1992) argues that this is just a stretching, not a transformation, of social planner models. Second, it assumes that extant policies reflect an equilibrium of economic and political forces (Johnson 1995). It also assumes that policies and public resources are already Pareto-efficient, and studies using this approach essentially measure marginal rates of transformation along the Pareto frontier (Bullock 1994). The accumulation of these strong assumptions can be easily challenged against realities of policy and political constellations, as much of the other literature reviewed in this chapter suggests.
6. The attribution meant here is that rural populations may (rightly or wrongly) make a connection between improvements they experience and investments or policies the government undertook.
7. Harstad and Svensson (2011) study lobbying activities and corruptive activities in a joint framework. They distinguish these two in that corruptive behavior seeks to bend the rules, while lobbying behavior seeks to change the rules. Both types of activities are subsumed under rent-seeking activities.
8. It is disputable whether public investment spending is a useful measure of targeted spending. This is explicitly discussed in the study.

9. Most of the analyses discussed in this chapter are, however, better contextualized by probabilistic voter theories than by the median voter theory, as the analyses for the most part imply that citizens—for a range of reasons—prefer policy outcomes in a nondeterministic way. "Better," however, does not mean "perfectly." Both the probabilistic voting and the median voter theory presuppose functional democracies with competitive electoral systems, and these are not the relevant context in the case of agricultural (and other) public spending choices in many developing countries.

# References

Abler, D. G., and V. Sukhatme. 1998. "The Determinants of Wheat and Rice Policies: A Political Economy Model for India." *Journal of Economic Development* 23 (1): 195–215.

Acemoğlu, D., and J. Robinson. 2001. "Inefficient Redistribution." *American Political Science Review* 95 (3): 649–61.

Adem, T. 2012. "The Local Politics of Ethiopia's Green Revolution in South Wollo." *African Studies Review* 55 (3): 81–102.

Akiyama, T., J. Baffes, D. Larson, and P. Varangis. 2001. "Commodity Market Reforms: Lessons of Two Decades." In *Regional and Sectoral Studies*. Washington, DC: World Bank.

Anderson, K. 2009. *Distortions to Agricultural Incentives: A Global Perspective, 1955–2007.* Washington, DC: World Bank.

Anderson, K., and Y. Hayami, eds. 1986. *The Political Economy of Agricultural Protection: East Asia in International Perspective.* Sydney, Australia: Allen and Unwin.

Anderson, S., P. Francois, and A. Kotwal. 2015. "Clientelism in Indian Villages." *American Economic Review* 105 (6): 1780–1816.

Araujo, C., F. Ferreira, P. Lanjouw, and B. Ozler. 2008. "Local Inequality and Project Choice: Theory and Evidence from Ecuador." *Journal of Public Economics* 92 (5–6): 1022–46.

Arcand, J., and L. Bassole. 2007. "Does Community-Driven Development Work?" Draft. CERDI-CNRS, Université d'Auvergne, and EUDN.

Arcand, J., and M. Fafchamps. 2012. "Matching in Community-Based Organizations." *Journal of Development Economics* 98 (2): 203–19.

Austen-Smith, D. 1997. "Interest Groups: Money, Information, and Influence." In *Perspectives on Public Choice: A Handbook*, edited by D. C. Mueller. Cambridge, U.K.: University of Cambridge Press.

Bale, M. D., and E. Lutz. 1981. "Price Distortions in Agriculture and Their Effects: An International Comparison." *American Journal of Agricultural Economics* 63 (1): 8–22.

Banful, A. 2011. "Old Problems in the New Solutions? Politically Motivated Allocation of Program Benefits and the 'New' Fertilizer Subsidies." *World Development* 39 (7): 1166–76.

Bashaasha, B., M. Najjingo Mangheni, and E. Nkonya. 2011. "Decentralization and Rural Service Delivery in Uganda." Discussion Paper 01063, IFPRI, Washington, DC.

Bassett, T. 2001. *The Peasant Cotton Revolution in West Africa: Cote d'Ivoire, 1880–1995.* Cambridge, U.K.: Cambridge University Press.

Bates, R. H. 1987. *Essays on the Political Economy of Rural Africa.* Berkeley, CA: University of California Press.

Becker, G. 1983. "A Theory of Competition among Pressure Groups for Political Influence." *Quarterly Journal of Economics* 98 (3): 371–400.

Beghin, J. C., and M. Kherallah. 1994. "Political Institutions and International Patterns of Agricultural Protection." *Review of Economics and Statistics* 76 (3): 482–89.

Bergh, S. 2010. Assessing Local Governance Innovations in Morocco in Light of the Participatory Budgeting Experience in Brazil: The Case of 'Civil Society' Federations (Espaces Associatifs) in Al Haouz Province." *Journal of Economic and Social Research* 12 (1): 113–38.

Besley, T., R. Pande, and V. Rao. 2012. "Just Rewards? Local Politics and Public Resource Allocation in South India." *World Bank Economic Review* 26 (2): 191–216.

Binswanger, H., and K. Deininger. 1997. "Explaining Agricultural and Agrarian Policies in Developing Countries." *Journal of Economic Literature* 35 (4): 1958–2005.

Blackburn, K., N. Bose, and M. E. Haque. 2011. "Public Expenditures, Bureaucratic Corruption, and Economic Development." *Manchester School* 79 (3): 405–28.

Bowman, A. 2011. "Mass Production or Production by the Masses? Tractors, Cooperatives, and the Politics of Rural Development in Post-Independence Zambia." *Journal of African History* 52: 201–21.

Bräutigam, D. 2004. "The People's Budget? Politics, Participation, and Pro-Poor Policy." *Development Policy Review* 22 (6): 653–68.

Bullock, D. S. 1994. "In Search of Rational Government: What Political Preference Function Studies Measure and Assume." *American Journal of Agricultural Economics* 76 (3): 347–61.

Burgess, R., R. Jedwab, E. Miguel, A. Morjaria, and G. Padró i Miquel. 2015. "The Value of Democracy: Evidence from Road Building in Kenya." *American Economic Review*, 105 (6): 1817–51. doi: 10.1257/aer.20131031.

Casey, K., R. Glennerster, and E. Miguel. 2012. "Reshaping Institutions: Evidence on Aid Impacts Using a Pre-Analysis Plan." *Quarterly Journal of Economics* 127 (4): 1755–1812.

Chinsinga, B. 2011. "Seeds and Subsidies: The Political Economy of Input Programmes in Malawi." *IDS Bulletin* 42 (4): 59–68.

Chirwa, E. W., M. Matita, and A. Dorward. 2010. "Targeting Agricultural Input Subsidy Coupons in Malawi." Working Paper, School of Oriental and African Studies, University of London, London.

Coate, S., and S. Morris. 1999. "Policy Persistence." *American Economic Review* 89 (5): 1327–36.

Dasgupta, A., and V. Beard. 2007. "Community-Driven Development, Collective Action, and Elite Capture in Indonesia." *Development and Change* 38 (2): 229–49.

Deacon, R. T. 1978. "A Demand Model for the Local Public Sector." *Review of Economics and Statistics* 60 (2): 180–202.

De Gorter, H., and J. F. M. Swinnen. 1998. "Impact of Economic Development on Commodity and Public Research Policies in Agriculture." *Review of Development Economics* 2 (1): 41–60.

——. 2002. "Political Economy of Agricultural Policy." In Vol. 2 of *Handbook of Agricultural Economics*, edited by B. Gardner and G. Rausser. Amsterdam: Elsevier.

De Janvry, A., H. Nakagawa, and E. Sadoulet. 2009. "Pro-Poor Targeting and Electoral Rewards in Decentralizing to Communities the Provision of Local Public Goods in Rural Zambia," Working Paper, University of California, Berkeley, CA. http://are.berkeley.edu/~esadoulet/papers/Zambia-Jul09.pdf.

De la Croix, D., and C. Delavallade. 2009. "Growth, Public Investment and Corruption with Failing Institutions." *Economics of Governance* 10 (3): 187–219.

Doner, R. F., B. K. Ritchie, and D. Slater. 2005. "Systemic Vulnerability and the Origins of Developmental States: Northeast and Southeast Asia in Comparative Perspective." *International Organisation* 59 (2): 327–361.

Drazen, A., and N. Limão. 2008. "A Bargaining Theory of Inefficient Redistribution Policies." *International Economic Review* 49 (2): 621–57.

Dunne, J. P., and R. P. Smith. 1984. "The Allocative Efficiency of Government Expenditure: Some Comparative Tests." *European Economic Review* 20 (1–3): 381–94.

Feeny, S., and M. McGillivray. 2010. "Aid and Public Sector Fiscal Behaviour in Failing States." *Economic Modelling* 27 (5): 1006–16.

Fernandez, R., and D. Rodrik. 1991. "Resistance to Reform: Status Quo Bias in the Presence of Individual-Specific Uncertainty." *American Economic Review* 81 (5): 1146–55.

Feyzioglu, T., V. Swaroop, and M. Zhu. 1998. "A Panel Data Analysis of the Fungibility of Foreign Aid." *World Bank Economic Review* 12 (1): 29–58.

Francis, P., and R. James. 2003. "Balancing Rural Poverty Reduction and Citizen Participation: The Contradictions of Uganda's Decentralization Program." *World Development* 31 (2): 325–37.

Grossman, G. M., and E. Helpman. 2001. *Special Interest Politics*. Cambridge, MA: MIT Press.

Harstad, B., and J. Svensson. 2011. "Bribes, Lobbying, and Development." *American Political Science* Review 105 (1): 46–63.

Ismihan, M., and F. G. Ozkan. 2011. "The Political Economy of Public Spending Decisions and Macroeconomic Performance." *International Journal of Economic Perspectives* 5 (2): 163–74.

Jayne, T. S., D. Mather, N. M. Mason, J. Ricker-Gilbert, and E. Crawford. 2015. "Rejoinder to the Comment by Andrew Dorward and Ephraim Chirwa on Jayne, T. S, D. Mather, N. Mason, and J. Ricker-Gilbert. 2013. 'How Do Fertilizer Subsidy Programs Affect Total Fertilizer Use in Sub-Saharan Africa? Crowding Out, Diversion, and Benefit/Cost Assessments.' *Agricultural Economics* 44 (6): 687–703." *Agricultural Economics* 46 (6): 745–55.

Johnson, R. W. M. 1995. "Modelling Government Processes and Policies in Agriculture: A Review." *Review of Marketing and Agricultural Economics* 63 (3): 383–93.

Keefer, P., and S. Khemani. 2005. "Democracy, Public Expenditures, and the Poor: Understanding Political Incentives for Providing Public Services." *World Bank Research Observer* 20 (1): 1–27.

Keefer, P., and S. Knack. 2007. "Boondoggles, Rent-Seeking, and Political Checks and Balances: Public Investment under Unaccountable Governments." *Review of Economics and Statistics* 89 (3): 566–72.

Khemani, S., E. D. Bo, C. Ferraz, F. Finan, and C. Stephenson. 2016. *Making Politics Work for Development: Harnessing Transparency and Citizen Engagement.* Washington, DC: World Bank.

Kjaer, A. M. 2015. "Political Settlements and Productive Sector Policies: Understanding Sector Differences in Uganda." *World Development* 68: 230–41.

Krueger, A., M. Schiff, and A. Valdes. 1988. "Agricultural Incentives in Developing Countries: Measuring the Effects of Sectoral and Economy-Wide Policies." *World Bank Economic Review* 2 (3): 255–72.

Labonne, J., and Chase, R. 2009. "Who Is at the Wheel When Communities Drive Development? Evidence from the Philippines." *World Development* 37 (1): 219–31.

La Ferrara, E. 2002. "Inequality and Group Participation: Theory and Evidence from Rural Tanzania." *Journal of Public Economics* 85 (2): 235–73.

Le Maux, B., Y. Rocaboy, and T. Goodspeed. 2011. "Political Fragmentation, Party Ideology, and Public Expenditures." *Public Choice* 147 (1–2): 43–67.

Lindert, P. H. 1991. "Historical Patterns of Agricultural Polity." In *Agriculture and the State: Growth, Employment, and Poverty in Developing Countries,* edited by C. Timmer. Food Systems and Agrarian Change Series. Ithaca, NY: Cornell University Press.

Liverpool-Tasie, L., and H. Takeshima. 2013. "Input Promotion within a Complex Subsector: Fertilizer in Nigeria." *Agricultural Economics* 44 (6): 581–94.

Lunduka, R., J. Ricker-Gilbert, and M. Fisher. 2013. "What Are the Farm-Level Impacts of Malawi's Farm Input Subsidy Program? A Critical Review." *Agricultural Economics* 44 (6): 563–79.

Mani, A., and S. Mukand. 2007. "Democracy, Visibility, and Public Good Provision." *Journal of Development Economics* 83 (2): 506–29.

Mason, N., and T. Jayne. 2013. "Fertilizer Subsidies and Smallholder Commercial Fertilizer Purchases: Crowding Out, Leakage, and Policy Implications for Zambia." *Journal of Agricultural Economics* 64 (3): 558–82.

Mason, N., and J. Ricker-Gilbert. 2013. "Disrupting Demand for Commercial Seed: Input Subsidies in Malawi and Zambia." *World Development* 45 (May): 75–91.

Moehler, D. C. 2010. "Democracy, Governance, and Randomised Development Assistance." *Annals of the American Academy of Political and Social Science* 628 (1): 30–46.

Mogues, T. 2015. "Political Economy Determinants of Public Spending Allocations: A Review of Theories, and Implications for Agricultural Public Investment." *European Journal of Development Research* 27: 452–73. doi:10.1057/ejdr.2015.35.

Mogues, T., and D. do Rosario. 2015. "The Political Economy of Public Expenditures in Agriculture: Applications of Concepts to Mozambique." *South African Journal of Economics* 27 (3): 452–73.

Mogues, T., and A. Erman. 2016. "Institutional Arrangements to Make Public Spending Responsive to the Poor—(Where) Have They Worked? Review of the Evidence on Four Major Intervention Types." Discussion Paper 01519. Washington, DC: IFPRI.

Mogues, T., S. Fan, and S. Benin. 2015. "Public Investments in and for Agriculture." *European Journal of Development Research* 27 (3): 337–52.

Mogues, T., B. Yu, S. Fan, and L. McBride. 2012. "The Impacts of Public Investment in and for Agriculture: Synthesis of the Existing Evidence." Discussion Paper 01217, IFPRI, Washington, DC.

Mulligan, C., R. Gil, and X. Sala-i-Martin. 2004. "Do Democracies Have Different Public Policies than Nondemocracies?" *Journal of Economic Perspectives* 18 (1): 51–74.

Niskanen, W. 1971. *Bureaucracy and Representative Government*. Piscataway, NJ: Transaction Publishers.

Nylen, W. 2014. *Participatory Budgeting in a Competitive-Authoritarian Regime: A Case Study (Maputo, Mozambique)*. Cadernos Instituto de Estudos Sociais e Económicos (IESE) 13E. Maputo, Mozambique: IESE Scientific Council.

Olper, A., J. Falkowski, and J. Swinnen. 2014. "Political Reforms and Public Policy: Evidence from Agricultural and Food Policies." *World Bank Economic Review* 28 (1): 21–47.

Olson, M. 1965. *The Logic of Collective Action: Public Goods and the Theory of Groups*. Cambridge, MA: Harvard Economic Studies.

———. 1985. "Space, Agriculture, and Organization." *American Journal of Agricultural Economics* 67 (5): 928–37.

Omuru, E., and R. Kingwell. 2006. "Funding and Managing Agricultural Research in a Developing Country: A Papua New Guinea Case Study." *International Journal of Social Economics* 33 (4): 316–30.

Pack, H., and J. R. Pack. 1990. "Is Foreign Aid Fungible? The Case of Indonesia." *Economic Journal* 100 (399): 188–94. https://ideas.repec.org/a/ecj/econjl/v100y 1990i399p188-94.html.

———. 1993. "Foreign Aid and the Question of Fungibility." *Review of Economics and Statistics* 75 (2): 258–65.

Pan, L., and L. Christiaensen. 2012. "Who Is Vouching for the Input Voucher? Decentralized Targeting and Elite Capture in Tanzania." *World Development* 40 (8): 1619–33.

Persson, T., and G. Tabellini. 2000. *Political Economics: Explaining Economic Policy*. Cambridge, MA: MIT Press.

Proost, S., and V. Zaporozhets. 2013. "The Political Economy of Fixed Regional Public Expenditure Shares with an Illustration for Belgian Railway Investments." *Regional Science and Urban Economics* 43 (5): 808–15.

Rangarajan, M. 2009. "Striving for a Balance: Nature, Power, Science, and India's Indira Gandhi 1917–1984." *Conservation and Society* 7 (4): 299–312.

Ranis, G. 2012. "Vertical and Horizontal Decentralization and Ethnic Diversity in Sub-Saharan Africa." Center Discussion Paper 1017, Economic Growth Center, New Haven, CT: Yale University.

Rao, V., and A. Ibanez. 2005. "The Social Impact of Social Funds in Jamaica: A 'Participatory Econometric' Analysis of Targeting, Collective Action, and Participation in Community-Driven Development." *Journal of Development Studies* 41 (5): 788–838.

Rinaudo, J. D. 2002. "Corruption and Allocation of Water: The Case of Public Irrigation in Pakistan." *Water Policy* 4 (5): 405–22.

Shall, A. 2007. "Sub-Saharan Africa's Experience with Participatory Budgeting." In *Participatory Budgeting*, edited by A. Shah. World Bank Policy Research Report. Washington: World Bank.

Song, Z., K. Storesletten, and F. Zilibotti. 2012. "Rotten Parents and Disciplined Children: A Politicoeconomic Theory of Public Expenditure and Debt." *Econometrica* 80 (6): 2785–2803.

Swaroop, V., S. Jha, and A. S. Rajkumar. 2000. "Fiscal Effects of Foreign Aid in a Federal System of Governance: The Case of India." *Journal of Public Economics* 77 (3): 307–30.

Swinnen, J. F. M., H. de Gorter, G. C. Rausser, and A. N. Banerjee. 2000. "The Political Economy of Public Research Investment and Commodity Policies in Agriculture: An Empirical Study." *Agricultural Economics* 22 (2): 111–22.

Takeshima, H., and L. Liverpool-Tasie. 2015. "Fertilizer Subsidies, Political Influence, and Local Food Prices in Sub-Saharan Africa: Evidence from Nigeria." *Food Policy* 54: 11–24.

Ting, M. M. 2012. "Legislatures, Bureaucracies, and Distributive Spending." *American Political Science Review* 106 (2): 367–85.

Tridimas, G. 2001. "The Economics and Politics of the Structure of Public Expenditure." *Public Choice* 106 (3–4): 299–316.

Von Cramon-Taubadel, S. 1992. "A Critical Assessment of the Political Preference Function Approach in Agricultural Economics." *Agricultural Economics* 7 (3–4): 371–94.

Wade, R. 1982. "The System of Administrative and Political Corruption: Canal Irrigation in South India." *Journal of Development Studies* 18 (3): 287–328.

Walker, T., J. Ryan, and T. Kelley. 2010. "Impact Assessment of Policy-Oriented International Agricultural Research: Evidence and Insights from Case Studies." *World Development* 38 (10): 1453–61.

Walter, H., and B. Wolff. 2002. "Principal-Agent Problems in Irrigation: Inviting Rent-Seeking and Corruption." *Quarterly Journal of International Agriculture* 41 (1–2): 99–118.

Weinstein, L. 2011. "The Politics of Government Expenditures in Tanzania, 1999–2007." *African Studies Review* 54 (1): 33–57.

Wong, S. 2012. *What Have Been the Impact of World Bank Community-Driven Development Programs? CDD Impact Evaluation Review and Operational & Research Implications.* Washington, DC: World Bank.

World Bank. 2008. *World Development Report 2008: Agriculture for Development.* Washington, DC: World Bank.

————. 2010. *Uganda: Agriculture Public Expenditure Review.* Report 53702-UG. Washington, DC: World Bank.

————. 2015. World Development Indicators database, World Bank, Washington, DC.

Zhang, X., S. Fan, L. Zhang, and J. Huang. 2004. "Local Governance and Public Goods Provision in Rural China." *Journal of Public Economics* 88 (12): 2857–71.

# Index

Boxes, figures, and tables are indicated by *b*, *f*, and *t* following the page numbers.

contributions of agriculture to, 13*b*
drivers of growth, 2, 45
extractive industry sectors and, 234
Growth and Transformation Program
(GTP), 161, 186
Growth Enhancement Support Scheme
(GESS), 174, 186, 187
Guinea
expenditures in, 251, 252
off-budget funding of agricultural
sector in, 238
political instability in, 233
rates of return in, 98
Gulati, A., 109
Gurara, D. Z., 156

**H**
Harrigan, J., 218*n*25
Harstad, B., 295*n*7
HarvestChoice, 116
Hazell, P., 107, 130–31
household-level effects of input
subsidies, 189–99
crop yields and production, 150*b*, 191,
193–94*t*, 196–97
enduring effects, 151*b*, 195*t*, 199
fertilizer and improved seed use,
150*b*, 189–91, 192*t*
food security and nutrition, 150*b*,
194*t*, 197
incomes, assets, and poverty, 150*b*,
194–95*t*, 197–98
soil fertility management practices,
151*b*, 195*t*, 198–99
human capital
building, 9, 51–52
productivity-enhancing effects
of, 105–6, 113
in research and development, 78–79*b*

**I**
IFDC. *See* International Fertilizer
Development Center
income
agricultural productivity growth
and, 1, 3, 5, 48

in agricultural sector, 151*b*, 201*t*,
203, 250, 251*t*
discretionary, 82*b*
fertilizer subsidies and, 84, 153
input subsidies and, 150–51*b*,
194–95*t*, 197–98
India
allocation of public funds in, 285
development assistance
in, 280, 281
dissemination of technology in, 21
fertilizer use in, 134, 216*n*6
irrigation infrastructure
in, 84, 107
political preference function as
applied to, 279
public resource allocation in, 275
rate of return on investments and
subsidies in, 109, 110–11*t*
research and development in, 18
subsidies in, 24*b*, 28
Indonesia
community-driven development
in, 290
development assistance in, 281
fertilizer subsidies in, 28
informational technologies, 117–
18*n*10, 159
Inocencio, A., 108
input distribution systems, 128, 129,
150*b*, 158, 180
input subsidy programs
(ISPs), 125–81
as agricultural development strategy,
125, 126, 143
beneficiaries of, 153, 154*t*
cost of, 128, 129*f*, 156
crop yields and, 150*b*
decline of, 127–28, 143
elite capture of benefits, 150–51*b*,
174, 189, 197, 202, 275
evolution of, 130, 143–48, 144–46*t*
fertilizer. *See* fertilizer subsidy
programs
food price and production effects,
148, 151*b*, 152, 153

## Environmental Benefits Statement